Austria in World War II

An Anglo-American Dilemma

ROBERT H. KEYSERLINGK

McGill-Queen's University Press
Kingston and Montreal

ISBN 0-7735-0644-6 (cloth)
ISBN 0-7735-0800-7 (paper)

Legal deposit 2nd quarter 1988
Bibliothèque nationale du Québec
First paperback edition 1990

Printed in Canada on acid-free paper.

This book has been published with the help of a grant from the Social Science Federation of Canada, using funds provided by the Social Science and Humanities Research Council of Canada.

Canadian Cataloguing in Publication Data

Keyserlingk, Robert H., 1933-
Austria in World War II
ISBN 0-7735-0644-6 (bound)
ISBN 0-7735-0800-7 (pbk.)
1. Austria – History – 1938-1945. 2. World War, 1939-1945 – Austria. 3. Reconstruction (1939-1951) – Austria.
I. Title.
DB99.K49 1988 943.6′052 C88-090004-0

Contents

Preface

The further we move from the events of 1939–1945, the more the incubus of political legend makes it difficult to see the historical reality, the more the picture of what actually happened has become obfuscated.

Fritz Fellner, *Austrian History Yearbook*

The Austro-Hungarian Monarchy, heir to the millennial Holy Roman Empire, was torn apart by the victors in 1919. Rump Austria became one of the foci of contentious interwar European politics. The reduced First Austrian Republic's existence as a nation and country became a European problem closely tied to central European security as a whole and the continental balance of power. Its population's marked attraction after 1918 to an Anschluss or union with Germany and the country's faltering internal unity aroused deepening international concern. Although by 1938 a majority of Austrians opposed a Nazi-imposed Anschluss, there appeared little that anyone could do about it when it finally took place. Hitler's appropriation of Austria marked the first step towards eastward Nazi expansion.

What was the nature of Anglo-American reactions to the Anschluss and wartime Austria? How did the Western Allies plan to arrange Austria's postwar future to avoid prewar domestic and international weaknesses? Would a reestablished Austria once again pose an international problem? The answer appeared to be straightforward. As a recent American study of postwar Austria typically asserted: "Of all the issues arising from World War II, the future of Austria might have seemed the easiest for the Allies to settle, for on few issues was there greater agreement well before the end of the war."[1] The commonly-held view states that after the Anschluss and during World War II the Western Allies, together with the Soviet Union, treated Austria as a special case. Although Austria was amalgamated by the Nazis into the Third Reich in 1938 and Austrians fought in the German military or served in the Nazi structure, the Allies refused to treat it as a part of Nazi Germany. They were held to have championed an occupied Austria's right to be liberated and restored after the war as a free, democratic, and independent state. This attitude found its most notable formulation in the Big Three's 1943 Moscow Declaration on Austria, their first definite policy statement about a continental European country's postwar future. Hitherto this viewpoint has prevailed almost unchallenged.

Austrians have tried conscientiously to look at their post-1918 history, especially the Nazi period, with unjaundiced eyes. Recent Austrian domestic scandals, political corruption, and the furore aroused by the 1986 presidential election, led some foreign observers, and even moderate Austrians, to wonder out loud whether Austria deserved to be considered the special case it claimed to be. But the conviction that the Allies early in the war adopted the restoration of an independent Austria as a war aim remained untouched.[2]

Others have occasionally expressed puzzlement at the Allies' generous wartime treatment of Austria, but have not questioned it. Possessing no clear answer to what he saw to be a riddle, the well-known historian Gordon Craig recently fell back on a humorous but "not entirely frivolous" story once told by a similarly perplexed senior member of the U.S. Foreign Service in Austria. According to this expert, Austria received such strong Western support during and after World War II "because President Roosevelt and Winston Churchill had spent happy summers in their youth rolling down Austria's lush hills in lederhosen and were privately agreed that the Austrians were a jolly people who deserved better than the awful Germans."[3]

However, despite apparent unanimity, aspects of this version still remain unclear. What warranted dealing with Austria during the war as a special case? On the face of it, it seems unlikely that the discouraging interwar history of the Austrian republic and its Danubian neighbours should have inspired Allied political planners to restore a small state like Austria to its prewar status. Would they be able to avoid their earlier problems this time? Is it possible that the Western Allies' pro-Austrian statements during the war concealed a certain confusion of aims and decisional paralysis, or were meant to serve as propaganda devices rather than intended as firm political policy? Did the bitter ten-year Cold War confrontation between East and West over prostrate Austria influence retrospective views of the Allies' wartime Austrian policies? Are the roots of the Allies' ambiguous postwar treatment of Austria to be found in the wartime period? If the Allies had agreed to treat Austria as a liberated country, why then the long postwar occupation? "Certainly the Austrians themselves never expected the occupation of their country by Allied 'liberators' to last ten years."[4]

Few myths grow so easily and profusely as political myths, especially in wartime. By the same token, few illusions die harder than political myths. This book seeks to challenge the legend outlined above which affirms that the Anglo-American Allies intended to treat post-Anschluss Austria as a special case; that after 1938 the British and Americans remained faithfully committed to a sovereign Austria and to its restoration as an independent state. The author has sought to settle the question of Anglo-American attitudes towards Austria between 1938 and 1945 through research conducted in British, American, Canadian, and Austrian archives. The main British documentary material employed were official papers in the British Foreign Office, Cabinet, and Prime Minister Churchill's files in the London Public Records Office, and the files of the Royal Institute of International Affairs in London and Oxford. American sources included United States Presidential and Departments of War and State sources in the Hyde Park Franklin D. Roosevelt Archives and the Washington National Archives, the files of the Council on Foreign Relations in New York, as well as the personal papers of official personalities in the Library of Congress and academic archives. Canadian Cabinet, Prime Ministerial, and Department of External Affairs files were consulted in Ottawa. Vienna University's Institute of Contemporary History generously placed its library and other research facilities at my disposal. In the Vienna-based Documentation Centre for Austrian Resistance (*Dokumentationszentrum für österreichischen Widerstand*, or DÖW) I studied collections of Austrian exiles' personal papers, diaries, and newspaper clippings, and the centre's photostat collection of official British and American documents on Austria. The Austrian Foreign Office in Vienna answered my queries with dispatch.

Without generous financial assistance, this research would not have been possible. The author received an original grant to subsidize a research trip to Austria and Great Britain from the Austrian Academic Exchange program through the good offices of Dr Christian Jaekl, cultural and press representative at the Austrian Embassy in Ottawa. The University of Ottawa Graduate School Research Fund assisted summer research efforts in Europe. A multiannual Social Sciences and Humanities Research Council of Canada (SSHRCC) grant proved essential for completion of this project. Dr Elizabeth Mach, counsellor at the Austrian Embassy in Ottawa, and the SSHRCC cooperated in funding an international symposium organized by the author in Ottawa on this topic. Dr Mach also helped to procure some photographs for the book.

Many individuals, including archivists in Great Britain, the United States, Canada and Austria, kindly offered valuable assistance and encouragement. Karl Renner of Ottawa awakened interest in the topic. Professor Fritz Fellner of Salzburg University, the leading Austrian historian to question current research results on this topic, advised the author on numerous occasions and guided him on possible sources to be consulted. Professor Gerald Stourzh of Vienna University, the Austrian expert on postwar negotiations looking towards the 1955 State Treaty and Austria's liberation, assisted in elucidating the official record. Dr Guy Stanley of the University of Connecticut, the Canadian pioneer concerning the British view of the question, and Dr Reinhold Wagnleitner of Salzburg University, who extended Stanley's work, offered unflaggingly practical comments and encouragement. Professor Erika Weinzierl and her assistants at the Vienna University Institute of Contemporary History patiently guided the author through the literature. The DÖW director, Dr Herbert Steiner, an Austrian exile in wartime Great Britain, and his staff suggested sources at the DÖW and granted access to them. Dean Maurice Williams of Okanagan College, who has investigated Austro-Nazism, helped with criticism and advice. Professor Martin Rauchensteiner of the Vienna Military Historical Institute aided in military aspects of the subject, while Professor Brian Villa of the University of Ottawa placed his research experience in World War II Anglo-American military problems at the author's disposal.

The author especially wishes to thank those who helped to edit or publish his material on the Austrian question. The Vienna Institute of Contemporary History accepted some of my original ideas on this topic in its journal *Zeitgeschichte*. Professors Martin Kovacs and T. Yedlin of the Central and East European Studies Association of Canada and Alberta published several of my earlier studies. Dr Thomas Spira of the University of Prince Edward Island, an expert in interwar Austro-Hungarian problems and editor of the *Canadian Review of Studies in Nationalism*, offered invaluable direction on earlier printed efforts to formulate preliminary conclusions in his journal. His selfless editorial labours on the manuscript of this book greatly improved the final product. The McGill-Queen's University Press staff including especially editor Charles Beer were unfailingly supportive, instructive, and courteous. Final responsibility for content and for errors lies, of course, with the author. I am greatly indebted to my wife for her patience, support, and suggestions, as well as to my father, a journalist and author with a wide contemporary experience of the period.

Abbreviations

BCOS	British Chiefs of Staff
CAC	Country Area Committees, State Department, 1944–5
CCS	Combined Chiefs of Staff (Anglo-American)
CFR	Council on Foreign Relations, New York
DEA	Department of External Affairs, Ottawa
EAC	European Advisory Commission, London
FDR	Franklin D. Roosevelt Archives, Hyde Park, NY
FO	Foreign Office, London
FORD	Foreign Office Research Division
FRPS	Foreign Research and Press Service
JCS	Joint Chiefs of Staff (US)
JIC	Joint Intelligence Committee, JCS
MOI	Ministry of Information (UK)
OSS	Office of Strategic Services (US)
OWI	Office of Wartime Information (US)
PRO	Public Record Office, London
PWE	Political Warfare Executive (UK)
R & A	Research and Analysis Branch, OSS
RIIA	Royal Institute of International Affairs
SOE	Special Operations Executive (UK)

Kurt von Schuschnigg, last pre-Anschluss chancellor of Austria, 1934–8 (Austrian Bundeskanzleramt-Bundespresseamt [BKA–BPD], 810.007; Fl. Waldmann).

George Messersmith, U.S. minister to Austria, 1934–7 (FDR, NPX 80–275[6]).

Churchill and Roosevelt with their Combined Chiefs of Staff, Quebec, September 1943 (PAC, C26936).

Secretary of State Cordell Hull attending President Roosevelt's departure from Washington for Warm Springs, Ga. (FDR, NPX 48–22: 3710[47]).

Adolf A. Berle, Jr, assistant under-secretary of state (FDR, NPX 74–20: 1544).

Karl Renner, chancellor of the First Austrian Republic (1918–20); chancellor (1945); and president (1945–50) of the Second Republic (BKA–BPD, 001).

An Austrian "traitor" before the Nazi Peoples' Court, 1944 (BKA–BPD, 811.017, Osterreichisches Institut für Zeitgeschichte).

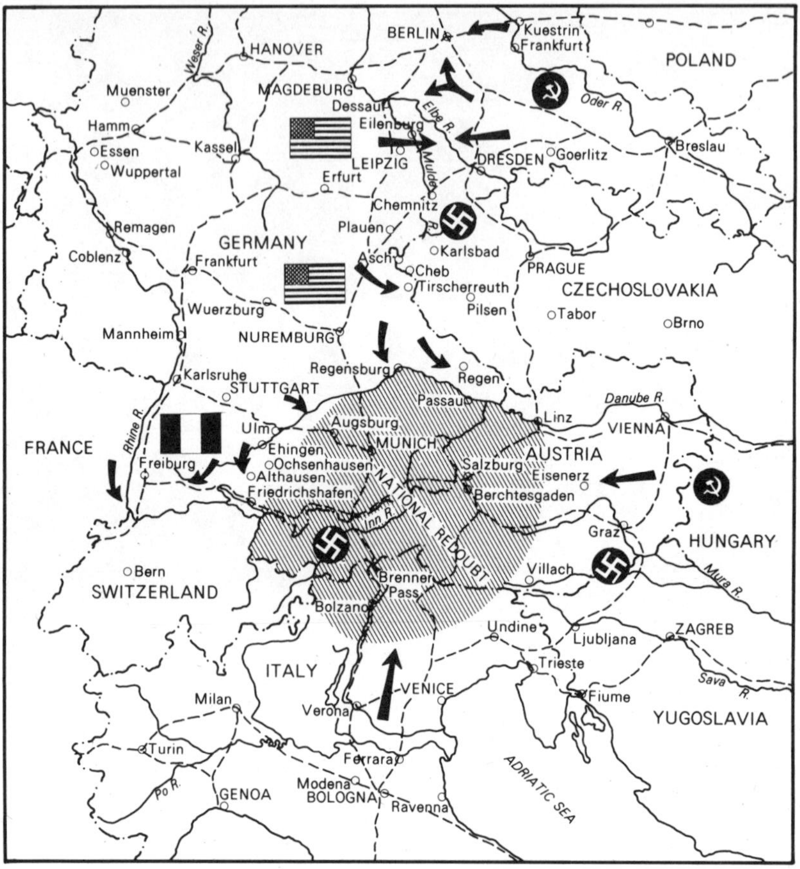

The feared National Redoubt supposedly encompassing Austria, 1945 (*New York Herald Tribune*, 19 April 1945).

Stalin, Roosevelt, and Churchill, Teheran, November 1943. In the background: Harry Hopkins, Foreign Minister Vyacheslav Molotov, Ambassador Averell Harriman, Ambassador Sir Archibald Clark-Kerr, Foreign Secretary Anthony Eden. (Note the usual absence of Cordell Hull at such Big Three meetings.) (FDR, NPX 48–22: 3626[9]).

Austria in World War II

Introduction

Undoubtedly the momentous events of World War II and the ensuing Cold War shifted global preoccupations. To what extent did these new concerns also create their own historical patterns? Almost a half-century after the Cold War arose as a historical and historiographical question, a comprehensive agreement on its origins is still lacking.[1] Recent scholarly debate in the United States has reopened the question.[2] Although these discussions touch upon vital wartime and postwar policies regarding central and eastern Europe, the subject of wartime British and American attitudes towards Austria has not been broached. This is surprising in view of that small country's strategic position as a bridge between east and west, complex German and Danubian ties, and faltering prewar record of internal instability and international weakness.

A great deal has been written about Austria up to the 1938 Anschluss, and again after 1945. But scholars have only fleetingly investigated the great powers' wartime plans regarding that country's postwar future. A brief inquiry into accounts of Anglo-American views of Austria between the Anschluss and 1945 reveals considerable interpretive discrepancy. On the one hand, most historians maintain that before 1938 the Western states became discouraged with Austria's debility and accepted Austria's *de jure* integration into the Third Reich with a mere shrug. However, after 1945 numerous authors recast Western attitudes into firm support in 1938 and after for an independent Austria. These postwar publications portrayed Austria as a friendly country cruelly occupied through Nazi force and liberated in 1945 by the Allies from the Nazi grip. The 1943 three-power Moscow Declaration on Austria was interpreted as demonstrating abiding Allied intention to reestablish an independent Austrian nation-state after the war. Typically a leading Austrian historian wrote in 1979: "Unquestionably, the most important document in the history of the founding of this [second Austrian] republic is the Moscow

Declaration. As a result of it, all the more-or-less vague Allied statements about the treatment of Austria issued before, during and after the war lost their significance."[3] This Moscow Declaration came to be considered a gauge of Allied wartime intentions concerning the restoration of Austria and was integrated into the legal-political basis of the Second Austrian Republic. Portrayals of prewar Anglo-American passivity turned into enthusiastic defence of Austria after World War II. Did this shift represent a true view of events in 1938 and during the war? Did postwar historical research uncover it, or was it rather spawned by wartime and postwar political considerations?

The danger lurks constantly that history will be misused for contemporary purposes. Whoever controls the present tries to manipulate the past in order to guide the future. Many people expect too much of their history and demand that it serve their present concerns. The past has been evoked variously as a source of national or racial myth, moral values, and experiential meaning, as an object of filial piety, and as a chart for the future. Controlling the contents of the past becomes particularly important during periods of sudden, dramatic reversals of foreign policy. As yesterday's enemies are converted into today's friends and allies, the integrity of conventional history is threatened. When World War II began in 1939, the Soviets were Hitler's allies. Two years later they joined the Allied anti-Hitler coalition. After 1945 Anglo-American disillusionment with the USSR grew, until these former allies again became enemies. Paradoxically, the defeated Germans and Austrians replaced them as friends or allies.

With each momentous shift, the participants sought precedent and sanction in the past. In a sense, as Benedetto Croce stated, all living history is contemporaneous. How we perceive our past is dependent upon contemporary events. History blends fact and interpretation, imbuing the present with satisfactory meaning. If current demands shift substantially, history, always an imaginative creation or interpretation in some ways, may well be summoned to satisfy new practical or emotional needs.[4] Some might argue that the pragmatic British and Americans would not react this way. Many observers stereotype America as an unhistorical society devoid of past bonds; a country in which anything is possible. But, as Vann Woodward has noted, the reverse is true. In fact, Americans often outdo others by substituting reinterpretable history for political theory. A case in point is the United States Supreme Court's routine discovery of ever new, flexible meanings in the eighteenth-century American constitution in order to accommodate policy shifts and needs over the years.[5]

The current view about positive Anglo-American attitudes towards post-Anschluss Austria certainly seemed to offer immediate postwar political rewards for the Western Allies and Austrians. It helped the Anglo-Americans to establish the legitimacy of their occupation presence in Austria, and to justify their postwar support for an independent Austria to be freed from Soviet control. Confident that the Austrians would prefer the Western system if released from four-power occupation, the Anglo-Americans could fall back upon the notion that they had always favoured an independent Austrian state. The new history also offered Austrians a way to distance themselves from Nazi Germany's crimes, and to retrieve their republican roots. In 1978 the Austrian historian Gerhard Botz observed that "present-day Austrian consciousness has very tenuous historical roots which for a long time made it possible for Austrians to occupy themselves with this period only in the face of great psychological and social resistance. Because of the Moscow Declaration and the presence of Allied occupation forces in the country, it was necessary to break as completely as possible with German fascism. As a consequence, the Austrians had a distorted view of their past for a long time after 1955."[6] If, according to the Anglo-American historical view, Austria had not been an integral part of the Nazi Reich after 1938, but had become a submerged and forcibly occupied state later liberated by the Allies, Austrians as a whole might escape postwar moral and legal accountability for the noxious actions of the Nazi regime. Domestic prosecution of indigenous National Socialists as well as requests for indemnities resulting from illegal Nazi actions in Austria might be moderated, and blamed upon external pressures or specific Austrian collaborators. State continuity and republican ideology could be retained, and Austrian anti-Nazi resistance integrated into Austrian national history.

It turned out upon closer scrutiny that postwar essays on the post-1938 Anglo-American view of Austria have been written largely by bureaucrats, jurists, politicians, and political scientists, not historians. These more contemporary-minded, practical individuals interpreted the Allied position on Austria between the Anschluss and the war's end. Understandably, they may have adopted positions that suited their governments' or clients' immediate interests. Their frequently abstract and animated debates rested on often ambiguously phrased public material as viewed through the lens of conflicting legal schools of thought or contemporary political concerns.[7] The experts of postwar Austria, mainly jurists and political scientists, ignored the primary historical record regarding the West's wartime attitude towards Austria, relying upon official public statements and acts instead. What is evidence differs for various people. Jurists, officials, and social scientists tend to accept authority's ready-made public statements. Authority is usually granted respectful attention; they listen to what authority chooses to tell them;

they allow authority to relate the story in its own way and at its own time. Historians, however, prefer to go behind the public scene; to subject documents and contemporaneous records to textual scrutiny and cross-examination.[8]

Now that immediate postwar concerns about Austria have faded, the diplomats and jurists have begun to depart the scene, stimulating a reexamination of the historical record. The Cold War no longer directly washes over the prostrate body of Austria. Today Austria is an independent, prosperous, and neutral republic. The main focus of political scientists has been upon Austria's postwar occupation and the road to the 1955 State Treaty. Perhaps it is time for a changing of the guard; for historians to try to pierce the protective shield of national interests, to revaluate official policy declarations, and, if necessary, to recast historical interpretation through the primary post-Anschluss historical record.

By and large, as Gerhard Botz noted, established Austrian historians long sidestepped the question of Austria's post-Anschluss period. When they finally took up this topic, they generally concentrated on domestic or Austro-German questions. Some investigated the status of Austrian refugees in Great Britain and the United States, asserting that they carried their vexatious prewar domestic loyalties into exile. Others analysed domestic Austrian affairs under the Nazis and documented the area's relegation to a backwater, provincial existence.[9] None systematically examined the Allied position during this period, especially the United States's attitude, except to comment upon the public and printed record. Over a decade ago, the Austrian historian Fritz Fellner judged this record so full of lacunae that it was a matter for speculation whether an independent American policy really existed at all or differed from the British position.[10] This topic is still so unclear that Gerald Stourzh, author of the most comprehensive history of Austria's postwar march towards national independence, utilized a passing remark uttered by New York's Cardinal Spellman as a major source of information regarding President Roosevelt's alleged postwar intentions in Austria.[11]

Several more general reasons may explain why professional historians in Austria and elsewhere have on the whole avoided the topic of the Western Allies' plans for Austria during World War II. There is no doubt that public and scholarly interest in southeastern Europe diminished dramatically after World War II, once the Soviets had taken over most of the area and closed it to Western scholarly access. After 1945 world attention focused mainly on Soviet Russia and the Cold War in Germany. Then again, after 1938 Austria no longer existed as a separate sovereign unit, and in a real sense vanished from view until well after 1945. Austria disappeared into the cracks between Soviet, central or eastern European, and German developments.

The analyst of World War II Anglo-American policy encounters additional problems produced by the nature of the wartime coalition and the disparity of sources, as many historians have discovered. Coalition warfare is complex and complicated, as much a source of confusion as of enlightenment and clarity. Foreign archives are distant and expensive to visit, and little pressure existed to question the official affirmative historical view of post-Anschluss Austria. As a result, Austrian historians spent much time and effort extolling or condemning pre-Anschluss Austrian historical personages before achieving a modicum of objectivity and national reconciliation, or they concentrated on pressing and difficult postwar questions.[12] Foreign authors contributed to these domestic historical revaluations, or also concentrated on the four-power postwar occupation, tracing the road from the war's end to the 1955 State Treaty.[13] The vigorous and unexpected postwar revival in scholarly Habsburg studies may also have played a part in deflecting attention from Allied attitudes towards republican Austria after the Anschluss and during World War II.[14]

Over a decade ago Guy Stanley, a Canadian doctoral student, and Elizabeth Barker, the British historical writer, were the first to use wartime archival material on Western wartime policy regarding Austria. They consulted the recently opened British Foreign Office files to investigate the British wartime view of Austria. Two years later an Austrian doctoral student, Reinhold Wagnleitner, carried on this work, concentrating on the end of the war and early postwar period.[15] But subsequent research on the topic has been insignificant, and has not followed up these important leads. Stanley's assertions regarding Great Britain's negative wartime Austrian policies failed to trigger a debate on the problem for the American printed record seemed to contradict them, indicating a more positive view of the subject. American primary sources were not studied. Nor has the Austrian question played a substantial role in discussions of the wartime origins of the Cold War. As a result, official postwar versions of Austria's post-1938 legal and political position and the Western Allied wartime Austrian policy have remained in place.

This study will investigate post-Anschluss and wartime Anglo-American intentions regarding Austria. The accepted postwar version, as this investigation will show, is not supported by the primary record. Much of the confusion stems from an inability to distinguish, as Stanley suggested, Allied wartime propaganda from political planning. It is indeed ironic that Austria suffered as a victim of this confusion in World War I, and benefited from it after World War II. We have only recently learned to distinguish the Allies' World War I propaganda pronouncements on the Austro-Hungarian Empire from political policy. Similar insights might have been applied to Allied statements concerning Austria in World War II. It has become evident that as late as 1918 Allied manifestoes demanding the dissolution of the Austro-Hungarian Empire did not reflect political policy, but were issued with the dual military purpose of sowing dissension among the Monarchy's national minorities and creating havoc in the hostile armies.[16] Whereas in the first great world conflict the use of propaganda as an instrument of war commenced fairly late, in the second global struggle propaganda and political warfare promised to replace conventional military planning and action by sapping enemy morale and destroying his will to fight. Only recently have scholars begun to expose the inflated claims made by political warriors during World War II, as a result of which military propaganda has often been mistaken for political policy.[17] This book will try to separate behind-the-scene political decisions by knowledgeable experts in the British Foreign Office and the United States Department of State from politicians' and propagandists' rhetoric aimed at domestic and enemy publics. Scholars have investigated Allied political warfare against Austria, but have not as yet tried to differentiate it systematically from political planning.[18]

This inquiry will try as well to demonstrate the congruity of British and American planning methods and political policies regarding Austria after 1938 and during the war, despite their different foreign policy styles and the absence of formal Anglo-American political structures resembling those created for military coordination. Anglo-American planning concerning Austria was always distinct from planning about Germany, taking place within the context of Danubian problems. This long-term planning was the result of a novel and fascinating collaboration engaging the most able official and scholarly personnel, many of them leading experts in southeastern Europe. For the first time, government officials cooperated closely in the planning process with outside academic experts from the Royal Institute of International Affairs (RIIA) in London and its sister organization, the Council on Foreign Relations (CFR) in New York. This unique and largely historical exercise in academic-official political forecasting induced planners to adopt a predominantly revisionist view of the Austro-Hungarian Empire and of the role of nationalism in the future of the Danubian region.

Long-term Western Allied attitudes towards Austria will be emphasized here rather than short-term, end-of-the-war expedients. Most current accounts of postwar Austria commence too late in the war to be able clearly to draw a line between long-term and tactical or occupational projects. Tactical Anglo-American differences about how best to achieve long-term goals have often obscured the basic long-range agreements. Because public statements towards the end of the war were phrased to meet the immediate needs of military occupation, they often hid long-term objectives. Occupation policies for Austria have been investigated elsewhere, although their wartime goals will need some revision in the light of what emerges here about the Allies' wartime planning.[19] Even had the actual course of the war not continually baffled wartime planners, their long-term schemes for postwar Austria would have created a set of alternative problems. Anglo-American planning for a Danubian federation, which continued as a goal to the war's end, encountered Soviet reservations. But it was not for this reason given up.

If it proves true that the British and Americans believed to the end of the war in a federative solution for the Danubian basin to include Austria, that the British still hoped in mid-1945 to fashion their own central and southeastern European policies by deploying reluctant American power to replace waning British strength, and that the Soviets encouraged an American presence in Austria to buffer the British and themselves, some light may be shed on one facet of the Cold War's beginnings. It would then be possible to grasp the full significance of America's disinterest in this complex region. If the Moscow Declaration on Austria represented wartime military propaganda, it cannot be employed to demonstrate American concern for the area before the onset of the Cold War. At the same time, it cannot serve as a clean bill of health for the Austrians between 1938 and 1945, or as a legal basis for a restored Austria. It is, of course, not surprising that the Austrians accepted the Allies' apparent gift, allowing them after the war to concentrate on national reconciliation and reconstruction rather than retribution for wartime activities, and to link up again easily with their prewar republican roots. The declaration's reincarnation served several postwar purposes. However, political expediency is not always coincident with historical accuracy.

CHAPTER ONE

The Anschluss Rejected

Based largely upon a vague and often ambiguous public Anglo-American record, the notion became entrenched after March 1938 among members of the public and scholars in Europe and the United States that the Anschluss had been rejected by the West; that consequently in the eyes of the West post-Anschluss Austria remained an occupied country eventually to be liberated by the Allies. This "occupationist" position still represents the majority view of the question among most Americans and Austrians. It has been opposed by the minority "annexationist" school of legal realists, who asserted that Austrian sovereignty had disappeared in 1938 and was replaced by German legal title. Hitherto these two interpretations have dominated discussions of Anglo-American policy towards the Anschluss and Austria. Both schools found some support for their position in the history of the interwar First Austrian Republic. If "occupationists" took consolation in the Schuschnigg government's courageous opposition to Anschluss in 1938, "annexationists" could point to the popularity of the Anschluss idea among Austrians between 1919 and 1938. The argument hinged as well on different assessments of the strength of historical Austrian patriotism.

Germany has posed a problem not only for the rest of the world, but for Germans and Austrians as well. Political cleavage has dominated German history. For a millennium Austria was part of the question, "What is Germany?" Historian Koppel S. Pinson explained: "In no other country in modern Europe [than Germany] did this struggle between centripetal and centrifugal forces take on such enormous proportions and attain such a quasi-psychological condition."[1] In 1806 Napoleon dissolved the overarching Holy Roman Empire, freeing the way for eventual Austro-Prussian competition for leadership. Neither the 1866 defeat of Austria by Prussia, nor its 1918 rout as an ally of Germany, in any way mitigated this dilemma.

Fundamental identity problems reappeared in German and Austrian history over the centuries. The question of who belongs to East and who to West Germany, and what precisely are their relationships with each other, is still debated today. Neither geography nor history has provided easy answers to these questions. Tensions between *klein-deutsch* particularism and *grossdeutsch* empire, drives to the south and east, fragmentation in the west, domestic cultural affinities and differentiations, all of them tempered by nationalism in the last century, have immensely complicated this issue. In 1438 the Austrian Habsburgs regained the German throne and then the imperial crown. Almost four hundred years later the French conqueror Napoleon Bonaparte irrevocably dissolved the Holy Roman Empire. The Austrian Empire partially replaced it in 1815 as a leading member of the German Confederation. Fifty years later Prussian Chancellor Otto von Bismarck united northern Germany and expelled Austria from the region, although he bound the new Second Reich in alliance to the Austro-Hungarian successor empire after 1871. The 1867 compromise between the Germans of Austria-Bohemia and the Magyars of Hungary created a Dual Monarchy, in which Austria and Hungary became respectively German and Magyar "nation-states," each, however, with a sizable minority of Slavs and others. National ascendancy in the two parts of the empire meant social and economic predominance for the two dominant peoples. World War I proved fatal to this empire and its German confederate. The common experience of defeat inevitably revived longings of union between Germany and the Austro-Germans. An issue which Bismarck had resolved by force fifty years earlier reappeared in strength. Five hundred years after the Austrian Habsburgs had assumed the imperial throne, small republican rump Austria disappeared in 1938 into Hitler's Third Reich through military invasion.

The desire for union, or reunion, with Germany attended the young Austrian republic's cradle in 1918–19. By October 1918 it had become increasingly clear that the Austro-Hungarian Monarchy would soon be driven out of the war and possibly into national dissolution, despite determined, last-minute attempts to turn it into a federal structure composed of its nationalities. By this time, however, the non-German minorities were seceding, which dashed the Austro-Germans' last-minute hopes of salvaging the empire as a federation under continued German leadership.[2] As a result of this calamity, Austria's German-speaking parliamentarians created a provisional assembly and proclaimed the independent state of German Austria. The German alliance was dissolved with Emperor Karl's agreement, and Count Andrassy, the last foreign minister, requested a separate peace from American President Woodrow Wilson. Austro-German deputies of all parties denounced this latter step. On 3 November 1918 the Entente imposed a tough armistice upon Austria. Eleven days later Emperor Karl renounced his political authority, and the next day the provisional national assembly unanimously proclaimed the German Austrian Republic.

Despite internal chaos and the bitterness of defeat and dismemberment, Austria escaped the experience of a Soviet republic resembling those of next-door Bavaria and Hungary. Many Austrians saw some hope that an eventual union might be achieved with their defeated ally, Germany. Once the federation idea collapsed, Austrian Socialists voted for union with fellow-Socialist Germany.[3] But in Paris the Austrian peace conference delegation chaired by the Socialist Karl Renner made little headway negotiating lenient peace terms with the victorious Allies. The Allies refused to sanction Anschluss, or union with Germany, a plan unanimously proclaimed by the provisional national assembly in November 1918. They also renamed the new Republic of German Austria simply the Republic of Austria. The creation of the First Austrian Republic in 1918–19 was apparently thrust upon the victorious Allies by circumstances. The Entente probably had no desire to destroy the Dual Monarchy until late in 1918. But by November 1918 the Allies saw no viable alternative to forming a separate Austrian state containing most of the German-speakers of the Austrian part of the defunct empire. It made no sense at all to the Allies to permit defeated Austria to join vanquished Germany in the name of self-determination. President Wilson suggested the formula that was finally adopted. Germany would recognize Austria's inalienable independence, and Austria would remain independent unless the League of Nations decided otherwise.[4] Austria became "ce qui reste," the state nobody wanted, a country little more than a "pathetic relic," according to the British historian Elizabeth Barker.[5]

Although Anschluss was forbidden, and this prohibition became part of the peace treaties, the idea of union with Germany refused to die and would frequently recur in the young federal republic. Would this diminutive state, heir to the weighty imperial name and traditions through Allied fiat, be able to master its serious historical, ideological, geographical, and economic challenges alone? In the midst of seething worries, would Austrians continue to consider the Anschluss solution a sound escape route? Resentment that the peace treaties excluded Bohemian, Moravian, and South Tyrolean Germans from the new Austria, fanned revisionist sentiment. Austrians doubted the new state's political and economic viability, and a native Austrian nationalism or loyalty to the republic failed to develop. Austria's domestic and international situation remained precarious and confusing. Nor did the West always understand Austria's deeply problematic history. The beaten

Austro-Hungarian Empire had appeared ripe for disintegration in 1918. The new Austrian Republic seemed to be no better. It threatened time and again to exemplify a failed experiment in nationhood. Allied disapproval and offers of economic support in the 1920s and 1930s helped to persuade Austrians to abandon the projected union with Germany for the time being and to persist in their radically reduced state. For some time to come Austrians would remain under the economic and political tutelage of the Western powers.[6]

In subsequent years a number of financial and economic crises aggravated the shock of the sudden collapse of the Austro-Hungarian Empire. The new state of Czechoslovakia inherited about 60 per cent of the old empire's heavy industry, while Vienna, the traditional imperial centre of trade, finance, and administration, lost its economic hinterland now in Czechoslovakia, Rumania, Yugoslavia — the Successor States — as well as in truncated Hungary. These new and remodelled countries further alienated themselves from each other and Austria by attempts to achieve autarky behind high tariff walls. After 1919 many observers pronounced Austria a nonviable economic unit that could limp along only through the infusion of continued Allied support.[7] A great deal of external aid, mainly from Great Britain and the United States, flowed into Austria, while the League of Nations virtually controlled the country's finances until 1926.[8] One disappointed Austrian compared Austria's postwar position to that of New York State, were it severed from the rest of the United States, isolated by the sea on one side and hemmed in by high tariff walls on the other.[9] A few over-optimistic League spokesmen tried to sustain the hortatory argument that Austria would soon become economically self-sufficient, but most experts remained unconvinced and pessimistic about the country's future.[10]

If Austria's economic situation was at best tenuous, domestic political life in the country remained fragile. Deep suspicion divided Austria's three major political parties, each nursing its own passionate ideological hatred of the others, and at different times entertaining loyalties beyond the country's limited frontiers. Party loyalty outweighed patriotism. The first election held in February 1919 produced a fatal balance between left and right: seventy-two Social Democrats, sixty-nine Christian Socials and twenty-six German Nationalists. Cooperation between the conservative Christian Socials and the leftist Social Democrats lasted only two years. Their differences became progressively more entrenched, in 1934 finally spilling over into a brutal civil war in which the left suffered defeat. A smaller, middle-class Pan-German party held the parliamentary political balance between 1922 and 1934. Each party had its own vision of Anschluss with Germany as a way out of current impasses. Austrian Socialists dreamed of union with their left-wing German brethren in an enlarged, German-speaking, socialist republic encompassing Germany and Austria. Christian Socials envisaged a fusion with their German conservative and Catholic Centre Party counterparts. Pan Germans favoured unification with Germany's nationalists.[11] Once the Socialists were vanquished in the 1934 Austrian civil war, Austrian conservatives banded together to establish an authoritarian, Catholic-oriented, and anti-Nazi regime. Socialists and conservatives abandoned advocating union with Nazi Germany as being an ideologically unacceptable solution for Austria's problems. Pan Germans, however, gradually slipped over to the Nazis for political and national reasons, and urged Anschluss with the Third Reich.[12] Many Austrian Pan-Germans and Nazis hoped that such a union would produce a federation, but were disappointed later when Hitler completely assimilated Austria.[13] At the same time some Christian Socials turned to nostalgic dreams of a larger, perhaps monarchical, Danubian federation once again centred in Vienna.

In sum, the modest Swiss model which the Allies had urged the Austrians to emulate remained unattractive to socialist, conservative, and nationalist groups, all of which viewed the Austrian Republic as a decadent, weak, boring structure, lacking historical roots and devoid of any future. The noted Viennese political journalist Gustav Stolper, for instance, pretended to see Austria's provinces as the only truly historic and political units. "German-Austria is not a historically-rooted organism," he intoned in 1921. "There exists no conception of an Austrian state. The Tyroleans, Carinthians, etc. consider themselves as separate states."[14] Indeed, after World War I the population of Vorarlberg voted to join Switzerland, while only 2 per cent in Salzburg and 8 per cent in Tyrol voted to join a new and independent Austria. In 1928 almost two-thirds of the members of the national parliament (*Nationalrat*) signed a petition favouring Anschluss with Germany.[15] Professor Hans Kelsen, father of the republic's original constitution, reluctantly concluded that union with Germany within a federative union was inevitable. Within this structure Austrians and Germans would be linked yet remain distinct. "It would be an act of ingratitude," he wrote in 1927, "if we became citizens of Germany without wishing to remain what we have been for centuries of joy and sorrow – Austrians."[16] Considered from a certain perspective, Kelsen's federative proposal might have been the budding of a frail sort of Austrian national identity; from another, it was merely a revival of older German *Weltpolitik* ideas. The post-1934 Dollfuss and von Schuschnigg authoritarian governments tried to stem any unification move towards Germany by promoting a vaguely republican Austrian nationalism with faint monarchical overtones. But they could not attract the loyalty of defeated Socialists, union-minded Pan-Germans, or most romantic monarchists.[17]

Austrians not directly involved in the economic or political process also wrestled with the knotty complex of Austrian identity. One of the interwar Austrian intellectuals' favourite hobbies was to devise models of existence other than the postwar republican. Was being an Austrian primarily a psychological state of mind compounded of religion, geography, and history, or was it a sort of cosmopolitan amalgam of Viennese, Bohemian, and Alpine cultures? Did it manifest itself as a subtle pessimism tinged with resignation; a psychological, purely cultural attribute not necessarily tied to the new and constraining political republic?[18] Some scholars opined that Austria had always formed an immutable part of German history, whereas others saw the country as being quite different from Protestant and Prussian Germany. Historian Heinrich von Srbik represented the former stream, reviving wide-ranging Metternichean notions of a "Central Europe" (*Mitteleuropa*) centred in Vienna, but including Germany as well.[19] On the other hand, disenchanted groups of young conservative extremists championed a revived Habsburg monarchy and defined Austria as baroque, Catholic, universal, and supranational. Uniformly opposed to Protestant and Prussian Germany, they were unable to generate much enthusiasm for truncated republican Austria.[20]

The internally riven Austrians experienced international abandonment as well. In a vain attempt to retain at least Mussolini's promised protection against Nazi Germany, in 1935 the Schuschnigg regime voted against League of Nations sanctions to be imposed on Italy in retaliation for the Italian dictator's attack on Ethiopia. As von Schuschnigg feared, these sanctions drove Mussolini into Hitler's arms, thus eliminating the only effective foreign support for Austrian independence.[21] In this sense Fascist Italy's annexation of Ethiopia led directly to the Nazi take-over of Austria. With Mussolini's somewhat reluctant acquiescence, Austria became Hitler's first foreign victim in March 1938. As an exiled Austrian historian sadly noted, imperial Austria's great motto must now be completely reversed. AEIOU no longer meant "All the world is Austria's subject" (*Alles Erdreich ist Österreichs Untertan*), but "The first [to be] lost is Austria" (*Aller erst ist Österreich vertoren.*)[22] A year later Czechoslovakia fell, and six months after that World War II began.

As a result of the Anschluss, the Austrian government ceased to exist, and Austria became a mere province of the Third Reich. The Nazis presented the union as a voluntary merger, and stressed that annexation had been a major plank in every Austrian political party's platform since 1918. The show of force occasioned by the purely ceremonial entry of German troops into Austria, the Nazis declared, was merely a catalyst to resolve the apparent impasse on the eve of action. A month after the Anschluss, in April 1938, the Nazi-sponsored plebiscite in Austria ratified the union overwhelmingly. And little wonder. The Nazis completely controlled the electoral operation, while Austrian hopes for acceptable treatment required a positive view of the new state of affairs. Not surprisingly, the Nazis achieved an over 99 per cent majority in favour of union with Germany. Austria thereupon disappeared quickly from public view, to reemerge seven years later following the dramatic defeat of Nazi Germany in World War II. Many Austrian nationalists and Austro-Nazis who had supported the Anschluss saw Austria's assimilation into the Third Reich as the fulfilment of the *Mitteleuropa* idea or Germanic *Weltpolitik*. Others were distressed as they witnessed their country reduced to a number of *Gaue* or administrative districts within the Reich.[23]

The international community's reaction to the Anschluss was ambiguous, but generally reflected at least rhetorical condemnation of Hitler's illegal manner of bringing about the annexation. Without much protest, Austria lost its membership in the League of Nations; foreign missions in Vienna either shut their doors, or more often, became consulates functioning through Berlin embassies or missions. The Munich four-power agreement of September 1938, which terminated the Sudeten question and eventually Czechoslovakia itself, appeared to accept unhesitatingly Germany's frontiers of that date. Did this muted international behaviour signify that these other states recognized the Anschluss; that Austria had disappeared in international law, and that German sovereignty replaced Austrian in the area?

The problem of Austria's legal position following the Anschluss became a fascinating conundrum for international jurists, who frequently consulted obscure political statements and international agreements, public records and legal judgments, only to arrive at contradictory conclusions. They acknowledged that political leaders enjoyed the prerogative of either recognizing or not recognizing changes in government, whether executed legally or otherwise. In the case of the Anschluss, Western political leaders failed to speak out as clearly as they might have, nor did their apprehensiveness lead to clear action. International reluctance to follow through with purposeful moves to counter the German invasion of Austria seemed to indicate either indifference or faint-heartedness. Statements were carefully phrased and replete with shades of meaning. After the Anschluss, political and official spokesmen showed on the whole little interest in defending Austria. Subsequent diplomatic and economic agreements with Germany seemed to recognize the new situation and did not live up to some politicians' initially negative verbal reactions to the Anschluss. As a result political scientists and legal specialists subsequently spent an enormous amount of energy and time speculating about what the various Western governments had in fact thought about the Anschluss, and whether they had recognized the Anschluss or not. Once the Austrian problem reemerged after the war, politicians could pick at will from among the conflicting legal opinions as they suited their purposes.

In 1938 the Western public generally deduced that their various governments had viewed the Anschluss as an act of naked force and brutality. The march of German troops into Austria seemed to symbolize all that was evil and reprehensible in the Nazi dictatorship. Although the British initially protested, they soon extended public recognition to the violent act. Upon being informed of the military action against Austria, the Foreign Office promptly handed the German government an angry note briskly rejecting the use of military force to invade a small neighbour in defiance of international treaties.[24] In the House of Commons Opposition leader Clement Attlee vehemently denounced the Anschluss as a brutal act of aggression, and urged all peace-loving states to rally together in the face of the current trend towards lawlessness. At the same time he carefully refrained from suggesting the use of British force to remedy the deplorable situation.[25] This apparently firm rejection of the Anschluss by government and opposition alike set the tone for subsequent discussions with the Hitler government about the Anschluss. While these negotiations continued, the British declared that they would only discuss unavoidable, vital business with the Third Reich. However, the British government's confidential dealings with Germany displayed a greater tolerance towards the Anschluss than did its initial public statement. The government never published its stinging answer to the German note regarding the union of Austria and Germany. The diplomats implied instead that Great Britain was prepared to begin official talks on replacing the old Anglo-Austrian treaties and agreements with new Anglo-German ones.[26] Even before the results of the April 1938 referendum were known, the British conceded publicly that Austria had disappeared as a state. The foreign secretary, Lord Halifax, informed the House of Lords that "H.M.G. are ... bound to recognize that the Austrian State has now been abolished as an international Entity and is in the process of being completely absorbed into the German Reich."[27] The British transformed their Vienna legation into a consulate general under their Berlin embassy. In May they informed the Germans that henceforth Anglo-German treaties might cover the Austrian area as well.[28] Two months later an Anglo-German transfer agreement shifted Austria's foreign debts to Germany.[29] Thus on the one hand the British government had indicated deep displeasure with the German invasion of Austria, but at the same time it had also decided to accommodate itself to the new situation, which was not likely to be reversed in the near future. What exactly had been the British reaction to the Anschluss?

Did the original note rejecting force represent the true British position, or were the transformation of the Vienna legation into a consulate and the trade agreements a recognition of Austria's demise? Before these doubts could be dispersed, attention rapidly shifted from Austria to the acute problem of Czechoslovakia's safety.

Once war started in 1939, the British government began to signal firm defence of Austria. In 1940 the Churchill government, with a mien of determination, announced its support for all conquered countries, including submerged Austria. Churchill was known to be an unreconstructed romantic, imbued with a deep nostalgia for the Austro-Hungarian Empire. His enthusiasm for things Austrian bubbled over on several public occasions. In an oft-cited Mansion House speech in November 1940, Churchill characterized Austria as the first country for which Great Britain had unsheathed her sword. "Our victory," he promised with deep emotion, "will supply liberation to all of them [the overrun countries]."[30] When accepting from Austrian exiles their gift of a field kitchen to the British war effort, the prime minister spoke of his unfaltering attachment to the Austrian cause. "The people of Britain," he intoned resoundingly, "will never desert the cause of the freedom of Austria from the Prussian yoke."[31] It was indicative of Churchill's heavily historical perspective that he still interpreted the struggle against the Nazis in terms of the war against the Germans of the Second Empire, who had all been subsumed by propaganda under the term "Prussians." The more restrained Foreign Secretary Anthony Eden noted in his memoirs that during the war he and his government colleagues had purposefully stood up for the Austrian cause. "We were certainly in favour of an independent Austria," he wrote, without elucidating further what he really meant.[32]

If the British appeared to adopt a negative public position on the Anschluss, there seemed to be even less cause for doubt about the United States's attitude on this issue. From the beginning Americans seemed unhesitatingly to reject the Anschluss. Far from the European scene, disgusted with the distant buildup of force, and swept by the winds of isolationism, the United States administration preferred to remain on an elevated plane, issuing pleas for a return to peaceful diplomacy and a principled world order. Its first official reaction to the Anschluss occurred several days after the event. Roosevelt's gentlemanly secretary of state, Cordell Hull, alluded somewhat elliptically to it in a wide-ranging, almost professorial speech before the prestigious Washington Press Club. From this national podium Hull voiced his country's unease with the militarization of world politics: "In common with all other nations we have, since the end of the World War, assumed a solemn obligation not to resort to force as an instrument of national policy. All this gives us the moral right to express our deep concern over the rising tide of lawlessness, the growing disregard of treaties, the increasing reversion to the use of force, and the numerous other tendencies, which are emerging in the sphere of international relations."[33] Despite this depressing analysis, Hull continued, it was not the United States's responsibility to consider countering force with force or to suggest specific actions to other countries to halt this undisciplined trend. The United States could not dictate how others should act, nor would it offer a program of its own: "There is one thing we cannot do; and that is to prepare and place before each country of the world a detailed chart of the course of policy and action which this country will pursue under any particular set of circumstances ... [This] would merely result in impairing our effectiveness in working for the one object towards which we constantly strive ... the establishment of a durable peace."[34] Hull failed to mention Austria by name, although his allusions to recent events were understood to refer to Hitler's invasion of Austria.

After a silence of several days following the Anschluss, the Austrian ex-minister in Washington informed the American government on 18 March that his country had ceased to exist as an independent state. Hull then announced publicly that the United States was closely monitoring the Austrian situation and was deeply worried about the ex-minister's note. At his next press conference Hull told reporters that peace was threatened, but refused to single out the Anschluss from among other world problems: "The extent to which the Austrian incident, or any other similar incident, is calculated to endanger the maintenance of peace and the preservation of the principles in which this Government believes is of course a matter of serious concern to the Government of the United States."[35] Hull was referring to the idealistic 1928 Kellogg-Briand Pact outlawing force and war as an acceptable means to solve international problems, and to the 1931 Stimson Doctrine of nonrecognition of territorial transfers brought about through force or threat of force in defiance of international treaties. Despite this cautious and general wording, Hull's distaste for the Anschluss appeared to emerge clearly.

Correctly gauging his country's hands-off sentiment, the secretary of state sensed that he could not go much further than he did. His official statements stressed the administration's dislike for dictators' methods of dealing with international problems, and the purely "technical" or "practical" nature of the American government's reactions to the Anschluss in the interest of American citizens. Hull's official answer to the ex-Austrian minister's announcement of the Anschluss reflected this line: "In view of the announcement made to the government of the

United States by the Austrian Minister of March 17, 1938, my Government is under the necessity for all practical purposes of accepting what he says as a fact and accordingly consideration is being given to the adjustments in its own practices and procedures in various regards which will be necessitated by the change of status of Austria."[36] These "adjustments" included the "practical step" of transforming the Vienna legation into a consulate general subordinate to the United States embassy in Berlin.[37] The note to Germany underlined that the United States accepted the Anschluss as "a fact," implying thereby that it had no legal status in the eyes of the United States.[38] Other "practical steps" quickly followed, including combining the Austrian immigration quota with the German, substitution of the German for the Austrian extradition treaty, and transfer of the Austrian debt to the Germans. On the issue of Austria's international debts, the United States seemed to take much the same line as the British. The official note to the German government stated that "in the case of absorption of a State, the substituted sovereignty assumes the debts and obligations of the absorbed State, and takes the burdens with the benefits."[39] Some have queried why the dubious expression "substituted sovereignty," which seemed to recognize German rule in Austria, was employed by a country that sought to distance itself from the Anschluss. But the government stressed that its overall tone and behaviour were dictated only by the need to conduct day-to-day transactions with Nazi Germany to protect the interests of American citizens.

In subsequent years the State Department refused to elaborate upon its original and somewhat inscrutable statements about Austria. Officials appeared either confused regarding the department's position, or with time they actually softened the line against Germany. A 1939 reply to a public letter of inquiry tried so earnestly to be balanced that its meaning was even less certain than that of the original documents: "The Government of the United States has accepted that Austria has ceased to exist as an independent sovereign state and that Germany is administering the territory of the former Republic of Austria."[40] On the one hand Austria had disappeared, while on the other the use of the word "administering" appeared to convey the impression that German rule in Austria was nothing more than a type of temporary occupation in the legal sense. The curious from among the public were generally urged to consult the department's 1938 diplomatic notes, the enigmatic nature of which had elicited the queries in the first place. When challenged directly in 1940 by a tenacious lawyer who still found these documents less than crystal clear, the State Department legal adviser, Green H. Hackworth, coolly cited again without further comment the original ambiguous diplomatic notes which had elicited the question.

"This Government had accepted as a fact the incorporation of Austria into the territories of the German Reich."[41]

During the first few months after the Anschluss, American diplomatic and administrative regulations allowed State Department officials to employ the terms "Austria" and "Republic of Austria." Then these designations were quietly dropped. The Americans did not grant permission for the creation of an official representative body for Austrian exiles in the United States such as existed for the exiled Ethiopians, who were permitted to staff a consulate general in New York.[42] This stonewalling of the Austrians was ascribed to the undemocratic nature of Austria's last government, or to the lack of any prominent Austrian personages in exile. The last Austrian head of state, Kurt von Schuschnigg, had voluntarily remained in Austria, where he was imprisoned by the Nazis, and for a long time no Austrian ex-minister resided in the United States.

Nevertheless, when the United States entered the war in December 1941, the American government took a number of steps which indicated a positive attitude towards Austrians. Most importantly, Austrian nationals in the country apparently were exempted from enemy alien regulations.[43] This ruling had been requested by Austrian exiles in the United States, and was warmly endorsed by John C. Wiley, America's last diplomatic representative in Vienna.[44] In President Roosevelt's radio message to the nation on 9 December 1941, explaining why the United States had entered the war, Austria was included in the list of countries forcibly occupied by Hitler.[45] In July 1942 Secretary of State Hull again spoke out at a special press conference about the United States's rejection of the Anschluss. Any post-Anschluss dealings with Germany about Austria, he reemphasized, had been merely in the nature of practical steps "in pursuance of its [the United States's] own laws designed to afford adequate protection to this country's interests in dealing with the situation presented by the imposition of military control over Austria, and the residents of Austria by Germany."[46] Hull stressed *de facto* acceptance of Nazi German control over Austria. By now, Hull reflected, everyone should be aware that the United States government had not approved of the coercion the Nazis had employed in 1938 against Austria. The government, Hull asserted, had been absolutely definite "as to the manner in which the siezure of Austria took place and to the relation of the seizure to the Government's well-known policy towards the taking of territory by force ... This Government has never taken the position that Austria was legally absorbed into the German Reich."[47] The mere fact that Hull organized a press conference to reiterate the official American position on Austria was taken to be a considerable boost for the Austrian cause.

In the following year it became evident that, as the fortunes of war shifted in favour of the Allies, the United States should begin to consider the future of countries occupied by Nazi Germany. Concerned that the Executive seemed unwilling to disclose fully to Congress Allied postwar plans, the House of Representatives commissioned a study of what was the country's past policy towards the Anschluss and what it ought to be towards postwar Austria. In early 1944 this study, based upon the American public record, revealed that the United States had indeed never recognized the Anschluss or German rule in Austria and intended to restore Austrian independence. To have done otherwise, it concluded, would have violated the American constitution and the dictates of international law. Thus the United States had continued after 1938 to recognize the existence of Austria as an occupied country to be freed as a result of victory.[48]

Several months earlier, in November 1943, the foreign ministers of Great Britain, the United States, and the Soviet Union, meeting together for the first time during the war, had taken an identical stand on Austria. At their Moscow conference they issued several policy statements, including a joint declaration on Austria. They proclaimed in it that the Anschluss was null and void, and promised to restore Austrian freedom and independence when the current war ended. However, the declaration contained an ambiguous passage which broached the subject of Austrian war guilt. In a sense this position contradicted the concept of Austria as an occupied country. But this unspecified guilt, which could be explained as being similar to that of other occupied countries forced by the Nazis to cooperate in the war, could be expunged, according to the three foreign ministers, if the Austrians engaged in anti-Nazi resistance.[49] This declaration's wording worried some critics. Had the Anschluss not been null and void before the Moscow Declaration? Was postwar Austrian freedom conditional upon the efforts of Austrians to implement their own liberation? What if their resistance was insufficent to please the Allies? Why did the Allies fail to establish official Austrian exile representations in their respective countries after issuing this declaration, as many Austrian exiles hoped? But these questions were mere phantoms when compared to the generous tenor the declaration adopted towards Austria. This top-level communication was the first, and the last, tripartite statement to appear about postwar Austria during the war.

What did all these Allied affirmations concerning Austria really signify? The official record of American diplomatic rulings for this period appeared in the State Department's multivolume series, *The Digest of International Law*, in the 1940s under the editorial direction of the department's legal adviser, Green H. Hackworth.[50] Appointed to the State Department in 1931, Hackworth had established a formidable reputation as his country's chief legal adviser under Presidents Hoover and Roosevelt and their secretaries of state, Henry Stimson, Cordell Hull, and Edward Stettinius, and was an ardent supporter of the rule of law in interstate relations. Following World War II he occupied the prestigious post of American representative to the International Court of Justice. Hackworth emulated Stimson's approach to international problems. It might be true that these liberal Stimsonian principles sometimes suffered defeat in practice, but as the eminent jurist P.C. Jessup pointed out in his review of the series, international law continued to operate and indeed to extend its influence: "Impotent to restrain a great nation which has no decent respect for the opinion of mankind, failing in its severest test of serving as a substitute for war, international law plods on its way, followed automatically in routine affairs, invoked, flouted, codified, flouted again but yet again invoked."[51]

This enlightened, Stimsonian attitude ought to have been reflected in the *Digest*'s analysis of the Anschluss and the post-Anschluss legal position of Austria. On the contrary, however, the *Digest* adopted a veiled phraseology and inexplicable silences concerning Austria. It refrained from celebrating negative American reaction to the Anschluss as a sterling example of the Stimson Doctrine or the sanctity of international law. It merely reprinted the official and public 1938 diplomatic notes regarding Austria without analysis or comment. Many relevant general sections of the *Digest* failed to mention Austria at all. That country was ignored in discussions regarding diplomatic recognition, annexation, or *de facto* and *de jure* governments. In fact, if many of the general doctrines in the *Digest*'s pages were read with Austria in mind, the principles expressed therein would apparently undermine the claim that the United States government truly upheld the existence and independence of post-Anschluss Austria.

Independent states, the *Digest* noted in the section on sovereign states, continued their legal existence until dissolved or absorbed by another political unit.[52] But when the Austrian ex-minister informed the State Department in 1938 that Austria had disappeared into Germany, he used the term "absorption," and official American notes had subsequently employed the term as well. Nor did the *Digest* consider Austria under the section dealing with recognition of the legitimacy of governments or the withholding of recognition.[53] When the *Digest* distinguished between *de jure* or legal sovereign governments and *de facto* or illegal regimes, it cited Ethiopia, but not Austria, as an example of an illegal annexation.[54] The series noted the growing tendency after World War I to renounce conquest as a means of acquiring territory, but again neglected to mention the Austrian example.[55] Why did Hackworth not trot out Austria as a helpful example of illegal conquest as he did with Ethiopia and Czechoslovakia?[56] Strangely, Austria appeared under legal annexations together with Ada-Kaleh (1913), Cyprus (1914), and Rhodes (1922). The *Digest* failed to analyse or explain the vague diplomatic rhetoric the United States employed in its dealings about Austria with Nazi Germany. Why was the transformation of the United States legation in Vienna into a consulate general under the Berlin embassy only a "practical step" in the American case, whereas for the British a similar change signified recognition of the Anschluss?[57] According to the *Digest*, the "fact" of Austria's annexation had resulted in German assumption of responsibility for Austria's external debts and the inclusion of Austria under existing German-American trade treaties.[58] But why did this shift of the Austrian debt to Germany result only in *de facto* rather than *de jure* American acknowledgment of German rule in Austria?

Other official State Department publications were also reticent about Austria. Most experts chose to interpret these few references to Austria or the long silences on the topic as proof that the United States did not recognize the Anschluss. The State Department's *Foreign Relations of the United States (FRUS)* for 1938 reprinted the country's diplomatic notes regarding the Anschluss addressed to Nazi Germany. A State Department letter reproduced in this volume implied that the United States would treat Austria's take-over as it had Ethiopia's in 1935, namely, through nonrecognition. There was no record of any follow-up or contrary decision.[59] According to the 1943 *FRUS* volume, Roosevelt told Eden that he favoured Austrian independence after the war. Roosevelt did not amplify his remark.[60] This exchange was followed by the November 1943 Moscow Declaration on Austria, after which silence descended on the issue, leaving the impression of a positive American policy on Austria.

The next major policy pronouncement on Austria took place in 1946. In April the Socialist president of Austria, Karl Renner, established a provisional coalition government with Soviet support. At first the British and the Americans distrusted his capabilities and Soviet connections. But by the fall of 1946 they decided to recognize the new government. As a result of this policy shift, the Americans resolved to rid their Austrian policy of any lingering ambiguities. In October Austria's foreign minister, Dr Karl Gruber, arrived for a first state visit to the United States. Following a long session with President Truman, who expressed warm support for the reborn democratic Austrian republic, Gruber was handed a State Department note, which purported to outline past American policy towards Austria and the administration's support for the fledgling Second Austrian Republic. This note advised Gruber that in 1938 the United States had considered the Anschluss null and void and that the country had never granted the annexation *de jure* recognition:

> The attitude of the United States to the military occupation of Austria by Germany and its formal incorporation in the German Reich in 1938 was always guided by this consideration (strong disapproval of Nazi attempts to force Austria into the Reich) and by the well-established policy of the United States towards the acquisition of territory by force. While, as a practical measure, the United States was obligated to take certain administrative measures based upon the situation created by the Anschluss, this Government consistently avoided any steps which might be considered *de jure* recognition of the annexation of Austria by Germany.[61]

This text replaced the original expression "absorption" with the word "annexation," which the State Department evidently thought better expressed the 1938 situation. According to this note, Austria continued in the eyes of the United States to exist as a legal entity; it remained an occupied state forcibly annexed by Nazi Germany. Consequently Austria was never at war with the United States, but on the contrary was seen as a friendly state liberated by the Allies: "The United States has accordingly regarded Austria as a country liberated from forcible domination by Nazi Germany and not as an ex-enemy state at war with the United States during the world war."[62] Much to Dr Gruber's delight, this statement was then made public, and referred to frequently in subsequent years as the official American position on the Anschluss and Austria during and after the war.[63] It melded smoothly with the legal and political doctrine which the Second Austrian Republic adopted in 1946.[64]

Discussion about Austria's status after 1945 came to be largely dominated either by legal scholars interested in litigation concerning property problems and state matters, or by politicians wrestling with dilemmas caused by the Cold War. Understandably, Austrians wished to distance themselves from their Third Reich involvement as much as possible. At the same time British and American officials had to compete with the Soviets for the loyalties of Germans and Austrians. It was important for the British and Americans to be able to point to a bold and confident historical position on Austria, based largely upon America's claim concerning nonrecognition of the Anschluss. This occupationist position promptly became elevated to legal and political dogma in the postwar West and in Austria. This doctrine maintained that an illegal, forcible act such as the Anschluss could not have enjoyed legal recognition because the annexation contravened international law. Consequently, Austria's sovereignty had been only temporarily suspended for the duration of the Nazi occupation, but not abolished. Therefore, the Nazis had never achieved true title in Austria. Austria was occupied after 1938 rather than integrated legally into the Reich. Even though it was a thoroughly illegal act in itself, the Anschluss might still have been "cured" later of its illegality and become a legitimate territorial transfer, but only if it had been recognized by the entire international community. However, claimed the occupationists, this was never the case. The Anglo-American Allies together with other countries had not offered this recognition, and therefore the act remained an illegal and unrecognized move in international law.[65] If there might have been any lack of clarity on this issue before the end of the war, after 1945 the United States and other countries opted strongly and openly for the "occupationist" argument. Nor should Austrians be tarred with the brush of responsibility for the war and Nazi atrocities.[66]

Most legal scholars reflected this occupationist view as regards Austria. Professor Robert Langer expressly cited the case of Austria as one of the best examples of the international community's moral insistence on the integrity of states and the need for treaties as the necessary basis for peaceful interstate relations. Like Albania, Czechoslovakia, Ethiopia, Poland, and the Baltic states before and during the war, Austria had not disappeared as a state following Hitler's illegal use of force, largely because of the United States' unconditional support for international peace and order.[67] President Wilson had attempted to introduce respect for democratic government and international law into global practice after World War I. President Hoover and his secretary of state, Henry L. Stimson, had followed suit in the 1930s with their nonrecognition doctrine during the Manchurian crisis.[68] Termed the Stimson Doctrine for short, this moral standard for interstate relations promised a more civilized and orderly international practice. Nations would be weaned from concentrating upon their own narrow self-interest, and force would disappear as a means of achieving objectives in international affairs.[69] In 1933 Roosevelt and his new secretary of state, Hull, adopted and continued to practise Stimson's ideas.[70] Accordingly, they must have unambiguously upheld Austria's right to a free existence.[71]

This benign view of the strength of international law became general during the postwar period in both the United States and Austria. Several noteworthy American doctoral theses in international law along these lines augmented these optimistic assertions.[72] The American scholar Robert Clute followed Langer by arguing strongly that Austria had survived as a state after 1938 largely because the United States had refused to acknowledge illegal acquisitions of territory.[73] Austrian legal scholars and politicians generally shared this view as well. If Austrians could demonstrate that the Third Reich lacked title in Austria, then Nazi laws and German property ownership in Austria were never valid, and Austria could automatically resume its prewar constitution and rights without the need to consult the international community, especially the Soviets, who claimed a veto in Austrian constitutional matters and title to ex-German-owned property in Austria.[74]

Adherents of a small "annexationist" school of legal realists disagreed with the occupationists. They conceded that the Anschluss had entailed a forcible transfer of territory. But they referred to the Nuremberg trials, which deemed the Anschluss the result of a belligerent act rather than an act of war.[75] This meant that technically the Anschluss was not a war-related act, despite Austria's occupation for the duration of the war. The Anschluss was undoubtedly illegal, agreed the annexationists. But complete *de facto* Nazi control in Austria meant logically the disappearance of Austria and *de jure* Nazi rule. As all Austrian institutions were abolished and Nazi institutions were substituted there, Austria was *de jure* absorbed into and annexed by the Third Reich. Legal positivists, such as the British jurist Karl Lauterpracht and Hans Kelsen, drafter of the Austrian republican constitution, rested their case on a platform of lofty legal philosophy, as did the occupationists. They claimed that real control of state power and actual possession were the basis of international law, not moral right. These theorists conceded that morality might play a role in the determination of international law, but only a minor one. Annexationists noted that in 1938 Austrians had not demonstrated much opposition to the Anschluss. Austrians could, of course, muster a number of plausible reasons for their compliance. Austria was small, and its international position hopeless. Socialists, liberals, Catholics, and even Jews, many acting in desperation, had overwhelmingly approved the Nazi referendum on union in the hope of decent treatment by Hitler in return. However, these grounds for accepting the union did not affect the fact that approval was given. Moreover, annexationists asserted, the international community had accepted the annexation as well.[76]

In view of Austria's unresisted absorption into Germany and the disappearance of all Austrian state institutions, the annexationists argued, Austria was politically and legally eradicated as a state in 1938. Austrians became German citizens and fought in Hitler's armies. Even after war started, the Allies failed to establish an Austrian government-in-exile or national committee. Thanks to these conditions, legal continuity between the First and Second Austrian Republics did not exist, because Austria had disappeared and become an integral part of the Reich. Strictly speaking, the Allies may not have been at war with Austria, but at the same time they could not have liberated it in 1945, because in that year Austria was still legally an integral part of defeated Germany.

Eventually these two opposing legal schools of thought became entrenched. Both groups utilized the same public sources, but interpreted their meaning in opposite ways. They confronted each other obstinately from their respective philosophical points of view. Factious legal discussions hardened into inflexible and resolute dogmas. Time did nothing to soften or alter their stance. At least, one would have expected, any postwar edition of the *Digest of International Law* would reflect America's unmistakably Stimsonian position on Austria, thereby helping to underpin the occupationist position. However, when the State Department finally published a revised *Digest* in the 1960s, the outlines of the Austrian picture appeared even more indistinct than two decades earlier. What had happened in the interim to the State Department's clear-cut 1946 statement to Gruber, which should have set the record straight once and for all? On the issue of the nonrecognition of forcible transfers of territory, such as Ethiopia, the new *Digest* stood as firmly as ever. But regarding Austria the *Digest* adopted an even more contradictory stance than had Hackworth's edition. Perhaps this shift from moralism towards legal realism reflected the United States's recently gained global experience and responsibility.

The new *Digest* gave equal weight to annexationists and occupationists, which implied that the legal issues under scrutiny remained open to discussion. Editorially, the *Digest* remained neutral, both occupationists and annexationists being cited at some length.[77] The noted realist, Ti-Chang Chen, was quoted, expounding the view that a *de jure* government had to be able to exercise "unrivalled control over the whole territory of a State."[78] States might still withhold *de jure* recognition over such control, but this then became a purely political decision rather than a legal act. A state's legal title derived from actual presence and control, and had nothing to do with abstract principles of right or short-term political considerations.[79] Hackworth was cited in support of this position as asserting that military occupation in war constituted sovereignty during the occupation period.[80] Once again the American diplomatic notes of 1938 concerning Austria were reproduced without any commentary.[81] Hull's 1942 statement on Austria and the 1943 Moscow Declaration were reprinted as well, but without any attempt to analyse them.[82]

In fact, this *Digest* edition seemed to tend towards the annexationist position. It produced new evidence from the war period which appeared to counter the claim that the behaviour of the United States in the case of Austria had been based on Stimsonian principles, or at the very least, that the situation was murky. An internal 1942 State Department memorandum written by an assistant legal adviser was considered important enough to be reproduced at length. This memorandum asserted that an internal departmental review revealed "that the government had probably recognized the Anschluss in fact," rather than merely *as* a fact. This opinion was based in part on a confidential letter Hull had written in 1939 to the attorney general on the subject of Austria. "These statements [of Hull's] indicate that the Department has in the recent past taken a stronger position than that Germany merely had *de facto* control of Austria."[83] As well, Green Hackworth was quoted in the *Digest* confidentially enlightening the secretary of state in 1942 that, in his view, Austria was an enemy country because of the Anschluss and in consequence of Germany's state of war with the United States.[84] The *Digest* also printed the text of the United States's 1946 recognition of the new Austrian government, which expressed the hope that "Austria might progressively *acquire* [author's emphasis] the status of an independent state."[85] A comment by John Foster Dulles on the 1955 State Treaty was also included which implied that Austria regained its independence only through that treaty: "It is possible to say that freedom and independence is [*sic*] being conferred by the four-power State Treaty."[86] Article One of that instrument apparently reinforced this view: "The Allied and Associate Powers recognize that Austria is re-established as a sovereign, independent and democratic state."[87]

How should this 1960s *Digest* information be reconciled with the prevailing public Stimsonian doctrine? These contradictions have never been properly compared or explained. What then was the actual British and American policy towards Austria after 1938? It is certain that annexationists, including the Austrian Hans Kelsen, believed in the suspension of Austria's international legal status in 1938, whereas the vast majority of American and Austrian jurists stood firmly behind the occupationist view.[88] This debate involving skilful jurists resulted from an ambiguous public record, interpreted according to the dictates of two diametrically opposed schools of legal philosophy. In order to surmount this impasse, it is necessary to move from the public to the primary record.

CHAPTER TWO

The Anschluss Accepted

Following his assumption of power, Hitler removed Germany from the League of Nations and began planning for expansion. In *Mein Kampf* and elsewhere he had referred to Austria as a bastard area that must be reunited with Germany. Under pressure from Mussolini, Hitler was forced in 1934 to dissociate himself from a *Putsch* by Austrian Nazis against the Dollfuss regime, thus preserving Austrian independence for four more years. Yet his original determination to unite Austria and Germany – *Ein Volk, ein Reich* – remained unshaken.[1] From the first, Hitler's program aimed at abolishing the Versailles system, of which republican Austria was one of the products. Hitler's gradualist policy to this end was almost flawless. By steadily increasing pressure on von Schuschnigg, he undermined Austrian hopes for rescue from the outside, convincing many Austrians and others that Anschluss was inevitable. This quiet approach promised Hitler the likelihood that Austria would fall into his lap like an overripe apple. However, pushed by von Schuschnigg's last-minute plebiscite challenge on the question of union, he decided to act. When 100,000 German troops marched into Austria, Nazi propagandists distributed pictures of wildly cheering crowds. First Austria, and later that year the Sudetenland, were supinely surrendered to Hitler's effective combination of threat and speed. None of the powers opposed to the Anschluss did more than lodge feeble protests against Austria's disappearance.

Whatever Western sympathies might have been in 1938 for the small and weak Austrian republic, the truth was that its government did not embrace democratic principles, and it was internationally isolated. Austria's resistance was greatly weakened by its Anschluss tradition, the subversive activities of pro-Nazi Pan-German groups, and the deterioration of Austria's position between the 1936 Austro-German "Gentlemen's Agreement" and von Schuschnigg's disastrous February 1938

Berchtesgaden meeting with Hitler. If in 1933 there had existed some willingness in the West to defend Austria's independence in league with Italy, after 1936 this resolve began to ebb. By 1938 many Western officials and political leaders had come to expect a union of Austria and Germany as a natural, inevitable, and perhaps even desirable evolution. Great Britain and the United States were by then firmly caught in the coils of appeasement and isolationism. Neither country seriously considered trying to halt Hitler's eastern expansion. Instead they hoped that through a combination of judicious treatment and concessions Hitler might still be coaxed back into the family of law-abiding nations. Both countries viewed Austria as a logical venue for German expansion, and as the area where Germany might be granted concessions that would result in a deeply desired continental settlement of all Nazi grievances. It will therefore be necessary briefly to review how the Anglo-Americans' shift towards appeasement or isolationism determined their reaction to the Anschluss.

The British may not have been fooled by Hitler's propaganda concerning Austria's national destiny and Austrian self-determination in 1938, but the loss of Italy as a potential ally after 1936, mounting German economic and military strength, desperate fear of war, and the conviction that Hitler might be tamed induced the British to avoid offending the Führer by attempting to protect Austria.[2] The British government recognized Hitler's "special interest" in Austria and hoped that flexibility on this issue would enable the great powers to reach a general European settlement. Oliver Harvey, Anthony Eden's principal secretary, reiterated in February 1938 what he had been long correct in assuming, namely, "that nobody would fight for Austria."[3]

Under Prime Minister Neville Chamberlain the British government adopted an appeasement policy towards the continental dictators. That curious mixture of guilt about the Versailles peace treaty and optimism regarding the likelihood of a general European settlement deluded the British into believing that all would be well if only Hitler's national demands were met. In Germany the Versailles legacy had bred bitterness and revisionism, of which Hitler was only the most forceful proponent. Hitler's insistence that German influence must be increased in eastern Europe was not ill-received everywhere. Despite Hitler's harshness in domestic and diplomatic practice, some British politicians and bureaucrats believed that by appeasing him they might avoid war and escape continuing British involvement in European affairs.[4] Some blamed the French for the over-strict enforcement of the 1919 peace terms. A few even hoped that Great Britain and the new, disciplined Germany might make common cause against Bolshevik Russia and its new ally France.[5] By prudently conciliating the Germans, the British might persuade Hitler to develop a responsible policy and allow Germany to be brought back into the family of law-abiding nations.[6] A final and all-embracing Big Power continental arrangement would permit Britain to concentrate on world trade and its vast imperial commitments elsewhere.[7]

The British remained preoccupied with their own problems. Imperial and global interests, partial disarmament, lack of reliable allies, and the debilitating effects of the depression made the search for a permanent continental accommodation seem desirable. The British keenly felt the increasing threat to their vast network of responsibilities from a new coalition of revisionist powers consisting of Italy, Japan, and Germany.[8] When Chamberlain became prime minister in May 1937, he firmly intended to terminate the country's tendency to drift in foreign affairs. He insisted on being his own foreign secretary and conducting, as he put it, his own "realistic" foreign policy. He frequently bypassed the cabinet and the Foreign Office in seeking reconciliation with Germany, preferring to seek advice from a small circle of intimates. His crusade for peace with Hitler could materialize only through direct negotiations, compromise, and some accommodation to Hitler's demands. In the European sphere Great Britain was not operating from a position of strength, as Chamberlain resignedly admitted in January 1938: "We must adjust our foreign policy to our circumstances."[9]

In this campaign to pacify the Germans, Chamberlain believed, Great Britain's potential allies would be a liability, and so he would have to proceed more or less on his own. He considered the French selfish. They only wanted to embroil the British on behalf of their own unstable domestic policies and crumbling east European alliance system. Chamberlain was not convinced that Hitler was a menace, but he knew for certain that Stalin was. The Americans were exploitative. They would demand concessions from the British in the realm of war debts and trade rivalries in return for assistance. In Chamberlain's calculation the United States at worst loomed as a potential threat to Britain's global status, and at best it was an unreliable ally. During World War I the British had been unable to protect their own economic interests, and stood by helplessly as the Americans took some of them into their own hands. President Wilson had brought the United States into the war, but much too late, and then he bungled the peace. As one well-informed member of the American Embassy staff in London observed in 1937, the British leaders seemed to want to dissociate themselves from the Americans in international affairs and not seek their support.[10] The British were deeply angered in January 1938, when President Roosevelt suggested the convening of an international conference before a set date to discuss outstanding international frictions, without first notifying the British. The idea was bound to fail, Chamberlain believed, because of its excessive idealism. As Chamberlain confided to his sister,"The plan appeared to me fantastic and likely to excite the derision of Italy and Germany."[11] Convinced that in any eventuality Germany was economically far too weak to sustain a prolonged war, Chamberlain believed that the British alone, or in concert with other European countries, might be able to reach an agreement with Hitler and the other Fascist regimes. Hitler's claims could not be dismissed out-of-hand, but should be dealt with in a business-like manner. The Führer must be treated as the representative and leader of a wronged nation with serious grievances.[12]

To assist him in carrying out his plans, Chamberlain gradually staffed the Foreign Office and leading diplomatic positions with his own men. Sir Horace Wilson, formerly the government's chief industrial adviser, became his main confidant, seconded through the Treasury to work directly for the prime minister. From this concealed position Wilson encouraged and facilitated much of Chamberlain's appeasement policy. It was Wilson who suggested that the appeasers' main obstacle at the Foreign Office, the Germanophobe Sir Robert Vansittart, since 1930 permanent under-secretary, be "promoted" to the new and largely powerless post of chief diplomatic adviser to the government.[13] The foreign secretary, Eden, saw through this stratagem, but did not defend Vansittart against Chamberlain's insistence that he take this new job. In January 1938, a few weeks before Hitler summoned von Schuschnigg to Berchtesgaden, Sir Alexander Cadogan, who was much more in tune with Chamberlain's views, replaced Vansittart.[14]

On 20 February 1938 it was Eden's turn to resign from office. The foreign secretary's deepening differences with Chamberlain over the Spanish civil war and relations with Hitler and Mussolini had caused increasing rifts within the cabinet. Chamberlain remained confident that congenial personal relations with Hitler and understanding of his revisionist expectations would eventually produce a settlement, but Eden had become more sceptical. Eden had wanted to broaden the number of countries involved in discussions with Hitler, whereas Chamberlain preferred to keep the dialogue on a personal, bilateral basis. On the day of Eden's resignation Hitler thundered in the Reichstag that Germany would soon demand more territory. He spoke in general terms about two countries on Germany's borders containing more than ten million Germans. No one could miss the reference to Austria and Czechoslovakia. While praising the Austrian Chancellor von Schuschnigg in his speech, Hitler avoided alluding to Austria's independence.[15]

Chamberlain replaced Eden with the distinguished ex-viceroy of India, Lord Halifax, who followed Chamberlain's line of thought in foreign policy matters. Lord Halifax had not acquired much foreign affairs experience, having served most recently as lord president of the council (cabinet). But in that position he had discreetly sided with Chamberlain. While as foreign secretary Eden had opposed the idea that the Nazis should be singled out for special treatment by personal or government envoys, behind his back Chamberlain had dispatched Halifax to size up Hitler at Berchtesgaden. On his first visit this gangling, distinguished British aristocrat had nearly caused a diplomatic incident by mistaking the short, dull-looking Nazi dictator for a footman. His haughty, condescending view of Hitler persisted. According to Arnold J. Toynbee, research director of the Royal Institute of International Affairs in London, Halifax regarded Hitler as he had the Indian "agitator" Gandhi earlier. They were viewed by Halifax as "both of them superbly exotic ... political 'mad mullahs'."[16] But Halifax agreed with Chamberlain that in order to secure Hitler's cooperation in a European settlement, the West must offer Nazi Germany economic and possibly colonial accommodations, and probably acquiesce in the Führer's demands regarding the Austrian and Czechoslovak questions. Lord Halifax not only believed this, but he told it to Hitler as well. He informed the Nazi leader that as far as the European continent was concerned, "Britain had no primary interests in eastern Europe."[17] Germany could perform a great service to Europe by preventing as best it could the "entry of communism" into Germany and the West.[18] Halifax's new under-secretary, R.A. Butler, was prepared to amplify this position. A few days after his appointment, Butler visited the German embassy in London to convey the message that a new and more conciliatory group now controlled British foreign policy. If under Eden the Foreign Office had been excessively pro-French, a new anti-French group now wielded power in London.[19] The Foreign Office thereafter encouraged its leading representatives abroad to adopt a new conciliatory posture towards Nazi Germany.

The British ambassador in Berlin, Sir Nevile Henderson, played a vital role in this policy shift. Henderson arrived in the German capital in April 1937 before Chamberlain came to power. It was a surprising appointment at the time, in view of his well-known pro-German views. He remained at his post until war broke out, then returned to London, a dispirited and broken man. Before his appointment to Berlin Sir Nevile had not been deeply involved in European affairs. He had not been comfortable as ambassador in Berlin under Eden, who had distrusted his approach to improving Anglo-German relations and several times had censured Sir Nevile for anti-French and pro-German statements.[20] Once Chamberlain had taken charge of British foreign policy, the British explained to the Germans their willingness to deal piecemeal with them on numerous contentious issues, including Austria, because they desired a peaceful European settlement. According to William Dodd, Sir Nevile's American counterpart in Berlin, Henderson actually encouraged Hitler on the subject of Austria. Dodd noted that Henderson went so far as personally to inform "the German government that England would make no objection if Hitler seized Austria."[21]

Four days after Eden's resignation as foreign secretary, the embattled but still unbowed Austrian chancellor announced in a well-publicized speech his intention to preserve Austrian independence in every possible way. In early March an Austrian plebiscite on independence would prove false Nazi claims regarding the existence of huge support within Austria for union with Germany. Von Schuschnigg felt confident that the Austrian people would resist the blandishments of the supporters of Anschluss. To Hitler's chagrin, von Schuschnigg adopted the principle of self-determination, which until then Hitler had employed against Austria.[22] Hitler was furious, and the world awaited his reaction. Henderson was still under the impression that Hitler was a reasonable man. The British ambassador reported from Berlin that he feared "that it will be difficult for Herr Hitler not to yield this time to extremist advice."[23] The Foreign Office had decided some time ago that Austria should not be defended. According to Cadogan, Austro-German union was inevitable, and he actually chafed at Hitler's hesitation in "solving" the Austrian question. "I almost wish Germany would swallow Austria and get it over with ... *what* is the good of brandishing Austria under Hitler's nose when we *can't* do anything about it?" Cadogan wondered. After all, were not Austrians and Germans similar in so many ways, and would not an Austro-German union accord with the nationality principle?[24]

On the day the Anschluss storm broke, 11 March, the British prime minister gave a luncheon party in honour of the recently named German foreign minister, Joachim von Ribbentrop, who was making his farewell rounds in London as ambassador. Chamberlain reiterated to von Ribbentrop his desire to "clear up" relations between their two countries. But just before luncheon two telegrams handed to Lord Halifax outlined Germany's demand for von Schuschnigg's resignation. Chamberlain ushered Ribbentrop into another room, agitatedly read him sections of the telegrams, and stressed the seriousness of the British government's view of the situation. He predicted that these threats and ultimatums would have deplorable effects on their respective countries' relations. Von Ribbentrop answered, probably truthfully, that he was unaware of this sudden crisis, but was certain that the situation would be resolved peacefully. Later that day Halifax visited von Ribbentrop, and emphasized the prime minister's distaste for this type of brutal diplomacy. Ribbentrop tried to soothe his visitor by repeating his morning assurances of a peaceful solution which would make Anglo-German relations even smoother in the future.[25]

At no point did the British seriously contemplate going beyond a protest to express their displeasure. When that same afternoon von Schuschnigg requested advice regarding how to react to the Nazi ultimatum, Halifax responded that the British government had condemned direct German interference in Austrian affairs, but that he could offer no further consolation or advice. "His Majesty's Government cannot," he pointed out to von Schuschnigg, "take responsibility of advising the Chancellor to take any course of action which might expose his country to dangers against which H.M.G. are unable to guarantee protection."[26] The next morning von Schuschnigg resigned, and German troops marched into Austria without a shot being fired.

British protests to Hitler were further weakened by the manner of their transmission in Berlin. The night before the Anschluss, London instructed Ambassador Henderson to inform the German government that if reports were true concerning a German ultimatum to Austria, the British government felt bound to protest in the strongest terms against the use of diplomatic coercion backed by force in order to create a situation "incompatible with its [Austria's] national independence."[27] Whether this protest condemned the threat of force or the threat to Austria's political independence remained uncertain. But Henderson was not in sympathy with von Schuschnigg. When the latter had announced the Austrian referendum, Henderson had tried to dissuade him from this "ill-conceived and ill-prepared folly." Henderson considered his instructions from London "awkward." If Hitler were to be impressed or stopped by a protest, Henderson's half-hearted manner of delivering it would not have achieved either objective. The negative reaction of the ambassador to his instructions and the shame-faced manner in which he carried them out became known in London, leading to a direct clash between himself and the Foreign Office. When Henderson presented himself to the German foreign minister, von Neurath, and to Field Marshal Hermann Göring, he tried to minimize the note's sting by placing the blame for the crisis on the shoulders of the Austrian chancellor rather than on the German government. Von Schuschnigg's sudden referendum call, he told the Germans, was a public challenge to them. He believed that "Doctor Schuschnigg had acted with precipitate folly."[28] Having verbally undermined his government's position, Henderson then conveyed the protest note. Von Neurath rejected the weak British protest out of hand, no doubt fortified by Henderson's personal remarks. He maintained that Great Britain lacked the right to establish itself as Austria's protector, inasmuch as Austria fell within the German sphere. Göring tried to conciliate the British by promising that German troops would be withdrawn from Austria "as soon as the situation became stable," and that free elections would be held.[29] When he learned of Henderson's conduct in Berlin, Halifax became so angered that he wrote a stiff reprimand. "You cannot but have diminished the force of the protest you were to make."[30]

But apart from verbal repudiation of force, Great Britain could do or wished to do little to reverse Austria's fate. Those in charge of the Foreign Office did not abhor the idea of an Anschluss as such. Rather it was the employment of brute force in the military invasion that threatened peaceful international relations. Halifax informed Parliament that although the government had not consented to Austria's absorption by Germany, or to Hitler's violent methods of achieving Germany's goals, the Third Reich's "special interests" in Austria had to be recognized. Nor did Lord Snell of the Labour opposition offer any more hope that aid would be forthcoming for Austria. As his party's spokesman he announced in Parliament: "For good or for ill – and I believe for ill – the fate of Austria has been sealed. We have to accept the situation as it appears before us; we have to accept the inclusion of Austria into the Reich."[31] On 14 March the Austrian legation in London informed the British government that the Austrian government had promulgated a law relegating Austria to the status of a *Land* (province) of the German Reich. That same day the German embassy delivered a similar note regarding a parallel German reunion law. According to this communication, former Austrian diplomatic representatives abroad would henceforth receive their instructions from German missions.[32]

Encouraged by the smoothness of the Anschluss operation, the British decided to exercise restraint. The government may have been shocked by Hitler's unsettling vehemence and speed of execution, yet the Nazis' apparently warm reception in Austria and German attempts to observe proper forms in legalizing the union soothed many British sensibilities. It was a widely held belief that Austria's demise had been inevitable. The real puzzle was that this had not taken place long ago. Intense pro-Anschluss Austro-Nazi and Pan-German activities had encouraged sentiment abroad that most Austrians desired union with Germany. Pro-Nazi factions had seized control of the province of Styria before the Anschluss, and on 11 March Austro-Nazis occupied strategic points throughout the country. These activities reinforced the impression abroad that Austrians were intensely reunion-minded. Many foreign observers were convinced that when the bloodless Anschluss occurred, it was as much a domestic act as the result of German military invasion.[33]

The Nazis immediately scheduled their own plebiscite for April. But even before its results became known, the British government decided to recognize the disappearance of Austria.[34] On 2 April 1938 Henderson approached the German government for permission to change the Vienna legation into a consulate general, in view of "the disappearance of Austria as a sovereign state."[35] Shortly afterwards Austrians voted 99 per cent in favour of the Anschluss. Despite Nazi intimidation, the British were prepared to accept the result as indicating that most Austrians apparently accepted annexation. According to Cadogan, "We might argue about the percentage in Austria that wanted or did not want the 'Anschluss' with Germany Nazi [*sic*], but we are always left with a more or less considerable residue that *did* want it. And we cannot ignore the fact that the Austrians are at least Germanic, with the same culture and tradition with a part of the Reich."[36] With that, the incident appeared terminated. Almost immediately, Nazi pressures on Czechoslovakia deflected public concern in another direction. The Austrian affair quietly faded from view.

Official British circles admitted that Austria had in fact legally disappeared as an internationally recognized entity, and that the British had no choice but to recognize this development *de facto* and *de jure*.[37] In subsequent years, when the British government held secret talks with German anti-Nazi opposition groups, who took the Anschluss for granted as a basic part of any peace agreement, Chamberlain did not contradict them. In September 1939 he quickly quashed discussions by Foreign Office officials regarding possible self-determination for Austria as being "fundamentally misguided."[38] In 1942 Sir Ronald Campbell, the British ambassador in Washington, informed American under-secretary of state, Sumner Welles, of Great Britain's *de jure* recognition of the Anschluss. The ambassador was uncertain, however, whether the Americans shared this view, and requested clarification.[39] Why would the British ambassador express doubt about the American view of the Anschluss, when staunch American rejection of it appeared to be a matter of public record?

British and American policies had not been coordinated before the Anschluss nor for a long time after that. In fact, if the British had ambivalent feelings towards the Americans during that period, many Americans including President Roosevelt reciprocated the sentiment. Roosevelt cherished the Anglo-American cultural community, but politically he was an Anglophobe who distrusted the alleged selfishness, snobbery, and financial power of the British ruling classes and their imperial policies.[40] Although Roosevelt appreciated the need for Anglo-American naval cooperation, he had no intention of subordinating United States policy to British objectives. He faced stubborn domestic issues, particularly the results of the depression. American disillusionment with the outcome of World War I, and fear of being pushed into another war, had launched the country on an isolationist course. Viewing himself as the spokesman rather than the arbiter of the American national will, Roosevelt practised caution in foreign affairs.[41] Until the Axis threat became much more serious, neither the president nor Secretary of State Hull felt inclined to favour alliances or collective security arrangements.[42]

Hull shared the president's conviction that American foreign policy options should be flexible and commitments avoided. A serious, meditative, frail southern gentleman of the old school, Hull sat in Congress for Tennessee from 1907 to 1921, and again from 1923 to 1931. He had had little schooling in foreign affairs and no diplomatic experience, when suddenly Roosevelt appointed him his secretary of state, largely for domestic political reasons. A keen-sighted congressman, Hull had previously shown a certain interest in foreign affairs and agreed to serve, despite his dislike of many of Roosevelt's domestic initiatives, in order to help bring some order into international relations. This principally meant concentrating on restructuring the global economic order. Hull was an economic internationalist, a true Wilsonian advocate of nonviolent change, free trade, disarmament, and self-determination as vehicles for a lasting world peace.[43] One of the obstacles in the way of such a settlement, he agreed with Roosevelt, was the British system of imperial preferences.[44] His aim was peace, even with dictators, to be achieved through free world trade and prosperity. To Hull dictators were simply evil men. Hull deplored "the rising tide of lawlessness in the world." He loathed Nazi Germany's extremism, rudeness, and anti-Semitism.[45] Yet it was not the task of the United States, he believed, to take a leading role in European affairs. That had to be left primarily to the Europeans themselves. The United States maintained some economic ties with Nazi Germany, but Hull could perceive few direct American interests in the area.[46] In contrast to France or Great Britain, the United States possessed the advantage of ideological and geographical distance from the complex tensions of the European continent. Although Roosevelt generally agreed with Hull about the large outlines of foreign policy, he was not attracted to Hull personally and intervened increasingly in the operations of his department. The two men maintained their distance. Roosevelt considered Hull indecisive, moralistic, imprecise, formal, and rambling, whereas Hull had little taste for Roosevelt's bustling and joshing manner and avoided imposing himself on the president.[47] Hull proved a weak leader at the State Department. Almost from the start Roosevelt meddled in its political and personnel affairs.

In time, some of Roosevelt's own diplomatic appointees and officials commissioned to deal with Germany became embarrassments as they came to share strong anti-Nazi views, thereby clashing with the official hands-off policy. Consequently, in late 1937, when Chamberlain began overhauling British foreign policy and replacing personnel, Roosevelt also began to replace anti-Nazi diplomats with pragmatic men congenial to his philosophy of neutralism. Defying Department of State advice in 1933, Roosevelt chose as his new ambassador to Germany William E. Dodd, professor of American history at the University of Chicago and president of the American Historical Association. Dodd was recommended to the president because he had pursued his studies in Germany and developed a deep admiration for German culture. Despite his lack of diplomatic experience, or perhaps because of it, Dodd, in Roosevelt's view, would sympathize with the new German chancellor, Adolf Hitler, and applaud his aspirations for Germany.[48] Dodd departed to occupy his post with high hopes for warm German-American relations.

But initial experiences with Nazi authoritarianism and brutality rapidly disillusioned and disappointed Dodd, who met Hitler once in 1933 but never again spoke to the chancellor. He steadfastly refused to attend the annual Nazi Party rallies in Nuremberg as a protest against Nazi methods of government. By 1935 he was stridently cautioning Washington not to trust Nazi promises of peace. The ambassador was convinced that Germany under Hitler aimed at "unlimited territorial expansion" in Europe.[49] He advocated the establishment of a collective security system as the only practical means to stop the dictator.[50] His advice from Berlin became more and more shrill and grating to his superiors. Apparently no one in Washington seemed inclined to follow it. Much to his own detriment, Dodd also angered American senators during 1937 by enthusiastically supporting Roosevelt's plans to pack the Supreme Court with administration supporters.[51] As a result, Dodd gradually lost favour in Washington.

The same evolution towards a self-conscious anti-Nazism can be seen in the case of the United States minister in Vienna, George S. Messersmith. Before his posting to Vienna in 1934, Messersmith had served as consul general in Berlin under Dodd, where he arrived at opinions regarding the Nazis similar to those of his chief. In Berlin Messersmith was supposed to concern himself with economic matters, but his long, garrulous reports included unfavourable political judgments of the Nazis.[52] Like Dodd he quickly came to detest the Nazis for persecuting their political and ideological opponents.[53] As early as July 1933 he warned Washington about Hitler's war preparations: "I think that the Department must be exceedingly careful in its dealings with Germany as long as the present Government is in power ... What they want to do, however, definitely is to make Germany the most capable instrument of war that has ever existed ... for the present this country is headed in directions which can only carry ruin with it and will create a situation here dangerous to world peace."[54] Messersmith's long, analytical -and basically correct – reports continued to underline Nazi immorality and aggressivity, repeatedly urging that American economic power be marshalled to force the Nazis to practise civilized behaviour.

Following the collapse of the 1934 Nazi putsch in Austria, Messersmith was named United States head of mission (minister) in the Vienna legation, whereupon he too sounded the alarm in Washington about the growing Nazi threat to Austria, the rest of Europe, and in the long run to the United States.[55] "One of the primary objects of National Socialism," he early noted, "has been to bring Austria under German domination."[56] This theme recurred constantly in his dispatches, as did his warm admiration for the threatened Austrians and their courageous Chancellor von Schuschnigg. He shared Dodd's view that only external economic pressure or a conservative revolt within Germany could stop Nazism and its expansion into Austria.[57] Messersmith watched sadly as Austrian independence slipped away through a combination of international indifference and increasing Nazi pressure on the small country. Little Austria was being slowly but surely dragged into the Nazi orbit, he reported, by sly Nazi manouevres such as the 1936 "Gentlemen's Agreement," which forced von Schuschnigg to take for the first time crypto-Nazis into the Austrian cabinet, and the 1937 Austro-German commercial agreement that gave Germany the whip hand.[58]

Neither Dodd nor Messersmith hesitated to expose Nazi duplicity and treachery. The Nazis hated both men, and by 1937 Washington also mistrusted their apparent rigidity. The State Department considered these two intransigent diplomats dangerous, and wanted to restrain them before they caused serious problems between Germany and the United States. Their unadorned interventionist rhetoric offended the prevailing American isolationist mood, which tried to avoid confrontation and involvement in Europe at all cost. By 1937 the president had targeted the State Department for a reorganization under Sumner Welles, with the clear intention of purging some of the activist diplomats. A member of the Eastern establishment, Welles was a graduate of Harvard University, a personal friend of the president, and his State Department appointee as assistant secretary of state in 1933. Welles became the president's confidant in the department with direct access to Roosevelt, a privilege denied Hull. Welles emerged as one of the main architects of the New Deal's Latin American "Good Neighbor" policy. To Hull's dismay, in 1937 Roosevelt named Welles under-secretary of state, a position he was to fill until forced out of office by a personal scandal in late 1943. Relations between Hull and Welles were never warm, and did not improve appreciably with Welles's promotion. Welles's new 1937 responsibility signalled the president's exasperation with Hull's Wilsonian views and with the State Department's foreign service activists. Dodd and Messersmith expected to be recalled.

In April 1937 Roosevelt informed the State Department that he would accept Dodd's resignation in the fall. The plan was temporarily shelved, however, because in the late summer the German ambassador in Washington lodged an official protest against Dodd's anti-Nazi statements. His anti-Dodd utterances were leaked to the press, perhaps by some of Dodd's enemies within the department, to show how Dodd threatened to implicate the United States in European affairs.[59] As a result Roosevelt postponed the date of Dodd's resignation in order to avoid the impression that he was yielding to Nazi pressure.[60] In November 1937 Dodd received his recall from Berlin and the more tolerant Hugh Wilson, currently minister to Switzerland, replaced him. Wilson was expected and prepared to take a milder line towards Hitler. The new ambassador decided almost immediately after his arrival that as an official United States representative he should attend the Nuremberg Party rally, as had the British and the French throughout the Nazi period. Dodd realized that his recall from Berlin meant a shift in United States policy. His comment on his replacement summed up his views: "Mr. Wilson ... was very welcome to the Nazis."[61] Dodd departed Berlin in December, and once home he immediately published a number of anti-Nazi articles and delivered speeches which mightily embarrassed Hull. Hull had welcomed the retirement, having referred to Dodd in an earlier conversation with the German ambassador as "somewhat insane" and a "sort of fool."[62] As far as Hull was concerned, Dodd had never been a loyal State Department employee, because, in a manner typical of Roosevelt's personal style of diplomacy, he had carried on a long personal correpondence with the president, bypassing regular State Department channels.[63]

At about the same time that Dodd fell from favour, the State Department decided to get rid of Messersmith in Vienna as well. Messersmith had discovered some time before that his bitter anti-Nazi tirades were being ignored and resented in Washington. To terminate this embarrassment, the State Department reassigned Messersmith in mid-1937 as an administrative assistant secretary of state in Washington. According to Sir Walford Selby, his British colleague in Vienna, this transfer deeply affected the Austrians, for whom he had always been a great reservoir of support and sympathy: "Perhaps the greatest loss suffered by the Austrian Government this year [1937] was the departure in July of the American Minister, Mr. George Messersmith. Nazi Germany feared Mr. Messersmith and through the tenure of his post he had given the most consistent support to two [*sic*] successive Chancellors."[64] With Dodd's and Messersmith's departures from Berlin and Vienna, the United States's two most perceptive diplomatic representatives vanished from the scene.

In his new Washington position Messersmith was excluded from the State Department's inner policy-making circle, and prevented from spreading his displeasingly harsh opinions about the Nazis. Defying his isolation from policy-making, he continued to send a steady stream of excessively long and deeply passionate warnings to Secretary Hull about the Nazis' wicked intentions. This made him a most uncomfortable colleague and caused him to lose whatever leverage he might once have had with his isolationist colleagues.[65] Jay Pierrepont Moffat, an engaging and conciliatory diplomat who emerged as head of the reorganized European division, was tendered the responsibility of controlling the hawkish Messersmith. Although junior in rank, Moffat received – and filed away – Messersmith's importuning memoranda concerning the dangers the world and the United States faced from Hitler, and the need for the United States to take an active role in restraining him.[66] George Kennan, who had done a stint in Vienna as Messersmith's political adviser and developed a deep admiration for him, especially admired him during this period for his honest and analytical approach to Nazi politics. He later testified that Messersmith's staunch character and clear vision had left an indelible mark upon him. Kennan lauded Messersmith as "incorruptible in his fight for what he considered right and decent."[67] Messersmith's judgments proved totally sound on Hitler. However, he learned that it is dangerous to be right when the boss is wrong. As a reward for the expertness and flawlessness of his predictions concerning the inevitability of war, after September 1939 Messersmith was still kept from European affairs and the following year was named American ambassador to Mexico.

When Messersmith was recalled in 1937 to Washington from Vienna, the State Department was deeply divided over policy, and in a stage of transition. Under Welles its directors were attempting simultaneously to mute anti-Nazi and anti-Soviet policies of the past. In an ironic twist, Messersmith's task in the State Department was to help dissolve the two independent West and East European Affairs divisions and combine them in a new unit under new personnel. The Division of East European Affairs had encountered the same problems as its Western counterpart. Robert F. Kelley, the anti-Soviet head of East European Affairs, finally collided with Roosevelt over the appointment of an "appeaser," pro-Soviet Joseph E. Davies, as ambassador to Moscow. George Kennan, then a member of the East European Affairs Division and a Kelley supporter, attacked this divisional unification plan as a purge instigated directly by the White House and expedited by the president's men in the department under Sumner Welles. He specifically excluded Messersmith from this group.[68] As noted above, Jay Pierrepont Moffat, who since Roosevelt's election had played a growing role in the department, was named chief of the new combined Division of European Affairs. He followed an line more congenial to Roosevelt.

Moffat's ideas about how best to deal with Hitler's Germany conflicted sharply with those of Dodd and Messersmith. Moffat had decided that the wisest policy for the United States to adopt would be to placate Hitler or at least remain neutral, and not to anger him with useless symbolic gestures. Regarding Dodd's refusal to attend Nuremberg rallies in protest against Nazi brutality, Moffat had written disparagingly that "if the British and French, who have far more at stake than we, go to Nuremberg, we could do likewise."[69] Moffat saw his task as that of preserving the United States from entanglements in European problems. "My personal perception," he wrote in November 1937, "is to prevent at any costs the involvement of the United States in hostilities anywhere, and to that end to discourage any formation of a common front of the democratic powers."[70] Moffat's style of diplomatic isolationism, which prevailed in the 1937 departmental reorganization, resembled markedly the concurrent Chamberlain shift in Great Britain. In both instances new men in influential positions heralded a milder course vis-à-vis Hitler and the Nazis, whatever personal revulsion they might have shared regarding the Nazi style of international politics.

Thus, before the Austrian pot began to heat up at the beginning of 1938, the neutralist "realists" had vanquished the interventionist "idealists" in the State Department.[71] Analysis of American public and congressional opinion had convinced the realists that most Americans would repudiate an "activist policy."[72] Taking Germany "into camp" at a cost even remotely feasible in terms of practical politics appeared unlikely. Offers to partially compensate Hitler would only be interpreted by the Nazis as a sign of weakness and would trigger additional demands. On the other hand, if the democracies clamoured too loudly for saner or more acceptable Nazi internal and international behaviour, Hitler would likely raise the level of his own churlishness.[73] The United States appeared powerless to resolve this situation. Was it worth the effort to try to intervene? Would intervention in European affairs not be counterproductive for American interests? Hull's pious preachings about the rise of lawlessness in the world had only frightened domestic public opinion and the press, and angered Hitler without curbing him.[74]

Departmental realists such as Welles, Moffat, and Assistant Under-Secretary of State Adolf A. Berle, Jr – a well-known Columbia University law professor, ex-member of Roosevelt's New Deal think-tank, and another Roosevelt appointee to the State Department – together shared Roosevelt's mistrust of Great Britain. They believed that Britain wanted to involve the United States in its problems for selfish reasons.[75] Consequently they distrusted all British urgings for American involvement in European power politics.[76] Instead they put their faith in a strong, viable Western hemisphere defence system built upon improved relations with Latin America: the "Good Neighbor Policy" which some of them had helped to shape. Surely the United States should remain aloof elsewhere, possibly offering its services as a neutral arbiter. Wars might rage elsewhere, but the western hemisphere could remain at peace. In this sense peace was divisible. The United States sought world peace on the honourable basis of disarmament and economic liberalism, but these wholesome concepts had not attracted Europeans, who insisted on dividing again into antagonistic factions. Now that collective security was dead, the United States could do little outside its own hemisphere.[77]

Within the limits imposed upon him by this type of attitude and the Neutrality Acts, Roosevelt still tried to cast about cautiously for some way of influencing world events. In late 1937 he urged Chamberlain to visit the United States. He weighed various suggestions for quarantining aggressors – and even blockades short of war.[78] The secret Anglo-American naval talks begun in January 1938 have been characterized as the first tentative British and American gestures to forge a future World War II alliance, but the rapprochement was very slight indeed.[79] Without prior British approval, Roosevelt proposed to convene an international conference to discuss disarmament and economic justice. At first the British rejected the suggestion, and then grudgingly approved it publicly. But their enthusiasm remained half-hearted. Roosevelt also offended the British by objecting to their recognition of the Italian conquest in Ethiopia. Thus the proposed conference never materialized, partly because Hitler's February 1938 purge of his conservative Foreign Office and military leaders radicalized German foreign policy. Roosevelt was forced to retrench his position. Publicly he distanced himself from Great Britain's appeasement initiatives, preferring rather to practise his own version of "biased neutrality."[80]

American reaction to the 1938 Anschluss must be evaluated against this background of abstention in Europe and suspicion of Great Britain. When the realists at the State Department discovered how naïvely Chamberlain had accepted the February 1938 German-Austrian agreement, which forced the Austrians to admit several pro-Nazis into the Austrian cabinet, they accelerated their withdrawal from the approaching Austrian drama to concentrate on hemispheric politics. Hitler seemed unstoppable. Russia was too weak, Great Britain too pliant, and France politically divided and bankrupt.[81] In early March, when von Schuschnigg unexpectedly revealed his plans to conduct a referendum, Washington's reaction was as negative as London's. The proposed referendum was not, according to the head of the European Division, truly democratic, and its announcement would indubitably drive Hitler to embrace desperate measures.[82]

Roosevelt's peppery secretary of commerce, Harold Ickes, was one of the few administration members disgusted with the State Department's lethargy and apparent indifference to Hitler's aggression against the established European order. Through its immobility the State Department appeared to countenance Hitler's expansionary ambitions. When he learned of the February 1938 German-Austrian agreement, Ickes was furious, and tried to induce the government to take a tougher economic line against Hitler. But Roosevelt demurred. Ickes then accused the State Department of acting like "some British fascists" in its treatment of Hitler. Ickes considered Hull so weak that he had even lost control over his own department, now dominated by cliques and factions, each with its own chief reporting secretly and directly to the president. Ickes took the Messersmith line by calling for increased American economic pressure on the Nazi dictator, but his outbursts had little effect.[83]

Meanwhile in Vienna, Messersmith's recall changed had little. The American chargé d'affaire, John C. Wiley, continued the Messersmith anti-Nazi line, for which he was roundly berated by Washington. Like his predecessor Wiley pointed to the near-certainty of a Nazi move into Austria in the foreseeable future, if the other powers did nothing to stop Hitler.[84] But nothing was further from Hull's mind than to involve the United States in any way in Austria's hopeless cause. Adolph Berle noted after von Schuschnigg's Berchtesgaden interview with Hitler in February 1938: "The German ultimatum to Austria has been accepted and I suppose ... Austria has fallen into the German camp."[85]

Wiley decided to issue his own statement of support for the beleaguered Austrian government. He may have believed that he was actually conveying his government's position. With some passion he informed the Austrian foreign minister that "my Government maintained a deep and sincere interest in the welfare of Austria and I was sure that it hoped earnestly that the Austrian Government would firmly resist threats against the independence of Austria."[86] This well-meant but imprudent public declaration of support for that small country shocked the State Department. Moffat was frankly aghast at Wiley's rashness and the implications other countries might draw from it. "We certainly can't be thought," he wrote, "whatever our sympathies might be, to assume any responsibility, legal or moral, in Europe at the moment."[87] As a result the reckless Wiley received a sharp message of rebuke from Hull: "I am somewhat concerned ... by the statement which you made to [Guido] Schmidt [the Austrian foreign minister] ... You should very carefully avoid, in the future, making any statements, which can possibly be construed as implying that your Government is involving itself, in any sense, in European questions of a purely political character or is taking any part, however indirectly, in the determination of such questions."[88]

The anticipated Nazi move into Austria finally occurred in mid-March 1938. When Adolf Hitler, surprised by the warmth of his reception in Vienna on 14 March, decided to unite the two countries immediately, American reaction was predictably abstemious. The State Department issued no statement, while officials pondered how to disguise American diplomatic paralysis. When the Americans finally responded, the British noted with satisfaction that the statement did not differ substantially from their own. In fact, the British maintained, they themselves had issued an immediate protest about the Anschluss, whereas the Americans remained silent, and then engaged in empty rhetoric to disguise their real sentiments. "The United States are usually behind us in these matters ... But they usually contrive to persuade the public that they are in fact doing much better than we are!"[89] State Department realists might have had their private reservations about Hitler's use of force in the Anschluss, but they feared involvement in basically unresolvable European affairs or in one of Great Britain's wars even more. They waited three weeks to see how the British would react to the Anschluss and its results before officially committing themselves. The realists released a few rhetorical generalities to the public in order to preempt the anticipated storm of indignation from idealists both within and outside the department. Eventually realists and idealists worked out a compromise of sorts, which in fact represented a victory for the realists. When the State Department finally issued a statement three weeks after the Anschluss, it closely resembled the British position.[90]

The post-Anschluss period was filled in Washington with hurried meetings and consultations. American administration officials offered vague public utterances, hoping to maintain some hold over public opinion. In a first flush of anger, Roosevelt wished to issue some sort of condemnation, but Under-Secretary Welles restrained him. According to Moffat, Roosevelt agreed to do nothing on the grounds that the American public would not accept a statement critical of the Germans.[91] The German ambassador in Washington had a very uncomfortable interview with Welles, who personally disapproved of Nazi aggression in Austria. At the same time, however, the ambassador realized that few officials were prepared to speak out against it. He reported to Berlin that even Hull showed "a certain understanding for the German action."[92]

In the meantime Messersmith informed Wiley in Vienna to sit tight and await the government's final decision, which would in all likelihood favour the Austrian cause. He compared the Austrian case with the

Ethiopian and Manchurian episodes. In both instances the government had invoked the Stimsonian doctrine of nonrecognition. In order to help anti-Nazi refugees in Vienna, Messersmith asserted, Wiley should stop pretending that he was replacing a minister, and function in future only as a consul general.[93] Wiley agreed with this advice. He worried lest the Nazis expel all Americans if the American government appeared to reject the New Order in Austria. That would dash all attempts to help refugees. For this practical reason Wiley urged the earliest possible *de facto* and *de jure* recognition of the Anschluss. In his view the United States only required a consulate general in Vienna to deal with refugee hardship cases produced by the Nazi take-over.[94] If Washington accepted his general recommendation, Wiley wrote, he wished to be transferred out of Vienna and replaced by a new man dispatched specifically as a consul with the consent of Germany. He hoped the State Department would do with him as other countries had done with their mission chiefs following the Anschluss. If he alone of the diplomatic corps remained, he would "stick out like a sore thumb," and he would certainly be considered by the new authorities as a friend of their enemies. Moreover, the Nazis could use his continued presence in Vienna as a "benediction" of the Anschluss rather than as a judicious bowing to necessity.[95] Hull responded by repeating his call for caution and composure, and especially for the avoidance of any public statement likely to entangle the United States in European questions of a purely political nature.[96] Wiley did not immediately receive his wish for a transfer. He was forced to wait until later that year before being posted as minister to Estonia and Latvia, which were to suffer a fate similar to Austria's.

The Anschluss question forced the State Department to consider how to balance neutralism and morality. How could the United States avoid European entanglements if it condemned the Anschluss? In February Adolf Berle had told the president that an Anschluss was "all to the good. Whatever can be done by diplomacy does not have to be done later by war." Unification of Germany and Austria "is probably necessary and not alarming."[97] Once the Anschluss had taken place, he advised Hull that the United States had no choice but to recognize the Austro-German union as a *fait accompli*. Now the department had to devise a diplomatic note that would satisfy Hitler, while at the same time for domestic purposes appear to rebuke him. The Anschluss itself had been inevitable, Berle thought. "We are not opposed to the annexation of Austria as such, but we are opposed to the oppressive nature of the Hitler government." In view of that regime's nature, there was precious little one could do to help Austria. Some might argue that the United States ought to recognize the Anschluss in return for concessions such as better trading rights. This ploy stood little chance of success, Berle concluded, "for Hitler is practically impossible to negotiate with along these lines."[98] Berle's realist colleague Moffat was less interested in the morality of the Anschluss than in the abstract legal problem of "when Austria legally ceases to exist." Moffat suggested inaction, thereby allowing intensive departmental discussion which would wear down the moralists to proceed. He considered proper timing and the appearances of legality more important than substance. One way these high-ranking State Department officials played for time was by claiming that the United States could not yet respond to the German notification of union with Austria until it received a similar notification from the Austrians, which was still outstanding.[99]

There remained the difficult question of what to say to the American public before the administration was clear as to what would be its final reaction to the Anschluss. Several weeks before the Anschluss Hull had agreed to deliver a major foreign policy speech at the National Press Club; in the meantime, the Anschluss had taken place, and he would now be expected to include a statement about the administration's reaction to this latest European event. Welles sought Roosevelt's view as to whether it would be wiser to keep quiet or to issue a vague statement. The press might ask uncomfortable questions. On the other hand, if the secretary kept his silence on Austria the repercussions might be even more embarrassing. The president decided that an apparently open approach would be best: Hull should meet the press and give his speech as scheduled. Domestic public opinion expected an official reaction to the disappearance of Austria, no matter how vague or rhetorical. "Domestic considerations," Roosevelt informed Welles, "outweigh foreign ones."[100] The object then was not to outline administration policy, which had not yet materialized, but to calm or control domestic public opinion.

When Hull subsequently met his regular press conference he took the high moral road and avoided specifics. He cited the Austrian incident as merely one example among many of a type which was "of serious concern to the Government of the United States."[101] Two days later a departmental contingent trooped to the National Press Club to hear Hull deliver his speech on foreign affairs.[102] He denounced violence in international affairs, a reference included in the text before the Nazis marched into Austria. Hull's careful generalities were not meant to serve as a direct challenge to Hitler's action in Austria, although they seemed to show a distaste for it. It was certainly true that the administration condemned the "rising tide of lawlessness, the growing disregard of treaties, the increasing reversion to the use of force."[103] But at the same time Hull took care to avoid outlining any American reactions to this catalogue of problems. Moffat was elated. The speech had generally struck the right note, although it might have been loaded with too many ideas, he believed. However, if anyone studied the text carefully, he would see American foreign policy emerge, if dimly. Hull's speech, Moffat concluded, pointed to the indubitable fact that the administration wished to avoid a positive American role in international affairs. In effect the United States had adopted a moralistic but clearly "hands off" policy regarding European affairs.[104]

Hull's speech may have pleased the neutralist press, but internationalist newspapers such as the *New York Times* and *Washington Herald* spiritedly assailed the secretary's passivity and condemned the statement that the United States had refused to associate itself with the British protest over the Anschluss.[105] *Newsweek* concluded that to all intents and purposes the United States had in fact recognized the Anschluss. In the event of future crises elsewhere the United States would shrink even further into its shell.[106] The influential Catholic weekly *Commonweal* labelled Hull a fanciful preacher, and wondered whether he could be trusted to lead the country through these stormy times. "Mr. Hull's principles provide an excellent norm of international morality," the magazine admitted. "But we regret that Mr. Hull did not clarify our foreign policy [even] to the extent of defining 'peace-loving nations'."[107]

However, these activist voices did not represent the majority view in the country. Most Americans did not regard the Austro-German union, however achieved, as improper or unnatural.[108] Many Americans, like numerous Austrians, had argued previously that a union of the two countries was the only practical way to solve Austria's long-standing economic and political difficulties. Most of the American press remained remarkably silent about the Anschluss.[109] American public opinion analyses in the fall of 1938 refuted activist claims that the country had shifted from isolationism as a result of the European crises of that year.[110] According to a large public survey, most Americans wished the administration to continue neutrality, especially towards Germany.[111] Only near the end of 1938 did the German ambassador begin to note a weakening of American isolationism. While most Americans had accepted the Anschluss, the Czech crises effected a change of mood regarding Germany.[112] By April 1939, following the German take-over of Czechoslovakia, 46 per cent of those polled believed that war with Germany was conceivable, while 54 per cent still did not.[113] These 1939 statistics represented a real shift of public opinion, but came far too late to aid Austria.

The first draft of an American note to the German government about the Anschluss adopted the approach of the British model; namely, protesting brutal Nazi diplomatic methods but not the result. Realists continued to plead for further delays since they wanted the note so phrased as to show that the Anschluss problem did not directly concern the United States. They held up discusions of the larger question of recognition by raising a number of immediate, practical problems such as the status of refugees and of the Vienna legation. In the meantime, both sides agreed to divulge nothing in public until a mutually acceptable package could be negotiated which dealt with all facets of Austria's "complete liquidation," as Moffat put it.[114] The realists planned to delay a decision until the British recognized, as the realists believed they would, the Anschluss. This strategy, if successful, would undercut the idealists' plea for American moral leadership. The realists maintained that the Austrian Anschluss was not analogous to either the Manchurian or the Ethiopian situation, when the State Department had invoked the Stimson Doctrine of nonrecognition. Besides, they held, rigid nonrecognition would harm American commercial and other interests in former Austria and in Germany. The realists' original compromise offer to the departmental idealists consisted of an agreement that Austria's absorption by Germany would be recognized, the American legation withdrawn from Vienna, and a statement condemning the Nazis' action included in the note.[115] In the end the two sides abandoned this compromise and adopted another. The Anschluss would not be recognized outright, but neither would it be denounced.

The Berle-Moffat group gained a week's respite through its insistence that some sort of official statement about the Anschluss be pried out of the Austrian ex-minister to the United States, Edgar Prochnik. For the Austrian head of mission in Washington, reputed to be a pro-Nazi, had almost immediately following the Anschluss turned over his legation to the Nazis. The building now flew the swastika. True, the German ambassador had conveyed his note informing the American government that the Anschluss had occurred, that Prochnik and his staff now served the German embassy, and that the former Austrian legation now belonged to Germany. But thus far Prochnik himself had not been heard from. A State Department official was delegated to find him and request him to inform the American government officially of Austria's fate. However, when approached Prochnik informed the State Department that he had received no such instructions from Vienna. Welles insisted that he be forced to act. The next day Prochnik, "with true Teutonic tact," as Moffat noted in his journal, phoned back to say that the German ambassador would call Hull about the matter. This was too much for the usually placid Hull. He angrily ordered the Austrian diplomat to deliver his own messages, even if only by phone.[116] So on 17 March Prochnik, presumably obeying the German ambassador's instructions, somewhat sheepishly phoned the Division of European Affairs rather than the secretary of state to confirm that he had – as everyone knew – transferred his legation to the German ambassador and now stood under his orders. This satisfied the State Department realists, who could now claim that the legal forms for territorial transfer had been respected.[117] Through this eccentric route the department finally obtained the type of Austrian diplomatic notice concerning the Anschluss required to pretend that the annexation had occurred not by force but more or less voluntarily. With this notification in hand, State Department officials continued their lengthy internal consultations on how best to formulate an official reply to the German note about the Austro-German union.

In the course of these discussions it seemed a sound idea to solicit the opinion of ex-Secretary of State Henry Stimson, creator of the so-called Stimson Doctrine of nonrecogntion of acts of international aggression. Should Stimson publicly support nonrecognition of the Anschluss, the administration would find it very difficult to resist such pressure. Stimson had left politics, was actively engaged as an influential lawyer in New York, and acted as a leading member of the prestigious private foreign policy research organization, the Council of Foreign Relations. For some time after his return to private life in 1933, Stimson had avoided taking positions in public on foreign policy. By 1935, however, Stimson was becoming so concerned at the course of international affairs that he began to speak out publicly against the rising tide of neutralism he saw in his country. He wrote an influential book for the council expounding his experiences as secretary of state and explaining the history of the doctrine of nonrecognition during the Far Eastern crisis of the early 1930s.[118] At the same time he informed the American Society of International Law that the United States had no other choice but to cooperate with other countries to prevent the approach of war.[119] In his continuing campaign for American leadership in the worsening international scene, Stimson objected to the neutrality laws and opposed the Nye Committee's one-sided investigation of the alleged influence arms manufacturers had exerted on the outbreak of World War I because it encouraged neutralism.[120] When refugees from fascist regimes began to arrive in the United States, including ex-Chancellor Heinrich Bruening of Germany, he made a point of befriending them, thereby keeping up-to-date on German and European affairs.[121] He welcomed any hint of an active American foreign policy such as Roosevelt's October 1937 Quarantine speech.[122]

Many public figures encouraged Stimson to invoke nonrecognition against the Anschluss. Ten days after the event, a group of prominent Americans approached him in order to garner his support for a petition they were submitting to the president calling for American nonrecognition of the Anschluss. However, much to the group's consternation,

Stimson refused on technical grounds to associate himself with the petition. It would be immodest for him, he replied, to intervene in the debate at this critical time, and it would be indelicate of him to embarrass the administration.[123] In the light of Stimson's immense reputation, this negative reaction completely surprised the group. Was his refusal merely political, as he claimed, or did it reflect other reasoning?

Perhaps Hull had heard through other sources of Stimson's refusal to step out in public in defence of Austria. Or perhaps he hoped to persuade Stimson to keep his counsel. At any rate, a few days later Hull decided to travel to New York to consult with him on how best to approach the Anschluss crisis. The two men had developed the habit of meeting informally from time to time to discuss current international problems. Opening the discussion, Hull outlined to Stimson the division of minds within the State Department, and asked Stimson whether he would recommend nonrecognition of the Anschluss. He was surprised – and delighted – to learn that Stimson firmly opposed nonrecognition of the Anschluss.[124] Stimson reviewed for Hull the historical circumstances of the doctrine's application in 1932 against Japanese territorial expansion into Manchuria. At that time nonrecognition had had nothing to do with alleged abstract legal or political standards of American foreign policy-making. As developed during the Manchurian crisis, the policy had been designed purely to rally domestic public opinion against the Japanese. Rejection of brutal force had deep ideological and moral roots in American history. But the nonrecognition option should be exercised only to galvanize domestic public opinion by appealing to its better nature in support of specific policies the administration enthusiastically supported. In the Anschluss question, however, Stimson could discern no adequate reason for trying to rally public opinion. In fact, it seemed to be both unnecessary and unacceptable in the circumstances for the administration to contemplate any practical or even moral measures designed to try to save Austria. Consequently he was prepared to promise Hull that he would have nothing to do with any public protest movements against the administration if it refused the path of nonrecognition. After their meeting, Stimson noted in his diary his advice to Hull against nonrecognition of the Anschluss. "I could hardly see how it [nonrecognition] fit," he wrote.[125] Hull could be well satisfied with his visit to the "oracle."

Armed with Stimson's own authoritative opinion and his promise of abstention from movements to pressure the State Department on the Anschluss issue, departmental realists felt much more assured of their own position. As a result of Hull's confidential talks with Stimson, the pro-Austrian petition to the president which Stimson had refused to support lost its momentum in Washington even before its presentation.

When Saul O. Levinson, the group's spokesman, appeared at the State Department with the petition following his visit with Roosevelt, he was easily fobbed off by officials acquainted with Stimson's views. Levinson harangued Hull about the United States's duty to refuse recognition to the Anschluss, and upbraided him for supineness in the face of that small country's open rape. He invoked the Kellogg Peace Pact and the Stimson Doctrine, both of which he protested outlawed international piracy, and demanded stern and immediate application of nonrecognition. Levinson was patronized, urged to go from office to office, and encouraged to outline his position for each new listener. He commented freely that Welles was the arch-villain in the piece, probably acting under the influence of the British. Moffat noted disdainfully in his diary that Levinson was "an interesting old man, but too garrulous and so convinced of his right and wrong as he sees them that he is unwilling to admit of any shading."[126] Predictably, Levinson's courageous visit to the lion's den had no effect on American foreign policy.

In the end the realists' delaying tactics proved effective and resulted in a victory for abstention concerning the Anschluss. This strategy of procrastination ensured a cooling of emotions and avoidance of an active American policy. Hackworth observed that worrying about Austria had little real value. "The fact remains that Austria has been absorbed by Germany."[127] Without fanfare Prochnik's name was quietly removed from Washington's diplomatic list at the end of March.[128] To the task of drafting the final version of the American diplomatic notes to Germany, the State Department assigned one realist and one idealist to the task, Jay Pierrepont Moffat and George Messersmith. They met many times to hammer out a mutually acceptable diplomatic formula, if possible. The realist carried the day. On 2 April 1938 the British diplomatic note on Austria to the German government was made public. It neatly coincided with the Berle-Moffat position, approaching the problem from a purely practical perspective. By announcing closure of their Vienna legation and the opening there of a consulate general under direction of the Berlin embassy, the British demonstrated that they accepted the union as a legal fact.

A day after the publication of the British note, Messersmith and Moffat presented their own draft diplomatic notes to Hull, who quickly accepted them in principle. The completeness of the realists' triumph was underlined by Moffat's single-handed editorial work during the next two days on the notes' final versions, which were to be dispatched to Berlin and released to the American public.[129] Their final phrasing resembled the British text, except that they remained vague about the legality of the Anschluss. This opaqueness was included to assuage the American public's sensibilities rather than to support any legal principle.

The Anschluss was treated as a "fact," which necessitated certain "practical steps." The notes contained no explicit expression of moral shock or reference to nonrecognition as had been evident during the Manchurian and Ethiopian crises. American and British "practical steps" coincided. The American Vienna legation became a consulate general "for the safeguarding of American interests" and to aid refugees, and the Germans were asked to take over the Austrian debt to the United States.[130] Again, Moffat prepared the press statement covering the 5 April issuance of the American notes, stressing American noninvolvement in European affairs. He demonstrated clearly his own opinion by lunching publicly the same day with a member of the German embassy. His diary record indicated that it was a friendly meal devoid of any friction over the American notes concerning Austria. Instead, Moffat noted that his German colleague was in "fine fettle" because he had just been chosen to return to Germany in order to accompany Hitler on his approaching visit to Mussolini.[131]

On the day the State Department released the text of its diplomatic notes to the Germans on Austria, the public campaign against the administration's "hands off" policy regarding the Anschluss reached its climax. A thousand angry demonstrators marched in front of the German consulate general in New York, hoping to influence the American government to protest the Anschluss. A large public petition was presented to Roosevelt begging him to issue an "open and affirmative announcement of the application of the diplomatic policy of nonrecognition with regard to the enforced annexation of Austria by Germany."[132] However, these public displays did not affect official policy.

In sum, both the American and British governments disliked the bullying tactics employed by the Third Reich in the Anschluss. But they accepted the annexation as an inevitable development once it had occurred. As late as 1944 Welles still blamed the Allies for having created in 1919 the conditions which led to the Anschluss. At that time they had failed to establish an economic federation between Austria and eastern Europe. Alone Austria had stood no chance of survival.[133] In 1938 leading British and American officials shared this view. An Anglo-American will to support Austria was lacking. No one in authority wished to endanger a possible settlement with Germany or become involved on the continent for the sake of a country with such a dubious future.[134] Both countries concealed their discomfiture over the Anschluss because their leaders felt it neither necessary nor possible to oppose Hitler over Austria. Ambassador Wilson reflected this sentiment in Berlin on 13 April when he stated that a real fear of war in Europe kept Americans from involving themselves in European affairs: "I know there are some things our nation will fight for. I believe there is a policy under wise leadership to keep the United States out of the great struggle. I admit the danger of our being drawn in; I do not admit the inevitability ... we earnestly hope and pray that no nation will make it impossible for us to realize this desire."[135] Not every member of President Roosevelt's cabinet concurred with the State Department's position on Austria. Secretary of the Interior Ickes refused to sell any more helium to Nazi Germany as a result of "Germany's ruthless and wanton invasion of Austria."[136] But he did not represent majority American opinion, and he and Hull had a violent showdown over this issue. Private foreign affairs experts such as Allan Dulles and Hamilton Fish Armstrong of the Council of Foreign Relations agreed that the United States could do no more than it had. The "Never Again War" philosophy still dominated domestic public opinion, which left the administration no choice "except to carry forward Secretary Hull's vigorous and courageous efforts to create a more normal psychology by restoring world trade to its usual channels."[137]

Nor was the State Department subsequently interested in shedding more light on this topic. Answers to public letters of inquiry simply repeated verbatim the 1938 diplomatic notes to the German government.[138] Its spokesmen alluded to Austria as a country which had "ceased to exist as an independent sovereign state."[139] Official internal correspondence showed an even bleaker picture. When the secretary of labor inquired what allegiance Austrians seeking American naturalization should now renounce, Hackworth pointed to Germany as "the present sovereignty."[140] In fact, in 1939 Hull confidentially revealed to the attorney general that the United States had fully recognized the Anschluss: "The Government of the United States recognizes that Austria ceased to exist as an independent state and has been incorporated into the German Reich and that Germany exercises *de jure* sovereignty over the territory of the former Republic of Austria."[141] By 1941 the American State Department appeared to be prepared to put out this view in public too. A draft official letter is still to be found in departmental files responding to private citizens' queries, which incorporated Hull's answer to the attorney general, but without any indication that it was ever sent. This letter was initialled by several of the divisions within the department, including the European and legal, concerned with this problem. At the very least, the draft indicated a new departmental consensus on the matter just months before the country entered the war.[142]

At the time of the Anschluss Great Britain and the United States were caught in the throes of neutralism. Neither country seriously contemplated halting Hitler's eastern expansion, but hoped to lure Germany back into the family of law-abiding nations by concessions or persuasion. These hopes did not disappear with the Anschluss. Roosevelt and Hull still dreamed of a future world conference to regulate outstanding problems with Hitler.[143] In the meantime, the State Department did not deny – at least internally – that the two countries had reacted to the Anschluss in a similar fashion. A 1942 State Department study regarding the country's reaction to the Anschluss reached the conclusion that the realistic stances adopted by the British and the Americans in 1938 were indeed similar. Both countries had found the methods Hitler used to bring about the Anschluss unacceptable and illegal, but they considered the result legal. Both recognized that Austria had disappeared as a state and had become an integral part of the German Reich. Therefore once war was declared against Nazi Germany, Austria also became enemy territory. The Americans may have reacted somewhat more ambiguously than the British, but only to calm domestic public opinion and to ensure that the Germans derived no benefits from trade preferences Austrians had enjoyed.[144] American officials admitted that they would have taken a stronger stand against Nazi Germany in 1938 had they foreseen that war would break out: "There can hardly be any doubt that we would have taken a more definite position as regards Austria if we had seen in the Anschluss the necessary first move in the strategy by which Czechoslovakia, Poland, Yugoslavia and Greece were conquered by the Nazis."[145] Britain and the United States did not reject the Anschluss. "Both the United States and Great Britain recognized the 1938 Anschluss of Austria and Germany by withdrawing their legations and establishing consulate generals."[146] American and British reactions to the Anschluss did not differ materially, although the Americans created the illusion through hinting at the Stimson Doctrine that they did.

Even Stimson did not recommend nonrecognition and he denied that a legal or diplomatic doctrine bearing his name existed. Anglo-American reactions to the Anschluss seem to cast doubt on the validity of some time-honoured principles of international law. But what is international law and how effective is it? The respected legal authority Georg Jellinek cautioned as early as 1905: "One can assert that nine-tenths of the traditional doctrines of international law are not actual international law."[147] Other legal experts have also warned against accepting without thorough examination the assumption that political or legal doctrines express scientific truths.[148] The collapse of League of Nations sanctions directed against aggressive powers, and the concurrent rise of the spirit of appeasement in Great Britain and neutralism in the United States, caused Anglo-American policies towards Nazi Germany and the Anschluss with Austria to evolve along similar pragmatic lines. How did Anglo-American reactions in 1938 towards the Anschluss influence the status of Austrian exiles and political planning once war began?

CHAPTER THREE

Austrian Exiles as Enemy Aliens

The Anglo-American alliance developed only slowly after 1939. What to do with Germany and Austria after the war long remained peripheral questions. Survival and Germany's defeat became first Great Britain's and then the United States's main goals. Little incentive existed to review or revise earlier Austrian policy. Neither Churchill nor Roosevelt desired to define Austria's postwar boundaries or future status during this early war period, when their own countries' futures were still far too uncertain. Their Austrian refugee and exile policies developed before Britain's entry into a formal alliance with the United States. These policies appeared somewhat ambiguous, although both countries generally tried to interpret them in a manner intended to show the world that the hosts wished to protect and offer refuge to Austrian exiles. Austrians made a point of demonstrating that their British and American hosts considered Austria a friendly country occupied by the enemy, and that they differentiated between the treatment of German and Austrian expatriates.

The primary record does not support exaggerated British and American claims of benevolence towards Austrians. After 1939 the British and the Americans, one at war and the other at peace until the end of 1941, slowly and haltingly evolved an alliance. During this glacial process they independently developed similar policies regarding the legal status of the Austrian exiles, and responded jointly to their aspirations to gain political recognition. Each state enacted administrative rulings which purportedly distinguished between German and Austrian exiles, but in fact Austrians remained classified as German citizens and enemy aliens until after the war. American policy-makers obscured this issue more than did the British. This Allied behaviour stemmed partly from British and American recognition of the Anschluss. However, the conduct of the Austrian exiles also had a good deal to do with this state of affairs.

Neither government cared to get involved too deeply with the splintered and quarrelling groups, especially in the wake of a few ineffectual attempts to unite them and to cooperate with them. As a result no Austrian group gained official recognition, nor did the two Allies contemplate the formation of an Austrian government-in-exile or a liberation committee. Most of the initial goodwill these organized Austrian exile groups enjoyed at the beginning of the war gradually dissipated.

Throughout World War II the British and American governments suspected one another's policies. In the war's early years Americans deplored the British blockade directed against Germany because they hoped for a negotiated peace settlement with the Germans once the Nazis were eliminated. The British, on the other hand, were resolved not to permit the Americans to secure undue economic advantage over them as they had during the previous conflict.[1] These apprehensions prompted Prime Minister Chamberlain in early 1940 to discourage the United States from entering the war lest Great Britain again become over-dependent upon or economically drained by the Americans.[2] This unsatisfactory relationship gradually improved, thanks to the efforts of Winston Churchill, appointed first lord of the admiralty in September 1939. From the beginning Churchill tried to awaken both countries to recognize their common cause. President Roosevelt began corresponding with the British statesman on 11 September 1939, and Churchill responded with enthusiasm. Throughout the war both men were determined to maintain this personal link, which enabled them usually to circumvent both the Foreign Office and the Department of State.[3] In May 1940 when Churchill assumed political control, Anglo-American relations were assigned top priority by his government as the continent of Europe disappeared under Hitler's control and Britain itself was threatened with invasion. Thereupon the United States moved to the centre of British concerns and became thoroughly immersed in British efforts to remain in the war.

Despite mutual suspicion, Great Britain and the United States had been cautiously and slowly edging towards cooperation after September 1939. In October Roosevelt declared the Western hemisphere a neutral zone, in the vague hope that this measure might aid the British war effort. Leading public opinion for the first time, Roosevelt revised the Neutrality Act by requiring all belligerents to purchase American goods, including arms, on a cash-and-carry basis. Roosevelt was prepared to allow the British and their allies to receive preferential treatment, but he laid down strict rules governing reimbursement. Although the British feared the economic consequences of these arrangements, they generally cooperated.[4] Roosevelt identified combat zones around the European continent, which United States ships, aircraft, and citizens were forbidden to enter. He exchanged fifty old destroyers for United States leases on eight British Caribbean and West Atlantic possessions.[5] The March 1941 Lend-Lease Act marked a turning point in Anglo-American relations. By then, British fears of economic domination by the Americans had dissipated. Harry Hopkins, Roosevelt's personal adviser, cemented the bonds between Roosevelt and Churchill during a 1941 visit to Britain and subsequently as head of the Lend-Lease program.[6]

Late 1941 saw the military element of the alliance fall into place. In the last half of 1940 many Americans felt that Britain might indeed survive Nazi bombing and invasion. By early 1941 American optimism wavered again.[7] Hitler's blockade had severely undermined the British war effort, while their empire in the Far East lay open to severe pressure from Japan. Iraq and Libya were threatened by German arms, and Hitler's spring offensive surged ahead almost unhindered in the Balkans. A leading State Department official wrote in May 1941 that the British are "damned near licked in the Mediterranean area."[8] Then in June 1941 came Hitler's massive attack against Russia. Russia's, then Japan's, entry into the war, and Hitler's declaration of war against the United States transformed the emerging Anglo-American relationship into a Russo-American-British tripartite alliance with three sets of aims and aspirations to be brought, if possible, into synchronization. The Russian invasion gradually reduced the direct German threat to Great Britain and eventually to the United States as well. This respite enabled the two countries to plan and fight a peripheral war until the great 1944 invasion of France could be organized.[9] Following the bombing of Pearl Harbor in December 1941, the United States found itself at war with the Axis powers and immediately entered into a close military alliance with the British, much to Churchill's and Roosevelt's satisfaction. Immediate strategic and military talks, the famous ABC discussions, created a coordinated Anglo-American military structure and strategy. The defeat of Germany and Italy and the defence of the Atlantic Ocean became the prime war aims for both countries.[10]

In the early stages of the war, when close Anglo-American cooperation still lay in the future, little rigorous thought could be given to Austria's future or the role of the Austrian exiles in it.[11] The British at first optimistically hoped that the war would be a short one. Militarily the British were unable to consider any major initiatives for the foreseeable future. Nor did they feel these would be necessary, because of an imminent internal collapse of the Nazis. Pressure applied to the Nazis from the outside in the form of a combination of economic blockade, propaganda offensive, and military threat would soon create such unbearable tension between the German people and the Nazi leaders that the Germans would rise up and bring down the evil regime from the inside.

In this way a bloody, costly invasion of the continent and fighting in World War I style could be avoided. A British force would need to land on the continent only to mop up once the Nazi regime had crumbled.[12]

In view of this early British war plan, which depended heavily upon internal revolt in Nazi Germany and Nazi-occupied Europe, German and Austrian exiles were seen as useful sparks to set off the revolt or inspire resistance at home. But the Austrian exiles in Great Britain and the United States did little to convince their hosts that they were willing to play this part, as they remained unable to unite around a common Austrian program. Some 90 per cent of the 10,000 refugee Austrians in Great Britain were either Jewish or apolitical or both, while among the active minority each feuding exile group looked to its hosts to arbitrate or to assist the group's political ends in its struggle with other exiles. Deeply riven by traditional loyalties and enmities brought into exile from prewar Austria, Austrian exiles demonstrated through their bitter factional jealousies that they shared no common loyalty able to bridge their prewar domestic resentments and divisions. Each doctrinaire group claimed to speak for the real Austria or Austrian interests, and its interests excluded the other factions. Most Austrian exiles at this early stage of the war opposed the reestablishment of the failed republic as it had existed until 1938. Finally, those who were most influential in exile politics, notably the monarchists and communists, did not seem to reflect the prewar political composition of non-Nazi Austria.[13]

In prewar Austria moderate socialists and conservative Christian Socials had formed the mass of the body politic, while communists and monarchists had constituted much smaller elements. The exile situation in Britain largely reversed this picture. Defeated in the 1934 civil war, Austrian socialists had turned more radical in exile. Under the influence of Otto Bauer, Revolutionary Socialists, as they began to call themselves, had already before the war begun to preach the notion of a pan-European or at least central European socialist revolution, which would make superfluous the need for a separate Austrian – or other – national state. Revolutionary Socialists generally refused to cooperate with other exile elements, in contrast to the minority moderate socialists. Some of these revolutionary themes attracted the Labour party's Hugh Dalton, who was the minister in charge of the economic blockade and political warfare. But the more conservative elements in the British government, and especially in the Foreign Office, were not fighting the Nazis in order to change the prewar social structure. Christian Socials had dominated the Austrian Republic's final years, yet almost none of their leading personalities went into exile. Most of the conservative leaders, including the last chancellor, Kurt von Schuschnigg, had remained in Austria, where they were imprisoned by the Nazis. Two other groups attained considerable influence among Austrian refugees. Communists became extremely active and well organized in Great Britain, and played a strong leadership role among Austrian exiles through their control of umbrella groups. They did not oppose the Nazis until the Third Reich invaded Russia in June 1941. Thereafter they supported Moscow's expansionist plans in eastern Europe, and to that end they entertained the notion of an independent but weak Austria.[14] At the other end of the political spectrum, Austrian monarchists, under the energetic direction of Otto von Habsburg, pretender to the Austro-Hungarian throne, and of his three brothers, initially had both Churchill and Roosevelt on their side. If Austrian Revolutionary Socialists preferred a large postwar European socialist federation, Austrian monarchists dreamed of a postwar Danubian federation under Habsburg rule, a sort of re-creation of the Austro-Hungarian Empire. At first the British tried to establish a nonpolitical Austrian Office in London, but secretly gave Austrian monarchists financial support and helped some of them to form a pro-Habsburg Free Austria Movement in Canada.[15]

Despite their internal rifts and lack of a cohesive national program, Austrian refugees as a group were considered loyal to the Allied cause. When the war began, the British investigated the trustworthiness of about 70,000 Germans and Austrians. The vast majority were found to be fully loyal. Some 55,400 were classified as *bona fide* refugees. Of the 70,000, about 64,200 were found to be "loyal anti-Nazis" and only 600 wound up in internment camps as possible security risks.[16] During the 1940 invasion scare the British authorities briefly interned approximately 25,000 German citizens, of whom about a third had Austrian origins. As a security measure several thousand suspected unreliables spent the next years in the Dominions. Once the panic subsided, most of them were returned to Great Britain.[17] On the whole, in practice the British authorities treated most Austrian exiles fairly liberally.

Eventually several thousand Austrians served under British colours during the war. About 1,500 Austrians joined the Pioneer, or construction, Corps, the only unit open to them at first. The government tried to form a separate Austrian unit within the Pioneer Corps, largely for propaganda purposes. However, this plan failed because of internecine Austrian bickering. Austrians were permitted to remain in the corps, but on an individual basis, scattered throughout the unit. Some of these men saw action in France; several were killed, and others captured. Once the 1940 invasion scare had passed other individual Austrians joined the Pioneer Corps, and later the regular armed forces. Some Austrians were granted permission in 1942 to serve overseas and to carry light weapons. Later that year Austrian individuals could enter the technical and some combat units of the British forces. Parliament decided in April 1943 that dependable enemy aliens would be able to serve in all branches of the British armed forces except the signal corps. By 1943 about 7,000 Austrian and German exiles, wryly labelling themselves "The King's Own Loyal Enemy Aliens," had joined the British military service. Before the war ended over 10,000 enemy alien men and women, of whom one-third or about 3,500 were Austrians, had become members of the British military establishment.[18] Despite this enviable pioneer and military record, Austrians were plagued by a reputation for being divisive and crotchety.[19] Following the collapse of a 1940 plan for an Austrian pioneer corps unit, the British took no further steps to assemble an Austrian military contingent, as they had done with nationals of other submerged countries. Of course, the Austrians, unlike other refugee groups, lacked a government-in-exile. But Austrian disunity also played a negative part in the exiles' status in Great Britain. The Foreign Office became convinced that no Austrian government-in-exile could ever be formed, and that even if one were set up, it would be unable to rally Austrians around the Austrian cause. Under the circumstances the British finally decided that a separate Austrian military unit would prove nothing less than an "unmitigated nuisance."[20] If Austrians could not submerge their political animosities, even in the face of a common mortal Nazi menace, they were better off scattered about as individuals throughout the various services.

This negative British view permeated all the government's relations with the Austrian exiles. The Foreign Office concluded that "the very slight advantage to be gained by granting the Austrians any concessions at all would be more than outweighed by counter-balancing disadvantages."[21] These British biases against Austrian refugees indubitably influenced official thinking about whether or not to reestablish an Austrian republic after the war.[22] By early 1941 the government had become convinced that it would be impossible to unify all Austrian factions. At the same time it lacked a definite Austrian policy. The British were still uncertain about the shape of postwar Austria, and unconvinced that reestablishing an independent Austrian state constituted a sound idea. It is not surprising, therefore, that the two parties were unable to develop a steady relationship.

A major internal Foreign Office policy paper in 1941 blamed the Austrian exiles for this asymmetrical state of affairs. In some ways, the paper conceded, Austrians could rightly claim that their country was a victim of Nazi aggression. Yet in other ways Austrians and Germans were disturbingly similar. This attitude explains why the policy paper lumped Austrian and German exile groups together. The British government despaired of disentangling Austrian exile politics and of granting recognition to any specific Austrian group. The British had no objections if any particular group of Austrian or German exiles banded together to support the Allied war effort. But in their view none could speak for all the exiles, let alone domestic opinion within occupied Austria: "Generally speaking, although there can be no question of official recognition for any group, HMG has no objection to the formation of such associations among the anti-Nazi Austrians and welcome any tendency to closer unity among German and Austrian emigres."[23] Nowhere did Great Britain's frustration with the exiles shine through more clearly than in this paper, which documented the government's inability to bring Austrians together. British representatives abroad received instructions to communicate this negative official decision about Austrian exiles to friendly governments, with the request that they adopt a similar hands-off stance.

Owing to these difficulties the British had few incentives to differentiate Austrian refugees from Germans. The 1941 Foreign Office report treated Germans and Austrians in the same category, and in the official mind they continued to be tied together. Nor did Foreign Office intelligence analyses regarding the domestic Austrian situation tend to change this rigid view. A 1943 report concerning Austrian domestic opinion found it to be as divided and passive as that of the Austrian exiles in Britain. True, indigenous Austrians were disgruntled with Nazi rule, but this antipathy did not seem to presage an emerging domestic unanimity about Austria's postwar future. The discontent might be tapped for its propaganda potential, but anti-Nazi sentiments had no positive political value. Domestic Austrian unhappiness had much more to do with anger at the German Nazis, who had appropriated the country's best jobs, and involved Austria in a long and bloody war.[24] This negative view of the Austrians was reflected in the Foreign Office's internal organization. Until nearly the end of the war Austrian affairs in the Foreign Office came under the jurisdiction of the Central, or German, Department under William Strang and later Oliver Harvey. The first member of this department to be responsible solely for Austrian affairs would not be appointed until late in 1944.

Churchill did not share his officials' negative view of the Austrians. He was not anti-Austrian in the same sense as he was anti-German. Churchill cherished a romantic historical vision of the Austro-Hungarian Empire, whose passing he had always regretted. For both historical and political reasons he favoured re-creation of this long-vanished political structure after the war. He was liable to enthusiastic public outbursts of a pro-Austrian nature, which kept his officials on tenterhooks. Even after this monarchical-federation scheme lost his officials' support, Churchill continued to cling to it. As late as April 1945 he still dreamed of aiding Austrian monarchists to resist a threatened Communist take-over in the recaptured country. Nothing came of this idea for once again Foreign office officials pointed out to Churchill that pro-monarchist action would threaten British interests in that region.[25]

Roosevelt too was fascinated by the imperial Austrian myth. During much of the war Otto von Habsburg, heir to the imperial mantle, lived in the United States, while his mother Zita, the last empress of Austria-Hungary, eked out a meagre refugee existence in Canada. Both were guests at the White House and the president's country estate, Hyde Park, in upper New York State, and the president obviously enjoyed Otto's company. Roosevelt considered Otto a royal refugee, treated him almost as an equal, and certainly as a personal friend. This close relationship worried the State Department in much the same vein as Churchill's attraction to the Habsburgs unnerved the Foreign Office.[26] Department of State officials were not certain whether presidential hospitality for the Habsburgs meant more than merely historical curiosity or personal respect, but they suspected it might. The State Department was as doubtful of the imperial family's political future as was the Foreign Office. "He [Otto] puts us to pains rather out of proportion to his prospects for achieving much as a political personality in the near future," a 1942 State Department memorandum grumbled.[27] The president employed royal titles in his correspondence with Otto, but as far as Hull was concerned Otto sojourned in the United States strictly as a private refugee with the same status as any other.[28]

During 1942 and 1943 Roosevelt and Secretary of War Stimson tried to circumvent the State Department in order to strengthen Otto von Habsburg's political standing. The effort backfired badly. Thereafter Roosevelt began to distance himself somewhat from the Habsburgs. In 1942 the United States Army began, as in Britain largely for propaganda reasons, to establish several national battalions. Without informing the cabinet, Roosevelt and Stimson decided in late 1942 to form an Austrian battalion as well within the armed forces. A 1,000-man Austrian unit would symbolize American concern for submerged Austria and would serve as a beacon to subjected Austrians and other central Europeans at home.[29] But the two conspirators' definition of Austria in fact turned out to be historic Austria-Hungary. Roosevelt appointed Otto von Habsburg officially to head the recruitment committee for this battalion, which would seek combatants not only from among ex-Austrian exiles, but among the various ethnic groups of the defunct Austro-Hungarian Empire as well.[30]

When this scheme was made public, the president expected a wave of enthusiasm to sweep the nation, and especially the various central European ethnic groups. Instead, the news caused an enormous shock wave of opposition, which soon consigned the scheme to oblivion. John

C. Wiley, last United States diplomatic representative in Vienna, immediately considered the idea mad. In the first place, a purely Austrian battalion would not be able to find enough recruits to fill it. "They [the Austrian monarchists] claim they can recruit at least 5,000," Wiley wrote in disgust, "personally I doubt they can assemble 50."[31] On the other hand, Wiley predicted that citizens of the successor states, once part of the Austro-Hungarian Empire, would explode with anger at such historic stupidity. To install Otto von Habsburg to lead the recruitment drive was to ignore the lessons of twentieth-century history and to take leave of one's political senses. Wiley's passionate denunciation of the Austrian battalion plan proved correct. Ex-imperial Austro-Hungarian nationality groups such as the Czechs and Hungarians were outraged by this proposal. They publicly denounced Roosevelt's scheme for this type of Austrian battalion and referred to Otto von Habsburg as a dangerous schemer and a meddler. The British, who had not been consulted and who had had their own disastrous experience in 1940 with a projected Austrian brigade within the British Pioneer Corps, were similarly appalled.[32] As Wiley had predicted, the number of recruits remained very low, outrage grew among central Europeans and Austrian republicans, and the affair turned into a public relations disaster. In a last desperate attempt to fill the thin ranks of the Austrian unit, Secretary Stimson tried to divert to the battalion, under duress, soldiers of central European origin already serving in the American army. But the public outcry continued to grow, threatening to scuttle the whole operation.[33] At last Roosevelt bowed to the overwhelming public pressure. In early 1943 he ordered that the Austrian battalion be quietly disbanded and its members dispersed throughout the American army.[34] When the administration finally extricated itself from the Austrian battalion scheme, few were happier than officials at the Department of State and the Foreign Office. Unwilling to blame his hero Roosevelt for the collapse of the plan, Adolf Berle, responsible within the State Department for domestic nationality groups, condemned the failed scheme as just another example of "Habsburg intrigues."[35]

Berle's opinion exemplified American officials' scepticism regarding Austrian monarchists in particular and other exile activists in general. Up to 1941 the State Department had directed its attention, appropriately enough, to the traditional peacetime task of representing American interests abroad. Hitler's advent to power created a large, new stream of refugees from the Third Reich. Between 1933 and 1939 the department issued some 350,000 refugee visas for entry into the United States, and consular officials disbursed thousands more before mid-1941 when Germany forced United States consulates throughout Nazi-occupied Europe to close. United States entry into the war severely curtailed the

State Department's overseas activities. Thereafter State Department officials were ordered to design domestic policies for the control and employment of the foreign refugees to whom they had earlier issued visas.[36] The functionaries soon discovered that this vast pool of refugees created a major ideological problem. For many of these exiles arrived in the United States with the firm intention of retaining their former nationality until the war ended. They expected to return home after the war, rather than become assimilated in their host country. Americans had always been extraordinarily sensitive about the influence foreign elements exerted in the United States, whether in the form of political propaganda or alien organizations. They often felt uneasy about harbouring people who did not mean to become Americans, but who continued to feel primary loyalty to a foreign homeland. Nor had they forgotten the sticky peace problems which arose after World War I, the result of questionable wartime commitments to active refugee national groups. The British in World War II shared some of these hesitations. Although the British government fairly quickly recognized free governments-in-exile, it did so largely for propaganda reasons, this time also remaining vague about specific postwar arrangements.[37] Although the American government encouraged the various anti-Nazi national groups to organize support for the Allied war effort, the State Department was certainly not enamoured of them.[38] The State Department experienced some difficulty in developing an affirmative policy on refugee national groups because basically its officials mistrusted them. They tried to keep the refugee groups as isolated as possible from the American mainstream and forbade American citizens of foreign backgrounds to join them. Breckinridge Long of the State Department's European division expressed this nativist view: "Personally, I would feel much easier about the future if we could get rid of *all* [foreign] groups, blocks and special interests."[39]

Despite these reservations, the Americans at first emulated the British by adopting a benevolent public stance towards Austrian refugees, convinced that they would quickly rally as a group around the Allied war effort.[40] Soon they learned about the disappointing British experiences with the feuding Austrian groups.[41] Their own 1942–3 misadventure with the Austrian battalion fuelled latent antipathies towards all exile organizations. Following this bungled episode, the Federal Bureau of Investigation (FBI) and the Foreign Nationality Branch of the Organization of Strategic Services (OSS) attached to the Joint Chiefs of Staff launched systematic investigations of Austrian exiles to see whether the British had appraised them correctly. The investigators hoped to distinguish the various groups' characteristics in order to determine why they seemed so unable to cooperate together. The FBI discovered that about 40,000 Austrian refugees had landed in the United States since 1938.[42] As in Great Britain, most of them ignored exile politics, especially as official American support was lacking. Although the FBI believed that they were probably all sincere anti-Nazis, at the same time they were so fragmented politically and ideologically that one could not discern any unifying Austrian national link. The FBI report included a detailed review of the Austrian battalion incident as proof of Austrian disunity. Its findings closely paralleled those of the British, except that in the United States the communists were not active or influential.[43] The far more detailed OSS report confirmed the FBI's conclusions. The various Austrian groups were much too splintered and politically inept to be taken very seriously, and therefore might not be of much assistance in psychological warfare. An almost complete absence of any true Austrian national profile or genuine patriotism made it impossible for the exiles to unite in a common anti-Nazi union. The report categorized the various small groups along ideological lines resembling those employed earlier by the British and the FBI.[44]

These disapointing experiences and studies undoubtedly left official American circles with little incentive to support the Austrians, even after the publication in 1943 of the Big Three Moscow Declaration on Austria which seemed to promise postwar independence.[45] As a result Austrians rarely exercised more than individual influence in Great Britain and the United States. For a while some monarchists gained an ear within the highest councils, and a few moderate socialists attracted elements in the British Labour party or among American progressives. But these personal forms of influence were too transitory and feeble to change what the Austrians considered uncaring or unreasonable official attitudes and rulings towards Austrians.

One of the most painful thorns in the side of Austrian refugees was the fact that Great Britain and the United States did not regard them as Austrian nationals and friendly aliens. Whatever personal sympathies they may have felt for these refugees from Nazism, the British classified them as German nationals and enemy aliens until well after the war ended. Until 1939 the British authorities continued informally to honour the refugees' old Austrian passports. But following the Reich's application in the summer of 1938 of German nationality to Austrians, they formally categorized Austrians as German nationals no matter whether they were Jewish or staunchly anti-Nazi. In the interval before the war, the British applied the same administrative restraints or concessions to German and Austrian refugees. Austrians remained listed as German citizens once war started, and therefore became enemy aliens as well. As a result, some Austrians were interned as being dangerous enemy aliens of German nationality.[46] Most Austrian refugees naturally resented being lumped together with Germans as enemy aliens, but they were unable to persuade the British to change their policy. The refugees chafed at British reluctance to acknowledge publicly their hatred of Hitler's evil system, of which they were among the chief victims. They felt humiliated at being forced to retain their despised German citizenship, pleading at least to be recognized as stateless. But the British refused to budge at all, even when a 1941 Nazi decree stripped German (including Austrian) Jews residing abroad of their German nationality. The Foreign Office insisted that this Nazi ruling could not affect the status of German refugees living in Great Britain. It was unthinkable in the midst of a war to honour Nazi laws or rulings or to allow Third Reich decrees to influence British administration of justice. Hence the 1941 Nazi decree relieving exiled Jews of German citizenship could not cause "people who are enemy aliens in this country to cease to be so and diminish the Crown's rights over them."[47] No matter how bizarre this argument must have sounded to the refugees, the government maintained this legal stance even after the end of the war.

Official nationality practice underwent a court challenge in 1944 when a group of interned Austrian refugees, including one Jew, sought release from internment by appealing the ruling to the High Court. The Big Three had signed the Moscow Declaration on Austria in late 1943, apparently labelling the Anschluss illegal and void. Surely in this new political climate the authorities would be willing to move on the issue of Austrian refugees' national status. The interned Austrians argued that the rules of *habeas corpus* applied to them on the ground that they had never accepted German nationality and therefore had not felt bound to renounce it. Therefore they should not have been classed as enemy aliens or interned without a fair trial. Nevertheless, despite publication of the Moscow Declaration on Austria and the certain knowledge that the Allies would soon win the war, the government opposed the Austrians' motion before the High Court. A leading Foreign Office legal adviser, acting as the principal government expert before the court, pleaded for retention of all Austrians in the German national and enemy alien category. He asked that the court keep the interned Austrians under lock and key. Bowing to the government's wishes, the High Court accepted the expert's position. Austrians remained classified as Germans and enemy aliens, and those interned did not gain release as they had hoped. Austrians could still be interned without a trial if they were considered a danger to the war effort.[48] They remained enemy aliens, despite the declaration's proposition that Austria had disappeared in 1938, on two apparently conflicting grounds: that Austrians had become German citizens and that Austria was held to be a country at war with Great Britain. In 1946 Britain recognized the new postwar Austrian government, but did not decide to terminate the state of war with Austria until 1947, after which the Austrian enemy alien classification was finally abolished.

Despite this legal impediment most Austrians were considered loyal to the Allied cause and benefited from some administrative concessions. These administrative measures did not affect the emigres' legal position in Great Britain, possessing propaganda rather than legal character. By December 1943, following the Moscow Declaration, ex-Austrians could reregister with the British authorities as Austrians rather than as Germans, even if previously they had been registered as Germans. They were required only to demonstrate that at one time they had possessed Austrian rather than German citizenship. Several months later in 1944 the government announced that Austrian prisoners-of-war would be held separately from German POWs. But these propaganda gestures, which some observers later misinterpreted as reflecting a radical shift in British policy favouring the Austrians, did not affect the Austrians' political and legal status within Great Britain one way or another.[49]

The Americans might have been expected to assume a more liberal position towards the Austrian exiles in view of the public impression they had fostered that the United States had not recognized the Anschluss *de jure*. But in practice there continued to exist a good deal of ambiguity about their status because of conflicting local decisions about their nationality. This shifting practice should have disappeared once that country joined the war in December 1941 against Nazi Germany. Certainly Austrian exile groups and their supporters in the United States hoped that this would be the case. Would not Austria now be recognized as a friendly occupied country and Austrian exiles openly accepted as friendly aliens?[50] The first official steps seemed to point in that direction. In 1939 the president announced that the FBI would assume responsibility for controlling dangerous enemy aliens, who were defined broadly as "natives, citizens, denizens and subjects of foreign nations and governments at war with the United States or which attempted an invasion of the United States."[51] If Austria was occupied or had disappeared, surely Austrians could not be included in this group? In the following year five million aliens in the United States were called upon to register with the government. The Austrians' contention seemed justified when they were permitted to register as Austrians, if they wished.[52] As soon as the United States declared war in December 1941 Attorney General Francis Biddle made public a presidential proclamation regarding the control of enemy aliens. Austrians were delighted to learn that they were not specifically mentioned as enemy aliens.[53]

At the outbreak of war Roosevelt moved quickly to establish a Presidential Advisory Committee on Political Refugees, which presented him with a report in mid-January 1942. In order to ensure that Austrians not somehow fall into the ranks of German citizens and enemy aliens, as in Great Britain, Austrian exile groups in the United States launched a public campaign to demonstrate their loyalty to their host country and the war effort.[54] The Presidential Advisory Committee, having weighed refugee rights against the need for national security, recommended that some classes of German refugees and Koreans, as well as a few others including Austrians, be classified as friendly aliens.[55] The following month the attorney general's regulations put into effect the committee's recommendations. Austrians and a surprising new category of persons termed "Austro-Hungarians" (former citizens of the defunct Austro-Hungarian Empire) were to be excluded from the requirement of applying for an enemy alien identity certificate, unless previously they had taken out Axis citizenship.[56] Many Austrians who had left Austria before the July 1938 German nationality law was proclaimed could rejoice. But many others found themselves caught under the regulations as Germans and enemy aliens because in order to leave German-occupied Austria they had been forced to accept German passports. In effect, it seemed that the passport held by a refugee upon entry to the United States determined his nationality.[57] In October 1942 the State Department added Italians to the classes of exempted aliens, thereby freeing them too from the duty of requesting an enemy alien certificate.[58] Polls revealed that Americans overwhelmingly favoured these rulings and were convinced of the loyalty of these foreign nationality groups to the United States.[59]

The attorney general's regulations apparently meant that Austrians as a national group were not to be classified enemy aliens. However, the Department of State and the Foreign Office deplored the attorney general's ruling as they understood it. The British feared that this declaration would impede a joint Anglo-American approach to the question of Austrian refugees. They also wondered if the Americans were considering labelling Austrians as neutrals and "de-recognizing" the Anschluss. Would the Americans, now involved in the war against the Nazis but ever prone to rhetoric, leave the British behind on the Austrian question?[60] The Department of State was as mystified by the attorney general's rulings as was the Foreign Office. Sumner Welles shared British concern because the attorney general had not sought the State Department's advice before issuing his regulations. Could this mean that the president was contemplating a shift in his Austrian policy? Welles believed firmly that the State Department and not a domestic department ought to make decisions about nationality questions and the legal consequences flowing from the country's foreign policy. It was certainly not within the attorney general's purview, he maintained, to set precedents in these matters. Welles was no more inclined than were the British to treat Austria as "occupied territory" and he was determined that the two countries' policies remain linked. No substantive change in the exiles' legal position would be tolerated.[61] When he broached this matter in cabinet, Welles was delighted to discover that its most important members including unexpectedly the attorney general shared his views.[62] Why then, Welles asked, had the Austrian exemption been made in the first place?[63] To the public the attorney general's enemy alien regulations appeared to reflect a well-considered official position on Austria and Austrian refuges. But behind the scenes officials from the State and Attorney General's departments quickly agreed that this ruling was legally meaningless. Attorney General Biddle was quite prepared to admit confidentially to the State Department that his ruling had been meant as a purely domestic administrative decision without any legal effect whatsoever. He had not attempted to preempt the State Department's nationality or enemy alien decisions, nor had he the power to do so. No legal, political, or even regulatory precedent flowed from this purely administrative act, which applied exclusively to one specific set of administrative regulations but not to the law establishing them. His exemptions had been purely "practical steps" freeing certain classes of anti-Nazis from specific administrative requirements.[64] This confidential explanation mollified the attorney general's colleagues in the Department of State and officials in the Foreign Office. However, the public remained ignorant of this secret agreement and consequently did not learn of this distinction between legal classification and domestic administrative or regulatory exception. Austrians saw only the latter and naturally assumed that they were not enemy aliens.

Still, the administration's reluctance to advance the Austrian cause in a manner that was politically meaningful left the question of the Austrians' true status less than crystal clear. In mid-1942 a rumour spread like wildfire within exile circles that the American government was about to reclassify Austrians as enemy aliens. Austrian groups galvanized their members, launched a write-in campaign, collected loyalty signatures, bought newspaper ads proclaiming their loyalty, and dispatched lengthy petitions to the president.[65] John Wiley, now a member of the OSS Nationality Branch and the exiled Austrians' chief supporter, fired off a long, impassioned personal letter to Hull. He vouched for the exiled Austrians' dedicated support of the Allied war effort and recommended that they continue to be recognized as allies in the anti-Nazi struggle. He reminded Hull that he knew from personal experience that the Nazis had occupied Austria against the will of its people. Now to classify Austrians as enemy aliens would only play into the hands of Goebbels and Hitler who could then boast that the Allies had finally recognized the Anschluss. Indeed, this was just the moment at long last for the United States to rise up nobly in defence of a free and independent Austria, Wiley maintained. "For both the British and American policies towards the Austrian question," Wiley complained, "have for some time been ambiguous." The British would not "de-recognize" the Anschluss. But, remonstrated Wiley, "American policy is scarcely less clear." Successive administrative decisions had wavered between treating Austria as a country temporarily subjected to enemy occupation and as a part of Germany. Austrian exiles in the United States were among the United States's best allies and constituted some of the firmest anti-Nazi elements in the country. Furthermore, he insisted, American public opinion in the United States was convinced of their loyalty as well. It was high time that the government abandoned its current flabby position on Austria and avoided compounding the error by terming Austrians enemy aliens.[66]

The Department of State reacted to the public campaign by deciding to initiate its own full-scale departmental review of the country's opaque position on the Austrian issue, looking towards a possible clarification or change of policy. A preliminary discussion paper prepared by the Division of European Affairs in May 1942 stressed that the Austrian question was one of the most complex in contemporary international affairs. Yet in some respects the situation was easy because Austria had completely disappeared. "The Austrian question is concerned with what is at least a geographical entity and a juridical status terminated by a single event, the Anschluss."[67] In view of the lack of an unequivocal American declaration of recognition, it was difficult to know whether recognition had been extended or not. The department's legal adviser would have to render the final judgment on the legal side of the recognition issue. A thorough investigation of past American statements and policy towards Austria appeared to affirm that "we accepted the Anschluss as accomplished, although we did have some misgivings." It was still too early in the war to be specific about Austria's future. The British had been remarkably cautious and the State Department had concurred with this attitude. Having thus far avoided making any commitments regarding Austria, the United States should not budge now. The division counselled no change and opted for the *status quo*. It was simply "not necessary to go into the matter at the moment." Austria would constitute an important topic at an eventual peace conference, but that lay far in the future. A more worrying factor was that the "ruthless and disquieting" Soviets seemed to be interested in moving into the area. Notwithstanding reservations about potential Soviet intrusion, it would be best to delay discussions about Austria's future.[68]

In the meantime could anything be done to buck up the morale of the Austrian exiles? Some improvement in the treatment of Austrians might also have a beneficial domestic and propaganda effect. Therefore the division recommended considering a move to classify Austrians as neutrals. However, the report continued, there existed no departmental consensus concerning how Austrian exiles in the United States ought to be treated. Those who considered Austria as part of Germany quite naturally preferred to see Austrians remain enemy aliens. For members of this group, it would be necessary first to "de-recognize" the Anschluss before Austrian exiles could be reclassified as neutrals. Others believed that it might be possible for the government to declare Austrians neutrals, while evading this political problem. In this case only a brief, bland statement regarding the Austrians' new neutral status should be issued to the press.[69] Derecognition of the Anschluss and neutral status for Austrian exiles defined the two separate camps within the department.[70] Legal Adviser Green Hackworth further complicated the matter by denying that the United States had recognized the Anschluss, while at the same time he rejected any change in the Austrian refugees' status. Hackworth claimed that "We have not recognized that Austria is *de jure* a part of Germany." As no explicit public statement of recognition was made in 1938, *de jure* recognition was still pending. Hackworth conceded, however, that he was reluctant to argue this point too strongly. At the same time he resisted any change in the refugees' domestic legal status. Although the Department of State's Visa Division classified Austrians as enemy aliens "on the understanding that the department had recognized the absorption of Austria by Germany," Hackworth preferred to invoke another, safer, if surprising, route leading to the same conclusion, namely, that Austria was now an ally of Germany: "I am not prepared to say that the same conclusion (that Austrians are enemy aliens) could not be based on other grounds, namely, that Austria is, to all intents and purposes, an ally of Germany in the present conflict."[71]

What did Hackworth mean? Did Austria still exist as an independent country which had freely associated itself with Nazi Germany in the state of war against the United States? This view meant pretending that Austria still existed – the basis for the occupationist view – but that it was really enemy territory because of Austria's decision to become allied with Germany, not owing to Nazi occupation. Such an opinion had in fact earlier surfaced during 1938 State Department discussions about the Anschluss, when the department insisted that the Austrian ex-minister indicate to the administration that Austria had united with Germany. In sum, Hackworth's position morally stigmatized 1938 Austrian behaviour in a manner not even adopted by annexationists. For Hackworth Austrian exiles fell within the class of enemy aliens covered by the provisions of section 21, title 50 of the United States Code, which defined enemy aliens as "all natives, citizens, denizens or subjects of a hostile nation or government." The act of allying themselves with Germany meant that Austrians had become German citizens: "I do not, therefore, see how we could regard Austria as other than enemy territory or how we could decline to regard residents of Austria or former nationals of Austria, who have become German nationals, as other than *potentially* [author's emphasis] enemy aliens."[72] Again, what did the word "potentially" mean? Hackworth offered no further explanation, but the tone of his argument demonstrated his intention of retaining Austrians as enemy aliens. Undoubtedly this weighty opinion took the wind out of any campaign to change the exiles' status in the United States.

Once Hackworth closed the avenues for legal or political movement in the Austrian affair, the departmental discussion moved to the subsidiary realm of propaganda. At the end of June the case reached Adolf Berle's desk, accompanied by the hopeful remark that any change at all in the Austrians' status would have powerful "psychological and political effects as bearing on the war against Germany." What this change should be, the note conceded, was no longer obvious, "without running up against too many legal complications or a too abrupt change in high policy." Perhaps all that could be done was to issue a positive-sounding but vague public statement implying that the country was moving forward "from the somewhat vague position in which the Austrian question was left four years ago." This matter required an early decision not only for propaganda purposes, but to clear up conflicting court rulings in several outstanding procedures concerning interned Austrians.[73]

The unresolved question was finally passed to Secretary of State Hull with Berle's recommendation that if no policy change occurred, or if one was only to be considered in the future, a nebulous public statement should be issued to sidestep all controversies. Repeating the traditional bland statements about Austria would not be helpful. "De-recognition," as Berle put it, still remained a possible option "as a matter of high policy." On the other hand, it would be safer to avoid having to make a political decision by announcing that – for domestic purposes only – Austrians would be considered as neutrals. Clearly this last option would have only a limited administrative effect, and be without any larger legal or political implications.[74] In order to resolve this tortuous question, Hull convened a meeting with representatives from the State, War, and Justice departments as well as the Selective Service branch. These high-level officials decided to accept Berle's recommendation to reject the derecognition and neutrality options. They agreed with his much safer recommendation instead to the effect that the secretary of state should issue a bold-sounding statement on the Austrian question whose rhetoric would hide total immobility.

Hull decided that the place to carry out this publicity stunt was his upcoming press conference of 27 July 1942. He opened that session by expressing to the journalists his regret at the confusion concerning exile Austrians which had apparently arisen because of conflicting administrative rulings concerning Austrians. Without specifying which practices he was referring to or clarifying which of these reflected true official policy, Hull went on to defend the government's administrative approach on the grounds of general public necessity. In other words, instead of clearing up the confusion he only noted it. He told the assembled newsmen that he preferred to move directly to the larger question involving the principles guiding the American attitude towards the Anschluss. On this issue, he announced firmly, the country's attitude was already well known. He was now prepared strongly to endorse this policy again and to reinforce it by repeating the United States's rejection "as to the manner in which the seizure of Austria took place and to the relation of the seizure to the Government's well-known policy towards the taking of territory by force." Hull thereupon announced: "This Government has never taken the position that Austria was legally absorbed into the German Reich." Hull pretended that he was uttering something quite novel, or at the very least dissipating a general misconception. But how did this statement differ in any way from the position taken since 1938? Defenders of the occupationist position found the mere fact that Hull took the time to speak out on Austria and the statement itself to be of great import. But Hull was as enigmatic in 1942 as he had been in 1938. No one had ever questioned that the Anschluss *per se* was an illegal act. The problem since then has been whether the United States had recognized the result. Nothing the secretary uttered at his press conference addressed this point. In fact, as noted above, this 1942 statement was carefully crafted to conceal behind empty rhetoric the fact that Hull had not budged at all on the Anschluss, the refugees' status in the United States, or Austria's future.[75]

The various Austrian groups were unaware of the true background of the statement or its motive. As a result they were at first quite taken in by it. They warmly praised Hull's courage and forthrightness, and wildly misinterpreted the statement as confirming American nonrecognition of the Anschluss, application of the Atlantic Charter's guarantees to Austria, and removal of any possible enemy alien stigma. However, when their representatives visited Hull to offer him their congratulations, they were unpleasantly surprised to find him cool, noncommittal, and unwilling in any way to expand upon or explain further what he had revealed to the press. They asked whether they might have misunderstood the intention of the press conference.[76] But Hull refused to be drawn out or offer further comment. Instead, he curtly referred them again to the vague 1938 diplomatic notes issued to Germany.[77] When the public too wrote in to find out more concerning the secretary's July 1942 pronouncement, the State Department also refused comment but returned copies of the 1938 United States diplomatic notes attached to a copy of Hull's press statement.[78] Insofar as any genuine change in the Austrian policy or the exiles' status was concerned, the entire exercise had been for naught. In the process, Hackworth had emerged as one of the "hardliners" in this dispute.

Emulating the example of his British counterparts, Hackworth refused to recognize the withdrawal of German nationality from Jews living abroad through the 1941 Nuremberg decree. He believed it imperative to maintain German and Austrian refugees, whether gentiles or Jews, within the classification of Germans and enemy aliens. The Jewish anti-Nazi refugees suffered doubly because Hackworth insisted that they did not come under American responsibility, but that as Germans they fell under the jurisdiction of the Swiss government which functioned during the conflict as the protecting power for German nationals and German prisoners-of-war. True, as far as their property was concerned the United States did not recognize Nazi decrees of confiscation. As Hackworth explained: "In support of this position reference was made to the right of the State Department to express policy towards the recognition of confiscatory decrees." However, he called attention to the State Department's note of August 3, 1942, to the Swiss legation in charge of German interests, which stated that "German aliens of the Jewish faith in the United States could not disavow the protection of the power which is in charge of the interests of the Government of which they are nationals."[79] Like the British, Hackworth was prepared to enforce his tough nationality views on Austrians in the courts.

Once the United States had entered the war, the American authorities interned several hundred Germans and Austrians including some of Jewish background as dangerous enemy aliens. They also interned some groups of Austrian refugee Jews who were sent from American protectorates such as Panama for safekeeping.[80] Austrians were astounded that Hitler's anti-Austrian and anti-Semitic policies might seem to find support in the United States. When interned Austrians sought to have the courts release them from internment, the State Department contested these legal challenges, thereby demonstrating its determination to uphold the status of Austrians as enemy aliens. Two important test cases involving interned Austrian Jewish refugees indicated how intently the Department of State defended its position on Austrian refugees. The first case dealt with a "native" of Austria, born in a part of the empire which became the Austrian republic in 1919; the second case involved a man born in what became Czechoslovakia in 1919, but who later became a naturalized Austrian citizen.

Frederick d'Esquiva was a "native" of Austria, and therefore liable under American law to be interned if he was considered to be dangerous to the war effort or disloyal. The term "native" designated the place of birth rather than of citizenship. "Natives" of countries at war with the United States were liable to internment. D'Esquiva was born in 1891 in the Austrian part of the Dual Monarchy. When Austria became a republic in 1919, he emigrated to France, where he resided as a stateless person. He never returned to Austria, but fearing a Nazi invasion of France in 1939 he made his way to the United States as a refugee. At the time of his arrival he allegedly registered as having "no nationality," but admitted having been an Austrian previously. He was interned as a dangerous enemy alien in December 1941 following the German declaration of war against the United States. D'Esquiva's lawyer did not dispute his client's Austrian origin, which made him a "native" of Austria. But he claimed that "natives" of Austria were not enemy aliens, because Austria had disappeared in 1938, the country was occupied by Germany, and hence Austria could not have been at war with the United States. Moreover, he contended, his client was not an Austrian citizen in 1938. And even had he been one, since the United States had never recognized the Anschluss d'Esquiva could not have become a German citizen following the Anschluss and the July 1938 German nationality law. Therefore he could not be considered a "native" of Germany, a country at war with the United States. D'Esquiva must be considered stateless, not an enemy alien, and deserved immediate release from internment.

The New York District Court ruled against d'Esquiva in June 1942 on the grounds that the Anschluss had been recognized *de jure* by the United States. "The acquisition of Austria by Germany was recognized by this country," the court ruled. "In the absence of any proof to the contrary, it must be assumed therefore that this government has officially recognized the consolidation of Austria with Germany."[81] As a result the ex-Austrian "native" became a German and enemy alien and hence liable to internment. In the following month Hull held his well-publicized press conference on Austria. As a result of what Hull said at that time d'Esquiva's defence attorney appealed the ruling on the ground that he now had the secretary's words to prove that the United States had not recognized the Anschluss in 1938. In preparation for his appeal the defence attorney wrote to Hull seeking official confirmation of his interpretation of the country's policy. Would the secretary not take this occasion to reaffirm and, if thought advisable, amplify his July declaration for the benefit of the court? Would he send the defence a clear reply to the question: "Has the annexation of Austria been recognized, or has it not been recognized, by the United States?"[82]

D'Esquiva and his counsel were bound to be disappointed at Hull's refusal to comply. Despite the July statement, the Department of State aided not d'Esquiva's but the prosecution's case. Hackworth set out the official argument against d'Esquiva in an internal departmental memorandum. He noted that d'Esquiva was indeed a "native" of Austria as of July 1938, when Austria was legally united with Germany and the German nationality law for Austrians was promulgated, and that d'Esquiva had not taken out a new citizenship. Therefore the German nationality law applied to d'Esquiva, Hackworth insisted and d'Esquiva had become a German citizen. Austria's annexation by Germany had a legal status accepted by the United States. According to Hackworth, after the Anschluss German nationality laws applied even to "native" Austrians.[83] In correspondence with d'Esquiva's attorney, however, Hackworth adopted a much more cautious tone. If the union of Austria and Germany were not "legal," he wrote, the effect of the German nationality law upon Austrians was to be regarded as legal.[84] The Justice Department made full use of Hackworth's advice. It argued before the appeals court that Austria was in fact a part of Germany, that d'Esquiva was both a "native" of Austria and a citizen of Germany, and that he was therefore an enemy alien without legal rights in wartime. As evidence of this it submitted to the court a confidential Hackworth letter dated March 1942 addressed to the Justice Department, which stated that for purposes of identifying enemy nationals, citizens, and subjects it must be kept in mind that Austria was *de jure* part of Germany.[85]

Faced with this official opinion, the court felt that it had little option but to accept that the evidence demonstrated that "this government has officially recognized the consolidation of Austria with Germany."[86] Apparently nothing in the secretary's July 1942 press statement contradicted this position. As the court pointed out: "But even if we give all proper weight to this statement, we cannot find in it anything absolutely decisive. The word 'legally' can hardly be given the same content with reference to intercourse among nations as it has in domestic law."[87] Even so, however, the court did not decide in favour of the government but remanded the case for further inquiry in the light of recent administrative rulings regarding Austrians which had muddied these waters. For new instructions had been issued in May and June 1943 by the Department of Justice which stated that for purposes of immigration and naturalization, aliens of "Austrian nativity and nationality" were no longer to be considered as natives of Germany. Moreover, the Treasury Department had just announced that Germans and Austrians would be distinguished from each other regarding foreign property ownership. In effect, the court was clearly not aware of the confidential agreement between the State and other departments that administrative rulings or exceptions by other departments were without effect upon the law regarding enemy aliens, which was in the hands of the State Department. Thus the court found itself in a state of confusion about the country's actual policy towards Austrians. The new regulations were considered to be sufficiently significant to prompt the court to reopen the whole Anschluss question. The appeals court asked the district court to investigate again whether or not the United States government had recognized *de jure* Germany's acquisition of Austria.[88]

But before this case could be resolved, a second litigation appeared to decide many questions about interned Austrian refugees, especially those of Jewish background. This suit posed the more straightforward question of whether Austrian nationals had become German citizens following the Anschluss.[89] Paul Schwarzkopf was an Austrian Jewish immigrant who had arrived in the United States in 1936. He was born in 1886 in Prague, then a city of the Austro-Hungarian Empire. When in 1919 Prague became the capital of the new Czechoslovak state, Schwarzkopf became a citizen of that country. A metallurgist by profession, Schwarzkopf later moved to Berlin and in 1925 became a German citizen. Two years later he moved to Austria and in 1933 became a naturalized Austrian citizen. Because of his place of birth, the United States admitted Schwarzkopf as an immigrant under the Czech rather than Austrian quota. By the time Hitler invaded Austria in 1938, Schwarzkopf had been an American resident for two years. In June of that year he declared his intention to apply for United States citizenship. This he did in September 1941, but his December 1941 internment as a dangerous enemy alien halted the process. Schwarzkopf's counsel, William S. Bennett, applied in May 1942 for a writ of *habeas corpus*, claiming that his client was not a German citizen and therefore not an enemy alien.[90]

This case involved two main questions. First, did Schwarzkopf become a German citizen through the July 1938 German citizenship law? Second, even if he had become a German citizen, had he lost his German citizenship through the November 1941 Nuremberg decree that denaturalized German Jews living abroad?[91] Once again the lower court asked the State Department for its expert advice. As before the State Department stuck to its guns, maintaining that Austrians had become Germans in July 1938. The department insisted that "Mr. Schwarzkopf should be regarded as a German citizen or subject."[92] The court decided to follow this expert advice and dismissed the Schwarzkopf writ for *habeas corpus*, and his defence attorney Bennett filed for appeal.

Bennett approached the State Department for more detail on why the government considered his client to be a German citizen.[93] The department refused to reply on the convenient ground that the case was under appeal in New York. The case involved the execution of a federal law by the state authorities and hence had to be decided independently at that level.[94] But there was no question where Hackworth stood in this case. Schwarzkopf had been permitted to enter the United States under the Czech quota, but at that time he had been an Austrian citizen. Therefore the 1938 German nationality law applied to him. The Nazi Nuremberg decree of 1941 had no force in the United States, and consequently Schwarzkopf had not lost his German citizenship. The United States had always refused to admit the applicability of any of these Nazi racial decrees to its own citizens and therefore could not act otherwise in the case of immigrants.[95] The Justice Department showed itself to be somewhat unsure of its case against Schwarzkopf. In preparation for the appeal the department again wrote to the Department of State requesting more detailed information about the nationality status of Austrians.[96]

When the Schwarzkopf case came up for appeal in mid-1943 Bennett did his best to undermine the government's chief arguments. He insisted that if a country changed its sovereignty, citizens living abroad had the right either to accept or to reject the new citizenship. Only if they formally accepted it could the new citizenship apply to them. Schwarzkopf had never become a German citizen because at the time of the Anschluss he resided in the United States and had not formally opted for German citizenship. Even if because of the Anschluss and the nationality law of 1938 he were considered as a German citizen, the Nazi Nuremberg decree of 1941 had taken German citizenship away from him. Bennett was disgusted with the State Department's position regarding *bona fide* Jewish refugees from Nazi persecution. An influential attorney with political ties to the Roosevelt administration, Bennett complained to his good friend Marvin H. McIntyre, Roosevelt's White House aide, that keeping Austrians classified as Germans was tantamount to performing Goebbels's dirty work.[97]

In this case the appeals court agreed with Bennett's arguments, and by doing so was able to bypass the contentious question of whether or not the United States had recognized the Anschluss. The court assumed that although Austria had disappeared as a state, the United States had not recognized this absorption. But the court refused to put much weight on this point. Instead it accepted Bennett's first argument about the necessity for voluntary adoption of a changed sovereignty. It ruled that "under generally accepted principles of international law Germany could impose citizenship by annexation (collective naturalization) only on those who were inhabitants of Austria in 1938."[98] But Schwarzkopf had left Austria two years before the Anschluss and had never given any indication that he elected to accept the new citizenship: "If the invaded country has ceased to exist as an independent state there would seem to be all the more reason for allowing its former nationals, who have fled from the invader and established residence abroad, the right of voluntarily electing a new nationality and remaining 'stateless' until they acquire it. In our view, an invader cannot under international law impose its nationality upon non-residents of the subjugated country without their consent, express or implicit."[99] Regarding Bennett's second point, the court agreed that even had Schwarzkopf acquired German nationality, the 1941 Nuremberg decree had divested him of it because of his Jewish background. In sum, the court decided that Schwarzkopf had not become a German citizen, but was a "stateless" individual instead. He was therefore not an enemy alien, *habeas corpus* was applicable to him, and he should be freed from internment.

D'Esquiva and Schwarzkopf were typical of interned Austrians who were either "natives" or citizens of Austria, and who had not chosen German citizenship after 1938. The rulings in their cases did not affect Austrians who after the Anschluss had had to leave Austria with German passports as German citizens, unless they were Jewish. These two court challenges posed the most important threat to the government's application of the enemy alien law to Austrians and Germans. In the d'Esquiva case, the government set the standards even though a final decision was temporarily delayed. The Schwarzkopf appeal was much more dangerous, for if it should stand Austrians who had not expressly chosen German nationality after 1938 as well as German and Austrian Jews could no longer be viewed as enemy aliens. Thousands would have to be released from this category and classed instead as stateless persons.

The decision the government had to make now was whether or not to appeal the Schwarzkopf case to the Supreme Court.[100] Once again the legal division dived back into the Anschluss marsh, collecting all official statements and opinions issued at the time and since. As before it failed to arrive at the clear-cut conclusion that the United States had not recognized the Anschluss. The issue appeared even more intractable than it had during the previous year.[101] Meanwhile other government branches pressured the State Department to issue an authoritative interpretation or render expert advice about how to deal with Austrian and German internees in the light of the two court decisions, one of which came out so powerfully against the government's traditional position. The director of the Alien Enemy branch insisted that he no longer knew what to do with d'Esquiva and Schwarzkopf, for whom he was responsible.[102] The attorney general admitted being similarly confused.[103] The Justice Department inquired if the State Department contemplated taking the Schwarzkopf case to the Supreme Court to determine whether the United States was bound to recognize the German nationality law of July 1938, as well as the effectiveness of the 1941 Nuremberg decree. At first glance it appeared to Justice that this was the route to follow.[104] However, the solicitor general, who until then had backed the State Department, became sceptical about the government's chances for success in the Supreme Court. In his view the appeals court had probably been correct in both respects. It seemed reasonable to assume that the July 1938 German nationality law need not apply to nonresident, nonelecting Austrians. The 1941 Nuremberg decree divesting absent German Jews of German citizenship probably applied because the state that granted citizenship could also take it away. It might prove tricky to go to court over the validity of the 1941 Nuremberg decree because the government appeared to have no clearly formulated political policy on this question, might seem to be doing the Nazis' work for them, and risked appearing anti-Semitic. Perhaps the government should consider beating a strategic retreat. By not remanding the Schwarzkopf case to the Supreme Court, the government could save the larger principle. If the appeals ruling were accepted rather than appealed, the appeals court's decision would apply only to the individual case, without affecting the law or its application in a universal sense. Would it not be "better that the question remain for the time being within the area of the political and administrative control of the Government?" suggested the solicitor general.[105]

Discussions continued within the State Department on what strategy to follow. It was now discovered, too late, that vital evidence against Schwarzkopf had been overlooked. It emerged that during the alien registration drive in 1941 Schwarzkopf had actually registered as a German, and therefore he could have been accused of accepting German nationality voluntarily at that time. However, even had this fact been known, the second point about the Nuremberg decree remained.[106] A member of the legal division lamented that it was "more difficult to uphold the Department's case in court than in administrative matters." The Schwarzkopf case was one of the most complex he had ever encountered and he no longer felt certain that the government had much of a chance for success if it appealed to the Supreme Court. If it decided to proceed with an appeal, the only grounds for pursuing the matter would be those of "public policy." Not to appeal could mean that the government might voluntarily have to reverse its contention that the Nuremberg decrees did not apply to Austrians and Germans of Jewish background. But to lose that case before the Supreme Court would make that change an absolute certainty.[107] An assistant legal adviser urged the government to appeal, arguing forcefully that the case ought to be pursued "as a matter of public policy." But in the end discretion proved the better part of valour inasmuch as the government wished to avoid being forced to clarify its vague Austrian policy and to lose its still-effective administrative weapons in the enemy alien question.[108] Although the conviction grew within the State Department that the Schwarzkopf decision concerning the validity of the Nuremberg decree might in fact have been consistent with international law, as the appeals court had suggested, the department was not prepared to admit this fact publicly. By declining to appeal to the Supreme Court the government would lose against the individual Schwarzkopf, but would keep its hands free in other similar cases.[109]

The State Department decided to follow the solicitor general's advice. By accepting apparent defeat in both the d'Esquiva and Schwarzkopf cases, it could save the broader legal issue concerning enemy aliens.[110] It issued administrative instructions that natives of Austria and persons born in that country were no longer automatically to be considered natives of Germany.[111] On 1 November 1943, the day the three foreign ministers published the Moscow Declaration on Austria, the State Department's chief legal advisers also gave up the fight in the Schwarzkopf case. It is interesting to note that these discussions over whether or not to appeal the Schwarzkopf case had proceeded quite unaffected by parallel State Department action on the Allied declaration on Austria, under consideration since July 1943. The Moscow Declaration on Austria called the Anschluss void and promised that country and its inhabitants liberation, freedom, and independence, but the drafting of these principles, in which the legal and European divisions were involved, never seemed to impinge upon the departmental discussions concerning the two court cases.[112]

That the government failed to appeal the d'Esquiva and Schwarzkopf rulings therefore did not signify support for Austria and Austrians. Nor is there any evidence that the Moscow Declaration triggered a change of attitude concerning them. This decision was guided strictly by administrative considerations. The government's general enemy alien position and practice remained unaltered. Austrians as a group continued to be treated as enemy aliens, remaining subject to apprehension and internment. As late as August 1944 the Department of Justice was still advising the War Department that Austrian aliens should be interned if they were considered to be "dangerous to internal security."[113] The gist of these two court cases was that the government suffered local tactical defeats, but retained its strategic position and manoeuvrability. Austrian refugees from Germany and Austria as a whole gained very little. Slowly over the next year, in individual cases the government began to apply the court ruling regarding the Nuremberg decree to refugee Austrian Jews, especially when outside the country.[114]

The British and American governments retained their ingrained negative views about the usefulness of Austrian refugees to the Allied war effort. They discovered, for instance, how apolitical most of them were and how divided were the rest. A national Austrian bond appeared wanting. As a result these Austrians exerted little direct influence upon their hosts, who classified them as German citizens and enemy aliens to the end. When some of then questioned or challenged the law, the government ignored or opposed them. The two Allies did not always understand or appreciate the similarity of their respective positions on Austrians, owing to differences in types of government and problems of communication. The American administration's "chaotic working conditions" shocked Eden's secretary, Oliver Harvey, who later headed the Foreign Office's German-Austrian section. He frequently proved unable to distinguish domestic rhetoric from official policy.[115] Had the Americans accepted the Anschluss even "more philosophically than we [the British] did?"[116] What did Hull's July 1942 press statement really mean?[117] Did the decisions in the d'Esquiva and Schwarzkopf cases and the government's unwillingness to appeal them indicate an American policy shift in favour of Austrians?[118] The Americans puzzled their British allies, who were not always sensitive to complex American constitutional nuances or domestic political pressures. However, during the process of their early postwar planning for Austria, both sides eventually came to realize that, despite differing national styles, their conclusions and forecasts respecting Austria proved remarkably similar.

CHAPTER FOUR

Early Planning for Postwar Austria, 1939–43

World War I leaders and officials had made little attempt before the war's end to work out a comprehensive Allied peace settlement. In World War II, by contrast, long-range planning commenced early under hectic and frequently chaotic circumstances. Initially the Western Allies faced a host of uncertainties which made planning for the future problematical. The first priority was to survive overwhelming Axis aggression and strength. They laboured within an exceptionally critical and fluid military framework, were out of touch with continental affairs, and had little to guide them but the past. The West did not fight World War II in order to engender radical social or political change, but to rescue prewar Europe and rebuild it on a sounder basis. The planners contemplated a European peace in which the same factors operated as before the war, although they hoped that the virulence of nationalism might have finally burned itself out. They were certainly unable at this early stage, with their own existence threatened, to envision that the war would end in such an unexpected fashion with a weakened Great Britain, a strong Soviet presence in eastern Europe, and a United States deeply embroiled in Europe's affairs.

In 1914–18 academics had been tied to the British war effort in the role of anti-German and pronationalist propagandists. At the end of the war President Wilson had brought together academics and others to assist in drawing up the peace terms. In World War II, however, statesmen hoped to avoid the mistakes of the previous conflict by from the outset engaging leading academic experts in international affairs in the process of planning for peace. The unique cooperation between official diplomatic planners and highly qualified academic experts tied to two private international affairs groups, the Royal Institute of International Affairs (RIIA) in London and the Council on Foreign Relations (CFR) in New York, reinforced an historical approach to successful peacemaking.

This attempt to project the past forward into an uncertain future raises certain uncomfortable questions concerning the relationship between the lessons of history and unexpected variables in human affairs. Paradoxically, many of the leading experts from the RIIA and CFR pressed into service in World War II were the same scholars who in World War I had championed the principle of nationalism as the only basis for a legitimate and secure peace in Europe. As a result of their interwar and World War II studies they had come to repudiate sharply some of the basic principles that had guided the adoption of the 1919 peace formula, especially the assumption that nationalism was the historically based and legitimate organizing factor to guide political life in central and southeastern Europe. Instead they formulated regional or federative solutions, which would neutralize the evil effects of nationalism.

A decade ago an Austrian historian labelled Austria "a nation sui generis" — culturally, ethnically, and politically distinct; no one's "errant offspring and lost province."[1] The wartime Western Allies would not have agreed with this statement, which was the product of a slow process spurred on by wartime and occupation experiences over the space of a generation between 1938 and 1955. Western wartime planners arrived at the long-term conclusion that an independent Austria was too weak on its own and instead should become a leading element within a Danubian federation. A corollary to this federative line of thought was the historical rehabilitation of the old Austro-Hungarian Monarchy. These decisions were taken within the Allies' political-diplomatic structures, but were not always reflected by military planning which sometimes ran on its own separate and parallel course, especially in the case of the American Department of War and its Civil Affairs Division. Despite Soviet hesitations, this federative program for Austria and its neighbours remained basic Western policy until the war's end.

At the best of times the unfolding of foreign affairs is a complex and difficult process to forecast. The task of planners is to ascertain what is likely to occur in the future and to formulate ways to cope with its development. Planners must assume that it is possible to imagine what the future will bring on the basis of present information. An experienced American official described forecasting the international future as "the art of thinking in ways that lead you to begin to do something now which will make the nation's position in the world scene better in the future."[2] But foreign affairs permit little control over men and events. It is difficult enough to identify historical trends, let alone understand their implications, recognize the true interests of a country, project coherent goals into the future, and choose the appropriate means to achieve them. These obstacles become critically difficult to overcome during a war, when immense new pressures bear down on peoples and governments. Yet, if change appears on the horizon, the desire to avoid harmful surprises dictates that an effort be made to study the nature of the altered conditions and formulate appropriate programs of action to cope with the new circumstances.

Foreign affairs bureaucracies have always demonstrated a disinclination to look beyond their day-to-day activities. Frequently, they unconsciously set up their own obstacles to thwart long-range planning. They revere diplomatic experience and bureaucratic specialization. They are heirs to the "harried parochialism" of having to respond to the most immediate daily demands confronting them.[3] Sharing an informal culture they stress the unpredictability of international events, and an intuitive approach to them based upon personal diplomatic experience. Diplomats usually favour short-range adjustments to long-term projections, which are frequently viewed as irrational and unwonted intrusions on short-term operations.[4] That is why sophisticated statesmen have consulted the views of outsiders, who do not have to maintain institutional loyalties, worry about disciplinary relationships within the official structure, or endure daily bureaucratic pressures. With greater conviction, frankness, and independence, external experts can offer long-term opinions or prognosticate about foreign affairs. But to be effective these outside forecasters must be "plugged into" the institutional decision-making process.[5] In World War II, both the British and the Americans experimented with the novel concept of attaching nonbureaucratic experts to their foreign affairs departments to help define the outlines of the future. It is important to study this new official-academic cooperation, for in some cases – and Austria was certainly one of them – the RIIA and CFR experts exercised an enormous influence on the policies adopted for the postwar era.

Before World War I the closely guarded arena of foreign affairs had been largely left to the secret machinations of professional diplomats or political leaders. But Wilson's 1917–19 "Inquiry," a group of scholarly advisers preparing for the peace conference, was a harbinger of change. Between the wars foreign affairs were opened up for the first time to public and academic scrutiny, creating a large pool of interested citizens and scholarly experts. People became curious to know how countries had tumbled into the bloody and costly war and then negotiated such an unsatisfactory peace. Publicly funded organizations sprouted to galvanize public opinion regarding international relations. Founded by scholarly British and American delegates to the Versailles conference, the RIIA and the CFR became especially influential between the wars. Other groups, such as the various League of Nations and peace societies, prospered as well. Many universities endowed new chairs of international affairs, and history courses stressed the study of diplomacy more than ever. Public political investigations studied the causes of the war and scrutinized the foundations of the peace. When war exploded once again in 1939 the RIIA and CFR almost immediately initiated their own studies on the future peace and offered their vast research and planning resources to the Foreign Office and the Department of State respectively. The offers were gratefully accepted, in this way encouraging a scholarly slant in the official planning process. This historical approach towards peace forecasting led the British and Americans to similar conclusions regarding Austria, despite their dissimilar foreign policy interests and styles.

Each country's policy reflected a diverse national style, a sense of foreign policy interests based upon respective national values, goals, interests, and strategies. Shaped by their different geographies, histories, national ideologies, and peoples, each coalition member viewed the world and its role in it distinctively. The development of warm personal relations, nearly intimate and usually secretive, between Franklin D. Roosevelt and Winston Churchill immensely aided, but also complicated, the Western alliance. On the one hand they shared a strong sense of the common culture and purpose of their two historic English-speaking nations.[6] On the other, this coalition also recognized the independence of the two partners. Neither country surrendered much of its sovereignty, although at Supreme Headquarters national viewpoints were remarkably submerged.[7] Churchill reputedly exclaimed once that there was only one thing worse than fighting with allies, and that was fighting without them. Practical considerations of self-protection and self-interest predominated, but did not always coincide. Each partner continually engaged in military and political calculations separately as well as in common. Significant differences of opinion eventually emerged over a whole range of questions, including what the main thrust of military effort in Europe and the political future of India, Asia, and Europe ought to be. The British and Americans were truly "allies of a kind," sometimes distrusting each other, concealing their intentions, and being unsure of the other's true motivations."[8]

Long versed in complex imperial and continental affairs, the British seemed to operate easily on the stage of global diplomacy. They recognized the international system for what it was: irrational, hostile, and ambiguous. National interests demanded intervention against rivals and to solve vital but intractable problems. The Americans were fortuitously separated by time, space, and history – and therefore belief -from such messy intrigues. Geography permitted them the luxury of invoking idealistic traditions of a normative nature in foreign affairs. They preferred to avoid coalitions and considered – at least until after 1945 – a free hand in foreign relations to be the normal state of affairs in international politics.[9] Consequently Americans often grew impatient with the ambiguities of power politics, preferring short-term diplomatic goals and "solving " temporary breaches in the naturally peaceful concourse of nations. They employed rhetorical pronouncements primarily to mobilize domestic support for international action. The contrasting national styles of the Allies in foreign policy praxis frequently puzzled them, and caused occasional divergences as they cooperated in the grand task of defeating Fascist Italy, Nazi Germany, and Imperial Japan.[10]

The wartime coalition functioned most effectively in technical, economic, and military matters, although hot arguments erupted, especially about grand strategy.[11] The economic and military aspect of the Anglo-American alliance became institutionalized especially through the Combined Chiefs of Staff (CCS) in Washington and Supreme Allied Headquarters later in the field, and remained effective despite differing military styles. The United States was primarily a continental power and consequently Americans were inclined to solve their military problems through overwhelming force employed on large land masses. Great Britain, an island power always short on manpower, had achieved its world position through maritime might and, whenever possible, by surrogate intervention on the European continent. Roosevelt generally gave free rein to his chiefs of staff in military matters, whereas Churchill tried to dominate his commanders. Yet despite these differences common military structures assisted in resolving disagreements and arriving at common military strategies and practices.

Political coordination proved to be much more problematical. National rivalries became fiercely evident as questions cropped up concerning the location and political benefits of a second front, relations with the Soviet Union, the future of Italy, Greece, and central Europe. Whereas Churchill tried to link military and political matters, short-term and long-term projects, Roosevelt preferred to compartmentalize them and concentrate upon winning the war. Churchill kept both military and political lines in his own hands, but as commander-in-chief during wartime Roosevelt was legally supreme only in military matters. Althought the constitution stated that the president might have political advisers including the secretary of state, many of his political powers were circumscribed and shared with the legislative branch. Churchill stressed the large international picture, while Roosevelt concentrated on the domestic front in support of his military leaders. Unlike the more sceptical Churchill, Roosevelt expected peace and harmony to reemerge naturally at the conclusion of victory over the arrogant disturbers of peace.[12] Churchill was always conscious of moulding the historical record, whereas Roosevelt intuitively shied away from committing himself. Later generations were often left to speculate about what Roosevelt's political policies and motives had been. Thanks to the lack of an Allied institutional political structure, the British and Americans were unable to develop coherent political coordination or unified political policies to match their highly successful military combination.

Little of detail and substance emerged publicly during the war to indicate the content of Western postwar planning. The public had to be content with grandiloquent rhetorical declarations, such as the 1941 Atlantic Charter, the 1943 Four Freedoms statement, and the 1945 declaration on liberated Europe. As a power with continental concerns, Great Britain was more interested in prognosticating the shape of postwar Europe, whereas Roosevelt preferred to enunciate grand principles and left the details to the war's end. Roosevelt's vacillation or silence on specific political issues, especially the future configuration of central and southeastern Europe, made it difficult for London or Moscow to know what these principles meant in specific cases.[13] Meeting initial resistance to their goals regarding neighbouring countries, the Soviets prudently desisted from revealing their postwar objectives. After June 1941 they were fighting for their very existence and desperately needed Allied military support and supplies.

Despite the fact that the Allies fought World War II as a coalition war without coalition policies, the Anglo-American political staffs made every reasonable effort to draft plans for the future.[14] The British hoped to avoid repetition of the Wilsonian peace, and they wished to prevent the evolution of a unilateral American Atlantic Charter scheme. The United States was chiefly concerned with arriving better prepared this time at the peace conference and with countering its allies' proposals with firm American policies.[15] Although the military and civilian leaders' time was largely occupied with day-to-day routine matters, British and American staffs began to study postwar problems as early as 1939.[16] British political planning centred in the Foreign Office, which maintained its predominant influence throughout the war. The Foreign Office produced the war cabinet's background planning papers and policy recommendations, on the basis of position papers from Professor Arnold J. Toynbee's RIIA wartime research branch, the Foreign Research and Press Service (FRPS), and its Foreign Office successor, the Foreign Office's Research Department (FORD). The FRPS, a research and eventually planning agency organized by Toynbee and staffed largely by academics, operated as a semi-independent branch of the RIIA at Balliol College, Oxford, between 1939 and 1943. FORD then took over this task when Toynbee and some of his staff joined the Foreign Office directly. Long-term British policies on Austria drafted early in the war under Toynbee's FRPS guidance and adopted by the war cabinet in 1943, set British policy for the ensuing period.

Early in 1944 the three-power European Advisory Commission (EAC) was established in London, in response to British suggestions and decisions reached at the tripartite Moscow Conference, to formulate Allied policies on surrender and occupation of enemy territories. The British EAC delegation received political instructions through William Strang, leader of the British Foreign Office EAC delegation.[17] New interdepartmental committees were established to draw up and coordinate short-term British policies regarding the surrender and civil administration of occupied and liberated territories. The best known of these groups was the Post-Hostilities Planning Sub-Committee under the chiefs of staff. These committees were largely interested in the military consequences of the war. They followed the political lead of the Foreign Office and worked within the framework of earlier FRPS papers and war cabinet policy.[18] When a special section was created within the Post-Hostilities group in 1944 to draw up details for an Austrian occupation, W.H.B. Mack of the Foreign Office's new Austrian section became its civil deputy commissioner responsible for political aspects.[19] Thanks to this closely knit network, the Foreign Office dominated both long- and short-term external political planning in Great Britain.

But even before the war began the Foreign Office realized that the small staff at its disposal would be unable to perform its usual routine operations and simultaneously satisfy new information and planning demands likely to be made upon it. During the Great War of 1914–18 the Foreign Office had not attempted to study the historical past and present systematic recommendations in order to determine options for the future. But as the war dragged on and the need for public support became imperative, the Foreign Office grew increasingly intent to demonstrate the war guilt of the Central Powers. Early in that war the Foreign Office established a four-man Political Intelligence Department under the eminent historian Sir James Headlam-Morley. On his staff were two young historians, Arnold Toynbee and Lewis Namier, as well as two Australian brothers, Allen and Rex Leeper.[20] Toynbee was set to work on Turkish affairs, concentrating on propaganda rather than history, as he later admitted. He edited the Blue Book on the treatment of Armenians in the Ottoman Empire, and he then collaborated with Lord Bryce on producing official propaganda concerning alleged German atrocities committed in Belgium and France.[21] Like others of that generation of academics, the Foreign Office propagandists believed strongly in nationalism as the force of the future and expected the old multinational empires in eastern Europe to vanish.[22]

Once the hostilities ceased these academics became deeply disillusioned with British hesitancy in implementing nationalist standards.[23] They believed that their noble schemes were distorted and bargained away by the politicians. Not only did many scholarly advisers from the same country meet for the first time in Versailles, but they encountered their counterparts from other countries as well. There they participated in the creation of a transatlantic Anglo-American Institute of International Affairs, dedicated to producing "objective, unpartisan and unemotional" studies on international affairs.[24] The founders hoped that better study and research by scholars concerning the mysteries of international relations might help prevent breakdowns in the international system such as they had just witnessed in the war and peace process.[25] The initiative for establishing this transatlantic group came from British historian Lionel Curtis, a founder of Milner's "Round Table" and a former Colonial Office functionary in South Africa.[26] Several leading Round Table members wound up on the Anglo-American Versailles delegations, including United States Round Table correspondent and historian George Beer, and an American Rhodes scholar, Whitney H. Shepardson.[27] Beer and Curtis organized the 30 May 1919 meeting at the Majestic Hotel, Paris, where they founded the Anglo-American Institute of International Affairs dedicated to "the study and formation of more enlightened concourse among the nations." Two of the three American steering committee representatives, Archibald Cary Coolidge and James T. Shotwell, were historian members of the "Inquiry."[28]

The founding of this institute represented the educated public's claim and perceived duty to become involved in foreign affairs, an activity hitherto considered the exclusive prerogative of government. The institute's studies would serve as an indispensable agent to promote more rational postwar international politics and prevent the pursuit of secretive, elitist cabinet policies. These diplomatic follies had landed the world in the mire of war in 1914. But geographical imperatives soon decreed that the transatlantic institute would be divided into two independent national organizations. Within a short time the American branch became known as the Council on Foreign Relations (CFR), while in Great Britain it emerged as the British Institute of International Affairs. Both groups retained warm ties with each other between the wars and hoped that similar organizations could be organized in other countries.[29]

Upon receiving a royal charter in 1925 the British organization became known as the Royal Institute of International Affairs (RIIA) or Chatham House after its London headquarters in St James Square. At first the Foreign Office "old guard" treated the RIIA with suspicion. As far as the professionals were concerned, this unsophisticated body consisting of enthusiastic amateurs wanted to poach upon the Foreign Office's private preserve. Initially civil servants were forbidden to join or even attend RIIA meetings. Over the years, however, the Foreign

Office realized the potential value of Chatham House as a pressure group in the more democratic postwar era, forming and guiding public opinion.[30] Between the wars the RIIA developed into the most powerful British stimulant for awakening public interest and encouraging academic research in international affairs. Its first publication, the massive, six-volume Temperley study of the 1919 peace conference, was followed by many other notable books over the next decades.[31] Under the guidance of Lionel Curtis and Headlam-Morley, who remained honorary historian at the Foreign Office, private funds supported these scholarly activities. One of the chief sources, the Rockefeller Foundation in the United States, also subsidized the parallel activities of the CFR. The RIIA's annual survey and chronology of international affairs, various documentary collections, the *International Affairs* journal, and regular press surveys proved invaluable for students of international affairs and created an excellent worldwide reputation for the institute.[32] In 1925 Toynbee joined the RIIA as director of studies.[33] By the late 1930s, much to the annoyance of Chamberlain, Toynbee had taken to issuing strong warnings concerning the Nazi menace.[34]

The year 1938 proved a great educator in Great Britain. The Austrian Anschluss and threats of war over Czechoslovakia caused some people to heed Cassandras such as Toynbee. The Foreign Office became aware that it could not keep pace with the Nazis' dynamic, hyperactive style of foreign policy initiatives. Its small staff was geared to traditional diplomatic activity. Foreign Office staffers learned that they were unable to meet any extraordinary crisis or task. It became imperative to improve the government's foreign intelligence and propaganda capability. At issue also was a developing bureaucratic struggle, an attempt to bring the country's foreign propaganda machinery, if it were to be expanded, under the wing of the Foreign Office and halt the creation of a projected Ministry of Information.[35] Rex Leeper, Toynbee's World War I propaganda colleague, who currently headed the Foreign Office News Department, hoped that any new overseas publicity tasks would be assigned to his department. With this in mind he solicited his influential friend Toynbee's advice and assistance.[36] The idea of engaging once again in propaganda work did not appeal to Toynbee, but he saw the possibility that the RIIA might be able to exert a considerable, and steadying, influence on government policy. If war came, the RIIA would probably be called upon to cooperate with the government. But this should take place under the institute's conditions: it might well function as an independent, scientific research group for the government. Toynbee and his directors agreed that they would rather close the RIIA than let it become an official propaganda tool. On the other hand, Toynbee was attracted by the opportunity to change the government's negative attitude towards himself and the RIIA, and to spirit his own ideas into the highest councils of British foreign policy-makers. By September 1938 he had registered success on both fronts.[37]

Some influential RIIA members balked at the notion that the institute should forfeit its highly prized independence by becoming too closely involved with the government. By this time the RIIA had managed to become self-sufficient and respected in its own right. It possessed one of the country's largest specialized libraries on world affairs, a competent staff with excellent research background, a vast international network of academic and political connections, and a first-rate record of publishing reputable books and other materials on international events. Eastern Europe specialists such as C.A. Macartney, I.F.D. Morrow, Elizabeth Wiskemann, and Robert W. Seton-Watson worked under the RIIA aegis.[38]

A compromise plan was finally worked out which hitched the RIIA's resources to the Foreign Office's needs, thereby indirectly ensuring RIIA influence over the government's foreign policies. Toynbee and Leeper agreed that international affairs experts from Chatham House and the universities would operate as a semi-independent, confidential information and intelligence gathering office for the Foreign Office. In return the government would subsidize the group's work through an annual grant of £80,000.[39] Toynbee reached an agreement with Balliol College to establish his new bureau on campus as the Foreign Research and Press Service (FRPS). Initially in charge of its Southeastern Europe section, which included Austria, was the renowned Professor Robert W. Seton-Watson, who had been the most powerful voice during World War I in favour of breaking up the Austro-Hungarian Empire and encouraging the emergence of the minority nationalities.[40] The RIIA and the Foreign Office formally confirmed this arrangement on the eve of war in August 1939.[41] However, almost immediately following the outbreak of war, the FRPS's work for the government came under fire. The press and public suddenly discovered what they assumed to be a nefarious government plot to exploit the wartime crisis in order to muzzle and lead public opinion. Toynbee was personally attacked in Parliament for his apparent opposition to national states. How could Britain fight to liberate states which one of its chief advisers judged to be of doubtful viability? Despite these criticisms and an initial cut in the government subsidy, Toynbee managed quickly to assemble in Oxford a large staff of 131 paid and volunteer academics and assistants. As the war progressed, the Foreign Office was able to increase the FRPS subsidy until by the end of 1942 it amounted to almost £70,000.[42]

Shortly after the Churchill government assumed power in mid-1940, the new minister of information, Duff Cooper, persuaded the war cabinet to form a Cabinet War Aims Subcommittee under the direction of the deputy prime minister and Labour party leader, Clement Attlee. It was given a very large mandate: "to make suggestions in regard to a postwar European and world system, with particular regard to the economic needs of the various nations, and to the problems of adjusting the life force of small countries in a durable international order."[43] These terms of reference made it clear that the small countries would have to conform to the demands of the postwar international order. The Foreign Office feared the competition from a planning group totally removed from its control. Moreover, the Labourite Attlee would probably promote left-wing social and political reform hostile to the more conservative world view advocated by the Foreign Office. Through bureaucratic manipulation it eventually succeeded in imposing restraint on what it regarded as over-zealous Labour hopes for radical postwar change.[44]

The solution lay with Toynbee, who had lobbied to replace this group with his own experts.[45] In preparation for this eventuality, at the end of 1940 Toynbee reorganized the FRPS's research structure on a new geographical basis with a separate unit called "The Danubian Countries" within whose purview fell Austria. Its head was Professor D. Mitrany, a Rumanian expert from Princeton's Institute of Advanced Studies, who had functioned in the FRPS as Seton-Watson's assistant. The Danubian section included other experts such as R.G.D. Laffran and C.A. Macartney.[46] The entry of the USSR into the war awakened new hope of a German defeat. Rex Leeper cautioned in July 1941 that a Soviet victory might completely subvert Great Britain's influence on the European continent, whereupon Stalin would make a bid for European leadership. Leeper considered it imperative for the British to make "as rapid progress as possible in defining the new kind of order in Europe for which they [the Allied governments] stand."[47] Toynbee had long been chanting the same tune.[48] Both interest strands criss-crossed at this point. The Foreign Office was keen to supplant Attlee's influence in the planning field and to integrate Toynbee's RIIA academic group more closely with official circles so as to increase Foreign Office planning capability, and to avoid the danger, as one member of the department expressed it, that the "long-haired people" from the outside might dictate the government's peace policy.[49] By the fall Eden had agreed that this reorganization would be useful and the Attlee War Aims Subcommittee research group was disbanded.[50] Toynbee's FRPS immediately took over the subcommittee's political research and planning tasks.[51]

Long before taking up the German question, officials pondered the problem of how to forestall another German, and perhaps Soviet, threat to weak Austria and splintered southeastern Europe. The FRPS was asked to determine whether the Danubian region should return to its prewar status, namely, that of a collection of independent countries, or whether these small units would stand a better chance to survive in the postwar world by aligning themselves in some type of eastern European bloc.[52] In order to expedite this assignment for the Foreign Office, FRPS researchers were given access for the first time to confidential political and consular documents. The Board of Trade also opened its files to the FRPS in order to shed light on the economic side of the Austro-Danubian question, or what the Foreign Office termed information "regarding the economic balance of [the] Austro-Hungarian Monarchy."[53] Foreign Office and FRPS perceptions of the Danubian question meshed easily. Official reports had long lamented this intractable problem which enabled Germany to infiltrate eastern European countries and exploit their interstate rivalries. The World War I victors had expected this region to become sufficiently strong and prosperous to resist German and Soviet pressures. But these hopes had been dashed in the interwar period.[54] Negative official views tallied with the pessimism of RIIA experts. As early as 1929 Toynbee had compared the situation resulting from the area's weakness and rivalries, including Franco-Italian competition in the Balkans, to the situation immediately preceding the outbreak of World War I. At an international conference two years later Toynbee demonstrated his departure from the principle of nationalism with these words: "We [groups like the RIIA] are at present working discreetly but with all our might, to wrest this political force called sovereignty out of the clutches of the local national states of our world ... In plain terms, we have to transfer the prestige and the prerogatives of sovereignty from the fifty or sixty fragments to the whole of contemporary society – from the local national states by which sovereignty has been usurped, with disastrous consequences ... I believe the monster [national sovereignty] is doomed to perish by our sword."[55] Robert Seton-Watson, once a proponent of regional national independence, had also realized by the 1930s that southeastern Europe's frontiers had to be adjusted or reduced in importance in order to arrange an economic or political union or federation.[56] Robert's son Hugh championed this cause during the war.[57] A 1939 RIIA study on southeastern Europe which concentrated specifically on the Nazi threat argued that geographical, political, economic, and national frictions had rendered the region impotent in the face of Nazi power.[58] Thus by 1939 official and academic thinking had converged in the notion of a federative solution in the Balkans and central Europe, if countries such as Austria were to weather the storm.

When the FRPS replaced the Attlee subcommittee in October 1941 it presented the Foreign Office with its paper on Austria and southeastern

Europe. This long overview and recommendations reflected the most astute Foreign Office and academic views on the subject. It was widely circulated through other government departments. Not surprisingly the report would have the region's countries form a multinational Danubian state after the war. Its approach was to devote most of its space to reviewing the sad national histories in southeastern Europe since 1918. The drafters made no attempt to speculate about the Soviet Union's possible role in that part of the world. This was not surprising because at the time the Soviets were battling for their lives and their survival was in grave doubt. Still, the proposal, if adopted, might counter not only a possible German threat, but resist eventual Soviet pressures as well.[59] By the time the war cabinet adopted the document almost unchanged as official policy two years later, the USSR's military situation had improved dramatically.[60]

The document viewed Austria as the keystone of the Danubian arch over the past five centuries. Its people were at one and the same time the most provincial and the most cosmopolitan in Europe. Before 1918 they had possessed no sense of national identity and they had failed to develop it subsequently. They were victims of imperial memories, deeply riven by local and ideological divisions. Austrians had proved unable to establish a viable state. Paradoxically, however, Austria's lack of overheated nationalism made the country much more rational than nationalistic Germany or the other Central European states. Southeastern Europe, or as the paper termed it, "Danubia," had finally succumbed to noxious nationalism. The national principle had obviously proved unworkable in "Danubia." Its people were too ethnically and religiously mixed, and too passionate. The FRPS historians and planners now admitted that in 1919 they had misapplied a sound Western idea, the national principle, under totally different and inappropriate conditions. The "enthusiastic application of Western ideas torn from their Western context" had obviously misfired. With this bold statement, Toynbee, Seton-Watson, and the other FRPS experts formally repudiated their former attachment to nationalism as the region's only possible solution. The League of Nations had provided interstate bonds that were wholly inadequate. The expected political and economic cooperation between these eastern European states had not materialized after 1918. An evolution towards economic union would have been mandatory for the well-being of all the states in the region, but interstate rivalries had rendered any such hopes unworkable. In the 1930s these rivalries enabled Germany to penetrate the area, first economically, and then politically and militarily. "The time for a healthy and independent Danubian union, in which Austria could have found her natural function as an experienced and cultured 'older brother' of the Successor States, had gone."[61]

Once promoted in its innocent youthfulness as the area's road to salvation, nationalism had instead turned into the disease of the age. What then of the future? Repeating the old mistakes would be suicidal. The failed 1919–39 experiment of completely independent eastern European states haunted the planners' thinking. Another Austrian Anschluss, the inevitable first step in German penetration of the area once again, had to be avoided this time. Austria had to be better protected and supported by the great powers and securely embedded in a more extensive political structure. To ensure success some supranational idea had to be imposed on the region. Ironically these former critics of the defunct Austro-Hungarian Empire now found themselves cast in the role of its defenders in more modern garb. One of the main derivatives of this new wisdom was the realization that the old multinational Habsburg state now seemed to have been much more successful than it had appeared to be before and during World War I. It was now time to realize that in 1918 "a more practical alternative appeared to be the maintenance of the unities of Austria and Hungary, but the application within them of national and cultural autonomy."[62] This historical revisionism led to the conclusion that the postwar interests of Europe, and of Austria and the Danubian states, would be best served by emulating the constitutional structure of pre-1914 Austria-Hungary, minus the Habsburgs this time. The FRPS recommended the creation of a Danubian federation supported economically and diplomatically by the Western powers. Federal institutions combined with local and cultural autonomy would create a large, tolerant state well able to survive economically and to defend itself successfully against any renewed German aggression. "It needed the cataclysm of this war to open the eyes of European public opinion to the need of Danubian unity." The paper assumed that not only the British, but also the various peoples of "Danubia," would have reached this conclusion by the end of the war. Churchill favoured the idea in general and no other arrangement appeared to be viable.[63]

The Foreign Office and the FRPS favoured the federative solution that might reestablish the various little Danubian units, but with diminished sovereignty within a larger economic and political structure. These federative opinions were underlined in early 1942 when the FRPS inadvertently released an internal working brief to the Foreign Office. This preliminary study of Austria's economic future contradicted the conventional wisdom that an independent Austria would not be economically self-supporting after the war.[64] Such iconoclasm unleashed an uproar in London. The Foreign Office objected principally because the report compared Austria to Switzerland and ascribed Austria's potential postwar prosperity to the country's thorough industrialization by the Nazis since 1938.[65] The FRPS immediately repudiated the paper and its directors rushed to apologize for this oversight. The brief was downplayed as being merely one person's private "first shot at the subject" and "not expert enough to justify the paper being taken seriously." In order to placate the Foreign Office and to prevent similar blunders in the future, the FRPS promptly discharged the unfortunate researcher. The Foreign Office expressed relief and all talk regarding a viable Austrian economic future was ended for the duration.[66]

Political planning at the Foreign Office in conjunction with the FRPS proceeded slowly amidst the day-to-day pressures of the war effort. As late as mid-1943 Eden conceded that routine wartime pressures forced him to be only superficially interested in future political plans, and that he remained eager not to commit himself to any specific course of action. Oliver Harvey, future head of the Foreign Office Central Department responsible for Germany and Austria, commented in August 1943 that "these subjects have been insufficiently studied by him [Eden] and [still] we are not ready. Brilliant empiricism and improvisation, which had served him so well in the turmoil of war, cannot replace solid work and thought."[67] One of the main topics that Harvey believed Eden had neglected was the puzzle of southeastern Europe. Yet as victory began to take shape the government became increasingly interested in determining the course of postwar policy.

The year 1943 was a critical one for the FRPS and for its policy recommendations on Austria. By this time the FRPS Oxford staff had grown to 177.[68] Convinced that the bombing danger to London had sufficiently diminished, Chatham House returned in 1942 to its St James Square headquarters, and was considering halting its annual subsidy to the FRPS on the grounds that the RIIA needed the money to recommence its own work. If the government needed the FRPS, it should pay all the costs itself. The Foreign Office replied that in view of the need to make postwar planning a more serious and confidential activity than hitherto, it preferred to amalgamate some of the FRPS staff directly with its own planning process. At first the Chatham House directors resisted a complete government take-over of the FRPS as "poor recognition of what has been done and [a] break in the wartime arrangement."[69] Yet in the end the choice appeared inevitable as both Toynbee and the Foreign Office agreed on this point. By December 1942 Lord Astor, chairman of the institute, and Eden agreed that the FRPS's permanent RIIA staff and library would be transferred to the Foreign Office until the completion of the peace treaties.[70] In mid-1943 the Foreign Office appointed some members of the FRPS staff including Toynbee temporary civil servants within its Foreign Office Research Department (FORD).[71] At the same time the Foreign Office recommended the FRPS's multinational Danubian concept to the war cabinet as being by far the "most attractive solution to the region's problems," and the cabinet adopted it as government policy. Because there were still too many imponderables in the equation, details could not yet be elaborated. For the moment they would have to remain in a "nebulous" state. It was not yet apparent, for instance, whether the Poles, the Czechs, and the Soviets approved of the plan. However, as the Foreign Office noted, it represented a solid target to be aimed at. "It is desirable to work for ... a Central (or south-eastern) European confederation" in which Austria would be placed, although matters did not need to be rushed.[72] In accepting the federative concept in June 1943, the war cabinet approved of both the goal and this informal schedule for implementation.[73]

This rehabilitation of the revised imperial Austro-Hungarian concept during World War II was to have a revolutionary effect on the thrust of postwar scholarly activity. After 1918 the Austro-Hungarian Empire was labelled a failure and academic interest between the wars shifted to the nationalities. At the conclusion of World War II, however, many FRPS and FORD experts returned to their academic posts and continued to write in the same vein about southeastern Europe as they had during the conflict. Toynbee's first postwar *Survey of International Affairs* echoed the 1941 FRPS paper on Austria and the 1943 cabinet decision. It again blamed the 1938–9 collapse in southeastern Europe on errors committed by the victors in 1919.[74] "The history of the Versailles system in eastern Europe," the *Survey* explained, "showed in microcosm what the League of Nations showed in the world at large, that sovereign states are incapable of disciplined co-operation for a long period in defence of a static international order."[75] Whereas between the wars scholars had ignored the Austro-Hungarian Empire in favour of the successor states, they now moved in the opposite direction. True to his wartime insights, historian C.A. Macartney warned the world in 1962 about the danger inherent in the desire of countries in southeastern Europe for national independence. Should Soviet control over the area disappear one day, Macartney doubted that the restoration of independent states in "Danubia" would offer a viable alternative: "To put back the fourteen national states of the interwar period, with their interwar frontiers would be to invite a repetition of the former failure ... the solution of the East European problem lies in the creation of some larger multinational state with special institutions appropriate to the special conditions of the area."[76] In this way the revised version of the Austro-Hungarian Monarchy and the role of nationalism continued to influence historical studies after 1945. The more historians stressed the negative aspects of nationalism and searched for supranational political models, the more intensive grew the interest in and nostalgia on behalf of the Austro-Hungarian Empire as a field of study and as a model for settling problems in Europe. This trend became transatlantic because the Americans arrived during the war at similar conclusions regarding Austria and "Danubia."[77]

Roosevelt, who has been accused of excessive improvisation and neglect of political planning, endeavoured to postpone many troublesome matters until the end of the war.[78] However, he did collaborate closely with Churchill and his Department of State officials conducted thorough wartime reviews of projected postwar policies. Roosevelt exchanged over 1,700 personal letters and messages with Churchill, attended nine wartime conferences, and even shared vacations with the British prime minister.[79] But their leadership styles differed greatly. Churchill performed at his best when working through a structured military and bureaucratic organization, even if he pursued his own pet trails from time to time or insisted on meddling in his officials' areas of responsibilities.[80] He presided over a centralized apparatus consisting of an Imperial Defence Cabinet Committee for military matters and a war cabinet which met regularly to prepare or adopt policies upon which the various ministries might draw for direction. In military affairs Roosevelt recognized his own lack of expertise and generally deferred to his Joint Chiefs of Staff Committee under General George C. Marshall, except for a few important strategic decisions regarding invasion plans in Europe during 1942 and 1943. When the two leaders met in December 1941 to coordinate their military efforts they adopted the British type of committee system in the Anglo-American Combined Chiefs of Staff.

But in domestic and political matters Roosevelt preferred to operate in an unstructured manner which often frustrated and confused his subordinates and allies. He had always been a helter-skelter administrator, and war did nothing to change his habits. As one historian commented: "He still conducted business in a flurry of telephone calls, personal conferences, formal correspondence cleared with appropriate agencies, informal letters cleared with no one, chits to secretaries and cabinet officers, evening conferences ... Roosevelt would not confine himself to administrative channels."[81] In this way Roosevelt dominated the governmental process when he wished. When he refused to make direct decisions or inform others of them, his advisers found it difficult to divine his policies or fashion their own to accommodate his programs. He refused to coordinate the political aspects of government. Reminiscing after the war, Henry Stimson observed that American wartime diplomacy could have greatly benefited if the United States had possessed a British-style war cabinet to parallel the effective military coordination of the American Joint Chiefs of Staff. Diplomatic and political problems were consequently split between military leaders ill-equipped to deal with them and various competing civilian government agencies.[82] This restless, shifting political environment suited Roosevelt's robust tastes eminently. It also allowed political decisions to be delayed as long as he wished in order not to strain the wartime alliance. He wished to avoid secret wartime commitments such as had been made during World War I. Much like Wilson, Roosevelt believed that contentious political issues could best be solved on a global scale at the end of the war through the international or world organization which he hoped to see established. Then the United States would exercise its own strong political role, a trend later to be augmented by control of atomic power.[83]

Despite his imperious nature and frequently eccentric behaviour, Churchill consulted regularly with his military and political cabinets, took their opinions into account, and relied on his foreign secretary. Roosevelt, on the other hand, was able to exercise all the personal prerogatives of what later became known as the "imperial presidency." His cabinet met irregularly and made few decisions. Secretary of State Cordell Hull was excluded from critical information and political decisions and did not accompany him to major interallied wartime meetings.[84] During the war Roosevelt's control of foreign policy grew, while personal appointees in the State Department further undermined the secretary of state's authority within the department. Roosevelt often bypassed Hull and depended on personal friends, assistants, or appointees, such as Adolf A. Berle and Sumner Welles, Harry Hopkins and Averell Harriman, for important political advice and confidential diplomatic activity.[85] Roosevelt's Map Room rather than the Department of State became the depository of important military and political decisions and records, many of which were never made available to the State Department.[86] Bureaucratic attempts to overcome this splintering of function and information such as the informal weekly meetings among the secretaries of state, navy, and war, or the more formal State, War, Navy Coordinating Committee (SWNCC) established in 1944, proved to be merely band-aid solutions which never adequately solved this problem of bureaucratic coordination and rivalry.[87]

During most of the war years little domestic pressure arose for the enunciation of clear postwar political policies.[88] Roosevelt's vacillation on specific political aspects of the international situation during the war, especially on the future of central and eastern Europe, fitted this mood.[89] For his officials, however, the nagging uncertainties regarding national policies due to ignorance of the president's intentions and the pervasive conflicts of authority among the executive arm's independent agencies created overlap and confusion. But it is incorrect to infer that

Washington failed to plan for the future. It is true that in Great Britain postwar planning enjoyed a respectful hearing in influential circles that usually led to the adoption of official policy. But even before the United States entered the war the prestigious CFR in New York and diplomatic officials in Washington undertook ambitious forecasting concerning the postwar world in order to avoid repetition of the country's and the State Department's unpreparedness for peace after World War I.[90] Before World War II the United States had had little experience in coalition warfare and serious political planning. During the previous war its army and navy had been only loosely attached to the Allied war machine and had functioned according to established military strategy with little direction from home. The Americans considered themselves as associates rather than allies and President Wilson drafted his general peace aims without systematic contact with the Allies. He did not involve the Department of State directly in his peace plans. Instead Wilson and Colonel House operated independently through the previously mentioned group of unofficial, largely academic advisers called the "Inquiry" to extemporize American peace positions at the end of the war.[91] During the 1920s and 1930s domestic disgust with the unsatisfactory evolution of the 1919 peace settlement and the intractability of European politics engendered a return to isolationism, which did little to prepare the country for a wartime alliance involving joint planning.

When the United States entered the war in 1941 its military establishment recognized the urgency of planning in coalition warfare. From the first wartime meeting of the Allied military during the January-February 1942 ARCADIA conference in Washington, the British challenged the Americans to define their military goals. The Americans were determined to remain masters in their own house, but discovered the weakness of their military team compared to the British organization. The antiquated War Board dating from before World War I was the only mechanism for coordinating the American armed forces. In 1941 this body operated without even a secretariat, and General Marshall's own staff required radical reorganization. Roosevelt barely knew his own military advisers whereas Churchill had been meeting weekly with his Chiefs of Staff Committee (BCOS) since the beginning of the war.[92] At ARCADIA the Americans failed to announce an "official" position and as a result found themselves at a great disadvantage. When matters of grand strategy arose the British confirmed their intention to launch a continental invasion. But they also spoke of "closing and tightening" the "ring" and of action in the Mediterranean and the Balkans as a "prelude" to an assault on Germany.[93] They gained American agreement to a "Europe First" strategy, although the British penchant for peripheral warfare caused intense discussion within the alliance during 1942 and

1943. These embarrassing experiences persuaded the Americans to form an American counterpart to the BSOC, the centralized Joint Chiefs of Staff (JCS), which cooperated with BCOS in the new Washington-based Combined Chiefs of Staff (CCS). General Eisenhower's mid-1942 nomination as supreme allied commander for the North African campaign and one year later as supreme commander for the European invasion tightly integrated the two countries' military efforts. Gradually the military balance shifted from the British to the Americans.

Roosevelt's main interest lay in facilitating the military aspects of the three-power coalition. The president was not in the least loath to issue ringing rhetorical statements to serve as rallying cries to further the military effort and set out general political principles. At ARCADIA he composed the hortative Joint Declaration of the Associated Powers or, as they became known, the United Nations.[94] In the same vein, at Casablanca in January 1943 he announced the doctrine of unconditional surrender. In Roosevelt's view many of these considerations had at least as much to do with military as with political problems. Yet specific political arrangements could not be swept away forever. In mid-1942 the British and Americans agreed to put aside Soviet claims to occupation of the Baltic states and to open a second European front. Other practical short-term political questions had to be faced from time to time. How should the United States react to the Vichy French during and after the 1942 North African invasion? If it proved useful to knock Italy out of the war, what should be the post-surrender situation in that country? Should Nazi satellites and allies be offered hints of an easier postwar treatment in order to weaken the enemy's war effort?

For a long time the president scoffed at long-range political planning and only reluctantly tolerated it. Ironically the main impetus for American postwar planning emanated largely from Roosevelt's own confidants in the State Department such as Sumner Welles and Adolf Berle. Berle like Welles enjoyed personal contact with the president and assisted in composing many of his policy speeches. He agreed with Welles that it was imperative for the United States to consider a more systematic ansd early approach towards formulating a peace program.[95] Although Roosevelt had his reservations about Welles's and Berle's excessive persistence, he valued these men as "a reflection of the idealism of the country about world affains."[96] In fact Welles and Berle proved to be a good deal more realistic than the president. As early as mid-1941 Berle advised Roosevelt that the State Department ought to begin considering postwar peace questions. The president agreed only half-heartedly: "I have not the slightest objection towards your trying your hand at the outline of the postwar picture," he informed Berle. "But for heaven's sake, don't even let the columnists know."[97] When the State Department persisted in its discussion of postwar political problems Roosevelt edged away. He complained to Attorney General Biddle following a November 1942 cabinet meeting that "Berle and Welles have been acting as impresarios and have been talking too much postwar stuff."[98] The State Department regularly submitted to and discussed with the president its progress reports on postwar planning, but no mechanism existed for making official policy decisions without the president's acquiescence. And as long as hostilities continued Roosevelt chose not to exercise this prerogative.

Roosevelt turned down the State Department's innovative suggestion in November 1942 that the Western Allies create a common planning board in London to facilitate Anglo-American political collaboration and act as a counterbalance to the Washington-based military Combined Chiefs.[100] The State Department feared that, in view of Roosevelt's reluctance to discuss political matters while hostilities continued, the British would gain the political initiative. In order to sway the president to their view, State Department officials attempted a gambit employing reverse psychology. They prepared a memorandum for his signature which acknowledged British political leadership in Europe. The key sentence was: "The Government of the United States has determined to recognize that Great Britain shall have the primary position in the political and economic reorganization of Europe." If Roosevelt disagreed with this statement, as surely he must, he would then adopt the department's alternative scheme of establishing an Anglo-American political planning body without delay through which the British could be controlled and American positions fostered. The department understood the risks involved in pursuing this strategem. If this policy of British leadership faithfully represented his opinion, he would probably find a good deal of support for it in public opinion. But either way the situation had to be clarified.[101] However, Roosevelt proved once again how difficult it was to pin him down against his will. He refused to rise to the bait. He refused to sign the memorandum, but he did not accept the State Department's alternative position. He went only so far as to agree that the State Department could expand its own planning process, while keeping it well under wraps.[102]

Roosevelt hoped to keep State Department planning focused on short-term objectives of direct value to the military effort such as occupation policies for France, Italy, and Yugoslavia.[103] To this end he burdened the department with an additional responsibility far beyond its powers. He mandated it not only to draft policies for territories liberated in the course of the war, but also to prepare itself to administer these areas. The State Department was ready to elaborate policies for these zones, but admitted that it was quite unequipped to implement them. As a result that latter task was handed over to the War Department which in April 1943 established a Civil Affairs Department (CAD) to administer occupied areas in the period before and after surrender. The CAD developed problems in getting its activities off the ground. In view of the military's lack of political experience, this agency took its general political directions from the State Department.[104]

Despite presidential reservations, the Department of State began its own review of possible postwar exigencies early in World War II. If there was to be an organization resembling the "Inquiry" in the United States, Hull was determined that this time it would be centred in his department. Earlier peace initiatives had demonstrated that the State Department's peace research capabilities were not high. It became involved in several failed attempts after 1938 to organize peace conferences between the opposing sides. Sumner Welles's 1940 tour of the various European capitals to assess the nature of possible peace terms was part of this drive to mediate the conflict. Even before war broke out the State Department had begun to think in terms of organizing a specialized internal planning group. It eventually created a fairly widely based Advisory Committee on Postwar Foreign Policy comprising departmental officials, congressional representatives, and external experts. The latter came mainly from the CFR, the RIIA's American twin. When the United States went to war in 1941, CFR members became directly involved in State Department planning groups.[105] In this manner, as in Great Britain, leading outside scholars and international affairs experts became involved in the official planning process, contributing a distinctive academic and historical approach to postwar problems.

Before the war the Department of State lacked a separate intelligence or research unit. In 1938 Harley Notter, a Stanford-trained member of the department's American Division and a specialist in Wilson's foreign policy, proposed the establishment of a research division within the department. As Hull had already been thinking along these lines, Notter's idea fell upon fertile ground.[106] Early next year Hull appointed Dr Leo Pasvolsky, a European trade specialist with a solid background in Danubian problems, as special adviser to the secretary of state in charge of problems of peace. Before joining the department in 1937, the Russian-born Pasvolsky had been a research scholar at the Brookings Institute and had written an influential book on the economic problems of Austria and the Danubian region in which he reached the same pessimistic conclusions as had Toynbee. He found little that was positive to say about the future of small Danubian states such as Austria unless they came to their senses and formed a regional federation.[107] In February 1941 the State Department established a separate Division of Special Research under Pasvolsky and his assistant Notter. Soon this division had acquired a staff of over sixty.[108]

Following the United States's entry into the war the department's postwar planning went through two main stages. In the first year-and-a-half after Pearl Harbor planners and consultants researched and prepared preliminary papers (P documents) mainly concerned with enemy countries and their satellites after defeat, including the period of military occupation and demilitarization. It is important to note that the topic of Austria was one of the first to be broached in this initial review. In the second phase of planning, from late 1943 to Hull's resignation the next year and his replacement by Edward Stettinius, senior officials reviewed a wide range of subjects based on preliminary conclusions arrived at in the first stage in order to reach final policy positions. The Division of Special Research was divided into two sections, one for political and the other for economic studies. Notter headed the first with assistant chiefs responsible for territorial, international organization, and security matters, and a special group for Central Europe. During the 1944 departmental reorganization undertaken by Stettinius postwar planning coordination was upgraded to a new Office of Political Affairs with several divisions. Pasvolsky was not summoned to head the new office as he had been appointed chief of the critical division responsible for planning the United Nations. By this time postwar policies for Austria and many other areas had become fairly well defined. This last phase of State Department planning involved discussions with other departments mainly on shorter-range questions of occupation, surrender, and the critical and delayed topic of the future of Germany. Significant work on these issues moved into lower level interdivisional Country-and-Area Committees (CAC), while the department's top policy review organ, the Postwar Program Committee, formulated the final political policy papers (PWC documents) in the last year-and-a-half of the conflict. Attempts were made to improve interdepartmental coordination on short-range occupation policies through the establishment of the State-War-Navy Coordinating Committee (SWNCC) at the assistant secretary level.[109] By the end of hostilities the State Department had completed 270 PWC papers representing 189 policy positions.[110] At this level American postwar planning was at least as substantial, although not as effective because of presidential reluctance to push these issues, as the British effort.

Like their British counterparts, State Department officials realized from the beginning that they were not trained for and did not have the time to devote to the sort of research needed to draw up peace proposals. So they decided to coopt external assistance with the required research and planning abilities, drawing in particular upon the influential CFR with its established scholarly contacts and reputation in international affairs. After the foundation in 1919 of the Anglo-American Institute of International Affairs in Paris, the American wing had at first languished. It soon sprang to life again by amalgamating in 1920 with a New York international affairs dinner club, the Council on Foreign Relations, whose name it adopted. The reconstituted CFR was composed largely of lawyers, businessmen and leading scholars whose original honorary president was Elihu Root, first president of the Carnegie Endowment for International Peace.[111] Despite their initial hopes for one Anglo-American transatlantic institute, the CFR and RIIA did not merge because of the growth in the United States of an anti-Versailles and anti-British feeling.[112] Historian Archibald Coolidge of Harvard University, who had attended the institute's birth in Paris, became editor of its journal *Foreign Affairs* in 1922 and was succeeded six years later by his assistant, Hamilton Fish Armstrong. The council and its journal soon became the most authoritative private forums for the discussion of international relations in the United States.

The CFR not only invited political and economic leaders to address its elite membership, but also organized study and discussion groups composed of members and external experts to research individual topics. Their conclusions were made available to government and selectively to the public through CFR-sponsored publications.[113] In this way before World War II the CFR linked influential private individuals and scholars with government. President Hoover and Secretary of State Stimson were original council members. Three of the seven members of Roosevelt's 1933 presidential inquiry into American foreign policy came from the CFR. Individual members of the State Department such as Welles, Berle, and Pasvolsky joined later by invitation. Among those council members later picked for positions within the State Department or for official international service were Ambassador Dodd in Berlin and wartime ambassadors John Winant in London and Admiral William Standley in Moscow, as well as the latter's successor, Averell Harriman. Stimson and Charles Warren headed the 1937 CFR study and discussion group on neutrality and Warren subsequently joined the Department of State in order to draft Roosevelt's neutrality legislation.[114] While America slipped into isolationism during the 1930s, the CFR generally stood for internationalism.[115] For instance, almost as soon as the internationalist George Messersmith arrived back in Washington from his diplomatic post in besieged Vienna as a new assistant secretary of state, he was asked to lead a CFR discussion group on European politics and the Neutrality Act. Perhaps to keep an eye on Messersmith, his isolationist colleague and chief of the State Department's European Division, J. Pierrepont Moffat, sat in on the discussions as well.[116]

When war erupted in September 1939, CFR director Isaiah Bowman, one of the United States's leading geographers, an ex-member of Wilson's Inquiry, and currently president of Johns Hopkins University, urged the council to assume the initiative in helping to prepare the United States for a cogent role at the next peace conference. His idea was that the CFR should undertake with the approval of the Department of State an in-depth study of American interests in war and peace and its results would be made available to the Department of State on a confidential basis.[117] The proposal to try to launch this scheme was adopted by the other CFR directors, several of whom then met with an enthusiastic State Department proponent of the scheme, George Messersmith, to discuss the best possible strategy for implementing it. the council's chairman, Norman Davis, one of Roosevelt's roving ambassadors, spoke to his friend Hull along similar lines. Messersmith, Hull, and Welles thereupon sat down together and immediately saw how the department could benefit from the services of this expert and experienced pool of researchers. They approved the project and informed the Rockefeller Foundation of their decision. In turn the foundation contributed $45,000 to underwrite the study, the first of several generous grants which between early 1940 and the end of the war exceeded $300,000.[118]

Basking in official approval and with a generous Rockefeller bequest in hand, the War and Peace Study project's steering committee commenced work. The committee, which included Versailles conference veterans Whitney Shepardson and Isaiah Bowman, established five subcommittees to investigate economic, political, territorial, armaments, and peace questions. Allan Dulles headed the armaments group, Bowman the territorial, and Hamilton Fish Armstrong the peace aims group. When they began their deliberations in early 1940 these five groups combined the talents of a number of unusually well-qualified volunteers -academics, financial leaders, and retired officials – with a structure of permanent, paid academic research secretaries. These CFR study groups dealt during the course of the next six years with officials from five government departments including the State Department and fourteen agencies and bureaus. Additional discussion groups fed into the subcommittees by considering specific topics and drawing up their own reports. Together these study and discussion groups eventually produced nearly seventeen hundred policy documents for the State Department and the president.[119]

As the war in Europe continued the CFR and the Department of State were brought into even closer collaboration through a convergence of interests. The council wished to influence government policy directly while Hull desired to strengthen and control the official peace planning process. When Pasvolsky became head of the department's peace forecasting group in 1940, he began to recruit CFR experts to serve as members of his new departmental planning committees. Pasvolsky became a CFR member himself and frequently travelled to New York to attend meetings of the council's economic and financial study group.[120] When in 1941 the department created a large, confidential Advisory Committee on Postwar Foreign Policy, it copied the CFR model of subcommittees. Officials, political personalities, and CFR experts were invited to join the Advisory Committee and its five specialized subcommittees, the intention being to exploit the CFR brain trust under the State Department's jurisdiction.[121] The original fourteen-member Advisory Committee contained five external members, four of whom were leading council members. Moreover, half of the State Department representatives on the committee already were or soon would be CFR members.[122]

When postwar planning began in earnest in early 1942 the State Department also adopted a departmental planning subcommittee structure like that of the CFR and some council members were asked to move directly into the department's planning structure. The CFR and State Department agreed as well that the the permanent War and Peace Study research secretaries would work half-time for the parallel State Department planning subcommittee. CFR chairman Norman Davis, head of the CFR study's steering committee, actually chaired the State Department's important security subcommittee, while Professor Bowman headed its territorial subcommittee.[123] Resentment at the CFR's growing influence over the State Department's planning process welled up and almost caused the resignation of Pasvolsky's assistant Harley Notter in September 1942.[124] But council members' prevalence did not diminish. When the Informal Political Agenda Group was established in 1943 to advise Roosevelt on the many conferences held that year, every participant but Hull was a CFR member.

Thus external scholars and experts in both Great Britain and the United States from the RIIA and CFR, the two sister organizations, not only assisted official postwar planning from the outside, but were to be found deeply embedded within the official planning process. Relations between the two bodies remained cordial throughout the war. From time to time RIIA papers wound up at the CFR for study and for transference of ideas through the council to the State Department. Several RIIA delegations met with the CFR during the war.[125] The participants in these meetings remained thoroughly convinced that a better peace could be achieved by uniting scholarly and business knowledge with official expertise. Through its system of presidential appointees, the United States was to continue this unique cooperation involving academics and diplomats past the end of the war.

CFR directors exerted an internationalist influence throughout the war. They firmly believed that the United States could no longer stand aloof from world affairs. The country could not escape a global role as it had attempted to do after 1919. The current European disaster demonstrated the folly of detachment only too graphically.[126] Before 1939 the United States had disapproved, albeit passively, of a wide variety of global territorial changes. In the future the country would have to become more actively involved in the direction of world affairs for the sake of peace. These experts at first expected the British Empire to emerge from the war considerably weakened or even to disappear, so the United States had little choice but to prepare itself to step into the breach.[127] If overheated nationalism had caused the present conflict, the harm might be remedied through the institution of postwar regional or global collaborative systems for which the United States would have to assume its fair share of responsibility, if only in a supervisory role.[128]

The subject of Austria cropped up early in the CFR's considerations and led to the by now familiar federative recommendation. These American experts firmly believed that the age of the nation-state and of balance-of-power in Europe was past. Europe had to leave behind its history of divisions and internecine strife and discover regional alternatives to the discredited polyethnic state system. An internationalist-oriented system would have to be either imposed or prodded into being and guaranteed after the war by Great Britain and the United States. Grave economic, social, and political problems would most certainly propel Europeans in this direction as well. Small-state combinations in eastern Europe would diminish historic national rivalries and checkmate German and Soviet encroachments. The Soviet Union would be less of a problem than Germany, these experts believed. In all probability the Soviets would want to cooperate with Great Britain and the United States in a universal postwar peace settlement.[129] They might be suspicious of European federation, but good will and recognition of Soviet interests would overcome this.[130] A 1945–6 CFR study of American-Soviet relations speculated about Soviet motives in eastern Europe, but stillrecommended that the West collaborate with the USSR. Such a gesture would still Russian suspicions regarding Western intentions and give the West the necessary leverage to promote eastern European federations and freedoms. However, by the time the report was ready for publication it was becoming apparent to many CFR members that the opposite Soviet reaction was in fact taking place. Finally the council decided that the more optimistic report would not be published.[131] In this way it is possible to see that the CFR's expectations concerning the political future of southeastern and central Europe began to shift, but this change took place only after Nazi Germany's surrender. Until that time the council's federative recommendations for Austria and the Danubian region still appeared reasonable and practical.

One of the CFR's initial undertakings was to catalogue the peace aims of the various European nations allied to the Big Three including Austria. It soon came to the realization that the Austrian case was not like that of the others. The council arranged a series of separate interview sessions at which spokesmen for each occupied country were invited to explain their postwar hopes. In the Austrian case, however, the CFR was constrained to organize not one but three separate sessions because the Austrian monarchists, democrats, and socialists refused to be heard together.[132] The committee heard little from the Austrians in favour of reestablishing the small republic. Monarchists and socialists proposed their own types of supranational postwar political entities for their region. Discounting the specific content of each plan, this was precisely the CFR position. As a result the CFR recommendation to the State Department was that Austria become part of a supranational Danubian federation, a recommendation that was to be repeated over the years.[133]

The question of Austria's and southeastern Europe's future was one of the first to be posed by the State Department's planners. Its coordinating political subcommittee ascertained in April 1942 that neither the United States nor Great Britain had made any commitments regarding Austria since 1938: "The United States and Great Britain have specifically assured each of the Axis [note Austria's categorization] countries, except Albania and Austria, that [its] independence will be restored after the war."[134] All postwar options regarding Austria, now an integral part of the Third Reich with a contingent of 400,000 men serving in the German army, were therefore open. This first review of American policy regarding Austria also admitted that the United States had accepted the 1938 Anschluss. "Both the United States and Great Britain recognized the 1938 Anschluss of Austria and Germany by withdrawing their legations and establishing consulate generals." Apparently only Russia favoured the notion of an independent Austria after the war, but it was unclear whether its motives were completely disinterested.[135] Subcommittee members were unable to support the concept of a reestablished independent Austrian state.[136] Welles suggested that Austria's future could only be considered within the European context. He mused whether "for the sake of Europe" it would be "realistically necessary to reconstitute some form of Austria?"[137] Clearly the committee wished to decide Austria's future in the light of how such a settlement would affect the peace and security of the continent. In view of this security preoccupation, committee members resolutely dismissed the idea of resurrecting Austria in its pre-Anschluss guise. Like their British counterparts they worried about the negative effect of an indubitably weak

Austria on overall European security. In searching for an answer to their dilemma, they made various suggestions involving some form of confederation or union with other southeastern and eastern European states. One proposal featured a possible Austro-Bavarian structure, another raised the possibility of a larger south German confederation to include Austria, and still another contemplated a continued union postwar of Austria and Germany.[138]

Pushed by its historical experts, the subcommittee spent an enormous amount of time reviewing the histories of Austria-Hungary, the Versailles-St Germain peace treaties, and republican Austria. Norman Davis, Isaiah Bowman, and Sumner Welles regretted that Austria and Hungary had not been joined in 1919 as Wilson had recommended. This time the victorious powers should force Austria and Hungary into some sort of Danubian confederation with the capital to be located in Vienna.[139] Members pondered whether Austria's prewar weakness and the Anschluss had resulted primarily from political or economic debility. Pasvolsky cited his own prewar research on Danubia, pointing to economics as the key to the Austrian problem. Had the Austrian economy been healthy, which it was not and probably would not be after the current war, the country's politics would have been stable as well. Hamilton Fish Armstrong challenged Pasvolsky's interpretation. The Anschluss, he insisted, had been virtually a natural event because Austrians and Germans were ideologically and culturally so similar.[140] Armstrong believed that in 1938 Austrian sentiment had overwhelmingly favoured the Anschluss and that this would once again be the case after World War II, although perhaps not immediately. As a precautionary measure Austria ought to participate in a new, federal German unit where it might exercise a benevolent influence balancing out Prussian militarism.[141] Subcommittee members typically refused to differentiate between German Nazism and traditional Prussianism — a common mistake at that time. Welles toyed with an older solution once propounded by the Austrian Christian Social chancellor, Mgr Ignatz Seipel, to the effect that Austria might tie itself to France and Italy to counteract Germany's weight.[142] But whatever the final specific arrangement, Welles made it clear that Austria would have to be tightly linked to other countries; that only within a federation might Austria find protection and security.[143] Most subcommittee members apparently agreed with the general principle that after the war Austrian views should be solicited. But this opinion was not given any priority. As Professor James Shotwell disparagingly noted, "Austrians are not politically minded."[144]

Only Hackworth argued briefly that an independent Austria might be worth considering. He claimed that from a strictly legal point of view the United States had not "tied itself down in public about the German absorption of Austria" and that "we have not outrightly recognized it." Presumably this meant that the United States might decide to go either way on this issue after the war. In the meantime this flexibility might prove a very useful lever. Welles criticized Hackworth strongly for his legalistic approach and for appraising the matter from the Austrian rather than the European perspective. Should Austria be reconstituted, the Allies would have to face the possibility of another Anschluss. If that happened, European stability and security would again be threatened. Even a union between Austria and parts of Germany was preferable to Austrian independence. It could be disappointing for the Austrians to be incorporated into Germany, but this solution might be best for both the Austrians and the rest of Europe. As Summer Welles reiterated: "We do not need to worry about that [an Austrian state]. The question was, what is best for international security?"[145] Welles alluded to the possible splitting up of Germany at a time when that country's fate had not yet been seriously discussed or decided upon. Hackworth replied that he did not personally favour reconstituting Austria. In fact, he thought, the other southeastern and eastern European states shared Austria's problem. It was time to begin to think of creating a sort of United States of Middle Europe after the war, following the model of the thirteen American colonies.[146]

During the summer of 1942 the planners turned their attention to another important political question, that of Germany, which they considered separately from the problem of Austria and eastern or southeastern Europe. In the meantime the Department of State parcelled out different aspects of the Austrian question to the other subcommittees dealing with economic, territorial, and security matters. The economic subcommittee was asked to investigate three questions: would Austria's economic future be most promising within one combined eastern European federation; in a twin-federation system, with Austria linked either to a northern or a southern unit; or as an independent state that would include Trieste?[147] The economic subcommittee's optimistic August 1942 report was judged superficial and was remanded for further study.[148]

Among the other possibilities for Austria, some posed the question whether parts of Germany might be united to Austria. In November the territorial subcommittee issued its report that opposed the partition of Germany. It suggested that Austria and the rest of the Third Reich's annexations be excluded from the postwar German state. Austria should find its place within an eastern European union.[149] The security subcommittee reported two months later that an independent Austria could be considered only if a strong and truly effective international security organization were created at the same time to support and protect it.[150]

Despite Soviet coolness to federation schemes in that part of Europe, a federal framework had to be devised for Austria and the other small Danubian countries, lest they replay their interwar tragedies — an unacceptable scenario from a security point of view. "The continued existence of small independent states in eastern Europe is probably not possible and is undesirable from the point of view of general security," the subcommittee concluded.[151] The optimum solution was considered to be a powerful international organization ensuring the survival of regional federations.[152] Although the subcommittees had to consider the possibility of an independent postwar Austrian state, they were unable to work up any enthusiasm for the idea. Bowman's territorial subcommittee was reluctant to enlarge and strengthen an independent Austria, should it be reconstituted after the war. It recommended that if an independent Austria were to be reestablished, the country ought to have its 1937 borders with the addition of South Tyrol from Italy for reasons of security.[153] Shortly thereafter this subcommittee made its recommendations on Germany. Should Germany be partitioned, certain portions of it might be assigned to Austria to make the latter a viable country. However, this was not a priority recommendation for, this subcommittee maintained, restoration of the prewar system consisting of independent Danubian states would only encourage eventual German or Soviet control. The USSR would probably conclude bilateral agreements with each eastern European state thereby tying each to the Soviet system, as had occurred with the Baltic states, which had then disappeared into the Soviet camp.[154] In the end the powerful political subcommittee rejected any plan for a German partition so that the unification of south Germany with Austria had to be abandoned in favour of an encapsulated Austria within a Danubian federation.[155] No matter how these planners considered the Austrian problem, whether from the economic, territorial, security, or political point of view, the same federative solution always popped up.

Once the Washington planners had sketched in the main outlines of American postwar interests, they strongly advocated that early discussions be launched with the other Allies concerning postwar arrangements. It would serve little purpose if each country adopted its own policies without attempting to coordinate them with the other powers before the war's end. The British warc cabinet adopted the same plan at about the same time. Should the Soviets raise objections regarding the creation of federations east of Germany, it was vital that their reservations be considered and overcome.[156] Adolf Berle knew the dangers of delaying political talks until after the invasion of Europe. "I am very clear that if we finally reach the continent of Europe without some prearranged understanding, there will be a fair chance that the conflict will take an entirely different form," he wrote in February 1943.[157] The USSR might prefer to deal with small independent states in eastern Europe, because they could be more easily linked to the Soviet system by bilateral agreements, and thereby Soviet control might be achieved over the whole region.[158] There was the possibility, on the other hand, that the Soviets might agree to a federative system or settle for a collective security guarantee for the area, if they could be persuaded that the West had no aggressive designs there, which it did not. Should the they be brought to accept the idea of east European federations, they ought to be permitted to exercise some influence over these political units. Even if at the moment the Soviet Union seemed to be opposed to the idea, an attempt should be made at the highest level to persuade it in this direction.[159] This advice was not pursued. Yet the American planners' objectives for eastern and southeastern Europe indicate that, in their minds, prosperity in this area of Europe would be achieved only through a regional federative solution and that Soviet acquiescence was possible.

The lessons of history and the behaviour of the Austrian exiles almost inevitably led the American planners to reach this supranational verdict. Exiled conservative and socialist Austrians supported a solution of this kind. Monarchists dreamt of a reconstituted Austro-Hungarian Empire, socialists of a federated and socialist Europe. One of the most influential and best-known Austrians in the United States during the war was Count Galigieri-Koudenhouve, leader of a Pan-European movement. He "converted" Roosevelt's secretary of the treasury, Henry Morgenthau, to the "death of nationalism" concept and to the inexorable triumph of European federalism. Although Morgenthau wondered whether in fact the mighty forces of European nationalism and separatism could be overcome, he suggested to Roosevelt that it might be worthwhile to attempt to form a United States of Europe after the war.[160] Roosevelt and the British ambassador, Lord Halifax, spent some time in the early part of 1943 discussing the merits of such a scheme and weighing the pros and cons of regional federations.[161] By mid-1943 separately-evolved American and British policies regarding the formation of federated southeastern European units to include Austria mirrored each other remarkably. "The policies of the American and British governments in respect to the Austrian question," a State Department memorandum comparing both countries' Austrian policies asserted in March 1943, "appear to be generally in agreement."[162] That summer the Americans received a copy of the official British policy on Austria just adopted by the war cabinet. Department of State officials immediately noted the coincidence of views. The British paper, they ventured, was "in general concordance with the Department's views ... an excellent exposition of the Austrian question."[163] The decision to separate Austria from Germany after the war was not difficult to reach; it derived automatically from Nazi Germany's defeat. The stubborn puzzle began with the question of what to do with the country after it was detached. The British and Americans concurred that Austria should not be entangled with south Germany, but instead should be immersed in a Danubian or eastern European federation.[164]

The two allies' overall views regarding the implementation of long-term goals for Austria remained unaltered, but they differed on tactics. They were uncertain, for instance, how to overcome Soviet hesitation concerning federations, and they had yet to decide the degree of their involvement in the projected regional system after the war. The British considered the Americans unrealistic about the growing Soviet threat in the Balkans and Central Europe, whereas the Americans still entertained hopes of a settlement with the USSR.[165] As well, Americans were somewhat vague concerning what political rights each ally ought to enjoy in liberated areas after the occupation period had elapsed. They apparently envisioned areas of "political gravitation," "open" spheres of interest or areas where a neighbouring great power might wield more influence than the others. Such a situation might arise east of Germany without necessarily endangering the West's ties with that region or with local federations. A September 1943 Department of State paper explained: "If a basis for long-term collaboration between the U.S.S.R. and the western powers should be established under which the former's great interest and political influence in the East European region was recognized, the Soviet leaders might feel that they could safely tolerate the existence of comparatively free economic relations between the western powers and the East European states."[166] At the Moscow Conference in October 1943, the American delegation supported the proposed Czechoslovak-Soviet treaty of friendship intended to serve as a model for close political and economic ties between the Soviet Union and independent eastern European countries, despite the fact that the Allies had agreed to make no firm political deals until the war's end. If the Soviets felt that the Czechs were friendly towards them, they would have no grounds to be suspicious of their ties with the West.[167] Early in 1944 the State Department's Advisory Committee on Postwar Foreign Policy reached a similar conclusion. Hamilton Fish Armstrong used the analogy of magnetism, or mutual attraction, in describing the Soviet position in postwar eastern Europe. Charles Bohlen cited the "doctrine of proximity," and others likened future Soviet involvement in the region to the American Good Neighbor policy in Latin America.[168] If the British still thought in terms of balance-of-power politics, they also favoured the establishment of regional political, economic, and security groupings or federations including Austria. Deference to local Soviet interests and the desire to cling to a limited role in an area of little direct American interest failed to dampen the Americans' desire for an accord with the British concerning Austria's long-term postwar future. The federal solution for Austria and other Danubian states under international auspices remained a favourite American aim.[169]

However, the president refused to open talks on these important matters with his Allies. He was not interested at that point in the war in risking political discussions with the Soviets that might somehow interfere with military efficiency. He cautioned in mid-1943 that "We must not relax our pressure on the enemy by taking time out to define every boundary and settle every political controversy in every part of the world. The all-important thing now is to get on with the war and to win it."[170] Thus American plans regarding postwar Austria functioned at best as a guide rather than as a formal policy such as the British had adopted.

One thing became amply clear during these Anglo-American ruminations about the future of Austria and central Europe. British and American federative policies definitely repudiated the Versailles peace treaty system and in so doing rehabilitated the concept of an Austro-Hungarian Empire in different guise. Several of the leading World War I European experts who favoured nationalism at the 1919 peace conference had come to see the error of their ways even before 1939. As they thought about the future of Austria and the Danubian region in general, the remarkable capacity of the peacemakers after World War I for getting things wrong did not escape their attention. Hopes that eastern Europe might develop strong, independent nation-states planted on the corpse of the Austro-Hungarian Empire had proved illusory. To rectify this error the World War II planners devised a reform plan, itself based on several imaginary propositions. They believed that their friends, the moderate nationalists east of Germany, would be chastened by the tragedies of the past decade and would agree to a program encompassing political, economic, and cultural reforms. The end result would be the resurrection of some sort of federative structure resembling the defunct Austro-Hungarian Empire. They also assumed that the region's inhabitants would gladly accept great power leadership because by the end of the war they would also realize the danger of over-heated nationalism. If Soviet approval of federations could be procured, the Western position in eastern Europe might be preserved as far as practicable. By 1943 British and Americans postwar planners had reached their analogous views concerning postwar Austria independently. They both wanted to avoid a postwar breakdown and power vacuum in that country and region, a situation that a revived Germany might exploit. They might have realized by 1943 that German defeat could lead to Soviet hegemony in central Europe. However, at that time the advantage still rested with the Germans, and their historic and military menace was sufficiently palpable to blind Western planners to the potential Soviet threat. Moreover, the Anglo-American planners still hoped to persuade the Soviets to go along with federation plans in eastern Europe. In view of the limited expectations for Austria, the Big Three foreign ministers' ringing Moscow Declaration that same fall, that Austria should be reestablished as an independent country after the war, seems more than a little surprising.

CHAPTER FIVE

The Moscow Declaration on Austria

Anglo-American planners had agreed by early 1943 that Austria and the other Danubian states would not be reestablished as they were after 1919. Instead they foresaw some sort of Danubian federation into which the Austrian area could be set. They assumed the existence of widespread dissatisfaction in eastern Europe with the interwar Versailles system, and a corresponding propensity to respond positively to a federalist concept after the war. Then why did the Big Three foreign ministers unexpectedly issue such a strong statement in favour of reestablishing an independent Austrian state after the war at their first wartime meeting, held in Moscow in October 1943? British and American planners had concurred earlier that this was the least desirable scenario of all possible choices for that small and defenceless country. It seemed illogical for them to advocate Austrian independence. Why issue a statement about Austria alone, while ignoring the fate of other more important countries? Why defend a country which the Foreign Office and the State Department considered to be part of enemy territory?[1] Why did the new American under-secretary of state, Edward Stettinius, inform the American cabinet during the Moscow Conference that the political agenda at Moscow was "apparently zero" and that the only topic was military?[2] This chapter will demonstrate that Stettinius's October 1943 assessment was indeed correct. Little of any political importance occurred at the Moscow Conference and no political decision was taken in particular concerning Austria.

At the time the Austrian declaration perplexed many observers as well. Why, queried one American journalist, worry about little Austria, when much larger issues loomed, such as Soviet Russia's projected postwar military presence in eastern Europe? Why had no agreement been reached with the Soviets regarding postwar conditions in eastern Europe? Apparently the Soviet Union had only conceded that some nebulous type of consultative process would take effect following its occupation of neighbouring countries. It could only mean that after the war the Soviet Union would hold the upper hand, particularly in eastern Europe. Why had nothing been said about Germany, Poland, the Baltic states, Finland, Rumania, Bulgaria, France, or even the Lowlands. Why was Austria the only country in central or eastern Europe singled out for a statement?[3] Was the Austrian declaration only a smokescreen, wondered another journalist, to hide acceptance of Soviet control in eastern Europe? In his view Stalin had scored an outstanding diplomatic victory in ensuring that only Austria and Italy were mentioned as countries to be liberated and democratized.[4]

What outside observers at the time could not know was that the Moscow Declaration on Austria fitted into a broad propaganda campaign directed against the Nazis. The declaration was issued as part of the Allies' political warfare attack on the enemy's morale in the Austrian area. Since the beginning of World War II propaganda and political warfare – morale-busting of the enemy – had enjoyed a much larger role than had been the case in World War I. Hitler and the West had learned the wrong lessons from that war, namely, that modern, mass-based conflicts were lost or won by the strength or weakness of morale behind and at the front. Both sides believed almost mystically that military action, coupled with appropriate propaganda campaigns and economic blockade, could fatally injure an enemy's morale and lead to internal collapse. It was a commonly held view in 1939 that the Germans and Austrians had collapsed in 1918 because of broken morale; that Hitler had risen to power through his own and his henchman Goebbels's mastery of political and rhetorical symbols; and that Hitler's military victories were the result mainly of exceedingly clever propaganda aimed at undermining his opponents' self-confidence. Certainly Hitler believed that military victory stemmed from one side's will triumphing over the other's. When the German forces exploded through the Low Countries and France in the summer of 1940, the West became riddled with tales of secret Nazi subversion and fifth column activities undermining Allied morale and ability to fight.[5] The Allied strategic bombing campaigns promised that German will and morale would be broken by this strategy, leading without bloody ground fighting to an early end of the war. American and British aviators were convinced that an invasion would only entail a mopping-up operation following the closing of the ring around occupied Europe and the bombing of Hitler's empire.[6]

Contemporaries greatly exaggerated the importance of political warfare in World War II. In fact Hitler gained control of Germany partly through rhetoric, but in large measure because the Weimar Republic was unable to solve real economic problems. He tapped German national sentiments and achieved foreign policy successes. Reports during 1939–40 of Nazi fifth columns were virtually all fantasies intended to explain away the crushing military defeats. Air power did not defeat the Nazis, as promised. As in Great Britain, air attacks only hardened the Germans' will to resist: German domestic morale did not crack and fighting continued longer than thought possible. On the other hand, the greatly feared and expected Nazi underground also failed to materialize after the war. Nazi and Allied victories and defeats came about through conventional – and sometimes unconventional – military means rather than through political warfare. Only when a real military threat was linked to deception did psychological warfare prove effective.[7]

As a result of their perception of the role of morale in World War II, the British, and later the Americans, placed immense faith in the efficacy of propaganda and political warfare. If linked with other weapons of war, these tactics might play a leading part in bringing the Nazi regime to its knees. During the war the Allies established large-scale propaganda and subversion apparatuses dedicated to the proposition that the Axis powers could be defeated by waging political warfare against them and eventually breaking their morale. Following the victorious 1939 Nazi invasion of Poland and during the 1939–40 "Phoney War" the British military establishment devised a novel war strategy based on a combination of blockade and propaganda. Deprived of physical means to strike at the Germans, the British sought and believed that they had found indirect methods to bring down the Nazi regime internally by attacking Germany's economic structure. British economic intelligence informed the government in 1939 that Germany's economy was in even worse straits than in 1918. It should be possible to repeat the victory of that year. Among numerous other benefits the inhuman bloodletting of World War I might be avoided.[8] The British estimated that if Germany were blockaded and bombarded with propaganda leaflets, the country could not hold out any longer than fifteen to eighteen months at the most. Cut off from essential war material and foodstuffs, drained to the limit by the war, Germany's "brittle" domestic economy would again collapse as in 1918 and Hitler's regime with it.[9] Hitler heard some of the same projections from his own experts. But he was convinced that he could solve Germany's critical economic problem by planning to launch swift and inexpensive blitzkrieg campaigns and capturing other countries' resources. As a result of the Nazi-Soviet pact and the conquests that followed, he could draw upon the resources of almost the whole of Europe including those of of his ally, the Soviet Union.[10] However, the British did not believe Hitler could save himself. A tight economic blockade and active propaganda would soon destroy the regime's internal unity and morale, and with it Nazi control over Germany and the occupied countries would crumble.

Even before the war influential voices had been raised in Britain demanding more energetic propaganda to counter Hitler's calumnies and to offer support for the many decent anti-Nazis in Germany.[11] But Chamberlain's government hoped that some arrangement or compromise might still be reached with Hitler. Consequently Chamberlain discouraged forceful propaganda campaigns or personal attacks against Hitler.[12] Bowing half-heartedly to pressure, Chamberlain permitted the establishment in early 1939 of a small, secret propaganda office (called Department EH after its location in Electra House) directly responsible to himself. Led by an aging Canadian, Sir Campbell Stuart, who had been a member of Lord Northcliffe's 1918 propaganda ministry, EH prepared propaganda leaflets to be dropped over Germany once war was declared. In October 1939 this little group of hesitant propagandists was handed over to Rex Leeper's revived Political Intelligence Department in the Foreign Office. A new Ministry of Information would convey the British message to domestic, neutral, and Allied audiences, while a Ministry of Economic Warfare would conduct the blockade against Germany.[13]

While Poland fell and Europe waited for Hitler's next move, no British bombs rained on Germany. Instead an economic blockade and a propaganda campaign were unleashed to show the Germans the folly of their government and the hopelessness of their situation. By February 1940 the Royal Air Force had scattered more than forty million propaganda leaflets over the Reich.[14] Despite criticism by some members of the war cabinet including Eden as to the real usefulness of these "leaflet raids" over Germany, the propaganda shower continued until May 1940.[15] This first stage of the war ended abruptly when Hitler burst into the Low Countries and France, and in Great Britain Churchill took over the reins of power from Chamberlain. Inventive and energetic, Churchill was steeped in European history. Immensely sensitive to publicity and impressed by the prevailing notion of the deadly morale-destroying effectiveness of the Nazi fifth columns operating behind the lines in Poland, Norway, and Western Europe, he extended Chamberlain's tame conception of propaganda warfare. The fifth column strategy must be turned against the enemy. Great Britain's own fifth column forces would be found among the many "decent" anti-Nazi Germans and the conquered nations of Europe. These angry, suppressed, and frustrated people should be encouraged to create "secret armies" to rise up against the "fragile" regime at the appropriate moment and to tumble the Nazi clique through a series of internal revolts.[16] Once the Nazis were sufficiently weakened by these uprisings, a small British army would return to the continent to mop up.[17]

Chamberlain had conceived of political warfare essentially in defensive terms, but Churchill imbued the strategy with an activist and aggressive edge, including increased bombings, subversions, commando raids, and a tighter economic blockade in addition to propaganda.[18] Churchill immediately reformed the war cabinet, chiefs-of-staff, intelligence community, and propaganda machinery. In June 1940 he created a top-secret, interdepartmental committee, the Special Operations Executive (SOE). This branch would prosecute political warfare aggressively under the leadership of Hugh Dalton, minister of economic warfare and his anti-German assistant, Sir Robert Vansittart, the government's chief diplomatic adviser. Special Operations was to specialize in subversion and propaganda in Germany and occupied Europe. It was to make armies appear out of nowhere in Germany and the conquered continental nations; to prepare "to set Europe ablaze." The next year this strategy was further refined and intensified by the addition of another interdepartmental group, the Political Warfare Executive (PWE), which took over Special Operation's propaganda work and focused more than ever on raising "secret armies" and encouraging revolt on the continent. Sir Robert Bruce Lockhart directed the PWE from within the Foreign Office's Political Intelligence Department, the new organization being linked to the SOE for subversion and to the Ministry of Information for propaganda at home and in neutral countries. At the height of operations he directed a large PWE staff consisting of 1,500 men and women, who devised political warfare policy for all British propaganda groups and aimed their own political warfare activities at Germany, its satellites, and the occupied countries.[19]

Churchill's political warfare program went considerably beyond Chamberlain's, but it functioned primarily in relation to morale-busting as a vital element in military action. The prime minister intended to do more than merely keep alive the oppressed peoples' morale. He wished to galvanize it, exert pressure upon the enemy, stab at the weak points in the Nazi empire, and inculcate in the "conquered" Germans and occupied peoples an active spirit of resistance. Meanwhile the British economic blockade would aggravate domestic shortages on the continent, and raise the level of discontent among the civilian population. Bombings, guerrilla raids, and sabotage attacks would demonstrate that the Nazis were not invulnerable. Aggressive war propaganda would constitute the fourth arm of the war effort. It would raise the spirit of resistance against the Nazis, and in time would lead to the hoped-for national revolts against the hated oppressor.[20] Churchill considered these combined efforts to be the only feasible strategy if the British were to bring down Hitler. The war cabinet's mid-1941 political warfare plan contained the following dramatic statement (underlined in the original): "*We therefore reach a very grave conclusion that unless Political Warfare as waged by the Political Warfare Executive – unaided by offensive military action – is able to cause disruption within Germany, the war probably cannot be won.*"[21] In this fashion the attack on enemy morale almost usurped the role of military action.

When the Americans first learned about these British political warfare organizations, some of them expressed scepticism. They even feared that Americans might be one of the targets as in World War I. Roosevelt, however, was as fascinated by the perceived results of political warfare as was Churchill.[22] As his original adviser in these matters, Roosevelt picked Colonel William ("Wild Bill") Donovan, a millionaire Wall Street attorney with much energy and enthusiasm but little taste for administration. Impressed by his ideas and eagerness even before the United States entered the war, Roosevelt ordered Donovan to form an American counterpart to the British SOE. In mid-1941 Donovan became coordinator of information, heading a new civilian information-gathering and analysis bureau.[23] Donovan considered his new office to be a propaganda and psychological warfare agency aimed not only at collating information, but also at using it aggressively against an enemy if need be. It enjoyed the assistance of British political warfare agencies with whom he saw eye to eye. Should the United States find itself at war, he was prepared to cooperate closely with them.[24] There followed several bitter bureaucratic battles with established agencies including the State and War departments, both of which resented the intrusion of the newcomer, and after December 1941 with still another competing civilian agency, the Office of War Information (OWI). Donovan's group was renamed the Office of Strategic Services (OSS), and eventually found its niche within the military establishment, at first attached to the American Joint Chiefs of Staff Committee (JCS) and in 1943 to the War Department.[25]

The OSS consisted of three main branches. Special Operations and Secret Intelligence conducted covert operations and psychological warfare, combining the tasks of the British SOE and PWE groups. As in Britain where SOE/PWE worked secretly, separated from the public Ministry of Information, another U.S. government organization, the Office of War Information or OWI, dealt with overt propaganda.[26] OSS's third division was the large Research and Analysis (R and A) section under the leadership of Professor William Langer of Yale University. R and A coordinated academic wartime studies much as FRPS under Toynbee did in Great Britain. By 1943 R and A had grown to over 1,000 employees. After a slow start it eventually discovered a fairly steady demand for its specialized historical and economic studies among the military, especially in the War Department's new Civil Affairs Division. Gradually its relations became more cordial with the State Department, and by 1944 it was cooperating with the department in long-term projects.[27]

In contrast to the situation in Great Britain, in the United States the military chiefs rather than the Department of State assumed direct control over the field of psychological warfare, an indication of its presumed importance for the military effort and of the State Department's reduced wartime influence. In March 1942, the JCS formed a Joint Psychological Warfare Committee (JPWC), which collaborated with the State Department to initiate psychological warfare, but under military auspices. The joint chiefs' first "Basic Estimate of Psychological Warfare," approved in September 1942, ordered the new committee to destroy the will of the enemy and damage its political and economic ability to continue the struggle. Early next year Donovan's OSS became an integral element of this military psychological warfare organization, while the OWI also performed special tasks for it as required. At the same time the chiefs approved a provisional field manual on psychological warfare. Large numbers of American psychological warriors were attached, starting with TORCH in late 1942, to field commands. In late 1943 and early 1944 they were formed into a new interallied Psychological Warfare Division under SHAEF in London, which grew enormously throughout this period.[28] By 1944 the OWI section alone possessed a staff of over 1,600 persons. During the Italian campaign this psychological division showered over 15 million leaflets over enemy lines; 9 million more would be dropped during the Normandy invasion, and 800 million additional ones over the next three months.[29]

If the Americans rejected what they saw to be British over-reliance on fanning continental revolts and forming secret armies to depose Hitler and his clique from within, they did agree that under certain circumstances the German population might be brought to rise up against the Nazi party, which the British termed the "soul of the enemy war machine."[30] If coordinated with major military defeats or mounting military losses, the OWI and OSS reported in early 1942, massive bombing and propaganda might destroy German morale. If the Germans could be brought to realize that total victory would forever elude them and that they themselves would now begin to suffer, the Nazi regime could crumble from within.[31] In many ways, the American psychological warfare plan echoed the British. It lumped together, for instance, the mass of decent, anti-Nazi Germans and Austrians with the peoples of the occupied countries.[32] The recommendations drafted by the JPWC for the JCS dwelt on Germany's morale breakdown in 1918 as a model for the current situation. Hitherto the most effective pre-World War II asset the Nazis enjoyed had been psychological, namely, "the defeatism, pessimism and pacifism bred in her [Nazi Germany's] enemies by the bitter experiences of 1914–1919." As the Nazis had so ably demonstrated since 1939, they were also able to win victories which were at least as much psychological as military achievements.[33]

Following the United States's entry into the war, it was natural that Anglo-American military planners consider how best to encourage the rapid collapse of German morale. During the first Anglo-American military conference held in Washington (ARCADIA, December 1941 and January 1942), at which was formed the Anglo-American Combined Chiefs of Staff (CCS), the British gave the Americans their plans for Operation Roundup to study. Although this British paper minimized the notion of secret armies and German revolt, it did assume the strong likelihood that German morale might disintegrate. Should this occur, Operation Roundup envisaged either a "fast-moving attack on an enemy ... weakened in strength and morale but still capable of resistance" or "an unopposed advance through a Europe in chaos."[34] The Anglo-American combined chiefs ordered a more detailed study of Operation Roundup, accepting it as the basis for offensive military planning.[35] Although the Americans and British differed on exactly how enemy morale would crack, this psychological approach remained an important element of all Allied war plans over the next few years. A sudden disintegration of the enemy always remained a distinct possibility requiring rapid military action to mop up the dispirited enemy forces. The CCS's first grand strategy paper, approved on 31 December 1941, treated subversion and propaganda as absolutely essential in wearing down Axis resistance. Since political warfare was viewed as so vital, they decided that future directives in this area would be decided upon and dispatched by the CCS.[36]

At this point in the war, many American political warriors were unconvinced that the Germans had reached the 1918 stage of psychological disintegration. In fact the president was informed that the Germans still had the psychological edge and were fighting the Allies successfully with this weapon. The Nazis wished to split the Allies and separate the people from their governments. Nazi propaganda in the United States focused on fomenting economic, religious, and racial divisions, while in Germany itself morale remained high. American civilian propagandists in the OWI suggested it was time to start turning this type of subversive activity against the Germans.[37] The American military leadership similarly thought German morale was generally healthy even though it may have been temporarily shaken by the military reverses of the 1941–2 Russian winter campaign and remained somewhat "listless." Written a month before the battle of El Alamein, this paper took into account effective German military advances during the summer of 1942. It was "dangerous to believe that the state of German civilian morale will at this stage appreciably affect the German war effort." Some strains might exist within Germany, but military victories reinforced by firm SS and Nazi party control kept the population effectively in line.[38]

This negative assessment concerning the immediate practicality of undermining German morale changed completely in 1943 as a result of the Western Allies' North African and Italian successes and the German defeat at Stalingrad. During the January 1943 meetings, the final CCS report included a phrase more reminiscent of British than American military rhetoric. It urged that the Allies assemble a strong force in Great Britain to be held "in constant readiness to re-enter the continent as soon as German resistance is weakened to the required extent."[39] By May Eisenhower recommended invading Italy so that bombers could for the first time attack Austria and southern Germany.[40] In the fall the Italians surrendered, the Russians stood near Kiev, and the first bombs fell on Austria. Stimson noted optimistically in his diary: "Germany is really on the toboggan."[41] The time appeared to have come realistically to envisage a breakdown in German military morale.

Anglo-American military leaders spent more time in 1943 discussing the military effectiveness of political warfare than ever before. At each meeting of the combined chiefs that year the topic was discussed in great detail.[42] That year must be seen therefore as the high point in the Allies' faith in psychological warfare. In early spring the JCS adopted an overall strategic psychological warfare plan submitted by the OSS, which promised to bypass the Axis military establishment by appealing to the war-weary populations of Germany and the rest of occupied Europe. In this manner the war would be brought to a speedy conclusion. "Psychological warfare employs *any* weapon to influence the mind of the enemy," a March 1943 JCS report asserted. "The weapons are only psychological in the effect they produce and not because of the weapons themselves ... They are effective because they produce dissension, distrust, fear and hopelessness in the minds of the enemy – not because they originate in the psyche of propaganda agencies."[43] From Algiers General Eisenhower endorsed implementation of these principles through improved JCS-CCS coordination. As a result, a combined ten-member Anglo-American group in Washington proceeded with this task. Its first assignment was to draft plans to trigger an Italian revolt and to create a campaign of deception to confuse the enemy regarding the projected Sicily landings.[44] In the broader European context the Americans believed that the Germans would retreat in Italy to beyond the Alps and attempt to hold fast on the eastern front. Breaching Hitler's Fortress Europe would not be possible by purely military means. Further German defeats coupled with crumbling morale in Germany and the satellites were essential. Only then would effective German military resistance melt away.[45] During the summer of 1943 reports began to circulate regarding shrinking German morale, mutinies in the German ranks, and growing despair on the home front.[46] The British suggested that it was high time to exploit the enemy's deteriorating morale.[47] For the first time British and American political warriors agreed that now German morale teetered on the edge.[48] By late summer the British had drafted surrender terms for Germany, but were unclear whether Austria should be included or receive special consideration.[49]

The Italian campaign demonstrated the failure of the political warriors to spark the hoped-for Italian revolt and early surrender. But this setback did not discourage the military leaders, who attributed the disappointing Italian performance to technical causes including lack of preparation time and inadequate coordination. They now insisted on improved organization and planning in this vital military field.[50] The Washington-based, reorganized, interallied propaganda group was ordered to become more dynamic in pursuit of its objectives, "to make decisions and issue broad directives on propaganda policies to the propaganda agencies of the two countries."[51] The last half of 1943, when the Moscow Declaration on Austria emerged, witnessed exaggerated predictions about the imminent collapse of Germany through military pressure and fierce political warfare. At this decisive juncture of the war the political warriors were called upon to help strike the decisive blow.

To achieve this objective the Allies vastly expanded political/psychological warfare and brought this action closer to the fronts. In September the British suggested that the CCS's centralized political warfare effectiveness be improved by the addition of three interallied theatre committees to execute policy: one in Washington responsible for the Pacific theatre, a second in London for Europe, and the third in New Delhi to cover southeast Asia.[52] The next month Churchill and Roosevelt sanctioned this reorganization.[53] Almost immediately the Washington and London committees began functioning in conjunction with the theatre commanders, but the New Delhi group never got off the ground because the Americans balked at being embroiled in British imperial policy.[54] The CCS noted at the end of 1943 with satisfaction that two of the new Anglo-American theatre political warfare units were operating energetically and efficiently.[55] The usually hesitant Hull, who now believed that the war would soon be over, tried to solicit Roosevelt's agreement to immediate inclusion of Russians in the London-based Anglo-American psychological warfare group. However, the military leaders refused to consider this idea on the ground that these were military not political committees.[56] At first these groups found it difficult to fit into the theatre planning structures and to coordinate their work with area military commanders. However, they assured themselves that in time they would surmount these problems.[57]

This late 1943 flurry of organizational activity demonstrated the military leaders' confidence that political warfare constituted one of the critical weapons in the last stage of the war. The assumption was that Germany and its satellites would collapse within the year. While Allied strategists planned the air offensive and the mid-1944 invasion against Germany, they thought it very likely that Germany might surrender even before an invasion. Under the code name RANKIN they had framed contingency plans for such an imminent disintegration. By late 1943 both military and political leaders were expecting an almost immediate collapse of the Nazi war effort.[58] Their hasty optimism confused some of the other allies and subject peoples, providing welcome ammunition for German propaganda.[59] The political warriors hewed to what was then termed the "Halifax line," which assumed that the war would shortly terminate as a result of broken German morale. Germany, they urged, was almost at the end of its rope. The London Political Warfare Committee confidently predicted: "The war effort of Germany cannot be sustained for long and even the terror machine of Germany will be unable to cope with the situation satisfactorily."[60] Yet at the same time resistance groups in occupied countries were reportedly fretting about Allied caution, and were impatiently awaiting more dynamic public messages of hope promising an early end to their occupation. Critics such as Ambassador John Winant in London supported the "Hardcrust line," which doubted the imminence of a German collapse.[61]

Would the winter of 1943–4 be the last of the war? If it was as so many expected, what was to happen in Germany following defeat? Despite the lack of political decisions, military planners pointed out the need for quick agreements on zones of occupation. Roosevelt refused to be drawn into this controversy. He believed that the Soviets and British would in all likelihood divide Germany into separate occupation zones, but rejected a British suggestion for a United States zone consisting of France, southern Germany, or areas to the east.[62] In November 1943 he announced that the War Department would be responsible for instituting postwar civil and relief administration in liberated areas, but he would not commit himself on postwar occupation or political issues.[63] However, this presidential activity regarding postwar relief indicated that Roosevelt too considered the end of hostilities not far off.[64]

Among all the links in the German strategic chain, Austria had long been identified as one of the weakest. Despite the lack of contacts within the country, Allied intelligence reports painted a picture of growing Austrian disaffection with the German war effort, especially when the fortunes of war began to turn against the Nazis. OSS chief Donovan informed Roosevelt as early as 1941 of Austrian distaste for the Anschluss, friction between Austrians and Germans, and open protests against a repressive regime, tight economic conditions, and food shortages.[65] Similar estimates of Austria's fragility within the Nazi system appeared in subsequent years. The PWE and OSS reported in mid-1943 that increasing "anti-Prussianism" seriously threatened Nazi rule in Austria.[66] Evidence existed that active sabotage and passive resistance within factories was on the increase.[67] The virulence of anti-Nazi sentiment was believed to be liveliest among the youth, who seemed to be abandoning the Nazis and joining clandestine groups throughout the country. Austria appeared to be the ideal target for Allied political warfare.[68]

The American press published from 1942 on dramatic though inaccurate reports describing daring resistance activity in Austria, desertions from the German army, and growing discontent among the Austrian population. The *New York Times* announced in October 1942 that "Hundreds of Austrians Join Yugoslavs," and one month later it published a series of articles purporting to report on guerrilla actions and mass military desertions by Austrians.[69] Further articles in March and April 1943 described tough Nazi reprisals to punish the faltering Austrian war effort.[70] During that summer more sensational pieces appeared on clashes between Austrians and Nazis, while the number of acts of sabotage was reputedly mounting rapidly.[71] By the fall, the combination of German military defeats and the initiation of Allied bombings in Austria was portrayed as rapidly undermining Austrian support for the German war effort.[72] Austrian exiles in the United States stoked these publicity flames by providing much of the information confirming the anti-Nazi wave in Austria, data supposedly gathered through their own secret channels.[73]

Allied intelligence analysts predicted towards the end of 1943 that an Austrian revolt was near. "Recent arrivals from Austria," a JCS intelligence report noted,"emphasize that the situation is now ripe."[74] By then even the Department of State acknowledged that "we ought ... to be examining the Austrian question with a view to doing something about it ... Austria is undoubtedly one of the weak links in Nazi Germany."[75] If these journalistic and intelligence reports were to be believed, it certainly looked as though revolt was near in Austria and that the time had come to strike a hard political warfare blow at crumbling Austrian morale. Political warfare rather than pro-Austrian sentiments motivated the consideration of a dramatic propaganda move against Austria.

Austria's 1943 inclusion in an American commemorative stamps series for subjugated Allied nations casts some light upon contemporary views of Austria. Many saw Austria's inclusion in this victory series as a further proof that the Allies supported the liberation of Austria, but the truth lies elsewhere. Roosevelt, an avid stamp collector, learned in the fall of 1942 that the Post Office intended to issue a stamp to honour occupied Norway. He suggested to the postmaster general a whole series celebrating the overrun but courageous occupied Allied nations. At that time Roosevelt's list did not include Austria or Albania.[76] In March 1943 Under-Secretary of State Welles heard of the proposal and expressed enthusiasm for it. When Welles recommended including Austria for political warfare purposes, the president agreed.[77] Originally Welles had recommended that only United Nations members should be included in the series, as the president had suggested.[78] Roosevelt had proposed that the series be issued alphabetically, but this would have made the Austrian stamp appear first which Welles opposed. Despite the Anschluss's date, he favoured instead commencing the series with Poland and Czechoslovakia and delaying the Austrian stamp because the Austrian situation was ambiguous, and after all Austria was still an integral part of Nazi Germany: "We believe it would be unwise to strictly follow this [historical] order, particularly for the first two stamps issued. In the lay mind, Austria is generally considered a part of Germany, and Albania a close associate. In the mind of the public, World War Two started with the invasion of Poland."[79] Following a lengthy correspondence involving the president, the postmaster general, and the Department of State, the decision was reached in April 1943 that the Albanian and Austrian stamps would come out last.[80] Thus in mid-1943 these victory stamps appeared in the following order: Poland, Czechoslovakia, Norway, France, Luxembourg, Albania, and Austria. Roosevelt received first-day covers of each stamp dedicated by the country's representive in the United States, but the French, Albanian, and Austrian covers remained unsigned. Whereas the majority of these stamps were meant to celebrate courageous occupied Allies in the anti-Nazi war, the Austrian and Albanian stamps were included for purposes of psychological warfare only.

The British fully shared in the increased awareness that Austria presented a fruitful field for political warfare against the Nazis. By the beginning of 1943 British political warfare organizations concurred that political warfare activity ought to focus on Austria. Without seeking Foreign Office assistance, they began in January 1943 to work out a propaganda declaration aimed at Austria. This document served as the first draft of the Moscow Declaration on Austria issued later that year.[81] At the same time the Foreign Office arrived at certain conclusions about Austria's political future as outlined in a previous chapter. These were so pessimistic in nature that propagandists would be hard-pressed to find anything positive in them to attract and stimulate resistance among indigenous Austrians. Austrian independence was a dangerous chimera. A semi-independent Austrian state would be viable only if it were embedded in some larger, protective structure.[82] Clearly the propagandists' objectives and the scepticism of the Foreign Office were diametrically opposed. When they heard of the political warriors' intentions regarding an Austrian declaration, Foreign Office officials immediately became worried because of the propagandists' tendency to draw up schemes independently of Foreign Office policy-making, probably resulting this time in inflated promises to the Austrians. Although the political warriors had been members of the Foreign Office's Political Intelligence Department since 1941, the "marriage" had not always been a happy one, because the propagandists continually developed new and startling initiatives of their own. Traditional-minded Foreign Office officials frowned upon many of these unorthodox activities, even though they grudgingly accepted them as necessary for the war effort. Political warriors did not always wait to calculate the political effects of their propaganda and subversion projects.[83]

The political warriors had an ally in Churchill, who — like Roosevelt — found rhetoric, publicity, indirect subversion, and unusual schemes of all sorts to be attractive. Churchill's usual advisers mistrusted the prime minister's moods, sudden explosions of ideas, and fascination with propaganda. Churchill supported the propagandists' plans to offer independence to Austria. Before an official British policy existed on Germany, he wanted to encourage separatist tendencies there. One Foreign Office official noted that the only way a decent political expert could salve his conscience and at the same time satisfy the prime minister's "unbridled lust" for propaganda was to leave it in the unscrupulous hands of the political warriors. So he minuted on their draft Austrian declaration, "ok for SOE to do so."[84] "Utterly unacceptable," noted another official. For if the PWE or SOE were permitted to commence another propaganda campaign on their own with the prime minister's support, the Foreign Office would indubitably be dragged into it. Eden agreed that it was up to the Foreign Office rather than the political warriors to formulate political and propaganda policy.[85] This was sound advice, but did not solve the problem of how to compel the propagandists to adhere to proclaimed policy without destroying the effectiveness of their propaganda undertakings.

In view of this hidden running battle between political "regulars" and propaganda "irregulars," two conflicting papers on Austria saw the light of day in early 1943. Most accounts have tended to blur the distinct origins and purposes of these two papers because they were formulated at about the same time. As a result their divergent political and propaganda purposes were not fully understood.[86] Foreign Office officials were crystal clear in their own minds that one paper represented official political planning, whereas the other dealt with the more occult world of political warfare. One was accepted by cabinet in June 1943 as official British political policy, the other represented merely a draft propaganda declaration still to be completed and designed for maximum military effectiveness. While the political policy paper on Austria soberly recommended against the reestablishment of an independent postwar Austria, the draft propaganda paper promised as much as possible to the Austrians including independence. The former reflected postwar policy, the latter was formulated as part of military strategy to foment a revolt against the Nazis in Austria. It represented a psychological attack on the enemy.[87] The substantive differences between the two papers proved to be too much for the Foreign Office, which tried hard to coordinate the propaganda paper with political policy, but with only limited success. In the process the propagandists' document became watered down until it lost its original, if dubious, appeal although it still appeared to promise postwar independence. Foreign Office caution left the propagandists disappointed. In the end they doubted whether the final draft could perform the political warfare task expected of it.

The Foreign Office's long political paper on Austria entitled "The Future of Austria" emerged following two years of rumination by Toynbee's FRPS and the Foreign Office regarding the Danube area and Austria. Adopted by the war cabinet in mid-1943, it became a long-term, official political policy. This paper recommended separating Austria from Germany after the war, but only as a first step towards establishing its final place within a Danubian federation supported by international guarantees. Independence from Germany would be only a temporary transitory situation until Austria found its natural place in such a federation. This development would compensate for the country's feeble economic, national, and political prospects. Even within such a federation Austria's prospects did not appear overly favourable. "It must be realized that whatever international guarantee such a State received, it will inevitably be weak and therefore a potential danger spot."[88] But the notion of Austria as an independent state was not "practical." As before, historical lessons and strategic considerations predominated. Whichever way one looked at it, Austria had always been the door to Danubia and any great power controlling Vienna would once again become master of the Danube region. Attached to Switzerland, Austria would bisect Europe. Strategically that country might either form an eastern salient for a resurrected and aggressive Germany or it could be a defence line against Germany. It was up to the victorious Allies to ensure that the latter alternative prevailed. The country would be politically and economically debilitated after the war, and little help could be expected from the weak reed of Austrian nationalism. Although a German people, Austrians by tradition were also Danubians and Europeans, a fact which deterred the evolution of purely Austrian nationalism. "This helps to explain why the great majority of Austrians can hardly be said to have been nationally conscious before 1918." Once the other Danubian states had turned their backs on Austria in 1918, the vast majority of Austrians almost by default sought inclusion in republican Germany. But Allied strictures had halted this trend. If by 1931 the attraction of Anschluss had "lost some of its appeal," the first real glimmerings of an Austrian nationalism appeared only after Hitler's accession to power in Germany. But it did not become explicit, and remained at a low level. "It would be foolish to ignore the fact that the Austrian republic of 1919–1938 did not succeed in arousing the patriotic devotion of its citizens," the paper stated. Most Austrians had welcomed Hitler. "When at last Hitler struck, the plebiscite of 10th April 1938 recorded over 99 per cent of votes for Anschluss," it reported without comment.[89]

Many Austrians had turned against the Anschluss, but not for national reasons. After the German occupation Austria was downgraded into a mere Reich province and later a number of *Gaue*. Austrians discovered that they were being dominated by Germans. As the war dragged on Austrians learned the painful lesson that perhaps they were different from Germans. Current discontent in Austria had little to do with a sense of Austrian nationalism. Austrians were driven by disillusionment and anti-German discontent, although they still fought loyally beside the Germans. Many probably wished to get out of the war and propaganda appeals to this sentiment might bear fruit. In view of these uncertainties regarding their real loyalties, the Allies should definitely not commit themselves in public concerning Austria's postwar political future. Any specific proposal, moreover, would further divide that country's warring ideological factions. "While the majority of Austrians are very probably united in their dislike of the Nazi regime," the document affirmed, nothing else united them, and consequently it was unlikely that Austrians would "make violent exertions for the sake of their freedom." At the war's end little real help could be expected from a war-weary people and returning exiles. Nazi rule had killed "altogether the tender plant of Austrian national sentiment." Unless outside powers took a strong hand, Austria would either collapse into internecine political chaos, fall apart into provincial particularism, or tumble into Germany's lap. "The conditions of 1918–1938" would be "reproduced after the war" and "the same conclusion [Anschluss] will follow." As a result "the best chance of maintaining Austrian independence probably lies in the ultimate association of Austria in some form of Central or

South East Confederation."[90]

Upon such timidity successful political warfare campaigns cannot be constructed. Little in this political policy paper lent itself to issuing a rousing call to revolt against the Nazis, nor were the Austrians expected by the Foreign Office to heed such a clarion blast. Whether Austrian resistance in the form of active sabotage activity and secret resistance groups -killing Germans, as the SOE liked to phrase it – would ever occur was more than doubtful given Austria's geographical position far behind the battle lines. However, British political warriors did not share Foreign Office dejection about the country and its people. They were certain that Austrians were ripe for revolt.[91] In January 1943 the PWE and the other political warriors began to think of ways to appeal to Austrians to help cast off the Nazi rule. Like the British propagandists at the end of World War I, they hoped to trade promises of freedom, national independence, and easier postwar treatment at the hands of the Allies, for Austrian cooperation in the war against the Nazis. If anyone hoped to awaken and inspire Austrian resistance, these main promises represented a bare minimum.[92] It was inevitable that the political warriors' need for inflated propaganda promises would clash with official Foreign Office political planning and policy. The propagandists watched in consternation and dismay as the diplomats chipped away at their propaganda proposals in the process surrounding them with qualifications and reducing them to mere shadows of their former selves. One Foreign Office critic expressed his colleagues' typical caution: "I think that a little ambiguity [regarding promises to Austria] is not altogether a bad thing."[93] Interdepartmental agreement was finally achieved, but, in the PWE's eyes, at the cost of making any promises to the Austrians far too conditional for effectiveness. The final result sounded more anti-German than pro-Austrian. Austrians might count on easier postwar treatment, freedom, and independence only if they admitted their own guilt, cooperated sufficiently in the judgment of the Allies against Germany, never again allowed themselves to be tied to Germany, and henceforth linked their future to that of their Danubian neighbours.[94]

Four short paragraphs comprised this July 1943 British propaganda compromise. The first two paragraphs made it clear that Austria's liberation was not a goal unto itself, but rather that it served military and anti-German aims. They read as follows:

> Austria was the first free country to fall a victim to Nazi ["Nazi" crossed through in draft] aggression.
>
> The Governments of the United Kingdom, United States of America and the Union of Soviet Socialist Republics do not regard themselves bound by any changes effected in Austria in and since 1938 and these Governments have as

one of their objectives the liberation of Austria from German domination. The PWE especially objected to the third paragraph because of its implication of war guilt and its threatening, conditional tone:

> In determining the future treatment of Austria it will be necessary to take into account the conduct of the Austrian people during the war. For this they have a responsibility which they cannot evade.

The conditional nature of the opening three words of the fourth paragraph — "Subject to this" made this text sound as though the victorious Allies would impose their own politically limited solution on Austria:

> Subject to this the Governments of Great Britain, the United States and the Union of Soviet Socialist Republics, having taken counsel together, hereby declare that they regard the *Anschluss* imposed upon Austria by Germany as null and void and that, being determined that Austria shall never again be allowed to become a strategic base for German aggression in Central and South Eastern Europe, they desire to see re-established a free and independent Austria which, in association with neighbouring states, shall be assured of that economic security which is the only basis for political freedom and lasting peace.[95]

One of the last paragraph's most positive assurances regarding economic security disappeared from later versions. "Political freedom" later became the much vaguer "freedom." Some of the anti-German rhetoric was removed as well, which made the document sound more pro-Austrian than originally intended. A call to Austrians to rise up against the Nazi occupiers and the promise of independence and support after the war should have formed, for the political warriors, the core of the declaration. But read in conjunction with the section on Austrian complicity in the Nazi war effort – contributed by the Foreign Office – the declaration turned from a message of hope into a threat. The draft now claimed that Austrians deserved much the same fate as the Germans after the war. Any hope that Austrians might have to be treated more gently than Germans would be conditional on their contribution to Germany's defeat. These awkward contingencies took most of the muscle out of the political warriors' proposed thrust.[96] Upon Eden's suggestion the cabinet agreed to submit a final draft for American and Soviet signature.[97]

When the Big Three foreign minister arranged to meet in Moscow later that year, the British decided that this might be the best opportunity to publish an Allied political warfare declaration on Austria. In preparation for this conference, the Foreign Office sent the American

Department of State in September copies of its two papers: the new political policy on Austria and the political warfare draft. It was noted regarding the former that British Danubian policy had "been crystallized and approved in principle to a greater degree than in the case of most of the other debatable areas on Europe," including especially Poland and Germany.[98] The Foreign Office hesitated to submit the two papers to the Soviet Union, especially the political policy which contained information regarding the projected establishment of federations in eastern Europe that would include Austria. It would be much easier to explain away the draft public declaration on Austria as just a propaganda ploy than the policy paper on federations, to which Moscow was known to be cool. This sensitive political question should therefore be remanded for personal negotiation in Moscow at a later date. In the end the Soviets were sent only the draft propaganda declaration.[99]

The Americans immediately understood the difference between the British policy paper and the draft propaganda declaration on Austria. They realized that one reflected official long-term political policy, the other was a political warfare exercise. On the political side of the question they agreed wholeheartedly with the British estimate of Austria's political future.[100] Adolf Berle worried about Soviet intentions in eastern Europe, as did other colleagues at the State Department.[101] They saw the Soviet Union pushing back the Germans successfully, while the Western Allies were still bogged down in the toe of Italy. Most hoped and wanted to believe that some understanding with the USSR would prevent the imposition of a rigid system on the people there. It was already clear that the Soviets would have a major voice in eastern Europe after the war and their security concerns in the area would have to be addressed. They would want to have some influence over the states to their west, but it was to be hoped that they would be content to remain discreet and exercise control only over their foreign policy.[102] The impending Moscow Conference and the subsequent Big Three meetings would initiate a lengthy negotiation process on these issues. The Soviets might not be averse to federations of independent states in eastern Europe if they could be convinced that these federations were not directed against them.[103] The Americans had yet to define specific goals in Europe, so that final territorial dispositions were best left to the end of the war.[104] Even so the State Department concurred with British pessimism about a reestablished Austrian state and endorsed the need for a confederation in which to place it.[105]

American military leadership was not greatly concerned about the changing military situation in eastern Europe. The JCS had just begun its military planning for the postwar period at that time. It did not foresee the need for an American presence in Europe after the war, but at this stage of the conflict concentrated on ringing North America with island bases to discourage any future aggressor from perpetrating a surprise like Pearl Harbor. It showed some interest in the European balance of power, but only for immediate military purposes. It experienced little unease with the notion of a postwar decline of British power and the corresponding growth of Soviet might.[106] Secretary of War Stimson's only advice to Europeans was to emulate the thirteen American colonies' example by establishing a United States of Europe.[107]

The Americans accepted the British view that Austria offered the most promising psychological target. By September Italy had surrendered, the Germans were bogged down in Russia, defeated in North Africa, and threatened in Italy. It was time to anticipate the next step. From Italy, Austria and the Balkans lay open.[108] In October OSS chief Donovan informed the president on behalf of the joint chiefs that the time had arrived to wage an all-out propaganda war against Germany since psychological warfare had not yet achieved much there.[109] In psychological warfare, Stimson complained, the Soviets had proven to be far ahead of the Western Allies, unencumbered as they were by the doctrine of unconditional surrender. The Soviets' Free Germany Committee, established in mid-1943 and composed of captured German soldiers, threatened to become a potent weapon in their hands.[110]

Roosevelt was much more attracted by political warfare possibilities in the Danubian and Balkan regions than has often been assumed. A quick German collapse in Italy and neighbouring regions might enable the Western Allies to shield these areas from Soviet occupation at no cost.[111] During the Quebec Conference in August 1944, at which Roosevelt and Churchill reaffirmed support for the 1944 invasion of France, the president asked about action plans in the Balkans and Danubia in the event the Germans suddenly withdrew. He informed Marshall, who opposed such schemes, that the military had to be ready to act in case of sudden German military disintegration: "Operations in the Balkans would be largely a matter of opportunity" and military planners must "be prepared to take advantage of them."[112] The British proposal for a propaganda attack on Austria attracted Roosevelt not only for strategic reasons, but also for its possible domestic repercussions. Much to his dismay Congress, and especially the Republicans, had begun to concern themselves with postwar questions. Roosevelt had an upcoming election to worry about and had to blunt these initiatives. He was reticent concerning public postwar decisions, and yet wanted to keep foreign policy matters in his own hands.[113]

In March 1943 Congress had ordered a study of the country's Austrian policy focusing on the Anschluss and postwar prospects.[114] Herbert Wright, a distinguished professor of international law of the "Stimsonian school," was chosen for this task. His research assistant was Willobad Plöchl, an ex-professor of law in Austria and a leading conservative exile, who advocated reestablishment of the Austrian republic. Plöchl had long been a thorn in the administration's side because of his activism.[115] Wright and Plöchl began collecting information and gathering testimony from individuals and government agencies with a view to publishing their report for Congress in the fall. Roosevelt tried to undermine this congressional study by letting slip that there might appear shortly a great power declaration on Austria. As Roosevelt had hoped, once the State Department informed Wright that such a declaration was under consideration Wright decided to delay completion of his report. The question of what was to be American policy for southeastern Europe was thereby removed from the election campaign. When published in early 1944, the study was able to praise the Moscow Declaration on Austria and laud the administration which had sponsored it.[116]

Wright's Austrian study was deeply influenced by his support for the Stimson Doctrine in international law and by the Roosevelt administration's apparent accptance of it in the Moscow Declaration.[117] Wright was convinced that the United States had not recognized the Anschluss. Since this was so, he concluded, the United States must favour a reestablished Austrian state. He was delighted that the Moscow Declaration on Austria apparently vindicated his view. Convinced that he had correctly grasped the country's past and present Austrian policy, Wright published academic articles to this effect afterwards.[118] He could not know, of course, that the declaration had been issued for propaganda purposes and did not reflect political policy. Nor could he have been aware that a good part of Roosevelt's motive for supporting the declaration was to eliminate congressional usurpation that sought to develop a firm Austrian policy and pressure the administration to formulate a clear policy for the region.[119]

Indeed, even if he had been serious in his intent to promise Austria postwar independence, the president lacked the constitutional power to issue a political pronouncement on the future of Austria without Senate approval. During their early 1943 meeting in Washington, Eden and Roosevelt had conducted wide-ranging political discussions regarding the future. They apparently agreed in principle that a federal system might be the best alternative for the small Danubian countries. At the conclusion of that meeting Eden delicately raised the question of whether the president possessed the constitutional authority during wartime to make binding agreements of this nature on his own. After some thought Roosevelt replied negatively. The best he could do was to cast his considerable political weight behind a program he advocated in Congress. Convinced that neither party could decide anything definitively, Eden dropped the subject.[120] To confirm the correctness of his views, the president asked Harry Hopkins to approach his Department of State foreign policy advisers for an authoritative opinion.[121] The reply he received stated that indeed he lacked the constitutional power as president alone to enter into prior international political agreements with other states. At best he could offer a pledge regarding the policy he might later recommend to the Senate.[122] However, as commander-in-chief during wartime, he could enter into military agreements with other powers regarding military campaigns and occupations and lay down guidelines for the military forces in dealing with independent or occupied states. He could decide to treat liberated or occupied countries, between surrender and a peace treaty, almost as if they were independent states. In this intervening period, if he determined that a specific territory "is so separated as to have become independent, he can recognize its existence by recognizing its government" without congressional approval. If Congress declined to fund a foreign post there, the president could appoint a military official or a civilian high commissioner with the personal rank of minister or ambassador. But he could not offer legal recognition to such a country or conclude prior political agreements in that area on his own. "The President has the power by military agreement to create a situation in which all of the characteristics of an independent state will be created except the recognition of the government."[123]

This ambiguous jurisdictional policy meant that, although he was constitutionally empowered to support an interallied declaration such as the one about Austria adopted in Moscow, either as a sign of presidential intent or as a military strategy, the president could not issue such a statement if it was envisaged as a political decision. The latter alternative, Roosevelt was happy to learn, would have to wait until the war's end and would necessitate approval from the Senate. Public opinion polls gave him much the same message: avoid political commitments during wartime. A 1943 presidential poll on this topic concluded: "There seems to be little eagerness to have President Roosevelt present a blueprint plan for the solution of postwar problems."[124] For Roosevelt the Moscow Austrian declaration lacked even declaratory weight, and possessed only domestic and military import. In fact the Big Three foreign ministers never even signed the declaration.[125] For the three Allies it represented only a propaganda ploy designed to speed the military end of Nazi Germany.

From its first version in July 1943 to its submission to the Americans in September the British draft went through several changes, at least one of which was aimed at eliciting American support for such a declaration. The original British draft aimed at arousing Austrian resistance to the Nazis, but as we have seen represented a partial Foreign Office victory over the political warriors. It avoided any mention of an Austrian state, remained vague about Austria's postwar situation, and included a third, conditional paragraph about Austrian war guilt and the necessity to do penance. The North American Department of the Foreign Office suggested that the first paragraph dealing with Austria's demise should include a reference to the Atlantic Charter in order to attract the Americans to this project.[126] Between July and September the issue was debated heatedly at the Foreign Office.[127] Finally reference to the Atlantic Charter was included in the draft, not because of any change of heart concerning its applicability to Austria but to secure American cooperation.[128] The term "Austrian state" was weakened to the circumlocution "people." Although the draft decreed the Anschluss null and void and spoke of a free and independent Austria, such independence was to be "in association with those neighbouring states," a phrase behind which hid the Foreign Office's concept of federations.[129] The third paragraph urged the Austrians to revolt, but at the same time contained the Foreign Office's direct reference to Austrian war guilt and conditional promise as to postwar treatment, a clause which the political warriors had tried to remove.[130] The draft promised that Austrians "will not be unduly punished for the past misdeeds of their country," while it offered "political and economic support and encouragement" as a "first step to the encouragement and maintenance of Austrian resistance to domination by Germany."[131]

When State Department officials in consultation with the American military leadership studied the British draft declaration in September, they found it generally appropriate for the military-propaganda task assigned to it. They suggested three changes, thereby indicating a kindred hesitancy about promising too much to the Austrians even for political warfare purposes. Despite British calculations the Americans rejected the reference to the Atlantic Charter since they did not believe that the charter applied to Austria. Austria's independence had disappeared in 1938 under uncertain circumstances. The Anschluss was not a warlike conquest by a hostile power, and Austria was enemy territory. Instead, they suggested, the Big Three could admit to being moved by the "spirit" of the charter and leave it to the public to infer what it wished, without obligating the Allies one way or the other at the end of the war. On the other hand they easily approved the proposed separation of Austria from Germany, which would inevitably follow as a natural consequence of Germany's defeat. By deciding to split the two, the Allies would not be pinned down as to what Austria's status would be after the war. Use of the word "liberated" in conjunction with Austria was not meant to have any political connotation for Austria's future, but only affirmed the intended separation of Austria from Germany.[132] The Americans found the second paragraph of the British draft much more to their liking. They accepted the declaration of the Anschluss as null and void and approved the need for a free and independent Austria to find its place "in association with" its neighbours. However, preferring not to convey the impression that this was to be imposed on the Austrians by the victorious powers, the Americans thought the promise would be more effective if the Austrians themselves were encouraged to choose this solution. Hence they included the word "themselves" in their version, which then read: " ... and thereby to open the way for the Austrian people themselves to find, in association with ... "[133] They begged off a more categorical statement about eastern European federations on the ground that American policy had not advanced far enough in that area to be more definite. federations in eastern Europe. Although they accepted the Austrian war guilt clause in the last paragraph of the British draft, they hoped at the same time to make the declaration more attractive to Austrians. Hence they suggested that the statement, "in the final settlement account will inevitably be taken of the part they play in assisting to expel the German invader," be altered to read, "in the final settlement account will inevitably be taken of their own contribution to the liberation of their country." In sum, the Americans approved of an Austrian declaration for purposes of pursuing political warfare, and it was this amended version which the British submitted to the Moscow Conference as their draft proposal.[134]

If the evolution of the draft declaration shows that it was developed for military-propaganda rather than political reasons, another indication of this can be seen in the draft agendas for the foreign ministers' Moscow meeting. If indeed the Austrian declaration had been meant as one of the Allies' first political war pronouncements, it would have loomed much larger than it did in these agendas and would have been raised under the heading of the Danubian rather than the German question. The fact that Austria appeared on the agendas only under the German rubric has led some authors to the incorrect conclusion that Austria was discussed as part of the German political question.[135] In fact at the Moscow Conference debates concerning Germany were not political but military in nature. This supports the contention that the Austrian declaration was meant to be part of the foreign ministers' military discussions regarding how best to defeat and later occupy a defeated Germany.[136]

This military approach to the Austrian question – and indeed to the other topics as well – became evident in the negotiations about an agenda for the Moscow meeting. Of the various Allied drafts the British version was the longest reflecting the wish to broach both military and postwar political-territorial topics at the same time. It contained a heading for Germany which omitted Austria and another entitled "Future of Poland and Danubian and Balkan countries including the question of confederation." Austria did not specifically appear under the latter item either, but judging from the war cabinet's political policy on Austria that topic would have come up under this heading.[137] The American and Soviet draft agendas avoided all mention of specific territorial items, although the American version broached the technical question of the mechanism to decide these questions at a later date. Four short items comprised the American list: general security, treatment of Germany and other European enemy countries, economic reconstruction, and methods for dealing later with specific economic and political issues resulting from the war. The first item covered military questions such as the opening of the second front in 1944. The next item dealt mainly with surrender and occupation policies in Germany and other enemy countries. Immediate postwar survival logistics were to be discussed under the third heading, and the final point included the principles upon and the organization through which the Allies would arrive at economic, political, and security decisions for the postwar period. These four sections lacked details, but clearly the Americans thought primarily in terms of immediate military decisions and did not consider the foreign ministers' conference as a place to secure agreement on the postwar political composition of Europe.[138] The Soviet draft agenda dealt exclusively with military aspects of the war. It consisted of only one item: namely, how militarily to shorten the war by opening a second front.[139] Following further exchanges a common Anglo-American agenda emerged. In accordance with the American suggestion this included a military item on Germany and other enemy countries. Austria appeared here for the first time as a military target. This final Anglo-American draft agenda indicated that the American and Soviet military approach rather than the attempted British military-political strategy had prevailed.[140]

Roosevelt realized that for domestic reasons he would soon have to at least appear to say something about an American policy towards the European question, even if in general rather than specific terms. It was imperative that he be seen to move on this issue in view of rising public and Republican interest in postwar international arrangements and the approach of an election year. Even ex-isolationists in the Republican party such as Senator Arthur Vandenberg had begun to request cooperation with the administration on postwar foreign policy issues, while the party adopted the Mackinac Charter in September 1943 declaring for the first time its support for American participation in a postwar international organization. Since the spring Hull had negotiated unsuccessfully with the Senate Foreign Relations Committee to procure its general agreement to vague administration policies. Roosevelt now saw the Moscow Conference in part as a means to solve domestic problems resulting from his own public reticence about the postwar settlement. Hull proposed several general declarations on postwar freedoms, American willingness to cooperate in an international security system, and Allied determination to free Austria. These pronouncements would go far towards blunting domestic challenges to Roosevelt in the foreign affairs field. Best of all they could be issued without prior Senate approval and credit for them would go to the president. At the same time, Roosevelt expressly ordered Hull to keep away from specific territorial and political questions at the Moscow Conference. Roosevelt reserved these matters for his meeting with Churchill and Stalin at Teheran in the following month. This arrangement suited Hull in part because of his penchant for principles over practice, but also as a result of the late decision that Hull instead of Welles was to head the American delegation, leaving the secretary of state inadequately briefed on specific questions.[141]

By this time the State Department had indulged in postwar political planning for over a year and had established a special Policy Planning group to prepare for the Moscow meeting. But because the administration desired to avoid territorial questions at Moscow, none of the specific political recommendations were discussed in that forum. Furnished with State Department planning documents on Germany just in case the topic should surface, Hull took no documentation concerning Austria except for the draft declaration.[142] Hull's main concern was not to be enticed beyond general discussions such as his "Four Freedoms." In his memoirs Hull expressed his gratitude that at Moscow the Soviets had abstained from raising specific political matters. They "never once raised the question that had disturbed us the previous year; namely, the settlement at this time of postwar frontiers."[143] Averell Harriman, America's new ambassador in Moscow, who attended and reported on the conference sessions, later concurred that territorial questions were not discussed in Moscow. The Soviets, he believed, probably intended to maintain their 1941 frontiers. Perhaps they did not intend to go farther if they could develop close relationships with states on their western border, and if they believed that an international security organization would protect Soviet frontiers.[144]

The American delegation to Moscow was very much a last-minute arrangement. Harriman's nomination as ambassador in Moscow was approved only on 7 October, and he had to be sworn into office in all haste at the London stopover on 11 October en route to Moscow. The original choice for delegation leader had not been Hull with whom

Roosevelt had cool relations and who had never accompanied the president to a major conference. Originally Roosevelt had selected Sumner Welles, the department's most experienced political planner and his appointee there, to occupy this position. However, just before the delegation's departure Welles had to be reluctantly dropped when rumours of his homosexual activity suddenly made him a political liability and Hull insisted on a showdown. At first Roosevelt hoped that Welles would still go to Moscow, but Welles's own refusal on 25 September and Hull's insistence ended this plan. Hull's role in Welles's dismissal did nothing to endear him further to the president, who sincerely regretted Welles's departure.[145]

Hull was ill most of the time while travelling to and residing in Moscow. The seventy-two-year-old statesman had never flown before and was so sick on the long flight that he had to be treated by a physician during the conference. He set out on his gruelling flight on 7 October, flying via London and North Africa to arrive ten days later in Moscow. At the conference itself Hull concentrated on the Four Freedoms declaration, the planned international security organization, and the China question. Of his sixteen days in the Soviet capital he spent six in pushing the Soviets to accept China as a member of the great powers.[146] In Harriman's view this enormous effort represented far too much work for so little return. "He used all of his influence to get China accepted as the fourth Great Power. I thought he would have been better advised to apply his considerable leverage with the Russians in attempting to work out arrangements to safeguard the independence of Poland and other nations in Eastern and Central Europe, whose liberation was foreseen in a matter of months."[147] Hull followed Roosevelt's directives and so brought up nothing in the important political area.

At the conference the British at first tried to broach territorial questions. Despite his own hesitation, Eden attempted diligently but in vain to discuss with Hull and Molotov measures to avoid postwar great power friction or a division of Europe into rigid spheres of interest following military lines of occupation. He was especially concerned about the destiny of the small central and eastern European countries and hoped that the federation concept might offer an acceptable solution. In line with Toynbee-Foreign Office planning and war cabinet policy, he informed his opposite numbers that the disappearance of the Austro-Hungarian Empire had left the small successor states abandoned in a virtual limbo, a situation which could only be cured by a postwar pooling of their resources.[148] But owing to Hull's reticence and Molotov's sole driving concern that the Western Allies open a second front, this initiative failed. Molotov appeared lukewarm to the concept, expressing reservations about this proposal without completely turning it down.[149] Eden tried to assuage his fears by promising that these federations would not be turned into a cordon sanitaire against the Soviet Union. In reply Molotov offered his personal guarantee that the Soviets would not divide Europe into separate zones.[150] Ignoring his own department's positive advice concerning federations, Hull stated the general principle that the area's small nations should have the right to decide their own fate after the war.[151] The practical side of this principle did not interest him at all. "I don't want to deal with these piddling little things. We must deal with the main issues," he reminded his colleagues.[152] As a result of the Hull-Molotov agreement not to discuss the "piddling" territorial details in eastern Europe, the topic of Austria was not raised at the conference as a territorial or political question.

Several key decisions adopted at Moscow further demonstrate the American and Russian interest in postponing political decisions until the war's end and help to pinpoint the military nature of the Austrian declaration. Two in particular recognized military reality in eastern Europe. On the one hand the Western representatives agreed that peace feelers from the Nazi satellite countries in eastern Europe would be referred to the Soviet Union, and they generally were thereafter.[153] On the other hand the American preference for one-sided Western military government in Italy became the model for a similar Soviet arrangement in eastern Europe. As the Americans considered the Italian occupation strictly a military operation, the Allied commander-in-chief in Italy would enjoy decisive authority in that country's control commission. Although the Soviets gained some influence in Italy it remained largely symbolic and they later imposed similar limits on Western influence in eastern Europe. As long as the war continued it seemed only natural for the Soviets to exercise control in eastern Europe to match the Western Allies' influence in the west.[154] Finally the Soviets agreed to Hull's four-power declaration on freedoms only after they had gained withdrawal of clauses permitting Anglo-American intrusion into the affairs of eastern Europe.[155] These important decisions at the Moscow Conference regarding eastern Europe demonstrate that the foreign ministers agreed only on military decisions or general principles.[156]

Only towards the end of the conference did the topic of Austria arise briefly in connection with deliberations on the defeat and occupation of Germany under item 7 of the agenda entitled "Treatment of Germany and Other Enemy Countries in Europe." The foreign ministers tentatively recommended that Austria's postwar borders be those of 1937. In the same breath they declared that this did not represent a political decision because Austria's postwar status was "a matter which should come within the purview of the general settlement."[157] Like the other areas incorporated into Germany after 1937, Austria was expected to fall away from the imperialistic and defeated Third Reich. But its final destiny could be decided only at a subsequent peace conference. This purely negative concept of Austrian separation from Nazi Germany did not contradict Anglo-American planning about Austria to date. But it cannot be interpreted as a political recommendation since it was meant only as a statement about the expected military consequences of Germany's lost war. The foreign ministers referred practical short-term questions dealing with Germany's surrender and occupation to a new body they established in London, the European Advisory Commission (EAC). This tripartite body was expected to take not political but only military decisions about the occupation of Germany. The political aspects of the German question would also be resolved at a peace conference in the future.[158]

In its final form the Austrian declaration was prepared by the conference's drafting committee. It used the Anglo-American draft as the basis even before Austria arose for discussion at the conference.[159] The American delegate on this committee was Green Hackworth.[160] The final draft of the declaration on Austria was presented to the conference, as mentioned above, under the military rubric of Germany and enemy countries. The foreign ministers studied it very briefly, accepting it quickly and without comment. It was considered so unimportant in any meaningful political sense that it was not even mentioned in the reports filed by Ambassador Harriman to Washington concerning the talks carried on under this agenda item.[161] Nor did his final report which included the text of the Austrian declaration contain any comment about it.[162] Had this declaration been a unique political-legal document, the first of its kind to emerge from three-power discussions, such silence would have been remarkable. But as a mere political warfare paper without political weight it received the minimal attention it merited from the foreign ministers.

The Austrian declaration adopted in Moscow deviated somewhat from the Anglo-American draft. The original proposal for an Austrian state "in association with" its neighbours yielded to a vaguer formulation. It called upon the Austrian people and their neighbours to search jointly for political and economic security. This phrase could be flexibly interpreted either in the British federative sense or in the Soviet context of ensuring a friendly system on the Soviet Union's western borders. The British detected four other major deviations from their original draft. To their regret, although it had been included for the Americans' sake, all reference to the Atlantic Charter had been dropped.[163] In a second paragraph the ambiguous term "Austrian people" had become "Austria" under Soviet insistence, probably in order that war guilt might be attached later on to an Austrian political structure which would then be forced to pay reparations.[164] According to Philip Mosley, a member of the American delegation, the Americans and British tried unsuccessfully to resist this particular change. But this view has been challenged.[165] Third, Austria's 1938 link with Nazi Germany ceased to be a union and became an outright annexation, much to the later puzzlement of the "occupationist" school. And finally, the references to the coresponsibility of the Austrians for the war and their moral obligation to expiate war guilt by a cleansing resistance effort were toughened. Austrians were not merely asked to "remember" these facts about their cooperation in the Nazi war effort but forcibly "reminded" of them. In deference to Soviet propaganda terminology which distinguished between Germans and the Nazi regime, Germany became "Hitlerite Germany" in the final text.[166]

The final wording of the Austrian declaration issued on 1 November 1943 read:

> The Governments of the United Kingdom, the Soviet Union and the United States of America are agreed that Austria, the first free country to fall victim to Hitlerite aggression, shall be liberated from German domination.
> They regard the annexation imposed upon Austria by Germany on March 15 [*sic*] 1938, as null and void. They consider themselves in no way bound by any changes effected in Austria since that date. They declare that they wish to see re-established a free and independent Austria, and thereby to open the way for the Austrian people themselves, as well as those neighbouring states which will face similar problems, to find that political and economic security which is the only basis for lasting peace.
> Austria is reminded, however, that she has a responsibility for participation in the war on the side of Hitlerite Germany, and that in the final settlement account will inevitably be taken of her contribution to her liberation.[167]

The declaration was issued to the public without fanfare or helpful explanation, unlike the Four Freedoms declaration and other conference decisions. This silence invited speculation about the purpose and meaning of the Austrian declaration. Most journalists mistook the declaration for a political document and agonized about its intent. Some saw it as a positive signal for postwar democracy. But others expressed reservations in view of Austria's past weaknesses.[168] New York editorialist Paul Mellon questioned the necessity for an Austrian declaration and assailed the foreign ministers' silence concerning the other countries situated between Germany and the Soviet Union. He feared this meant that "Russia will hold the major hand particularly in eastern Europe."[169] Drew Pearson concurred with this analysis. The foreign ministers' mention of only two "enemy countries," Italy and Austria, highlighted a tragic decision by the West to write off the Baltic States, Poland, and the rest of eastern Europe.[170] Several other journalists, on the other hand, perceived the real purpose of the Austrian declaration. The *New York Herald Tribune* termed it "their [the Allies'] best and brightest instrument for breaking down the crumbling structure of Hitler's empire of evil."[171] The *New York Post* labelled it a "revolution" to be employed "as a military weapon against Hitler."[172] Felix Morley of the *Wall Street Journal* also correctly assessed the declaration as possessing little or no political weight. At best such declarations were "a statement of executive intent ... it is not improbable that there will be some reservations on the one pertaining to Austria."[173]

American cabinet members certainly understood that the declaration on Austria had only military rather than political significance. While Hull was at the conference his deputy Stettinius briefed cabinet members that the foreign ministers were not about to make any political decisions in Moscow.[174] Stimson agreed that any such exercise would be both foolish and premature. Conditions now demanded military decisions and cooperation, and it was far too early for political negotiations. Before political matters relating to the postwar period could be taken up the war had to be won and the economic future studied. He was sure that the current talks about Austria had nothing to do with politics. On 28 October he wrote in his diary, "They are all thinking of cutting Austria away from Germany. Well, if they restored Austria to her position in which she was left by the Versailles arrangements twenty-five years ago, why they would reduce her again to a non-sustaining state, *and they don't seem to have that in mind at all* [author's emphasis]."[175] Hull revealed as much confidentially to the press upon his return to Washington. He admitted "off the record" that the declaration had been published solely for propaganda purposes and was certainly not official administration political policy. As he told the journalists, " ... (off the record) there were definite manifestations in Austria against the German Nazis which might prove very embarrassing for them, and that some of his associates had felt that some way of intimidation could be helpful in a practical way. (end of off the record)."[176] What irritated Stimson about the conference decisions was Hull's approval of the establishment of the interallied EAC in London to draft surrender and post-surrender military policies for the Allies. Hull had not consulted Stimson regarding this point. Stimson believed that such a commission would undermine the decision-making power of each ally. Stimson was later pointedly to ignore the EAC. Hull tried to placate his cabinet colleague by explaining to him that the EAC idea had materialized at the last minute and had to be decided on the spot. But this excuse only partially mollified Stimson.[177] The Austrian declaration, on the other hand, elicited no reservations or even comment from Stimson or his colleagues.

Polls revealed that the American public knew little and cared even less about the Austrian declaration. According to an OWI survey conducted a few weeks after the end of the Moscow Conference, most Americans polled were aware that a conference had taken place but knew very little about what had actually transpired. Generally they believed that Allied unity had been improved through this first Big Three foreign ministers' meeting. But 39 per cent of those questioned could not recall even one specific decision reached, 9 per cent erroneously assumed that the conference had agreed to demand the unconditional surrender of Germany, and only 1 per cent had even heard about the Austrian declaration.[178] Austrian exiles on the other hand were ecstatic and assumed that the declaration was a passport to international recognition for Austria. They were convinced that now at last the Allies would take them and their cause seriously.[179]

The political warriors who had originally suggested a strong declaration on Austria for political warfare purposes were convinced that in its current diluted form the declaration could not help to launch an Austrian revolt against the Nazis. The PWE believed that the promises were too conditional and that the Austrians would demand far more specific political and economic details regarding Allied plans before they would become "activist." If nothing more could be said in this respect, it might be best to terminate plans for a political warfare campaign against Austria: "Indeed, if it is run hard now and elicits no response, it may well spoil our chances of appealing effectively for action at a more appropriate moment."[180] As further details about Austria's future were not forthcoming, the PWE decided on its own in March 1944 to cease appeals to Austrians to revolt until the moment "for the supreme blow," as the PWE put it.[181] By mid-1944 the political warriors had totally reversed themselves from the previous year. Now they reported that "the overwhelming majority of Austrians" were "not prepared to take any personal risk."[182] A resigned Foreign Office official, fed up with the interdepartmental bickering over Austria, noted in July 1944: "Were it not for the strategic importance of keeping Austria separate from Germany, we would let this flabby country stew."[183]

American psychological warfare professionals shared their British colleagues' disappointment with the Austrian declaration. Some tried to interpret the declaration as "a glancing blow at the unity of the German Reich," but the JCS admitted three weeks after publication of the declaration that it had missed its originally hoped-for effect. Indigenous Austrians had apparently failed to take notice of it. The JCS questioned whether the collapse of morale or the revolt expected to result from the declaration in conjunction with the initiation of bombing raids on Austria would take place. Current intelligence reports indicated that the effect of the threatening third paragraph might be just the opposite of what was originally intended. More Austrians might become afraid of Allied revenge for their complicity in the war than were inspired to revolt. In addition the extremely vague offer of independence, lacking any specific political or economic details or international guarantees, was not attractive to them. It seemed to leave Austria as in 1919 facing a bleak future alone. In retrospect the clear offer of a federation of which Austria was a member might have been a more effective alternative. Recently captured Austrian soldiers appeared not to have heard of the declaration at all. This meant that more pamphlets containing the declaration should have been dropped over enemy lines. But it is doubtful whether these propaganda pamphlets would have delivered any positive results. The declaration itself was too ambiguous. Had the Allies provided a clearer definition of postwar policy towards Austria, these pamphlets and propaganda broadcasts might have stood a better chance of success. In its present form the declaration differed not at all from Allied statements made to the other satellites of Nazi Germany.[184] In December 1943 the interallied military propaganda division in Algiers which was responsible for propaganda against Austria forwarded this message to Washington: "To point out the consequences to Austria of a long war does not of itself constitute strong inducement to take strong measures to break loose from the German yoke." The Austrian needed another, more generous statement about Austria's future "couched in terms appealing to Austrian listeners and readers of leaflets, to stimulate him to action."[185]

If the public could rejoice in the Moscow and Teheran spectacles of interallied unity and promises of Allied liberation, and Austrian exiles could interpret the declaration on Austria as a major politicai-legal document proving the Allies' staunch support for their occupied country, for the political warriors it represented a missed or failed opportunity. They had originally dreamed up the idea for psychological warfare purposes and in the end it was they who were most disappointed with it. Paradoxically those who in 1943 misinterpreted the declaration's intention in a political sense would later, as the war wound down and postwar political problems loomed larger, find further justification for it but again for the wrong reasons. The Western Allies landed on the continent in mid-1944, surged quickly through France towards Germany, and slowly came to an agreement with the Soviets on how to occupy Germany and Austria. In the process they searched for appropriate public statements, no matter how rhetorical they might be, to conceal or justify changes in policy regarding central and eastern European affairs. Thus the Austrian declaration was revived and insinuated into the public consciousness imbued with a political flavour originally unintended for it. However, in the confidential opinion of Anglo-American political leaders this public reinterpretation of the Austrian declaration did not thereby turn it into political policy. Austria remained enemy territory, defeated as part of Nazi Germany, and unlikely to be reestablished after the war as a sovereign state.

CHAPTER SIX

National Redoubt and Liberation

The astonishing prowess of the German army and the disappointing record of the British land forces in the early years of World War II had so impressed Churchill that he preferred to avoid a decisive test of strength with the enemy. Since the beginning of the war Churchill and the political warriors had favoured fomenting revolts on the continent and had contemplated landings at numerous places to enable the conquered peoples and satellites to rise and fight alongside liberating Allied troops. Victory could be achieved through these alternative methods, which included triggering internal convulsions in Germany and Austria through a combination of political warfare, German military losses, economic privation, and Allied bombing campaigns. The 1943 Moscow Declaration on Austria had been conceived as a political warfare weapon to assist an early Allied entry from Italy into Austria. For a short time it appeared likely that the Western Allies would arrive in Austria ahead of the Soviets. In November 1943 most British and some American leaders including commanders of the American 15th Airforce stationed in Italy had reckoned that the invasion OVERLORD in France would be neither desirable nor necessary. It might be better to push the Germans quickly across the Po river, take their airfields, and deploy Allied ground forces in Austria.[1] However the war in Italy bogged down. Rome fell only in June 1944 and the Allies failed to reach the Po river until next the year. The dismal record of Allied progress in Italy, even before the transfer of seven divisions to France in late 1944, does not suggest that even with these larger forces the Allies could have broken into Austria and the Balkans from Italy. As Allied military progress towards Austria remained limited the insurrectionary goal of the Moscow Declaration on Austria proved to be utopian and so it gradually lost its original importance. The war was not to be won by indirect methods such as behind-the-lines revolts nor was Austria to become a battlefield until the very end in April 1945.

The war wound down agonizingly slowly far away from Austria. In 1943 Austria's position had been of prime strategic importance. By the next year, however, Austria again became isolated from the main battlefronts as the western military drive shifted its focus from Italy to France. In 1944 the vast Soviet military machine opposing the Germans in the east consisted of 525 divisions or five million men. The Western Allies fought their way after D-Day through France and the Low Countries with 45 divisions, 12 of which were British.[2] Finally in early 1945 costly advances against bitterly resisting German forces brought the Western Allies face-to-face with the Soviets at Torgau in the ruined heartland of Germany. At the same time German forces in Italy started separate surrender talks, which might have opened the road for an Anglo-American sprint to Vienna, but these feelers came to naught.[3] The Soviets entered Austria first in March 1945, captured Vienna, and then struck north into Czechoslovakia. Not until late April 1945 did American forces arrive in Austria from the northwest.[4] If the Western Allies had been able to invade France in 1943 instead of 1944, they might have been able to occupy most of non-Soviet Europe including Austria while Stalin still fought Germans on his own territory. But this argument remains at best speculative since D-Day did not in fact occur before June 1944.[5] Even so the Anglo-Americans might have reached Prague and Vienna first in 1945 from the west had their capture appeared desirable on political grounds and been militarily feasible. But Soviet wartime sacrifices and desire for security had enabled Stalin to create a favourable public opinion in the West and to exploit western naïveté regarding the Soviet Union's intentions in postwar eastern Europe. Moreover, it was feared that Austria's Alpine heartland would become the stage for the Nazis' last suicidal stand.

During the last eighteen months of war, therefore, Austria lost much of its value as an Anglo-American military and political warfare target, while long-range political planning generally yielded to immediate military concerns regarding invasion, surrender, and occupation policies. Unfortunately for Austrians, not only did their country remain unoccupied by the Allies until almost the end of the war, but when the Germans refused to collapse as rapidly as predicted the political warriors reversed themselves on the topic of Nazi morale. Where previously they had touted poor morale as the weakest link in the Nazi chain, now they turned indomitable morale into the Nazis' greatest asset allowing the Germans to continue fighting against all odds. In the process Austria turned into a symbol of a newlydiscovered iron will to fight to the end. The chosen field for a mythical Nazi Götterdämmerung, or suicidal last battle against the Allies, and a bloody guerrilla warfare to be pursued by fanatical Nazi "werewolves," they predicted, would be Alpine Austria. These military and political warfare developments combined to render the declaration's propaganda goal of eliciting Austrian resistance to the German war effort unattainable.

Since 1939 political warriors had repeatedly insisted that German and Austrian morale was about to crack and that the end of the war was near. The Moscow Declaration on Austria was meant to be one of the final nails in the Nazi empire's coffin. But the promised Austrian resistance failed to materialize. The cowed and demoralized population behind the Alpine lines could do little apart from mounting a few courageous and scattered actions near the war's end. Nazi control over Austria remained brutallly effective to the end. Nor did publication of the declaration influence further Anglo-American postwar planning for Austria. As outlined above, before the Moscow Conference the Western Allies had viewed Austria as an integral part of the German Reich with little prospect of a viable independent postwar existence. If the Moscow Declaration had been a political rather than a propaganda statement, it should have had a dramatic effect on subsequent Anglo-American planning for Austria and the Austrian exiles. If after publication of the declaration the Western Allies truly considered Austria an occupied country to be liberated by the Allies and reestablished as an independent state, the qualitative difference between pre- and post-Moscow Conference planning for Austria should have been evident. But the Western long-term view of Austria remained unaltered, even though some of the public rhetoric increasingly conveyed the impression that it had changed. Despite massive Soviet advances into eastern Europe, the Western Allies clung to their original federative schemes for postwar Austria.

At first Western military leaders maintained high hopes for the effectiveness of the Moscow Declaration despite the political warriors' unhappiness with the vague formulation of the text. In November 1943 Allied military headquarters in London dispatched a special psychological warfare team to the Italian front to exploit the declaration by appealing to Austrians via repeated radio calls and pamphlets to assist in their own liberation. But their activity produced no visible returns.[6] The propagandists showered the German troops among whom were scattered many Austrians and Austrian civilians with the declaration text, while at the same time they conveyed to their superiors their lack of faith in the effectiveness of the declaration in its current form. They requested in vain fuller guidance regarding what the declaration meant in practical terms and how they should best exploit it.[7] In its present wording, they complained, the declaration could even prove counterproductive because by suggesting that the Allies intended to dismember

Germany, it might induce the Austrians and Germans to close ranks. In this sense it could actually serve as fodder for the Nazi propaganda machine.[8] If the Allies wished the declaration to have a positive echo among the Austrians, they would have to explain its vague terms much more fully and provide more practical detail. Then the declaration might become a plausible model for encouraging other "satellites" (*sic!*) to revolt and increase the Nazis' sense of isolation among untrustworthy populations.[9]

But as Austria's relative military importance in Allied priorities declined during 1944, Western leaders lost interest in that area. As they came to realize that little likelihood of an early Allied invasion of Austria and consequently of the need for a domestic Austrian revolt existed, the declaration gradually lost its utility as a political warfare weapon. In the meantime intelligence agency reports remained universally negative on the declaration's influence within Austria. Allan Dulles's Bern OSS office judged in January 1944 that the declaration had had "no profound effect within the country." Left-wing socialists within and outside of Austria still toyed with the idea of a pan-European revolution. Liberals and Catholics were not tempted by the offer to return Austria to isolated independence within its post-1919 boundaries. All Austrians distrusted Allied peace promises, having had one searing experience in World War I. They were not prepared to risk their lives in a revolt so that Austria might become a mere province of Czechoslovakia or perhaps the Soviet Union. They were discouraged by the apparent lack of clarity and detail that plagued Allied postwar policy for Austria. They were also bewildered as to what was expected of them despite tight Nazi control, and wondered how the Allies expected them to extricate themselves from the trap in which they found themselves.[10] One of the last OSS reports to concern itself with the Austrian problem, written in late January 1944, claimed that not enough able-bodied men remained in Austria to carry out sabotage and underground work. Austrian losses in World War II had already exceeded those of World War I. Nor were Austrians in a position to do anything themselves because the ruthless Nazis tightly controlled the area. The implied threat that a revolt was a vital condition for favourable postwar treatment merely confused the Austrians and weakened the offer. The Allied call for a revolt "seemed unrealistic to Austrians themselves."[11] New ideas and specific postwar policies for Austria were needed to attract the Austrians. The offer of independence alone held little attraction: "Unlike the Czechs or Poles, the Austrians have no passionate or positive national feelings."[12]

The British also became resigned to the absence of a positive Austrian response to the Moscow Declaration. They too saw that the combination of the slow Allied advance through Italy, tough Nazi police control, and the weakness of Austrian patriotism sapped the will for sabotage or resistance activity even if Austrians were tired of the war. PWE propagandists switched from the previous year's enthusiasm for Austrians to despondency about their future prospects and in the process began to sound very much like Foreign Office officials. They were evidently unconvinced that even after the war the Austrians, if left on their own as the declaration hinted, would be very dependable. They predicted that once the war's bad memories had faded away Austrians would probably again favour Anschluss. In all probability this would take place fairly rapidly because the Allies would treat Austria as a defeated enemy rather than as a liberated country.[13] To counter this, the Allies would have to hide their reservations concerning Austria's unreliability, at least appear to support independence, and rapidly impose the federative solution no matter what Austrians themselves wanted. "The mass of Austrians are probably so politically childish that their opinions on the question [of their future] are worthless."[14] It was quite apparent to the western propagandists that the Western Allies had failed to appeal to Austrians as effectively as the Soviets, who utilized Austrian exiles to offer their non-Nazi compatriots outright freedom and independence without punishment.[15] The Foreign Office's weekly political warfare directives to British propaganda agencies continued to make no distinction between Austria and Germany, including Austria under the heading of "Germany" until late 1944 and thereafter under "Germany and Austria." Only in the last month of the war did Austria merit a separate subheading of its own, no longer tied to Germany but under "Occupied and Liberated Countries."[16]

In view of their propaganda experts' advice, the Anglo-American combined chiefs agreed with the conclusion that the political warfare campaign against Austria based upon the Moscow Declaration was heading nowhere. In early 1944 they too announced that it was "unrealistic" to expect Austrians to revolt because "they are not in a position to do anything effective at the moment."[17] The CCS endorsed the opinion that the Moscow Declaration would have no effect in Austria, not only because the Austrians were powerless, but because they mistrusted the Allies as much as the Germans.[18] When the time came in April 1944 to consider drawing up a psychological warfare strategy for operation OVERLORD, which included trying to incite the occupied peoples and break the Germans' and satellites' will to continue the war, Austria was no longer even mentioned.[19] When this was drawn to the attention of the military planners their response was passive: "A section on Austria would be useful, but not essential."[20] In the end Eisenhower and his staff grudgingly conceded that because it was still official Allied policy to exploit the Moscow Declaration, Austria should be included as a target for psychological warfare.[21] The OWI drafted a new and more positive statement aimed at the Austrians, but the State Department rejected it as being too soft for Austria was still enemy territory. Although the State Department and General Eisenhower agreed that a new public statement on Austria was essential if the Allies hoped to secure effective Austrian assistance behind German lines for the forthcoming invasion, they were only halfheartedly prepared to work towards one. Nothing came of this weak initiative as Roosevelt finally vetoed the idea as unnecessary.[22] The optimistic 1943 political warfare ambitions for Austria had almost completely disappeared.

Despite a few flurries of interest in Austria, no material change of western policy became evident in the last stage of the war. Encouraged by Austrian exiles, the American press continued its coverage regarding the imminence of an uprising.[23] It reproduced the Soviet Union's strong calls to Austrians to rise up against their Nazi oppressors.[24] In September 1944 Cordell Hull thundered a warning to Austrians that if they wanted postwar freedom they would have to turn immediately on the Germans.[25] Following Hull's lead, Eisenhower issued a call in October for Austrians to dissociate themselves from the Nazi war machine.[26] But at this point the Allies were still pushing across France or into Poland, far away from Austria. As the Western Allies drove into Germany and the Soviets into Hungary in late February 1945, the British chiefs of staff and the PWE briefly ventured the opinion that Austria "was probably more vulnerable than other parts of the Reich to moral attack." But again the suggestion went nowhere because no decision could be reached about possible further promises to Austrians.[27] Nor did one emerge from the Yalta Conference in early 1945. On the eve of the seventh Anschluss anniversary in March 1945 Acting Secretary of State Joseph Grew reminded Austrians harshly that they were directly responsible for participating in the war, and cited the need for redemptive signs of resistance if they hoped for reasonable postwar treatment.[28]

As the Allies prepared to break into Austria in early 1945, some resistance groups came to their notice. The mayor of besieged Vienna promised the Soviets a revolt in April which did not materialize.[29] Small groups of resisters united in an Austrian National Committee named 05 bravely carried out some guerrilla actions and tried to instigate cooperation with the Allies. But the Allies knew too little about them and were unwilling to make great efforts to help them or announce any specific commitments concerning Austria's future. Whatever the courage of their individual members, the Austrian resistance groups' military effectiveness did not impress the Allies.[30] When in March 1945 *Time* magazine queried the Department of State whether the increased Austrian sabotage and resistance could be considered "sufficient" in terms of the Moscow Declaration, it received only the vaguest of answers: "This was not a matter which could be discussed in such terms, that the Moscow Declaration did not prescribe a specified tonnage of contribution to be delivered within a specified period, that it merely stated that the Austrians' own contribution to their liberation would come into consideration, that the time during which this contribution could be made was still running, and would continue to run on for some time to come, and that naturally everybody hoped that the Austrians would continuously do everything in their power to bring about their own liberation."[31] No further details could be provided, the correspondent was informed. A secret 1945 PWE directive was equally vague about the relationship between Austrian resistance activity and Austria's future. Resistance groups should be encouraged, but "without committing us to support of one party or another."[32] In the Western Allies' view this internal resistance proved disappointingly weak and without much consequence for postwar Austria.

Austrians were caught in a world of hard military fact and stringent Nazi control which made resistance unlikely. Austria's distance from the main battle fronts further complicated its situation. But one of the main factors in the Anglo-Americans' shift in 1944 away from interest in Austria was their abrupt reversal on the subject of Nazi Germany's morale. German military resistance remained strong despite a string of individual defeats. This suggested that Nazi morale was not about to shatter quickly. As a result the psychological warfare experts did an abrupt about-face. They began to drop their claim that German morale was "brittle" and shifted boldly to the opposite conclusion. Where once they had denigrated the Nazi will to resist, they now inflated Nazi morale into an almost mystical force. Despite huge German losses which resulted in reduced capabilities for offensive and defensive action, the propagandists now insisted that the fanatical Nazis were forcing the dazed population of Germany and Austria to fight on even past surrender. Failure of the July 1944 officers' coup showed that 1944 would not be a repetition of 1918. Apparently the Nazi party leadership remained in firm control.[33] The CCS estimated in August 1944 that "the civilian population alone has neither the courage nor the capability to risk revolt, even if it is beginning to appreciate the hopelessness of continued resistance." Little indication was evident of either an imminent German collapse or surrender, the CCS concluded.[34]

Thus in the year after publication of the Moscow Declaration the Western Allies almost miraculously transformed Nazi morale from one of the enemy's chief weaknesses to one of his most effective military weapons. Despite the apparently weakening German military position, the CCS estimated in January 1945 – quite wrongly, it proved – that Nazi resistance would indeed become stronger because the retreating military forces enjoyed the advantage of interior lines. The strongest elements in the German strategic situation, it was believed, were the political and psychological forces which united the majority of the German people behind the total war effort. The Nazis could postpone defeat by "a fanatical refusal to accept defeat and a skillful employment of such resources as they have." This being the case, an Allied triumph remained elusive. In attempting to comprehend continued German resistance in a seemingly hopeless situation, the CCS became an unwitting dupe of Goebbels's total war propaganda. It listed the following psychological causes of the enemy's unflagging military effort: the Nazi will to resist; strong German patriotism (presumably including Austrians); effective Nazi control behind the lines; fear of unconditional surrender and the destruction of Germany; hope of an Allied split over central and southeastern Europe; and Allied failure to end the war earlier as frequently and publicly announced. The Germans (and Austrians) showed little inclination to break the Nazi grip and take active steps to end the war: "While antagonisms, susceptible to development by Allied psychological warfare, clearly exist within the National Socialist state, none of these antagonisms is at present strong enough to endanger the national cohesion, or to elude the strict, efficient Nazi control apparatus."[35]

A mere month before the German surrender the CCS was still sticking to its estimate that the war against Nazi Germany might drag on for some time yet. "One of the strongest elements in the German strategic situation continues to be the political and psychological forces which have united the majority of the German people behind the total war effort." Morgenthau's revengeful postwar plans relegating Germany to being an agricultural area bolstered Nazi resistance.[36] The CCS envisaged a frightening German capacity for continued fighting, agreeing that the Nazis were unlikely to surrender. Even if central Germany were lost, the Nazis were prepared to exploit the geographical advantages of the Austrian Alps and their own formidable will power to pursue a bitter and protracted guerrilla war in the so-called National Redoubt. The military did not take seriously rumours of a native Austrian resistance.[37]

Some British political warriors suggested a last attempt in February 1945 to draft another more efective call to Austrians to throw off the Nazi yoke. Such a declaration they hoped might undermine last-minute Nazi resistance in the National Redoubt of Alpine Austria. But nothing came of this plan because Allied leaders no longer believed an Austrian revolt likely.[38] While Western newspapers published encouraging news stories about large-scale Austrian revolts, most propaganda advisers and military chiefs discounted them.[39] Psychological warfare had come full circle and turned upon its practitioners.

The notion of fanatical Nazi resistance in a National Redoubt consisting largely of Austria dominated much of Eisenhower's thinking in the final weeks of the war. By mid-April 1945 the British and Americans had reached another critical point in their series of disagreements about military strategy. Once again they differed about where the main thrust of the next Allied attack should be directed. Churchill urged that their forces shift northwards to capture Berlin. Eisenhower on the other hand thought it more important first to clean up German resistance in north and west Germany, especially in the Ruhr area, and then to attack south towards the feared National Redoubt in the Bavarian and Austrian Alps. Berlin was to be left to the Soviets. When his chief of staff, General Bedell Smith, reviewed the Western military situation on 21 April 1945, the battle of the Ruhr, a large double-pincer operation, was just winding down. Soviet and American troops were within a hair's breadth of meeting each other on the Elbe river. Eisenhower believed that Berlin had lost its military importance. The National Redoubt in the Bavarian and Austrian Alps appeared to be the last seizable Nazi bastion still to be breached. Smith admitted that not much was known about the Redoubt but he was convinced that the struggle for it was necessary and would be savage. It was rumoured to be honeycombed with virtually impregnable underground defence systems. Hitler was thought to be there, and once his troops from southern Germany and Italy had withdrawn into it he would command a vast army of over 100 divisions. From the bowels of the Redoubt he could also continue to command by radio his large armies in north Germany and Scandinavia. Two American armies were poised for the assault, but the area would be extremely difficult to enter. In Smith's estimation the German command was "Just as good as ever. Very high order." Victory could still be months ahead. The capture of Berlin and Prague had been covered by previous three-power agreements, but the area of this southern redoubt comprising parts of Austria, north Italy, Yugoslavia, Hungary, and Czechoslovakia was not, in General Eisenhower's view. So Anglo-American forces could occupy the zone without risking confrontation with the Soviets.[40]

The American 7th and 3rd Armies turned south while French forces attacked the National Redoubt from the west. A few hundred Germans offered resistance at Lake Constance but were quickly overrun by the French.[41] Otherwise the fighting between the end of April and 5 May was of no operational or military importance.[42] Truck accident casualties were higher than those caused by fighting. Ignoring large pockets of largely passive German troops the Americans rushed ahead through Austria to meet up with the Soviets, who had stopped several weeks previously along lines outside of Vienna. The German army in Italy surrendered and advance parties of British soldiers from Italy crossed into Austria on 8 May. On that day a million German (including Austrian) soldiers surrendered in Austria. The National Redoubt had proved to be a hollow shell.[43] But this could not have been foreseen. Austria had appeared in 1943 to be a soft, disintegrating part of the Third Reich. Instead it became one of the last areas of Nazi Germany to surrender and the fantasy site of an awesome, fanatical last stand of truly Wagnerian proportions. The expected internal Austrian resistance arrived very late and was believed to be of little military value.[44]

The Moscow Declaration became little more than an embarrassment and a source of some confusion as the war drifted away once again from Austria, especially among the Allied military leaders who were not always privy to the political intentions of their governments. As far as the military were concerned Austria was still as part of enemy Germany and derived its postwar status not from the liberation of that area but the terms of a German unconditional surrender. Allied forces in Austria were told by the CCS in February 1944 that they would have their occupying powers "conferred in the terms of surrender imposed on Germany ... You will prepare your plans on the assumption that the territory involved is that of an enemy belligerent and your mission is to obtain and maintain military control over such territory." At the same time the CCS warned local commanders that the Allied governments "might direct that the position of Austria will be that of a liberated territory, which it is proposed to restore to the condition of an Independent and Democratic State."[45] In other words, the military were led to assume that Austria was enemy territory, but that the politicians might later decide to interpret the Moscow Declaration as a promise to reestablish that country as an independent state. They showed themselves as confused about their governments' intentions as they were clear about their own. The question remains: were they correct in envisaging a possible political change of attitude towards Austria?

As noted above, the Moscow Declaration had not been conceived as a legal or political document. Moreover, the British and Americans appeared to agree about Austria's shaky prospects as an independent country. Why therefore did the United States begin to declare its public political support for Austria in 1944? For this American policy shift is one of the reasons why the myth of strong American support since 1938 for an independent Austria circulated so effectively after 1945. The grounds for this American policy change were twofold. They may in part be found in Roosevelt's reluctant bending to British and Soviet pressure during 1944 to participate in an Austrian occupation. Second, the president continued during the election year 1944 to lure uncommitted liberal internationalists to the Democratic party by emphasizing

American concern for postwar Europe, and to turn away Republican criticism that he might try to override American and others' national interests in his drive towards a new internationalism. As a result of these considerations the government began to emphasize the Moscow Declaration on Austria and American participation in an Austrian occupation. The British followed suit for reasons of their own. In order to justify their participation in the Austrian occupation they too pretended publicly that their actions stemmed from the political promises rendered in the Moscow Declaration. However, a closer glance at confidential Anglo-American thinking demonstrates that nothing had changed and that the British and American Austrian policy continued as it had been since before November 1943.

As far as postwar agreements about eastern Europe were concerned, compromise would be dependent upon good will, a commodity often in short supply among great powers. The British did not have to convince the Americans that the best solution for postwar eastern Europe was a system of interdependent democratic political units. The issue between the Western Allies was not so much long-term aims as it was the type of policy or plan of action most likely to achieve these goals. Long-range planning in Britain and the United States, especially for eastern Europe, remained remarkably constant and similar in nature. This agreement on larger goals was often taken for granted in the heat of debate about tactics, creating an atmosphere of suspicion and irritation. Uncertainties existed about the course of the war. Americans disliked British imperialism and concentration on balance of power problems. The British sometimes differed from Americans on questions of military and political strategy and saw them as curiously indifferent to hard political realities.[46] By 1944 pressure had begun to build for postwar decisions and widening differences emerged between the Anglo-American Allies. Whereas Churchill tried to broach postwar territorial problems during this last stage of the war, Roosevelt continued to believe that controversy about a postwar settlement was best postponed. Churchill preferred a common Anglo-American approach towards the Soviet Union, while Roosevelt worried that such tactics would give Stalin the impression that they were "ganging up" on him. The result was that final solutions generally followed lines of military occupation with the addition of British influence in Greece and the Middle East. The Western powers' inability to effect change in areas under Soviet rule in eastern Europe gradually reestablished long-range Anglo-American consensus. Indeed by late 1944 Stimson's think-tank Operations Division was even prepared to recognize that one of the war's goals was the upholding of the British Empire and its interests on the continent of Europe.[47] For the British it was essential to link the Americans closely to postwar European affairs.[48] Austria was a weathervane for America's shift towards military and then political involvement in middle Europe. In the process the Moscow Declaration on Austria was infused with a new meaning not originally intended for it.

Western planning for postwar Austria had taken place within the southeastern European rather than German context. The Anglo-American Allies had expected to reach Austria before Germany, and until almost the end of the war Anglo-American occupation elements for Austria were based first in Algiers and then Italy rather than being attached to the London-based SHAEF. Whatever the vagaries of war during 1944 and 1945, the long-term federative goals for Austria did not materially change, although it became increasingly clear that Soviet approbation of them would be necessary. Securing this agreement was regarded as difficult but not impossible. The reality of Western federative policy for postwar Austria remained hidden behind the rhetorical screen of the Moscow Declaration. Allied military planners could be forgiven for taking the Moscow Declaration into consideration when drawing up an occupation policy for Austria. Far be it from them to question political policy as they understood it. For them the main short-term aim of a postwar occupation of Austria was "to ensure an orderly and sound return to consititutional government." Because the war against Nazi Germany ended in an unexpected manner, long-term forecasting was knocked into a cocked hat by circumstances.[49]

It is perhaps not surprising that Foreign Office staff assigned to Austrian and German responsibilities towards the end of the war held that the Moscow Declaration had been a propaganda failure. Looked at coldly, nothing in it suggested a novel and favourable postwar political or economic deal for Austria.[50] They maintained their scepticism about the viability of an independent Austria and were unable to move beyond earlier federative plans. But now the PWE strengthened this negative view as well by reporting that Austrians wished to see the end of the war and were ready to repudiate the Anschluss, but only because Germany was losing the war. It considered that Austrians were not attracted to the concept of independence, although they could recognize the postwar benefits they might derive if the Allies treated them differently from the Germans. In fact, the Anschluss spirit was still alive and well, if perhaps in a more democratic form. Despite their cynical if understandable calculation that independence would lead to better postwar treatment, Austrians still secretly believed that Austria could not function as a viable country alone and should find its postwar place attached to a democratic Germany. They might resent "Prussians," but they had no faith in their own political institutions, which had disappeared in 1938. Except for the hiccup of the Bismarckian Reich, history had made

Austria a part of Germany. "If events [in 1871] had developed only slightly differently, Austria might have been the kernel of the German Reich and Prussia the German-speaking state left out." The PWE repeated Foreign Office stereotypes about the "softness of the Austrian character" and the absence of patriotic feelings. It admitted that the Austrians were still notoriously divided among themselves and "more disposed to talk than to act."[51] In effect, towards the end of the war the British psychological warriors concurred with the diplomatic officials that the Moscow Declaration had missed its propaganda target, that its promises were politically unrealistic, and that the Austrians lacked the national bonds on which to build a state.

The Moscow Declaration, as one might expect, was not in the eyes of the British government either a legal or a political document. It neither "de-recognized" the Anschluss nor constituted a political promise of Austrian independence at the end of the war. A Foreign Office legal expert expressed this thought clearly in January 1945: "The unfortunate statement that they [the foreign ministers in Moscow] regarded the annexation of Austria as 'null and void' was in law either meaningless or wrong, and cannot have meant that they regarded the independence of Austria as re-established, which would be inconsistent with the rest of the Declaration."[52] The Foreign Office looked at the declaration until the end of the war simply as a propaganda instrument, and an abortive one at that. As late as the fall of 1945 it secretly instructed the Dominion governments, which were apparently bewildered by the Western Allies' hesitation towards the new Renner government, that they were not in any way obliged by the Moscow Declaration to recognize that government because the declaration had been released in 1943 exclusively for political warfare reasons, and therefore carried not the slightest political or legal weight.[53] Nor did the legal situation of the Austrian exiles in Great Britain change after issuance of the declaration. Again for propaganda purposes only, the British permitted Austrians in 1944 to register with the authorities as Austrians instead of Germans if they could present proof of pre-1938 Austrian nationality. Many were unable to do so. As in the United States several years previously, this decision was considered to be an administrative change lacking any legal or political meaning.[54] In view of their political position concerning Austria, the British and American governments agreed anew not to encourage the formation of any unified Austrian front in their respective countries or to offer even unofficial support to individual Austrian committees or groups. The exiles' lengthy tradition of bitter infighting, they noted, had dissipated whatever Anglo-American good will might once have existed.[55]

The Anglo-American leaders continued to back the federative idea for the Danubian region, even though the Americans tended to take a much more hands-off attitude to the area than did the British. Churchill, who was unwilling to cede eastern Europe to Soviet control, made two Moscow trips in 1944 in order to come to some postwar arrangements with Stalin. There he worked out the famous "percentages" agreement regarding the victorious powers' weight of influence in different countries. At first Roosevelt was willling to condone the arrangement because he had little interest in the area and believed that these decisions covered only the war and occupation periods.[56] In August 1944 the president informed his military chiefs that he was not interested in the region. He preferred that the Soviets "establish a kinship with the other Slavic people."[57] It was "unwise to plan military strategy based on a gamble as to political results."[58] Even though by mid-1944 Hull had begun to suspect that the Moscow-Teheran high point of American-Soviet relations might be passing, he too wished to shield the United States from eastern Europe's problems if possible.[59]

Churchill's views concerning Soviet intentions in eastern Europe did not alter British federative plans for Austria. In February 1944 the Foreign Office drafted a memorandum regarding Austria's future which recommended that it receive additional territory from South Tyrol, but did not support Austrian independence. The Post-Hostilities Sub-Committee accepted this position and agreed that it would recognize Austria within its 1937 borders only for the purpose of drafting surrender conditions.[60] Six months later, in October, a Postwar Reconstruction Committee policy paper echoed the traditional British theme discounting Austrian nationalism. Strong regional loyalties were paired with an internationalist tradition; "the middle term (*i.e.*, national) of Austrian feeling is almost missing ... the Austrians, as a German people, share the common German tendency to interpret nationalism in terms of stock rather than of State." When by 1938 the international or Danubian option was closed to them, this German sentiment triumphed. As a result "the German army drove into Austria with an unrestricted impetus which almost suggested that it was being sucked in to fill a political vacuum." It was probable, despite current Austrian unhappiness with the Germans, that at the war's end an independent Austria, once again a dangerous political and economic cripple, would desire to move towards Danubia or would suffer a renewed attraction "towards a reconstituted Germany at a later stage."[61]

When Churchill returned from his October 1944 talks with Stalin regarding the future of eastern Europe and the great powers' postwar spheres of responsibility, he still hoped that the Soviet leader might not completely oppose a confederation of some sort in which Austria and perhaps some southern German states would be members. He reported to Roosevelt: "Contrary to his previously stated views, he [Stalin] would be glad to see Vienna as the capital of a federation of south German states ... As you know the idea of Vienna becoming the capital of a large Danubian federation has always been attractive to me, though I should prefer to add Hungary, to which Uncle Joe is strongly opposed."[62] Churchill's abiding faith in the central importance of Austria in a Danubian structure was far more optimistic although not different in substance from that of the political planners. As late as July 1945 the British still held that Austria could survive only within a strong eastern European federation or customs union. Such an organization might tend to injure short-term British interests in the area. Nevertheless, the Foreign Office maintained, a federative policy alone could ensure stability in the region, thereby protecting Great Britain's most important communication routes to the eastern Mediterranean and the Middle East.[63] Although by this time the Soviets had occupied much of the Danubian region, the British did not surrender this goal because any other alternative seemed unacceptable. This policy helps to explain British reluctance to recognize the 1945 Renner government.[64]

The United States government also continued to hold that the Moscow Declaration on Austria possessed no legal or political character. Three weeks after publication of the declaration an American lawyer representing Hans Rott, head of the conservative Free Austrian Movement in North America and one of the last surviving members of the Schuschnigg cabinet, visited the Department of State. Deeply moved and encouraged by the declaration, he inquired whether the moment had not arrived to establish a representative Austrian committee with Rott as a member. However, Hackworth, himself one of the declaration's drafters in Moscow, bluntly informed him that the declaration had not made Austria an ally of the West like other occupied countries. Instead, that country remained both in fact and in law an integral part of the Nazi empire. "The situation of the former Austrian government is not analogous to that of Norway, Belgium etc.," he told his disappointed visitor. Hackworth underlined this stance subsequently by circulating a memorandum to other State Department officials asking that they not even accept a visit by ex-minister Rott in order to avoid "misinterpretation." For, according to Hackworth, Austrians were simply Germans cooperating in Nazi Germany's war against the United States.[65] Even if the symbol of Austria as an occupied country could have proven to be a useful propaganda weapon, the exiles would have been incapable of forming a common Austrian front because of their bitter internecine feuds.[66]

Similarly, when in April 1944 Otto von Habsburg suggested that another former Austrian minister now residing in Brazil be recognized by the Allies as an official Austrian representative, the State Department again rejected the idea not only for legal but also for practical reasons: "... nor have we believed that it would be useful at this time to have any Austrian representative recognized by this government."[67] The department could not stop the president from fawning upon Otto, but it took a very dim view of the relationship. Nor did the president bother to enlighten the department about the content of his discussions with the ex-archduke, which further worried his officials.[68] Typically Roosevelt and the American intelligence community cooked up a scheme between them to permit Archduke Karl Ludwig to visit Portugal in early 1944 in an attempt to coax Hungary out of the war. The archducal mission lacked the State Department's knowledge or consent. When rumours of this trip surfaced, one of the assistant under-secretaries reacted worriedly: "Something is going on here, which will undoubtedly explode before long."[69] Nothing much came of this initiative, and when in October 1944 Otto decided to leave the United States for Great Britain no one was happier than the secretary of state.[70] Unable to see any usefulness either to the war effort or to postwar Austria in any of the Austrian exile groupings, the State Department and the Foreign Office kept their distance from all of them to the end of the war.[71]

If the Allies reacted so negatively to wartime Austria and the Austrian exiles, why did the Americans begin during 1944 to speak favourably in public of the Moscow Declaration's promise of Austrian independence? The answer lies in their hesitant but increasingly positive response during that year to their allies' requests for American participation in the postwar occupation of Austria. Allied disagreements during much of 1944 concerning which occupation zones they would take in Germany and Austria had stemmed largely from Roosevelt's original determination to acquire a short-term northwestern rather than southern occupation zone in defeated Germany, and to refuse any coresponsibility for the occupation of Austria. Behind the American position on occupation zones lay matters of communications, and reluctance to be closely involved in monitoring the peace in certain parts of Europe. For their part, the British and Soviets offered the Americans a southern German and an Austrian zone, hoping to involve the Americans in those areas. As we have seen, at the Moscow conference the Big Three had decided that the forum for discussion of Allied surrender and occupation policies would be a new tripartite body, the London-based European Advisory Commission (EAC). Foreign Office officials wanted to ascertain that Allied military surrender and occupation policies meshed with political programs. But the EAC's mandate did not include establishing political policies for the postwar era. Nor was such coordination likely or possible on the American side.[72]

Roosevelt had decided in November 1943 on a six-month military government in occupied enemy territory after surrender. But what this meant in detail was unclear. Military government had few precedents in American history, and hence its terms of reference or how military necessity would be balanced against the welfare of the governed were uncertain. The War Department suspected the EAC as a State Department creature designed to undermine the military's prime responsibility for occupation and surrender affairs, and consequently was reluctant to share information and decisions with it. The Washington-based State-War Committee, which was supposed to mesh civil and military policies in the form of instructions to the American EAC representative in London, was unable to resolve the domestic impasse.[73] Nor did the president care to push the contending parties in Washington towards policy resolution for use in the EAC. It sufficed for Roosevelt that the American public should perceive his London EAC delegates apparently cooperating with the other Allies. Operating largely in the dark about Washington's policies, Ambassador John Winant, chief United States delegate to the EAC, struggled unsuccessfully to present a coherent American position to the other Allies.[74] The British were especially proficient in offering policy papers, and even the Soviets were more effective at formulating their views than were the Americans. Winant's frustrations in London were legion.[75] This helps to explains why in September 1944 Henry Morgenthau could step so easily into the American political vacuum with his own plan for Germany.[76]

Not only did Roosevelt disagree with his allies about where the American zone of occupation should be in Germany, but his reluctance to participate in a postwar occupation of Austria was at first strong. As noted above, neither Roosevelt nor his advisers were at first particularly concerned that eastern Europe would fall, at least temporarily until a peace conference, under Soviet occupation. Lt. Gen. Sir Frederick Morgan's 1943 RANKIN plan continued in force during 1944. It assumed that Soviet Russia would occupy eastern Germany, whereas the Americans would be responsible for southwestern Germany and Austria. But the Americans would not ratify this arrangement. Because the JCS could not agree that American units should be involved in the occupation of Austria, British troops from Italy were temporarily assigned to this role.[77] In February 1944 President Roosevelt formally rejected a CCS suggestion that favoured an American occupation zone in southern Germany and Austria.[78] He foresaw problems of communications for a southern German zone, and believed that the American public did not want American troops to police central Europe, but rather that they be used sparingly in Western Europe and in the main quickly transferred to the Pacific war. Roosevelt wrote to Winant in response to his plea for a presidential policy decision on British and Russian offers to share the occupation of Austria with the Americans: "I can only add that political considerations in the United States make my [negative] decision [about an Austrian occupation] conclusive."[79] In early May the JCS still maintained that southeastern Europe was a British and Soviet but not an American responsibility. It named Austria specifically as one of the areas in which the United States was not interested.[80] Winant disagreed vigorously with this hands-off policy. He had become convinced that the British and Soviet offers made sense because sooner rather than later the United States must decide to share the postwar responsibility for both Germany and Austria with its Allies. However, Roosevelt firmly ordered Winant to obey his earlier decision that only northwestern Germany be assigned as the American zone, and he issued Eisenhower a directive to that effect.[81]

Nevertheless, in mid-1944 Roosevelt suddenly changed his mind. Under British and Soviet pressure, he first accepted the principle of an American involvement in the occupation of Austria and later the southern German occupation zone. External and internal reasons account for Roosevelt's turnabout. Growing tensions over Poland and Soviet-occupied eastern Europe began to show in frayed relations with the Soviets, which might require clear occupation lines and an American presence farther eastwards if the United States hoped to wield any postwar influence in the region. In May the JCS Strategic Survey Committee recommended that the United States consider acceptance of British and Soviet requests for an American element in the Austrian occupation. It gradually dawned on Americans that they might be deprived of any influence in countries under Soviet occupation such as Bulgaria and Rumania because their occupation forces were not directly involved in these places. Americans should therefore realize that the question of actual rather than merely symbolic occupation was "of direct concern to the United States." Without American mediation, the JCS foresaw and Roosevelt feared, British-Soviet friction in southeastern Europe and Austria "might lead to postwar disunity among the three powers ... [and] might even affect adversely their solidarity against Germany."[82]

Compelling domestic reasons having to do with the upcoming November presidential election also helped to change Roosevelt's mind on American participation in the postwar occupation of Austria. Since the beginning of the year, as noted above, Roosevelt had avoided public pronouncements regarding American postwar policy. Austrian exiles and indigenous Austrians were mystified at the president's silence concerning the future of their country. Why had nothing more been said following the Moscow Declaration "to point the way more clearly to a constructive solution of the Austrian problem"?[83] But with the election approaching, Roosevelt believed he would have to declare himself on the issue of foreign policy, in particular the question of a more active role for the United States in the postwar era. In order to attract independent voters such as the liberal Republicans, who he estimated made up about 20 per cent of the electorate, Roosevelt proposed to move on foreign policy. One way to do this was to offer strong support for a postwar United Nations organization, while at the same time stilling fears that his internationalism might threaten sovereign states' rights.[84] Thus the administration was prepared to demonstrate at least rhetorically a greater concern for eastern Europe including Austria.[85]

At this moment, Winant decided to bring his own personal influence to bear upon the president in order to change his mind on American participation in an Austrian occupation. The British and Soviets in the EAC had already come to an agreement to divide both Germany and Austria into tripartite occupation zones. Faced by this united front and as usual lacking clear instructions, Winant had had to refuse American cooperation in Austria. Deeply opposed himself to this negative stance, Winant decided in May 1944 to fly to Washington and appeal directly over the heads of the warring officials to the president. To his surprise Winant discovered that the president, impelled by both military and electoral considerations, was now willing to bend. However, he would still countenance only a symbolic American presence in Austria. Hull and Stimson were not at first informed of this presidential decision, although Winant claimed later that he had discussed the matter informally with General Marshall during his visit in Great Britain. From Stimson, Winant had heard that the JCS had accepted the necessity of establishing clear demarcation lines between the Allied occupation zones, and of having Americans participate directly in the occupation of countries where they wished a voice. The omnibus occupation question in southeastern Europe was "of direct concern to the United States."[86] As Winant reported to Hull almost a month later: "On the last day I was in Washington, I accordingly took up the matter with the President and obtained his permission to agree to the tripartite control of Austria on the understanding that I would in no way commit us regarding the size of the contingent that we might be willing to contribute to this occupation ... The objective of importance is to establish the line between ourselves and the Russians and that we have been able to accomplish."[87]

With Roosevelt's agreement in hand, on 31 May Winant announced in the EAC that the United States had agreed to the implementation of a three-power occupation in postwar Austria at the national level, meaning by this the deployment of a token American detachment in Vienna.[88]

Once again, Roosevelt neglected to inform his secretary of state about this change of course. Hull first heard of this decision from an early June memorandum issued to the department by the British Embassy in Washington. This British note read in part as follows: "The United States representative on the EAC, however, stated at the meeting of the three representatives on May 31st that he was authorized to accept the proposal for tripartite occupation of Austria."[89] The perplexed Hull demanded an explanation from Winant, who rehearsed for him his unhappy position on the EAC. Constantly functioning without clear instructions from home, he often found himself disadvantaged in that body. Faced with a decision which required prompt action, he had decided to visit the president and had procured his agreement to the policy statement made in the EAC regarding the Austrian occupation.[90] The ancillary question of whether the United States army would occupy the northwestern zone in Germany, as it had requested, or would accept the Anglo-Soviet offer of the southwestern zone adjoining Austria, remained unresolved until September 1944 when Roosevelt again bowed to his Allies' pressure and accepted the latter plan at the Quebec Conference.

Once the president had decided to become involved in the Austrian occupation, American public policy towards Austria began to change dramatically. In late June this shift became apparent for the first time at the official level in a military planning paper approved by the president and the JCS and dispatched to Winant in London.[91] Austria was described as an essential strategic area for the United States in postwar Europe: "Austria's strategic position in Europe makes her future political status in relation to her neighbors a matter of paramount concern to the United States and to the international community."[92] Policy for the first time seemed to echo the Moscow Declaration. Following this new approach, the paper stated that the United States had never recognized the Anschluss, and labelled Austria a victim of Nazi aggression and an occupied state. "This [new Austrian] program is premised on the view that Austria, as a victim of Nazi aggression, was never legally incorporated into the Reich." As the United States had not recognized the Anschluss *de jure*, Austria was not an integral part of the German Reich. The United States therefore favoured Austria's restoration as a free state, "subject only to such limitations upon its sovereignty as are shared by all states or are clearly in the interests of international security."[92] This last statement left an escape hatch open for a federative Austrian future, reflecting doubts some Americans still entertained concerning Austria's viability as a sovereign state. Anyone taking up the story at this point might be excused for believing that this had always been American policy. In fact, however, this was a novel, convenient, and deliberate reinterpretation intended to justify or give a covering justification for the recent occupation decision.

In the late summer, this new version of the United States's Austrian policy was passed on to American legislators. As part of his successful campaign to create a bipartisan foreign policy, thereby removing the topic from the electoral campaign and undercutting his Republican opponent Thomas Dewey, the president continued to encourage Hull to meet with Democratic and Republican Congressional foreign policy leaders. His task was to convince them of Roosevelt's determination to act quickly and decisively to guarantee the coming peace and the re-establishment of the European state system after the war, by force if necessary. Thus when in August 1944 Senator Arthur H. Vandenberg, leading Republican member of the Senate Foreign Relations Committee, inquired what exactly the government's view was on the Anschluss, Hull sent him an unusually uplifting reply. Hull cleverly alluded to Professor Wright's half-forgotten 1943 congressional study on Austria as though it reflected uninterrupted American policy. "This document," he wrote the senator, "contains an exhaustive study of the legal aspects of the annexation [*sic*] of Austria by Germany as well as the policy of the United States towards the annexation." Hull went on to claim that the United States had, of course, always supported a free and independent Austria, and was committed to reestablishing it after the war. Although forced by circumstances in 1938 to accept the Anschluss as a *fait accompli*, the United States had steadfastly refused to recognize it: "This position was never considered to constitute *de jure* recognition of the Anschluss however. The attitude of the United States was constantly guided by its policy of refusing to recognize acquisitions of territory by force in violation of treaty obligations."[94] For the first time, moreover, Hull applied the provisions of the 1941 Atlantic Charter to Austria, a sovereign state which the Germans had illegally occupied, and which would be liberated and reestablished as a state by the victorious Allies. Obviously the vagueness of previous administration statements concerning Austria now stood Hull in good stead. Without having to contradict himself, he could pretend that the United States had always remained faithful to the principles of nonrecognition which Stimson had enunciated in 1932.

That these sentiments represented a convenient reinterpretation can be seen by comparing them to political planning just prior to this period. Five months before Roosevelt's mid-1944 change of course over Austria, an OSS document commissioned by the War Department and based upon State Department views had reiterated traditional American policy. The Allies were free of any firm political commitments regarding Austria's future. The main problem after the surrender would be to develop a specific Austrian national consciousness and economic health, "which are not yet apparent." Nor would legal continuity be established between the prewar republic and any postwar state, should one be created. The only correct historical, legal, and political conclusion was that "Austria had ceased to exist as a legal and administrative unit in February [*sic*] 1938."[95] The interdepartmental Postwar Committee had echoed this position just prior to the June policy shift. Independence would not be a sound basis for Austria's future since it would only cause economic problems and raise the Anschluss question again as the dominant political issue.[96]

Following the apparent shift on Austria in mid-1944, the same older misgivings concerning Austrian independence surfaced in confidential political planning circles. Even the more positive approach announced in the June 1944 paper was accompanied by cautioning that Austria must never again become an international ward. Its "*initial*" (the word is italicized in the original text) independence "is not a prescription against future economic and political relations" with its neighbours, which might assume "a political federation or even a merger of sovereignties."[97] This cautious phrasing was far from being a vote of confidence for a reestablished sovereign Austrian state. In August the OSS described postwar Austria as "a provisional state," having, if possible, "an entirely new framework." For reasons of sheer practicality, in the immediate post-surrender period the Allies would apply the pre-authoritarian 1920–9 Austrian constitution.[98] A major State Department planning report next month plaintively asked: what had the Moscow Declaration really meant? It complained that the declaration "poses the Austrian question without specifying a clear-cut solution." Nothing in it prohibited a federative union between Austria and other neighbouring states, or even a future Anschluss with Germany. Austrians were disappointed with the Allies, who had refused publicly to clarify any of the burning issues raised by the declaration; or "to point the way more clearly to a constructive solution of the Austrian problem." Austrian independence, as formulated in the Moscow Declaration and interpreted in Hull's letter to Vandenberg, clearly held no appeal for State Department planners. Even if the Allies forced Austria to be independent, the report continued, the Austrians themselves still questioned the notion of a separate sovereignty. They might wish to cast off the Nazi yoke, but a strong sense of national identity and enthusiasm for renewed autonomy were sadly absent. The war might have taught some Austrians to moderate their internal political squabbles, but the economic viability of Austria and its security as a state could be considered only within the framework of an integrated, strong, and non-nationalistic Europe. It was unlikely that these conditions would be present, and so it appeared inevitable that an independent Austria "will become a theater of conflict if power politics prevail." To protect it against its neighbours' rivalries, Austria should be attached to other states or neutralized, "if such encroachments upon its sovereignty were deemed necessary."[99]

Nor did the problem of Austria's relation to postwar European security disappear overnight from the planners' considerations, Indeed, they probed this issue in some detail. They showed that their pre-Moscow Declaration intentions for Austria were still very much alive. Having weighed the nation-state answer for Austria and found it wanting, State Department officials decided that just about any arrangement would be better for Austria and the rest of Europe than unfettered independence. Once again they felt that a union with other states appeared mandatory and could materialize in three different ways. It might take the form of a customs union, as long as this economic arrangement was neither exclusive nor viewed with suspicion by others as being a step towards an unacceptable political Anschluss. Second, in their concern for security they recommended a second Anschluss with a democratic Germany. Although full union with Germany would remove an independent Austria from the map, this infusion of Austrians might weaken militaristic and ultra-nationalist forces within Germany. An added attraction of this solution was that the Germans would be compensated for anticipated substantial territorial losses in the east, thereby dulling their possible resentment against the peace settlement. Austrians would certainly be better off and would enjoy more security within a reformed Germany, and even the Moscow Declaration did not ban a future, democratically ratified Anschluss. For the moment this route was barred because of Austrian revulsion towards the first Anschluss. Moreover, neighbours such as Czechoslovakia and Yugoslavia would probably oppose it. Yet much in Austria's culture and history as well as the Austrians' need to be associated with another large political entity spoke in favour of a second Anschluss, given the right circumstances. These preconditions included a general European security system, a democratic Germany, and a sufficient time lapse to permit bad memories to fade and for everyone to accept the idea that a democratically combined Germany and Austria would not necessarily threaten peace. Finally, a union linking Austria with some of the southern German states might at some stage become practical should the Allied leaders decide to dismember Germany. However, this last proposal was regarded as the least attractive of the three.[100] It is remarkable that, at this late stage in the war, American planners still seriously considered federative and indeed Anschluss scenarios for Austria, and that they continued to prefer the Danubian federative project. They understood by a Danubian federation the re-creation of the vanished economic and political unity and security of the Austro-Hungarian Empire. Austria's neighbours seemed to oppose it at present because the promised advantages did not seem sufficient to outweigh or overcome reciprocal national antipathies. Evidence was also lacking that the Austrians desired to become members of such a confederation. Still the Western Allies kept this plan in mind because some solution other than independence had to be devised for Austrians.[101]

Meanwhile the issue of Austria as a boundary area separating the Allies in southeastern Europe continued to dominate American discussion about Austria. In August the president again rejected an American occupation zone in southern Germany. Despite his agreement the previous May to a symbolic American presence in Austria, his insistence on the northern location of an American zone in Germany made any effective American participation in the Austrian occupation unlikely.[102] But when in September Roosevelt bowed to his allies' pressure and accepted a southern German occupation zone abutting onto Austria, realistic planning for the small American occupation element in Austria at the national level could begin.[103] Responsibility for organizing the American unit for Vienna was entrusted to Mediterranean command. A political adviser, John Erhardt, joined the group in November.[104] An accompanying military instruction decreed that Austria together with Albania, also a first-time member of this list, as well as Czechoslovakia, Greece, Poland, and Yugoslavia were to be treated as occupied and liberated states. .[105]

An American unit in Vienna was not enough in the eyes of some experts. Winant continued to urge from London a larger American military presence in Austria because recent developments in southeastern Europe had demonstrated that Austria was much more than a local question. That country's destiny was deeply intertwined with future world security and American influence in middle Europe: "A few months ago we believed that a small Vienna contingent would suffice. But Soviet dominance in Bulgaria and Rumania have shown that without a physical presence there is no control." Winant had little faith in Allied control commission agreements unsupported by a military presence: "Possession is 9 points of the law." Failure to be on the spot and arrive at prior agreements would only "lead to a grab as grab can policy." Without a more impressive American presence in Austria, a certain and strong Soviet influence would cause problems in the American occupation zone and elsewhere in Germany. It was essential therefore for the United States to adopt the full Anglo-Soviet zonal projects and take an active occupational role in Austria.[106]

Finally in December 1944 Roosevelt took the step and gave in to Anglo-Soviet wishes for a full tripartite occupation of Austria. He informed Stettinius: "I have yours of December sixth about zones in Austria. Please take this up with the Joint Staff. I would be willing to accept a zone next to Bavaria – in other words, touching the German zone which has been allocated to us."[107] The JCS informed American military headquarters in Italy of this decision and explained that plans for an American zone in Austria were in preparation.[108] Yet specifics were slow in coming and were still unavailable to the CCS or to the American military in Italy as late as March 1945.[109] By April it appeared likely that some of the earlier assumptions might have to be changed, since American military penetration of Austria would probably proceed from the north rather than the south. Because of the fear of fanatical resistance from within the National Redoubt, American entry into Austria was expected through southern Czechoslovakia, outflanking the Alpine stronghold.[110]

In preparation for an American presence in the defeated Third Reich, the OSS busily drafted the first civil affairs guidelines for military government in occupied Germany and Austria. Often confused afterwards with American political planning, these civil affairs instructions were designed only as administrative guides for the military during the occupation stage and were not meant to prejudice or necessarily reflect political decisions. They were based on the assumption that Austria would be split away from Germany, occupied by and administered under military government as though it were a state, and denazification procedures commenced. The OSS guides made it quite clear that these assumptions and measures were military in nature, applicable only as long as military occupation remained in force.[111] The State Department also drew a clear line between temporary occupation arrangements and Austria's long-term legal and political status. Short-term practicality demanded treating Austria as an independent state, but that was not necessarily to be its final status. "For present purposes," the department's legal division explained in April 1945, Austria's prewar treaties would be considered valid. It was now correct to state publicly that the United States had never extended *de jure* recognition to the Anschluss, and that Austria "had continued to exist as a separate sovereign state" never at war with the United States. Like other subjugated countries, Austria would now be considered a liberated state, with all its pre-Anschluss obligations, rights, treaties, and constitutional laws. However, the legal division cautioned, this current official opinion was subject to change in response to future long-term political decisions.[112]

State Department officials were aware that they were being called upon to adapt past policies to current concerns. They were under pressure from the army, which had to occupy the country, to clarify American policy on Austria and to drop ambiguous references to treating Austria "like a liberated country." Following recognition of the new Austrian government (not state) in late 1945, they slowly began to shift completely, if reluctantly, to a positive public stance on Austria. One of the first visible results was the 28 October 1946 statement handed to Dr Karl Gruber on his first United States trip. Another was the decision to appoint Erhardt as minister to Austria backdated to January 1946. They admitted confidentially among themselves that this historical revisionism would be useful in countering Soviet intransigence over Austria.[113] But they held that these decisions were temporary political exercises devoid of long-term commitments. They could again be reversed at a later stage if circumstances including Soviet behavior should later change. Recognition of the Renner cabinet as representing Austria's legitimate government did little to kill the federative idea as a long-term goal for Austria. As one of the department's legal experts expressed the administration's continuing freedom of choice in the Austrian question, "The expression 'recognizes' is a word of art with a technical legal connotation, but here also the act of recognition is determined by the political decision."[114] However, this position became increasingly useful as the wartime Allies quarrelled concerning Austrian reparations and other occupation questions. If Austria were considered to be a friendly, formerly ex-occupied and liberated, independent state with its own constitutional laws, reparations could not be legally demanded by the USSR, and Soviet demands for veto power over new constitutional laws could be negated.[115]

As the Cold War's grip on Austria tightened, what the Americans had foreseen as temporary military government policy unexpectedly hardened into a long-term political one under the pressure of circumstances. As a corollary to the working hypothesis of an occupied and liberated country, Austria became technically absolved of responsibility for the Nazi era. A 1948 Washington directive informed the American military commander and high commissioner for Austria that "Your Government, therefore, does not consider the Austrian Government responsible for the acts of the Nazi regime or its representatives during the effective period of the Anschluss."[116]

The British decided to be almost as flexible towards Austria as the Americans, and for similar short-term reasons. In May 1944 the two Western Allies had agreed that Austria was a part of Germany and that the German surrender document would cover Austria as well. The draft British proclamation to the Austrians read: "To the people of Austria: 1. The Allied forces enter Austria as victors inasmuch as Austria has waged war as an integral part of Germany against the United Nations."[117] But later in the year the Foreign Office suggested that a softer approach could be taken where it served British purposes. "Where we want to be severe with Austria, we should regard her as a part of Germany ... Where, on the other hand, we want to encourage Austria, emphasizing her liberation rather than the need for purging and control, we should use new proclamations or orders specifically drafted for Austria."[118] Thus when the final proclamation came to be issued in 1945, the Western Allies chose the more positive approach and claimed that they entered Austria not on the basis of the German surrender instrument, but as representatives of the United Nations coming to liberate a friendly country.[119] However, this benign proclamation and occupational practice in Austria did not connote any significant change in British political thinking about Austria and its responsibility for the Nazi regime. When the question arose whether or not Italy and Austria might be represented after the war on a United Nations' war crimes commission, the British rejected the suggestion. The Foreign Office reiterated, in confidence, that Great Britain had recognized the Anschluss, that "Austria as a whole" had contributed to the German war effort, was not a member of the United Nations, and possessed no officially recognized political body abroad. Like the Italians, Austrians would have to "work their passage back home."[120] American and British legal minds met on this issue in 1946. As a secret American report stated: "the fact is that the country has stagnated since the end of the war ... Austrians are not unaware of their own faults and their past ideological mistakes for which retribution must be made."[121] However, as the American "occupationist" theory came to be increasingly emphasized, this scenario appeared less and less likely. Still, the British remained less forgiving towards the Austrians than the Americans, refusing to adopt the exculpatory "occupationist" approach to the same extent. As a Foreign Office legal expert had written in late 1944: "There is no doubt that from a legal point of view, Austria is enemy territory," and the British did not deviate from this position for some years after the war.[122] In fact, Great Britain and most of the Dominions considered themselves to be legally at war with Austria until the late 1940s. On the other hand, when the British realized by 1946 that an Austrian treaty would probably not be obtained within a reasonable time because of Soviet opposition, they too gradually adopted a public position similar to that of the Americans; namely, that Austria was a liberated country.[123]

The truth was that both the British and the Americans shared a deep scepticism concerning Austria's right to obtain preferential treatment on the basis of that country's record, and they shared the opinion that in the long run an Austrian state would be precarious and dangerous to European security. Therefore they insisted even past the end of the war on a federative long-term solution for Austria. They saw the need for some temporary postwar Austrian administrative structure, even if

Austria's future probably lay within a southeastern or Danubian federation or perhaps even as part of a democratic Germany.[124] But, as the Americans stated firmly in January 1945, "independence alone, however, would not be an adequate basis for Austria's future."[125] As late as July 1945 the British advocated a Danubian federation in which Austria should be placed. Only a broader political organization would ensure Austrian political and economic stability, and above all protect Great Britain's vital communication routes to the eastern Mediterranean.[126] Whenever the Western Allies envisaged an independent Austrian state in 1944 and 1945, they carefully labelled it a "provisional state" lacking legal continuity with pre-Anschluss Austria. This arrangement proved useful in the short run for occupation purposes. However, the Allied occupation lasted many more years than had been expected as the wartime alliance fell apart. For a decade Austrians waited for genuine freedom and independence while the Cold War was fought over the prostrate country. In this manner, short-term policies adopted just before the war's end for short-term domestic or military purposes became frozen into place in the ensuing period. The postwar occupation, difficult as it was for the Austrians, put paid to wider Anglo-American plans for the country. Austria's loyalty to the West and its growing success as a state in these years gradually transformed Anglo-American disdain and distrust into genuine admiration and support.

Conclusion

The 1938 Anschluss of Austria with Germany alerted the world to the exposed position of the small country sharing frontiers, history, and culture with its larger Germanic neighbour to the northwest. An acute aspect of the Austrian question lay in the danger such a weak and dispirited Austrian state posed to the international community. The defeated country had resented the form of independence thrust upon it by the victors of World War 1 at Versailles. It was also riven by ideological dissension and financial incertitude, and came to see itself surrounded by hostile neighbours. The Western powers had to intervene repeatedly to stave off political and economic collapse. Only after the Austrian economy gradually recovered with the help of League of Nations loans did pressure for union with Germany temporarily subside. The 1929 depression again caused enormous economic dislocation, social tension, and class war in Austria, and reopened the Anschluss question. The country's renewed internal problems and the threat from Nazi Germany became sources of profound concern to the other European states for which they possessed no easy remedy. These dilemmas led directly to the entry of German troops into Austria on 12 March 1938.

Scholars have recognized the existence of some ambiguity in the West's reaction to the Anschluss, but have chosen to stress the element of moral rejection. They maintained that once the war started against Nazi Germany, the West strongly rejected the Anschluss and came to support the notion of an occupied Austria to be liberated by the Allies and reestablished after the war as a sovereign, independent state. The 1943 Moscow Declaration on Austria emerged as proof of these Anglo-American intentions. It termed the Anschluss null and void, spoke of Austria as an occupied country to be freed by the Allies and restored to independence after the war, and called upon Austrians actively to assist in throwing off the Nazi yoke. However, a review of the primary record indicates that the benign Anglo-American "occupationist" view of post-Anschluss Austria and its corollary that the Western Allies supported the reestablishment of Austrian independence after the war are erroneous. This study has outlined two main reasons for the confusion; the first stemming from a misunderstanding of the interaction of wartime political warfare and planning, and the second from the upgrading of wartime propaganda to political policy during the radically changed circumstances of the Cold War.

Seemingly tidy conclusions concerning Anglo-American reactions to the Anschluss and intentions for postwar Austria derived for the most part from overlooking the Allies' two-track system of issuing public propaganda statements, while conducting elaborate political planning at a different level. These two activities frequently contradicted each other, but the conflict is largely resolved by keeping serious postwar planning separate from political-psychological warfare. Western planners remained committed not to reestablishing Austrian independence, but to fitting Austria into a larger federative structure. For their part, political warriors drafted the Moscow Declaration on Austria as a military weapon designed to raise rebellion behind the Nazi lines. In other words, the declaration was conceived for purely military reasons rather than as an international agreement with legal or political ramifications.

In 1938 both the British and American governments recognized the Anschluss not only in fact but also in law, and they upheld this position throughout the war. The British proceeded somewhat more overtly than the Americans, who obfuscated the issue behind a discreet screen of moral rhetoric concerning the Stimson Doctrine of nonrecognition of forcible territorial changes in violation of international treaties. Both governments despaired of Austria's survival in 1938 and doubted that they could do anything for the isolated and fragile country. In many ways they regarded the Anschluss as a long-expected event, almost inevitable for reasons of culture and power politics. It seemed at the moment more important to appease Hitler in order to restore Germany to the family of nations and avoid further continental problems. If Austria had to pay the price for peace, the cost was not considered too high. Because the Anschluss was recognized, Austria was considered enemy territory throughout the war, and Austrians were placed in the category of German nationals and enemy aliens. However, neither the British nor the American government made any effort to enlighten their respective publics regarding these political calculations.

What of Austria's postwar status? Scholars have noted the existence of early World War II federative plans for southeastern Europe including Austria, but believed that these schemes had lost their attraction by 1943. In particular, the 1943 Moscow Declaration seemed to offer genuine national independence to Austria. Yet why was Austria picked out as the first central European country to become the subject of a formal interallied political agreement, long before the Allies had answered much larger questions regarding the general future of Germany and Europe as a whole? This question puzzled some observers at the time and subsequently. In fact, it turns out upon closer scrutiny that a federative solution for the region and Austria remained to the end of the war the most attractive one for Anglo-American statesmen.

The interests of central Europeans did not rank high among British and American priorities. If Churchill thought about the region at all, it was as a side-show whose problems could best be solved by reference to a supranational historical model he respected, namely, the Austro-Hungarian Empire. Besides working to win the war, he hoped to preserve as much as possible of British national and imperial power. Primary British interests lay in the eastern Mediterranean and the Middle East. By keeping the Soviet Union fighting and by trying to arrange for some sort of postwar balance of power on the continent, a compromise of sorts might be found for central and eastern Europe. As several scholars have recently demonstrated, Churchill's assessment of Stalin and communist doctrine could sometimes be erratic and ill-informed, while American abstention forced him to try on his own to arrive at agreements with the Soviets.[1] Thus British federative plans lingered on and were shored up by "percentage agreements" regarding postwar East-West influence in the area. The fate of the large region was not seriously discussed at critical wartime Allied conferences until Yalta, which then merely blessed the *de facto* partition of Europe. Apart from Poland, Americans evinced even less interest during the war in the large central and eastern European problem. Politically isolated in the 1920s and 1930s, the United States was not equipped at the outbreak of World War II to act as a world power. Its army consisted of just over three divisions, while the concept of fortress America dominated thinking until 1942. Even though subsequently Roosevelt and the American people slowly moved towards the notion of the United States as one of the "world's policemen," the notion was regional and did not include eastern Europe. For the Americans too, vague federative notions persisted in setting the tone for the region's future, including that of Austria, to the end of the war.

Before and during World War I the Allies had stressed the legitimacy of nationality as the chief organizing principle in central and eastern Europe. But during World War II a return to the *status quo ante bellum* of independent states in the Danubian region seemed unthinkable. Nationalism had wrought its damage there, and heeding it again would only lead to history repeating itself. Both the British and the Americans agreed that the passionate eastern European nationalism of the interwar years must not be allowed free rein after the war. The individual states had proven to be alarmingly weak and factious, permitting rampant, expansionary, "Prussian" German nationalism to move easily into the region.

The Allies' lack of faith in restored Austrian independence stemmed not only from the Versailles system's legacy in eastern Europe and the failed history of the First Austrian Republic, but from their experience with the several groups of feuding Austrian exiles within Great Britain and the United States. Intent on continuing their prewar ideological struggles in exile, and not attracted until very late in the war to the concept of a revived Austrian state, the deeply divided Austrian refugees were unable to prove to their hosts that they shared a common national bond. Thanks to the combination of Austria's disappointing past record and the squabbles of the exile groups, who never exerted a strong positive influence upon Allied policy-makers, the Western Allies found the concept of renewed Austrian independence unattractive.

The 1938 Anschluss had publicized Austria's twentieth-century nationality crisis. It seemed to demonstrate the shallowness of the republic's national roots and the Austrian people's constant temptation to seek larger and more attractive alternatives to the sagging political and economic structure bequeathed by the Treaty of St Germain. Was Austria destined to follow the particularist tradition within the Germanic world as a separate political unit, or would it seek a future within a modified reprise of the vanquished Austro-Hungarian Empire, a regenerated socialist Europe, or even a large democratic Germany? What criteria would be used in this quest?

Publicly Washington and London demonstrated little interest in eastern European federations. However, assisted by some of the best available academic personnel, Anglo-American officials envisaged the virtual recreation of the multinational Austro-Hungarian Empire, but without the Habsburgs. Once considered parasitical, the old imperial idea underwent a remarkable rehabilitation during World War II as academic and official planners sought multinational and regional solutions to the seemingly intractable problems of European nationalism. The concept of a Danubian federation, developed separately by the British and Americans and without reference to as yet undeveloped planning for Germany, became a long-term Anglo-American goal by 1943 and remained a general objective until the end of the war -and indeed, beyond it – no matter how tentative or imprecise were its details. A larger regional federation such as the Danubian would include and protect small states like Austria, render the region more prosperous and secure, and free it from harmful nationalistic passions. The adoption of this policy represented a major shift in Anglo-American thinking. Although the Western Allies remained uncertain about the specific features of their political plans for a federated Danubian region including Austria, they pursued the scheme as a realistic goal. They were unable to address the thorny question of how to achieve the federative goal in detail because of the fluid nature of the war and the expectation that a peace conference would deal with these matters within the framework of a world organization. They believed that the goal of a self-supporting and closely-knit Danubian area would surely appeal to all parties involved because of the presumed ability of such a federation to resist renewed German blandishments and threats, and to overcome traditional political fragmentation and competition. Somehow, the Allies hoped, the Danubian people, including the Austrians and the victorious Soviets, would recognize the value of this federative scheme.

The Allies' public promise in 1943 of future Austrian independence must be seen against this political background. It did not represent serious Anglo-American planning, but formed part of a broader military strategy of fanning revolts by the continent's suppressed yet latently explosive populations against their Nazi oppressors. As the Anglo-American forces fought their way up Italy towards Austria in late 1943, they expected soon to knock on Hitler's Alpine door. Active anti-Nazi resistance in Austria would seriously threaten Germany's war effort in a vital economic and military sector. The Moscow Declaration was meant to trigger an Austrian revolt. It did not reflect or change Anglo-American political planning for Austria, which had been established long before along federative lines.

Concerned lest this propaganda statement might, as in World War I, commit the Allies to policies they did not support, political officials tried to emasculate, thereby distorting, the declaration's purposes. From a political warfare point of view, the Foreign Office and State Department erred in trying to water down the propaganda effect of the declaration and protect too diligently their freedom of action after the war. Produced in the crossfire between political warriors and political officials, the final declaration pleased neither group and proved to be an example of failed political warfare. In retrospect, the goal of raising widespread revolt within Austria appears utopian. Caught deep behind the battle lines until the end of the war, cooperating with or intimidated by the tough Nazi police system, Austrians were hardly in a position to undertake large-scale sabotage or resistance actions against the Nazis, whether or not they wished to do so. In fact, as two American political warfare experts admitted at the end of the war, German fighting morale did not collapse until about April 1945.[2] During 1944 the war again moved away from Austria, whereupon the Allies quickly lost interest in the Moscow Declaration.

A further reason why the occupationist myth about Austria has survived in such resounding health is that after the war it came to serve the purposes of both the Allies and Austrians. Research into the wartime and Cold War periods continues to be active – more so among American than British scholars because the period represents the rise of American and the diminishing of British power. It seeks to explain the great and unexpected shift in power relations on the European continent and to expose some of the stratagems created to cope with it. When East and West found themselves face to face over the prostrate body of Austria, it became expedient to pretend that the Moscow Declaration in fact reflected genuine political intentions. In order to overcome the great tension between wartime aims and a radically different postwar reality, the declaration on Austria was employed as an historical bridge leading directly from war to occupation. The Moscow Declaration's ambiguities lent themselves to later reinterpretation, when the international balance of power underwent a radical and unforeseen change. Thus as in World War I a propaganda statement came to be applied as political policy at the end of the war.

Whereas the British sought to influence the area directly after the war, the Americans treated it as primarily the responsibility of their allies. President Roosevelt only slowly and hesitantly agreed to American participation in the occupation of Austria. In so doing, he admitted the need for clear demarcation lines between the zones, hoped to act as mediator among the Allies, and saw domestic electoral rewards resulting from a more forward-looking policy for peace. At the same time further experience with other Allied control commissions under Soviet supervision elsewhere in central and eastern Europe began to indicate that without a military presence little scope remained for non-Soviet influence in the area. Once implicated in the occupation of Austria, Americans preferred to think of it as a temporary measure without long-term political importance. American military plans for the postwar era envisioned a ring of off-shore bases around the North American continent and a friendly Europe, but excluded long-term occupation schemes or political responsibility in Europe, and particularly in Austria. The British, on the other hand, hoped to shore up their influence in central and southeastern Europe by deploying reluctant American power to reinforce their own waning strength. Stalin, it appears, encouraged an American presence in Austria as a buffer between the British and the Soviets. However, the occupation of Austria did not end as quickly as expected, nor could interallied agreement as to the country's future be reached.

In this way postwar Western policy towards Austria and the Second

Austrian Republic's self-image came to be anchored in the occupationist thesis. Largely the work of Anglo-American propagandists, political scientists, international jurists, and statesmen, this interpretation served to justify the Allies' continuing presence in Austria. It also acted as a welcome buttress for the Austrian people, who wanted to sever their connections with the recent Nazi past and construct a new political framework for their country. Once the Allies decided to stress Austria's wartime occupation together with its liberation and restoration to national independence rather than dwell on its unification or cooperation with Nazi Germany, the door was opened to a new, more positive Austrian self-image. The Austrians accepted the Allies' gift of a clean bill of national health, which enabled them to concentrate after the war on national reconciliation rather than large-scale retribution for questionable wartime activities. Postwar Austria thus derived substantial legal and moral benefits from the occupationist theory. Small wonder that the Moscow Declaration came to be referred to in Austria with all due reverence. But at the same time Austrians were forced to experience the bitter difference between public declarations and political reality. For the vagaries of postwar East-West relations and the four-power occupation of Austria did not fulfil the apparent promise of the Moscow Declaration. Only after successive disappointments did the Austrians manage in 1955 to escape the inheritance of sceptical Allied perceptions about their country's prospects and restrictive occupation policies to discover their own true national independence and neutrality.

The swift and unexpected advent of the Cold War completely changed the postwar scenario predicted by Anglo-American planners. As a result they discovered to their chagrin that history is not always a reliable aid in predicting the future. During the war emminently qualified diplomatic officials and academic experts had conducted extremely thorough historical seminars in the belief that a study of the past would reveal how to build a better future. In the process of trying to rectify past mistakes they sought to reconstruct Europe again within a familiar historical framework. However, with hindsight, it is possible to conclude that they paid insufficient attention to new, emerging ideological and power relationships pointing towards the postwar presence of the United States and the Soviet Union in the heart of Europe. One of the leading historical lights in the planning process during World War II, Arnold Toynbee, ruefully reflected towards the end of his life that planning for the future on the basis of history rests on weak foundations. "I don't think that anyone can apply this past experience," he stated, "even if one can accumulate a large number of examples of it, to the future and make predictions on the strength of it. Our knowledge of the 'variables' will never be complete enough."[3]

Appendices

SYNOPSIS

1 *Great Britain and the 1938 Anschluss*

- a. British Protest to Germany, 11 March 1938
- b. British Protest in Berlin, 12 March 1938
- c. Halifax Reprimand to Henderson, 12 March 1938
- d. Chamberlain Statement in the House of Commons, 14 March 1938
- e. Halifax Statement in the House of Lords, 16 March 1938
- f. Chamberlain Speech on the Anschluss, 8 April 1938

2 *The United States and the 1938 Anschluss*

- a. State Department Press Release, 19 March 1938
- b. Answer to German Notes, 21 March 1938
- c. Stimson on Nonrecognition of the Anschluss, 4 April 1938
- d. Note to Germany on the Anschluss, 5 April 1938
- e. Note to Germany on Austrian Indebtedness, 5 April 1938

3 *The 1943 Declaration on Austria*

- a. British Policy and Draft Moscow Declaration, 28 August 1943
- b. American Response and Draft Moscow Declaration, 9 October 1943

c. The Moscow Declaration on Austria, 30 October 1943

4 *Post-Moscow Declaration: Anglo-American and Austrian Views, 1943-5*

a. Austria an Enemy State (American), 23 November 1943
b. No Austrian State Continuity (American), 6 January 1944
c. Austrian Nationalism (British), 23 April 1944
d. Reestablishment of an Austrian State (American), 14 August 1944
e. Austria within a Federation (American), 11 January 1945
f. State of War with Austria (British), 18 January 1946
g. Austrian Foreign Minister's Reaction to the American Statement on Austria of 28 October 1946
h. British Reaction to the October 1946 American Statement on Austria

Appendix 1

GREAT BRITAIN AND THE 1938 ANSCHLUSS

a. *British Protest to Germany, 11 March 1938*[1]

Viscount Halifax to Sir N. Henderson (Berlin), 11 March 1938.

Please represent to German Government that, if this report is correct, His Majesty's Government feel bound to register protest in strongest terms against such use of coercion, backed by force, against an independent State, in order to create a situation incompatible with its national independence.

As I have already pointed out to German Minister of Foreign Affairs here, such action is bound to produce gravest reactions of which it is impossible to foretell the issue.

I am informing the French Government that this protest is being made in case they wish to act likewise.

b. *British Protest in Berlin, 12 March 1938*[2]

Sir N. Henderson to Viscount Halifax, Berlin, March 12 1938.

I greatly regret failure of my efforts to prevent series of events as regards Austria. It can however be stated that everything that could be done short of direct threat of force, was done to save Austria from the consequences of Dr. Schuschnigg's ill-conceived and ill-prepared folly. French Ambassador was handicapped by non-existence of French Government so that the brunt of battle fell practically entirely on myself and my personal interventions with Baron von Neurath and Field-Marshal Göring, as well as written communication to the former, constitute in my view the utmost that could be done. I did not attempt to see the Chancellor because firstly I had no doubt but that some excuse would have been found to put me off until after the accomplished fact and because interview on March 3 left no shadow of doubt that my representations would have led to no result. I felt it undesirable to expose His Majesty's representative to this double rebuff.

I warned both Baron von Neurath and Field-Marshal Göring that German action would inevitably do irretrievable harm in England in respect of any attempt on our part to come to an understanding with Germany. Both professed to deplore this while asserting that their action was unavoidable in view of Dr. Schuschnigg's provocation.

c. *Halifax Reprimand to Henderson, 12 March 1938*[3]

Viscount Halifax to Sir N. Henderson (Berlin), 12 March 1938.

I am disturbed to see from your telegram No. 97 that you told General Göring that you "reluctantly agreed that Dr. Schussnigg had acted with precipitate folly" in ordering a plebiscite. It may well be your personal view, as stated in your telegram No. 98 that "Dr. Schuschnigg has let us all down badly by his rash decision taken without consulting members of his Government," and you are of course entitled to express that view in your communications to me. But I cannot help feeling that by the admission to General Göring quoted above you cannot but have diminished the force of the protest you were instructed to make in my telegram No. 79.

There was not, I think, any doubt as to my own views on the subject of the plebiscite. They were fully set out in my telegram No. 71 in which I recorded my remarks on this subject to Herr von Ribbentrop and it is of first importance that any communication you make to German Government should conform to the instructions you receive from me and to the attitude I myself adopt in my communications to German representatives here.

In general I think it desirable that in any discussion you may have with General Göring or others, you should be particularly careful that you do not go beyond any instructions given or diminish in subsequent conversation force of any protest you may be instructed to make.

d. *Chamberlain Statement in the House of Commons, 14 March 1938*[4]

... His Majesty's Government have throughout been in the closest touch with the situation. The Foreign Secretary saw the German Foreign Minister on 10th March and addressed to him a grave warning on the Austrian situation and upon what appeared to be the policy of the German Government in regard to it. In particular Lord Halifax told him that His Majesty's Government attached the greatest importance to all measures being taken to ensure that the plebiscite was carried out without interference or intimidation. Late on 11th March our Ambassador in Berlin registered a protest in strong terms with the German Government against the use of coercion, backed by force, against an independent State in order to create a situation incompatible with its national independence. Such action, Sir Neville Henderson pointed out, was bound to produce the gravest reactions, of which it would be impossible to foretell the issue. Earlier that day I made earnest representations in the same sense to the German Minister of Foreign Affairs, with whom my Noble Friend also had two further conversations on that day.

... It might seem unnecessary to refute rumours that His Majesty's Government had given consent if not encouragement to the idea of the absorption of Austria by Germany, were there not evidence that these are being sedulously put about in many quarters. There is, of course, no foundation whatever for these rumours. The statement which I have made shows clearly that His Majesty's Government emphatically disapprove, as they have always disapproved, actions such as those of which Austria has been made the scene.

... The House may desire me to repeat what our position in regard to Austria was. We were under no commitment to take action *vis-à-vis* Austria, but we were pledged to consultation with the French and Italian Governments in the event of action being taken which affected Austrian independence and integrity, for which provision was made by the relevant articles of the Peace Treaties.

... It is quite untrue to suggest that we have ever given Germany our assent or our encouragement to the effective absorption of Austria into the German Reich. We had, indeed, never refused to recognize the special interest that Germany had in the developement of relations between Austria and herself, having regard to the close affinities existing between the two countries. But on every occasion on which any representative of His Majesty's Government has had opportunities to discuss these matters with representatives of the German Government, it has always been made plain that His Majesty's Government would strongly disapprove of the application to the solution of these problems of violent methods.

... The hard fact is – and of its truth every hon. Member can judge for himself – that nothing could have arrested this action by Germany unless we and others with us had been prepared to use force to prevent it. I imagine that according to the temperament of the individual the events that are in our minds today will be the cause of regret, of sorrow, perhaps of indignation. They cannot be regarded by His Majesty's Government with indifference or equanimity. They are bound to have effects which cannot yet be measured. The immediate result will be to intensify the sense of uncertainty and insecurity in Europe. Unfortunately, while the policy of appeasement would lead to a relaxation of the economic pressure under which many countries are suffering today, what has just occured must inevitably retard economic recovery, and, indeed, increased care will be required to ensure that marked deterioration does not set in.

e. *Halifax Statement in the House of Lords, 16 March 1938*[5]

... The problem of Austria, of course, has been with us ever since the War ended with the break-up of the Austro-Hungarian monarchy, leaving a small German Austria stranded in the Danubian plains ... They [successive British governments] have never supposed that the *status quo* in Austria could be maintained for all time. They have been perfectly willing to recognize the special interest of the German Government in relations between Germany and Austria. Therefore they have been perfectly willing to contemplate revision of the Peace Treaties ... I have never in any conversation I have had with German leaders taken any line but this: that, while I did not suppose that anyone in this country was concerned to maintain the *status quo* in Europe for all time, what they [resisted was that this change] should be made in Europe by violence, or by something approaching violence, that might lead to incalculable consequences.

... It was, indeed, the desire to avoid such sharp disturbance, I suppose, that in part moved the framers of the Treaties to do what they did. They recognized the special position of Austria and the peculiar problem that it represented owing to its purely German character. They foresaw, I imagine, that Austria might at some time wish to join Germany. But they also realized that such a union, involving, as it would, the transfer of something like 32,000 square miles of territory and something like 7,000,000 human beings from one sovereignty to another would cause a serious and, in certain cases, a dangerous shifting of the balance of power in that part of Europe ...

... I do not fancy that even he [Lord Cecil] would say that any British policy short of war could have checked the events of the last ten days ... That [Austrian] independence, in complete disregard of treaty provisions, has disappeared overnight, and the world, therefore, has been presented with a *fait accompli* in a fashion and in a setting of accompanying circumstances for which I can recall no parallel in history ...

These facts, I suggest, must be squarely faced, and the conclusion that I reach is that the League, though it has a perfect legal right to interest itself in the question, cannot conceivably do anything at this moment which would compel Nazi Germany to turn back from the course on which she has now embarked. His Majesty's Government are therefore bound to recognize that the Austrian State has now been abolished as an international entity and is in the process of being entirely absorbed into the German Reich. They do so indeed without waiting for the plebiscite, the result of which, in view of the circumstances in which they are going to be held, is a foregone conclusion ... [end of statement on Austria]

f. *Chamberlain Speech on the Anschluss, 8 April 1938*[6]

Our policy is not one of dividing Europe into two opposing *blocs* of countries, each arming against the other amidst a growing flood of ill-will on both sides, which can only end in war. That seems to us to be a policy which is dangerous and stupid. You may say we do not approve of dictatorships. I think, perhaps, most of us in this room do not approve of them, but there they are. You cannot remove them. We have to live with them, and to us in the Government it seems that, while we must continue to arm until we can get a general agreement to disarm, it is only common sense that in the meantime we should try to establish friendly relations with any country willing to be friends with us. We should take any and every opportunity to try to remove any genuine and legitimate grievances that may exist.

... I mentioned just now those events which took place just a month ago [in Austria], and which terminated in the inclusion of Austria in the German Reich. I do not think that the people of this country would want to interfere in a case where two States desired to join together, but there were features about the methods which were employed in this particular case of union which were extremely distasteful to His Majesty's Government, and which profoundly shocked public opinion.

Appendix 2

THE UNITED STATES AND THE 1938 ANSCHLUSS

a. *State Department Press Release, 19 March 1938*[1]

Department of State Press release no. 132.

On March 17, 1938, the Minister of the Republic of Austria, Mr. Edgar Prochnik, informed the Department of State that, as a result of the developments which have occurred in Austria, that country has ceased to exist as an independent nation and has been incorporated in the German Reich; that therefore the Austrian mission to this country, of which he had been the head, has been abolished; and that the affairs of the mission have been taken over by the Embassy of Germany. The German Ambassador has informed the Department of State that he has assumed the functions hitherto performed by the Minister of Austria.

The events pertaining to the changes which have taken place in the status of Austria will necessitate, on the part of the Government of the United States, a number of technical steps, which are now being given appropriate consideration.

b. *Answer to German Notes, 21 March 1938*[2]

Handed by the United States Ambassador (Wilson) in Berlin to the German Foreign Minister, 21 March 1938.

Excellency: I have the honour to acknowledge the receipt of your notes dated March 14 and March 16, 1938, respectively, quoting a German law of March 13, 1938 and referring to the status of the Austrian Minister and the

Austrian Legation in Washington. I have taken note of the contents of these communications.

Accept, Excellency, the renewed assurances of my highest consideration.

Signed: Cordell Hull

c. *Stimson on Nonrecognition of the Anschluss, 4 April 1938*[3]

Mr. Hull asked me to come and see him at twelve o'clock today. I spent an hour with him ...

He told me of his difficulties with Great Britain.

He asked my views about the application of non-recognition to Austria. I told him I could hardly see how it fit. He told me confidentially that England was going to recognize Ethiopia and how he had protested against it. I told him how I had used non-recognition not as a legal concept but as a successful slogan to rally the League of Nations at a time when they were afraid to use their own machinery and also for use as a punishment upon the adjudication of guilt by the Assembly of the League at Geneva. He followed this very sympathetically. I told him I saw clearly his difficulties in fitting the doctrine into the present situation and was not surprised at all at the problem. At the same time it had served a very useful purpose as a prop for morals in the public mind and care should be taken not to lightly injure it. He fully agreed ...

He expressed himself very warmly about the importance of my keeping on with the work which I had done with the people on the Hill and how grateful he was for it and how he would try to follow it up ...

d. *Note to Germany on the Anschluss, 5 April 1938*[4]

Secretary of State to Ambassador (Wilson) in Germany, Washington.

Please address a formal note to the German Foreign Minister as follows:

Excellency, I am directed by my Government to inform Your Excellency as follows:

On March 17, 1938, the Minister of the Republic of Austria, Mr. Edgar Prochnik, informed the Department of State that, as a result of the developments which had occured in Austria, that country had ceased to exist as an independent nation and had been incorporated in the German Reich; that therefore the Austrian mission, of which he was the head, had been abolished; and that the affairs of the mission had been taken over by the Embassy of Germany. The German Ambassador has informed the Department of State that he has assumed the functions hitherto performed by the Minister of Austria.

The Government of the United States finds itself under the necessity as a practical measure of closing its Legation in Vienna, and of establishing a Consulate General. In the circumstances I am directed by my Government to request provisional consular status for Mr. John C. Wiley, Consul General; Mr. John H. Morgan and Mr. John H. Lord, Consuls, and Mr. G. Frederick Reinhardt and Mr Thomas R. Flack, Vice Consuls.

Accept, Excellency, the renewed assurances of my highest consideration.

We plan to give the text to the press at 1 p.m. Washington time April 6th.

Please repeat to Vienna for information.

e. *Note to Germany on Austrian Indebtedness, 5 April 1938*[5]

The Secretary of State to the Ambassador in Germany (Wilson), 5 April 1938.

Please deliver the following note to the German Foreign Office.

In view of the announcement made to the Government of the United States by the Austrian Minister on March 17, 1938, my Government is under the necessity for all practical purposes of accepting what he says as a fact and accordingly consideration is being given to the adjustment in its own practices and procedures in various regards which will be necessitated by the change of status of Austria.

In this connection I have to notify the German Government that the Government of the United States will look to it for the discharge of the relief indebtedness of the Government of Austria to the Government of the United States under the Debt Agreement signed May 8, 1930, and the Moratorium Agreement signed September 14, 1932 between the Government of the United States and the Government of Austria.

... [there follow details of Austrian indebtedness]

... This Government will expect that these obligations will continue to be fully recognized and that service will be continued by the German authorities which have succeeded in control of the means and machinery of payment in Austria. The welfare of numerous Austrian citizens is directly affected and this Government will appreciate prompt assurances on the subject.

We plan to give text to the press at 1 p.m. Washington time April 5th. Please repeat to Vienna for information.

Appendix 3

THE 1943 MOSCOW DECLARATION ON AUSTRIA

a. *British Policy and Draft Moscow Declaration 28 August 1943*[1]

The British Embassy [Washington] to the Department of State, 28 August 1943.

The attached paper entitled "The Future of Austria" has been considered by His Majesty's Government who would be glad to receive any comments on it which the United States Government may wish to offer.

It may be observed that the paper contemplates two stages in the future development of Austria after the war: first, the re-creation of an independent Austria, and second, the subsequent association of Austria with some form of Central or South-Eastern European confederation ... [Soviet dislike of confederations, which may be overcome] ... Indeed His Majesty's Government see an advantage, if it is at all practicable, in bringing about such an inclusion [of Austria in a confederation] as soon as possible after the war has ended, before there is time for opinion to harden on other lines. As the tide of war turns increasingly in favour of the United Nations, the possibility of causing embarrassment to Germany by encouraging resistance and sabotage in Austria improves. Anti-German feeling appears to be growing and there is some evidence that active resistance to the German regime is on the increase. On the other hand opinion in Austria seems to be aimless and in need of reassurance regarding the aims of the Allies for the future of the country. With this in mind and in the hope that the United States and Soviet Governments will be prepared to agree in principle to the re-creation of an independent Austrian state after the war, His Majesty's Government has prepared as a basis for discussion the draft of a declaration to be issued jointly as soon as possible by His Majesty's Government, the United States Government and the Soviet Government, making clear their desire to see re-established a free and independent Austria. A copy of this draft is attached and His Majesty's Government would be glad to receive as soon as convenient the United States' views upon it.

His Majesty's Government are also consulting the Soviet Government on this subject.

[Enclosure]

Revised Draft Declaration

Austria was the first free country to fall victim to Nazi aggression. In 1938 the Austrians were deprived by the Nazis of the right of self-government set forth in the Atlantic Charter, and re-affirmed by the United Nations.

The Governments of the United Kingdom, the Union of Soviet Socialist Republics and the United States of America are determined to liberate the Austrian people from German domination. Having taken counsel together in the spirit of the Atlantic Charter, they hereby declare that they regard the union imposed upon Austria by Germany on the 15th of March 1938 as null and void. They regard themselves in no way bound by any changes effected in Austria since that date. They declare that they wish to see re-established a free and independent Austria, which shall enjoy, in association with those neighbouring states which will be faced with similar problems, the political and economic security which is the only basis for lasting peace.

The Austrian people must, however, remember that they have a responsibility which they cannot evade, and that in the final settlement account will inevitably be taken of the part they play in assisting to expel the German invader.

b. *American Response and Draft Moscow Declaration, 9 October 1943*[2]

The Department of State to the British Embassy, 9 October 1943.

The Department of State has examined with attention the document attached to the *aide-mémoire* of the British Embassy of August 28.

The status of Austria as set forth in the Foreign Office's secret paper "The Future of Austria," and the observations made therein as to the prospects for a viable independent Austria are in general concordant with the Department's views.

The Department is also agreeable to the proposal that a declaration concerning Austria be made jointly by the British, Soviet and American Governments. In substance the draft text submitted with the *aide-mémoire* as a basis of discussion would be acceptable to the Department. Since, however, the American Government has not yet had occasion for a definite statement of policy on the matter of federations or confederations in Central and Eastern Europe, the Department would prefer that the text of the declaration should not carry the implication that Austrian independence is to be conditioned by "association with neighbouring states," however desirable it may be that the way should be left open for Austria's inclusion in some regional structure.

The Department wold like to make two further comments, both matters of drafting rather than substance. First, it believes that the clause

"The Governments of the United Kingdom, the Union of Soviet Socialist Republics and the United States of America are determined to liberate the Austrian people ... " would be interpreted to indicate an action taken regardless of the will of the Austrian people, or without expectation of any Austrian contribution to the achievement of this libration. Second, the opening paragraph might well be recast since it refers to events preceding the formulation of the Atlantic Charter.

With these considerations in mind the Department has prepared a variant text of the British draft declaration. The alternative draft is attached hereto, for the Embassy's examination.

[Enclosure]

Having taken counsel together in the spirit of the Atlantic Charter, the Governments of the United Kingdom, the Union of Soviet Socialist Republics and the United States of America are agreed that Austria, the first free country to fall victim to Nazi aggression, shall be liberated from German domination.

They regard the union imposed upon Austria by Germany on the 15th of March 1938 as null and void. They consider themselves as in no way bound by any changes effected in Austria since that date. They declare that they wish to reestablish a free and independent Austria, and thereby to open the way for the Austrian people themselves to find, in association with those neighboring States which will be faced with similar problems, that political and economic security which is the only basis for lasting peace.

The Austrian people must, however, remember that they have a responsibility which they cannot evade, and that in the final settlement account will inevitably be taken of their own contribution to the liberation of their country.

C. *The Moscow Declaration on Austria, 30 October 1943*[3]

The Governments of the United Kingdom, the Soviet Union and the United States of America are agreed that Austria, the first free country to fall victim to Hitlerite aggression, shall be liberated from German domination.

They regard the annexation imposed upon Austria by Germany on March 15, 1938, as null and void. They consider themselves in no way bound by any changes effected in Austria since that date. They declare that they wish to see reestablished a free and independent Austria, and thereby to open the way for the Austrian people themselves, to find that political and economic security which is the only basis for lasting peace.

Austria is reminded, however, that she has a responsibility which she cannot evade for participation in the war on the side of Hitlerite Germany, and that in the final settlement account will inevitably be taken of her own contribution to her liberation.

Appendix 4

POST-MOSCOW DECLARATION 1943–5:

a. *Austria an Enemy State (American), 23 November 1943*[1]

Department of State, Legal Adviser, memorandum re: visit of Mr. Crotty, associated with Austrian exile Hans Rott who hoped to be recognized as temporary head of an Austrian government.

I told Mr. Crotty that I doubted the wisdom of undertaking to recognize Mr. Rott as the head of the former Austrian Government in view of the fact that that Government for all intents and purposes has been out of existence for more than five years; that the situation of the former Austrian Government is not analogous to that of Norway, Belgium, etc.; that Austria as a country is definitely in the war on the side of Germany and against the United States; that it would be somewhat incongruous for us to say that there is a fugitive Austrian Government in the United States cooperating on the side of the Allies in view of the actual internal situation in Austria itself, and the historical background; that while the Moscow Declaration, with respect to Austria, contemplates the re-establishment of that country as an independent state, this is to take place only after Austria has been liberated from German domination. I called his attention to the statement in the Declaration that Austria has a responsibility for participating in the war on the side of Germany, and that in the final settlement account will be taken of her own contribution to her liberation. I said that in the present state of the war it seemed to me premature to discuss the question of a government of independent Austria since much remained to be done in the military and administrative fields before the question of a legitimate government comes to the fore.

... Mr. Crotty expressed agreement with what I had said ... Finally, he asked whether I would be willing to express the same views to Mr. Rott, whom he desired to bring to the Department. I said that I thought that it would not be desirable for anyone in the Department to confer with Mr. Rott, although this was not entirely within my bailiwick, for the reason that it might give rise to undesirable speculation in various quarters and might well be misinterpreted. He likewise agreed with this.

(Department of State, Legal Adviser) Green H. Hackworth

b. *No Austrian State Continuity, 6 January 1944 (OSS draft)*[2]

The major problems are the establishment of a new state and the creation of favorable conditions for the development of a specific Austrian national consciousness.

... Because the Anschluss had integrated completely the Austrian political structure into the Third Reich, Austria had ceased to exist as a legal and administrative unit in February 1938 [*sic*], a fact acknowledged by the foreign powers. There exists therefore no legal continuity between the old Austrian Republic and the new state to be established. This conclusion is not only required by a correct legal construction of the historic events, but it recommends itself also for political considerations. Any other construction would lead to the thorny problem of which Austrian constitution should be deemed valid ...

c. *Austrian Nationalism, 23 April 1944 (PWE directive)*[3]

Summary

This study brings up to date the P.W.E. paper "Opinion and Morale in Austria" dated 6 Jan 1943, the findings of which are confirmed.

Austria is not to be regarded as a mere part of Germany, but also not as an ordinary satellite or occupied country. The difference may be expressed by saying that the Austrian has a local patriotism even stronger than that of a Bavarian, but no real *national* feeling in the British, French or even Bavarian sense. Genuine desire for local autonomy is probably almost universal; the Anschluss is unpopular, even among Austrian Nazis, because it proved to involve unexpected domination by "Prussians." Desire for national independence, though present, is probably less deep-seated. It is due partly to the association of Anschluss with war, which followed in the next year, leading to the association of Austrian independence with conditions of peace. It is considerably encouraged by the belief that an independent Austria would receive more favourable treatment from the victorious Allies than a part of Germany. Many intelligent Austrians do not believe that Austria is capable of permanent independent existence. Continued attachment to a democratic Germany is favoured particularly by the parties of the Left. Attachment to Bavaria on the one side or the states of the Danube basin on the other is favoured (1) by advocates of a revived Habsburg empire and (2) by those who believe that the Allies would forbid a continuation of the Anschluss. Many dislike the prospect of attachment to the Danubian states on any terms implying the equality of German-speaking with non-German peoples.

The natural "softness" of the Austrian character and the weakness of the patriotic motive for unreasoning hope combine to produce greater pessimism regarding Germany's chances in the war in Austria than in Germany proper. There seems also to be much more active opposition to the Nazi regime in Austria, to which the authorities replied during 1943 with a policy of mass executions. But it is possible that this opposition is largely ineffective. In the first place, Austrians are more disposed to talk than to act. In the second place, the opposition is divided against itself regarding the objectives to be aimed at.

d. *Reestablishment of an Austrian State, 14 August 1944 (OSS document)*[4]

A. The Present State of Austria

Austria has ceased to exist as a state and as a social and economic entity. It is even doubtful whether an Austrian national sentiment comparable to that of other European nations exists.

The Non-existence of the Austrian State

The Anschluss completely integrated the Austrian political structure, both on the national and local levels, into the Nazi organization of "Greater Germany," thus destroying Austria as a legal and administrative entity.

... The rule of the Nazis and Austrian participation in the war have created a desire for seperation from Germany, based on the hope to escape from the consequences of defeat. The Moscow Declaration will probably re-inforce this attitude. However, the demand for Anschluss is likely to become again a dominant issue in Austria, if independence were followed by continued economic deprivation and if union with Germany would strengthen the position of any significant Austrian political group ...

B. Problems under Military Occupation

1) To establish Austria as a state, though only a provisional one, with the frontiers of 1938;

2) To establish a provisional government, though only as an instrument ...

a) *The Creation of a Provisional State*

The establishment of an Austrian political organization will necessitate the creation of a provisional state to furnish the basis both legal and pragmatic for the formation of a free and democratic Austrian government.

... The view has been entertained that the enactment of the 1920–1925–1929 constitution is mandatory in order to provide for the legal continuity of the new Austrian government. Legal continuity, however, is a mere fiction and is, besides, not even desirable ... In view of these considerations, it would seem desirable to provide an entirely new framework for the independent Austrian state. In the provisions for the establishment of this state, military government should adopt the basic provisions of the Austrian constitution of 1920–1925–1929 as a provisional arrangement, yet without specific reference to this constitution.

e. *Austria within a Federation, 11 January 1945 (U.S. State Department)*[5]

This review is based on previous memo (PWC 218, 217A) of 8 June 1944, which was reviewed by the joint Chiefs of Staff and approved by the President.

... Independence alone, however, would not be an adequate basis for Austria's future. The continuation of the revived state will depend on a solution of its political and economic relations with its neighbours. [This may consist of special economic relations, political federation] or even a merger of sovereignties, provided that such an arrangment is approved by the parties concerned and is acceptable to the international organization.

f. *State of War with Austria, 18 January 1946 (Dominion Affairs)*[6]

Austria

In New Year broadcast to the Austrian people Dr. Renner expressed disappointment at absence of Austria from list of countries with which, according to communiqué of Moscow Conference, peace treaties were to be concluded. He said that, on the one hand, there was no pretext for a peace treaty in the real sense, for there was no Austrian state when war began or ended and Austria[n] Republic had never made war; on the other hand a treaty was required to settle such questions as replacement for what Germany owed Austria, Austria's obligations to the Allies, part of Austrian national inheritance to remain to her, and scope and duration of the occupation.

2. In our view a peace treaty for Austria will be necessary. Recent recognition of Austrian Government and of restoration of Austrian independence does not terminate state of war. If this were not the case, it would mean that Austria was no longer bound by the terms of the German surrender which, on Dr. Renner's theory, would only have applied to Austria so long as she was part of Germany, whereas in fact newly recognized Government remains subject to terms of surrender. Moreover these terms constitute basis of Allied Council's existence ...

g. *Austrian Foreign Minister's (Karl Gruber) Reaction to the American Statement on Austria of 28 October 1946*[7]

In the meantime the American Goverment went ahead and decided on an important diplomatic step that was to improve our position considerably. For some time the European Division of the State Department had been busy working out a declaration that would grant [*sic*] Austria the status of a friendly country. This was the first [*sic*] really constructive step in the policy of a great power towards Austria, although a significant interlude had delayed its actual completion. When the State Department canvassed London and Paris on the proposed declaration, the former made known its opposition and nightly telephone calls were required to settle various differences of opinion. Behind the scenes it was whispered that the British wanted the Austrian question soft-pedalled.

Nevertheless, on 28 October 1946, on the occasion of my visit to President Truman, the State Department eventually published the declaration. It stated that:

In order to clarify the attitude of the US Government in this matter, the US Government recognizes Austria for all purposes, including legal and administrative, as a liberated country comparable in status to other liberated areas and entitled to the same treatment, subject only to the controls reserved to the occupying powers in the new agreement on control machinery in Austria of June 28th, 1946.

Pointing to our record the declaration added that in the United States view this was "adequate reason for all members of the United Nations to regard Austria as a liberated country."

h. *British Reaction to the October 1946 American Statement on Austria (Dominion Affairs)*[8]

Austria

My telegram circular D. 933 of lst November. After issue by United States Government of statement of 28th October about their attitude towards status of Austria, enquiry was received from the United States Government as to our views on the same question. United Kingdom Ambassador at Washington has now been instructed to inform State Department that whilst United Kingdom Government in virtue of their recognition *de jure* and *de facto* of the Anschluss of 1938 regard Austria as having necessarily inherited enemy status of Germany, so that technical state of war existing between United Kingdom and Austria must continue until it is specifically terminated, we have no desire to accord undue emphasis or significance to this fact at present time. And, although the

United Kingdom's formal position is thus somewhat different from that of the United States, we believe that there is no discrepancy between policies of the two Governments towards Austria ...

2. State Department is also being informed confidentially that, should Austrian Treaty be unduly delayed, we might be prepared to consider issuing unilateral declaration, similar to that just made by the United States Government, designed to abrogate the technical enemy status of Austria, in advance of conclusion of a general treaty ...

Notes

PREFACE

1 Cronin, *Great Power Politics and the Struggle over Austria*, 11.

2 Fritz Molden, "Bewältigen – nicht verdrängen," in Eberhard Strohal, ed., *Österreich: Was wirklich geschah: Fragen und Antworten und Fakten zur Zeitgeschichte* (Wien 1987), special issue of *Rot-Weiss-Rot* published for Austrians abroad, 2. Also "Der Staat, den alle wollten," ibid., 23. Renewed interest in researching Austria's postwar period, when both domestic pressures for the reintegration of ex-Nazis and external pressures for integrating Austria into the Western system overlapped, is evident in recent works such as Riedelsperger, *The Lingering Shadow of Nazism*; Rathkolb, "US-Entnazifizierung in Österreich," and "US-Medienpolitik in Österreich"; Knight, "Britische Entnazifizierungspolitik in Österreich;" Wagnleitner, "Die kulturelle Reorientierung Österreichs nach dem zweiten Weltkrieg;" and Meissl et al., *Verdrängte Schuld, verfehlte Sühne*.

3 In reply to Gordon Craig, "The Waldheim File", *New York Review of Books*, 9 October 1986, Professor Gerhard Stourzh of the University of Vienna wrote that the Allies saw Austria as a special case. Clearly not convinced, Craig asked "why there was any disposition whatsoever on the part of the Western powers to treat Austria as a special case. This still puzzles me." Ibid., "Letters," 26 February 1987. In 1985, Whitnah and Erickson also suggested that the Allies doubted early in the war whether Austria should be liberated because of the advanced nazification of the country. *The American Occupation of Austria*, 5. At the same time, they accepted – without explanation of the change – that in late 1943 the Allies committed themselves to Austria through the Moscow Declaration.

4 Cronin, *Great Power Politics and the Struggle over Austria*, 11.

INTRODUCTION

1 Hoff-Wilson, "The Future of American Diplomatic History," 11ff.
2 Gaddis, "The Emerging Post-Revisionist Synthesis on the Origins of the Cold War," 171ff; Gardner, Kaplan and Kuniholm, "Responses to John Lewis Gaddis, 'The Emerging Post-Revisionist Synthesis on the Origins of the Cold War,' " 191–204 ; Leffler, "The American Conception of National Security and the Beginnings of the Cold War, 1945–1948."
3 Rauchensteiner, *Der Sonderfall*, 15. A recent military history of United States occupation of Austria took the same position: " ... at length the United States officials repudiated Hitler's actions against Austria and agreed with Great Britain and the USSR in October 1943 to issue the Moscow Declaration, which energetically declared that Austria would be liberated and extended a better status than her German captors following the war." *The Occupation of Austria*: xi, 6ff, and 264.
4 Woodward, C. Vann, *American Attitudes to History*, 1–20, as reproduced in Winks, ed., *The Historian as Detective*, 24–38.
5 Becker, "Everyman His Own Historian," 221ff; Woodward, *American Attitudes*, 37–8.
6 Botz, "Comments" on papers by two North Americans on Austrian Nazis in 1938 and after, in *Austrian History Yearbook* 14, (1978): 175.
7 These will be more fully discussed in chapter 1.
8 Collingwood, *The Idea of History*, 249ff; Gottschalk, *Understanding History*, 41ff and 53ff.
9 Bollmus, "Österreichs Unabhängigkeit im Widerstreit," 56–75; Goldner examined the State Department files in the National Archives in Washington and those of the Franklin D. Roosevelt Library in Hyde Park, New York, for his book, *Das einsame Gewissen*, but admitted that he was unable to discover authentic American policy for Austria; Maimann's first-class study of Austrian exiles in Great Britain, *Politik im Wartesaal*.
10 Fellner, "Die aussenpolitische und völkerrechtliche Stellung Österreichs 1938 bis 1945," in Weinzierl and Skalnik, eds., *Österreich. Die Zweite Republik*, 1: 53–79. One of the best recent accounts is Rauchensteiner's *Der Sonderfall*, 15–32. Some work has been undertaken on Soviet attitudes towards Austria, but it suffers from a dearth of primary sources. See Stearman, *Die Sowjetunion und Österreich 1945 bis 1955*; Vogelmann, "Die Propaganda der österreichischen Emigration in der Sowjetunion"; Fischer, *Sowjetische Deutschlandspolitik im Zweiten Weltkrieg 1941–1945*; Aichinger, *Sowjetische Österreich-Politik 1943–1945*. For a view of the Free French policy towards Austria, marked by concern about Austria's postwar viability, see Lettner, "Die französische Österreichpolitik von 1943 bis 1946."
11 Stourzh's masterly *Geschichte des Staatsvertrages 1945–1955*, 4.

12 Ibid.; Rauchensteiner, *Der Sonderfall*; Verdross, *The Permanent Neutrality of Austria*, and his "Aussenpolitik," in Weinzierl and Skalnik, eds., *Das neue Österreich*, 1: 85–150.

13 See the papers given at the 1967 international meeting organized by the United States Committee to Promote Studies of the Habsburg Monarchy, reproduced in "The Nationality Problem in the Habsburg Monarchy in the 19th Century," especially the reports by Schroeder and Fellner about the growth of Habsburg studies in North America and Western Europe.

14 Bader, *Austria between East and West, 1945–1955*; Ewing, *Peace through Negotiations*; Luza, *Austro-German Relations in the Anschluss Era*; Mase, *Country without a Name*; Hiscocks, *The Rebirth of Austria*; Stearman, *Die Sowjetunion und Österreich*.

15 Stanley, "British Policy and the Austrian Question, 1938–1945"; Wagnleitner, "Grossbritannien und die Wiederherstellung der Republik Österreich," and "Diplomatische Dokumente zur Geschichte Österreichs 1918–1945"; Barker, *Austria 1918–1972*.

16 Kann, *The Multinational Empire*, 1: 341; Fellner, "The Dissolution of the Habsburg Monarchy"; Holborn, "The Final Dissolution of the Habsburg Monarchy"; Mamatey, "Legalizing the Collapse of Austro-Hungary."

17 Beer, "Allierte Planung, Propaganda und Penetration, 1943–1945," in *Das Burgenland im Jahre 1945*; Stafford, "The Detonator Concept", and *Britain and European Resistance*; Keyserlingk, "Otto Strasser in Churchills Strategie der nationalen Erhebungen, 1940–1942"; Balfour, *Propaganda in War 1939–1945*, 438–9.

18 Beer, "Alliierte Planung, Propaganda und Penetration 1943–1945," 67–88. Although referring to some OSS sources, this interesting article still leans mainly on the printed public record and secondary sources.

19 The most recent American book using Department of War, Civil Affairs Division material is Whitnah and Erickson, *The American Occupation*. See also Rauchensteiner, *Sonderfall*; Holborn, *American Military Government*; Donnison, *Civil Affairs and Military Government in Northwest Europe, 1944–1946*; Muir, "Austria," in Balfour and Muir, eds., *Four-Power Control in Germany and Austria, 1945–1946*; Erickson, "The Zoning of Austria"; Ziemke, *The United States Army of Occupation in Germany, 1944–1946*.

CHAPTER ONE

1 Fellner, "The Dissolution of the Habsburg Monarchy"; Holborn, "The Final Dissolution of the Habsburg Empire"; Kerekes, "Österreich zwischen Anschlusspolitik und Donaukonföderation 1918–1919."

2 Pinson, *Modern Germany*, 3–4.

3 Low, "Otto Bauer, Austro-Marxism and the Anschluss Movement 1918–

1938"; Leichter, *Otto Bauer*; Fletcher, "Karl Leuthner's Greater Germany."

4 Low, *The Anschluss Movement 1918–1919*, 7, 452 and 458–9; also his "The Anschluss Movement (1918–1919)" and *The Anschluss Movement, 1931–1938*.

5 Barker, *Austria 1918–1945*, 15; Mamatey, "Legalizing the Collapse of Austro-Hungary"; Kann, "The Defeat of Austro-Hungary in 1918"; Mamatey, *The United States and East Central Europe 1914–1918*; Schmid, "Amerikanische Österreichpolitik zur Zeit der Pariser Friedenskonferenz 1919"; Hausmann, "Die amerikanische Aussenpolitik und die Entstehung der Republik Österreich 1917–1919"; Macartney and Palmer, *Independent Eastern Europe*, 341 and 351; Fellner and Maschle, *St. Germain im Sommer 1919*; Andics, *Der Staat der Keiner Wollte*, 66; Lorenz, *Der Staat Wider Willen*.

6 Kleinwächter, *Von Schönbrunn bis St. Germain*, 145–6.

7 Schausberger, *Der Griff nach Österreich*, 82–3; Kerekes, "Die wirtschaftliche und soziale Lage Österreichs," in Neck and Wandruszka, eds., *Beiträge zur Zeitgeschichte*, 81–94.

8 Pasvolsky, *Economic Nationalism of the Danubian States*, 95–6; also his "Obstacles to the Union of Austria with Germany," 520–8.

9 Kleinwächter, *Selbstbestimmung für Österreich*, 30.

10 Layton and Rist, *The Economic Situation of Austria*, a report for the League of Nations; Hertz, *Zahlungsbilanz und Lebensfähigkeit*; Pasvolsky, *Economic Nationalism*, 577. For the minority view that the First Austrian Republic was economically viable, see Schausberger, *Griff nach Österreich* 83–7. See also Rothschild, *Austria's Economic Development between the Two Wars*; Suval, *The Anschluss Question in the Weimar Era*, 177; and Hiscocks, *The Rebirth of Austria*, 6.

11 Wandruszka, *Geschichte der Republik Österreich*, 405; Gehl, *Austria, Germany and the Anschluss, 1931–1938*, 60ff; Leichtner, *Zwischen zwei Diktaturen*, 41ff; Stadler, "Engelbert Pernsdorfer"; Neck and Wandruszka, eds., *Beiträge zur Zeitgeschichte*. The most recent and thorough bibliography of the whole Anschluss question is in Low, *The Anschluss Movement, 1918–1938*, esp. xivff.

12 Klemperer, "On Austro-Fascism," 313–17; Pauley, "A Case Study in Fascism"; and Botz, "Comments," *Austrian History Yearbook* 12/13 (1976/1977): 274–9.

13 Williams, "The Aftermath of the Anschluss," and comments by Gerhard Botz, *Austrian History Yearboo* 14 (1978): 159ff.

14 Stolper, *Deutsch-Österreich als Sozial- und Wirtschaftproblem*, 111.

15 Preradovich, *Die Wilhelmstrasse und der Anschluss Österreichs, 1919–1933*; Suval, *The Anschluss Question*, 169.

16 Wagner and Tomkowitz, *Anschluss*, 44, 62 and 94–9.

17 Kelsen, *Die staatsrechtliche Durchführung des Anschlusses Österreichs*, 7; Sweet, "Seipel's View on the Anschluss," 323.

18 Hantsch, *Österreich* ; Wandruszka, "Grossdeutsche und kleindeutsche Ideologie," in Kann and Prinz, eds, *Deutschland und Österreich*, 17.
19 Srbik, *Metternich*, 1; on his *Deutsche Einheit*, Ross, "Heinrich Ritter von Srbik"; and Kohn, "AEIOU."
20 Winter, *Rudolf von Österreich*; Suval, "The Search for Fatherland"; and Large, "Richard von Kralik's Search."
21 Zöllner, *Histoire de l'Autriche*, 510; Orde, "Grossbritannien und die Selbstständigkeit Österreichs."
22 Kohn, "AEIOU," 513–27.
23 Luža, *Austro-German Relations in the Anschluss Era*; Botz, *Wien vom Anschluss zum Krieg*.
24 *Documents on British Foreign Policy 1919–1939*, 3rd ser., 1: 21–3, Viscount Halifax to Neville Chamberlain, 11 March 1938 (see appendix). For more detail see Stanley, "Great Britain and the Austrian Question," and Wagnleitner, "Grossbritannien und die Wiedererrichtung Österreichs," 2ff; Wathen, *The Policy of England and France towards the Anschluss of 1938*; Clute, *The International Legal Status of Austria 1938–1955*; and Verosta, *Die internationale Stellung Österreichs*.
25 Great Britain, *Parliamentary Debates. House of Commons*, 333: 14 March 1938; also quoted in Chamberlain, *In Search of Peace*, 69–76 (see appendix 1).
26 Wendt, *Economic Appeasement*, 460–80.
27 Great Britain. *Parliamentary Debates. House of Lords*, 5th ser., 108: 16 March 1938, 178–80 (see appendix 1).
28 Clute, *International Legal Status of Austria*, 97.
29 Ibid., 98.
30 Holborn, ed., *War and Peace Aims of the United Nations*, 1: 193.
31 Klusacek et al., eds., *Dokumentation zur österreichischen Zeitgeschichte*, 426.
32 Eden, *The Reckoning*, 290.
33 The speech is reprinted in the United States Department of State publication, Hull, *Our Foreign Policy*; see page 2 for quote.
34 Ibid., 10.
35 United States, Department of State, *Press Releases*, 1: no. 133, 19 March 1938.
36 Secretary of State Hull to the German Ambassador, Washington, 5 April 1938, *Foreign Relations of the United States* (hereafter referred to as *FRUS*), *Diplomatic Papers 1938*, 1: 473 and 2: 483–4 (see appendix 2); also quoted in Langer, *Seizure of Territory*, 162.
37 *FRUS*, 1938, 1:473 and 2: 483–4.
38 Ibid.
39 Ibid.
40 Assistant Under-Secretary of State Adolf A. Berle to Burleigh and Beckworth,

7 June 1939, United States, National Archives, Washington, DC (hereafter referred to as NA), Department of State, Record Group 59 (hereafter referred to as RG 59), numerical files 863.01/628; ibid., 863.01/796, Legal Advisor's memorandum of 10 September 1943.

41 Ibid., 863.01/636, Hackworth to A. Ornstein, 30 March 1940.

42 Ibid., 865D.01/589, European Division memorandum to the Near East Division, 22 May 1941, and Wallace Murray to S.H. Bishop, 22 May 1941.

43 Ibid., 740.00115EW39/3248, Berle to Under-Secretary of State Sumner Welles, 27 February 1942.

44 Ibid., 863.00/5–2142, Czernin of Austrian Action, with four pages of loyal Austrian signatures, to Franklin D. Roosevelt, 10 May 1942; ibid., 863.01/6–342, John C. Wiley to Hull, 21 May 1942.

45 Ewing, *Peace through Negotiations*, 11.

46 Hull's press statement of 27 July 1942, Department of State *Bulletin*, 6: press release no. 386, 660.

47 Ibid.

48 United States, Congress, House of Representatives, House resolution 458 reported on by Mr. Jarman, 3 March 1943, Report no. 1228, House Misc. Documents, 10845. See also 1943 House Document no. 477, Wright, *The Attitude of the United States towards Austria*; Vandenberg, ed., *Private Papers of Senator Vandenberg*, 47 and 92–104.

49 *FRUS 1943*, 1: annex 6 to the Anglo-Soviet-American communique' of the Conference of the Three Foreign Secretaries, Conference document no. 42, 761; also NA, RG 59, 740.0011, Moscow/10–43. For a typical, later view, see "Austria Is Warned To Earn Freedom," *New York Times*, 12 September 1944, wherein Hull reminded Austrians that only an armed uprising "would insure the *creation* [author's emphasis] of an Austrian state."

50 M.O. Hudson, Professor of International Law at Harvard and a judge of the Permanent Court of Justice, reviewed the *Digest*, and found the series a "magnificent undertaking." At the same time, he included a very sane caveat to the effect that "its value for purposes of international law will depend upon the circumstances of its formulation." *Harvard Law Review*, 55 (1941–1942): 321.

51 Jessup, "The Reality of International Law," 253.

52 Hackworth, ed., *Digest*, 1: 127–8.

53 Ibid., 161–6.

54 Ibid., 127.

55 Ibid., 431.

56 *FRUS*, 1938, 1: 148. The United States did not recognize Italy's conquest of Ethiopia, although Hull and his assistant Welles split over this at the time of the Anschluss. Braddick, "A New Look at American Foreign Policy during the Italo-Ethiopian Crisis," 72–3.

57 *Digest*, 1: 448–9.

58 Ibid., 543–8; 5: 349–72.

59 Assistant Secretary of State George S. Messersmith to John C. Wiley, Chargé d'affaires, Vienna, March 1938, *FRUS*, 1938, 1: 451–3.

60 Ibid., 1943, 3: 35, Minutes of Roosevelt conversation with Anthony Eden, 22 March 1943.

61 Draft statement in James Riddelberger to Matthews, General Hilldring, and Secretary of State, "Status of Austria," 22 October 1946. Department of State Archives, West Europe: Austria files 1946–9 (released to the author), FW 863.00/10–1846, noted with approval by Acheson. Text quoted in Whiteman, ed., *Digest*, 5: 900–1; Gruber, *Between Liberation and Liberty*, 80–3. This granting of the "status of a friendly country" to Austria was, according to Gruber, "the first constructive act of a great power towards Austria." Ibid., 82 (see appendix 4).

62 Whiteman, *Digest*, 5: 900. Great Britain and most of the Commonwealth countries until 1947–1948 saw Austria as a country still at war with them. See Keyserlingk, "Grundsatz oder Praxis?" 227.

63 Department of State, West Europe: Austria, 1946–1949, "Policy and Information Statement on Austria," 3 February 1947, a secret memorandum issued jointly by the State and War Departments; see also ibid., Mr. Hickerson, European Division, to all State Department division chiefs, 21 June 1946.

64 Austrian Federal Ministry for External Affairs (*Bundesministerium für Auswärtige Angelegenheiten*), letter to the author of 30 March 1981, Nr. 517.0017/1–11,1/81. This letter referred the author for more information to Stephan Verosta's *Die internationale Stellung Österreichs*.

65 Wright, "The Denunciation of Treaty Violators," 526; idem, with the exiled Austrian Professor Plöchl, *The Attitude of the United States towards Austria*, Congress, House documents 10845 and 477; idem, "The Legality of the Annexation of Austria by Germany," 621. Note the interchangeability of the two words "occupation" and "annexation" at this early stage of the discussion. The distinction between the two terms only arose later; see Clute, *The International Legal Status of Austria*, and Langer, *Seizure of Territory*.

66 Concerning public official publications such as *FRUS* or the *Digest*, Perkins warned: "There is a large number of questions that the State Department publications leave unanswered; the omissions, as we shall see, are fully as striking as the inclusions." "The State Department Speaks," 124; Hyde, *International Law Chiefly as Interpreted by the United States*, 2: 1533–4.

67 Langer, *Seizure of Territory*; Marek, *Identity and Continuity of States*; Verosta, *Die internationale Stellung Österreichs*. For an indication of a recent shift away from this principle, see Galloway, *Recognition of Foreign Governments*.

68 Langer, *Seizure of Territory*, 163 and 285; Marek, *Identity and Continuity*

of States, 8 and 131ff; Clute, *International Legal Status of Austria*, viii and 42ff.

69 Ostrower, "Secretary of State Stimson and the League"; Current, "The Stimson Doctrine and the Hoover Doctrine."

70 Clauss, "The Roosevelt Administration and Manchukuo, 1933–1941."

71 Langer, *Seizure of Territory*, 163 and 285; Marek, *Identity and Continuity of States*, 8 and 131ff.

72 Grayson, *Austria's International Position 1935–1953*; Steefer, "American Attitudes and the Development of Policy towards Austria 1938–1945."

73 Clute, *International Legal Status of Austria*, 42ff.

74 Stadler, *Austria*, 256; Ermacora, *Österreichische Verfassungslehre*, 63–9; Jedlicka, "Verfassungs- und Verwaltungsprobleme," 136; Stourzh, "Die Regierung Renner."

75 International Military Tribunal, *Trial of the Major War Criminals*, 1: 291, 309, and 318–19.

76 Lauterpracht, *Recognition in International Law*, 87–97; Kelsen, *Principles of International Law*, 260–4; Chen, *Principles of International Law*, 262, 762–4; Whiteman, *Digest*, 2: 60ff, 754–65, 780–7. On nonrecognition, ibid., 604ff.

77 Whiteman, *Digest*, 2: 327–36.

78 Ibid., 1: 918–19, quoting Chen, *The International Law of Recognition*, 270–2 and 290–2.

79 Ibid.

80 Ibid., 2: 753, note; 783–7, 1125–6; 10: 540–98.

81 Ibid., 2: 327–8, 783; 5: 900–6.

82 Ibid., 2: 330.

83 Ibid., 328–9, R.S. Hill memorandum, 2 March 1942.

84 Ibid., 329 and 331, Hackworth to the Chief of the European Division, 3 June 1943, and to Hull, 23 November and 30 December 1943.

85 Ibid., 333, State Department *Press Release*, no. 342, 7 January 1946.

86 Ibid., 334–5, Dulles statement of 15 May 1955 in Vienna.

87 Ibid., 334. Others also held that Austria became a sovereign state in 1955. Hiscocks, "Austrian Prospects," 240; "Contemporary Practice of the United Kingdom in the Field of International Law," *Digest*, 1: 271–2.

88 "Independent Austria," 92–5; Jessup, "Force under the Modern Law of Nations," 91; Whiteman, *Digest*, 785–6.

CHAPTER TWO

1 Low, *The Anschluss Movement*, xii-xiii.

2 Orde, "Grossbritannien und die Selbstständigkeit Österreichs," 224ff.

3 Harvey, John, ed., *The Diplomatic Diaries of Oliver Harvey*, 108.

4 Offner, "*American Appeasement*," 234–8; and Wilson, *A Career Diplomat*, chapter three.
5 Dilkes, "Baldwin and Chamberlain," in Butler, ed., *The Conservatives*, 271ff; and Douglas, "Churchill and Eden, 1937–1938," 97–116.
6 Chamberlain to Mrs. Morton Price, 16 January 1938, in Feiling, *The Life of Neville Chamberlain*, 324.
7 Gilbert, *Britain and Germany between the Wars*, 70–1; Watt, "Appeasement," and "Roosevelt and Neville Chamberlain."
8 Drummond, *British Policy and the Empire*, and his *Imperial Economic Policy*; Ovendale, *"Appeasement"*, 4.
9 Gladwyn, *Memoirs*, 90; and Feiling, *Chamberlain*, 325.
10 Diary entry of 29 July 1937, Jay Pierrepont Moffat Papers, Diary, vol. 39. Moffat was counsellor at the American embassy in London at the time.
11 Chamberlain to his sister Hilde, 23 January and 6 February 1938, in Reynolds, *The Creation of the Anglo-American Alliance*, 19.
12 Ibid., 22.
13 Johnson, *Sir Anthony Eden*, 146.
14 Eden, *Facing the Dictators* , 521. Sir Alexander Cadogan was an ex-ambassador to Peking.
15 Eden, *The Reckoning*, 3–4.
16 RIIA, Toynbee, ed., *Survey of International Affairs*, 1937, 1: 338–9.
17 Halifax, *Fullness of Days*, 183; *Documents on British Foreign Policy*, 3rd ser., 1: document nos. 39, 44, 46, and 47.
18 Ribbentrop to Auswärtiges Amt, Berlin, 20 November 1937, *German Diplomatic Documents*, ser. D, 1: 75.
19 Gilbert and Gott, *The Appeasers*, 78–9.
20 Gilbert, "Two British Ambassadors," in Craig and Gilbert, eds., *The Diplomats 1919–1939*, 2: 537–8.
21 Diary entry of 2 June 1937, W.E.Dodd and Martha Dodd, eds., *Ambassador Dodd's Diary*, 417.
22 Eden, *The Reckoning*, 7; Middlemas, *Diplomacy of Illusion*, 58.
23 *Documents on British Foreign Policy*, 3rd ser., 1: 8 and 11.
24 Dilks, ed., *The Diplomatic Diaries of Sir Alexander Cadogan*, 47; also see diary entry of 16 February 1938, *Diaries of Oliver Harvey*, 91.
25 C.H.Fone, "Summary of British Policy on Austria," 7 August 1942, PRO, FO 371, 30942.
26 Quoted in Barker, *Austria*, 113.
27 Viscount Halifax to Sir Neville Chamberlain, Berlin, 11 March 1938, PRO, Cabinet Records (CAB), 13(38)2.
28 Fone, "Summary of British Policy on Austria"; *Documents on British Foreign Policy*, 3rd ser., 1: 25; John Gilbert, U.S. chargé Vienna, to United States Secretary of State, 10 February 1938, *FRUS, 1938*, 1: 404.
29 Fone, "Summary of British Policy on Austria."

30 *Documents on British Foreign Policy*, 3rd ser., 1: 110 and 115; Gilbert, "Two Ambassadors," 537–8.

31 Great Britain, *Parliamentary Debates (Lords)*, 5th ser., 108: 16 March 1938, 170–80 (see appendix 1).

32 *Documents on British Foreign Policy*, 3rd ser., 1: 538.

33 Pauley, "A Case Study," 272.

34 Halifax, Great Britain, *Parliamentary Debates (Lords)*, 5th ser., 108: 16 March 1938, 178–80 (see appendix 1).

35 Fone, "Summary of British Foreign Policy on Austria."

36 Dilkes, ed., *Diaries of Sir Alexander Cadogan*.

37 Foreign Office legal expert Williams, 20 January 1945, PRO, FO 371, C263/83/3.

38 Stanley, "British Policy and the Austrian Question," 34.

39 Sir R. Campbell, British Ambassador to the United States, to Welles, 2 March 1942, PRO, FO 371, 30942.

40 Roosevelt to Bingham, 11 July 1937, in Nixon, ed., *Franklin D. Roosevelt and Foreign Affairs*, 2: 554.

41 Steele, "The Pulse of the People," 195ff; Cohen, *The Public's Impact on Foreign Policy*; Jonas, *Isolationism in America*; and Dallek, *Franklin D. Roosevelt and American Foreign Policy*, 101ff and 154–5.

42 Jablon, "The State Department and Collective Security"; and Dallek, *Franklin D. Roosevelt and American Foreign Policy*, 155.

43 Bohlen, *Witness to History*, 129.

44 See his reaction above to the *Panay* bombing. Also see Drummond, "Cordell Hull," in Grabner, ed., *An Uncertain Tradition*, 184ff. Hull later wrote that economics not politics were the key to foreign affairs, Hull, *Memoirs*, 1: 525.

45 Offner, "Appeasement Revisited."

46 The United States' share of exports to Germany declined from 11.5 per cent to 7.4 per cent between 1936 and 1940, and the share of German exports to the United States fell from 5 per cent to 2.8 per cent. On the other hand, American investment in Germany rose from 3.4 per cent of all American investments abroad to 5 per cent. Ibid., 374–6; and Hull, *Memoirs*, 2: 304.

47 Bohlen, *Witness to History*, 129.

48 *Ambassador Dodd's Diary*, 9–10; Hull, *Memoirs*, 1: 183.

49 Dodd to Roper, 14 August 1934, FDR, Official File (hereafter OF), 523; Messersmith memorandum, 22 March 1935, Department of State, *Peace and War*.

50 Dodd to Roosevelt, 28 October 1933, FDR, President's Personal File (hereafter PPF), 1043; Dodd to Roosevelt, 8 February 1934, FDR, President's Secretary's File (hereafter PSF), Dodd file, box 10; *Ambassador Dodd's Diary*, 117 and 126; and Dodd, *Through Embassy Eyes*, 148.

51 Ford, "Three Observers in Berlin," in Craig and Gilbert, eds., *The Diplomats*, 2: 452–3.
52 Born in 1883 to lower middle-class parents of Germanic background in Pennsylvania, Messersmith's social and professional background cut him off from the establishment men in the State Department. As an ex-schoolteacher, Messersmith could at first only become a member of the lowly consular service. Dallek, "Beyond Tradition"; and Moss, "George S. Messersmith."
53 Shafir, "George S. Messersmith," 32–41.
54 Messersmith's report to the Secretary of State, 26 July 1933, cited in *Peace and War*, 191; Lloyd C. Gardner called this a "prophetic dispatch," *Economic Aspects of New Deal Diplomacy*, 98.
55 Moss, "George S. Messersmith," 240–1.
56 Messersmith, "A Resumé of Some of the Major Factors in the Economic, Financial and Political Situation Facing Europe Today," late summer 1934, George S. Messersmith Papers, no. 450.
57 Dodd to Hull, 28 February 1934, NA, RG 59, A/B 611.6231/320.
58 Moss, "George S. Messersmith," 246.
59 Ambassador Dieckhoff to German Foreign Minister Baron von Neurath, 5 July 1937, in *German Diplomatic Documents*, ser. D, 1: 627.
60 Roosevelt to Moore, 5 April 1937, FDR, PSF, Dodd file, 27.
61 Dodd, *Through Embassy Eyes*, 360; and Hull memorandum, 14 January 1938, in *War and Peace*, no. 103.
62 Dieckhoff to Neurath, 5 August 1937 and 14 January 1938, in *German Diplomatic Documents*, ser. D, 1: 627 and 679.
63 See FDR, OF, 523G; PPF, 1043: PSF, boxes 10, 19 and 27.
64 Selby, *Diplomatic Twilight*, 74.
65 Moss, "George S. Messersmith," 246.
66 Kennan, *Memoirs*, 83–4.
67 Ibid., 66.
68 Ibid., 83–4; and Propas, "Creating a Hard Line towards Russia," 225–6; and Kennan, *Memoirs*, 83–4.
69 Hooker, ed., *The Moffat Papers*, 97ff and 146.
70 Ibid., 183.
71 Diary entry of 31 January 1938, Moffat Papers, Diplomatic Journal.
72 Ibid., diary entry of 10 January 1938.
73 Ibid., diary entry of 18 January 1938.
74 Ibid., diary entry of 10 February 1938.
75 Ibid., diary entry of 30 January 1938; diary entry of 19 March 1938, FDR, Adolf A. Berle Jr. Papers; and diary entry, Henry L. Stimson Papers, Yale University, 28: 155.
76 Diary entries of 11 November and 13 December 1937, Moffat Papers, Diplomatic Journal; diary entry of 1 November 1937, in Berle and Jacob, eds.,

Navigating the Rapids, 148.

77 Reynolds, *Creation of the Anglo-American Alliance*, 28–9.

78 Cabinet meeting of 17 February 1937, in Blum, ed., *From the Morgenthau Diaries*, 1: 498; and Ickes, *The Secret Diary*, 2: 274–5.

79 Reynolds, *Creation of the Anglo-American Alliance*, 31.

80 Diary entry of 22 February 1938, Moffat Papers, Diplomatic Journal; and Dallek, *Roosevelt and American Foreign Policy*, 156.

81 Entries of 12, 13, 19,and 20 February 1938, Moffat Papers, Diplomatic Journal.

82 Ibid., 10 March 1938.

83 Diary entries of 19 February 1938 and 29 June 1940, Ickes, *Secret Diary*, 1: 321 and 2: 216.

84 John Wiley's report to the Secretary of State, 19 February 1938, FDR, PSF, 23; and T. Smith, US Military Attaché, Berlin, to Washington, 9 March 1938, FDR, Harry Hopkins Papers, 18.

85 Diary entry of 16 February 1938, Berle, *Navigating the Rapids*, 164.

86 J. Wiley's report to the Secretary of State, 14 February 1938, *FRUS*, 1938, 1: 391–2.

87 Diary Entry of 15 February 1938, Moffat Papers, Diplomatic Journal.

88 Hull to Wiley, 15 February 1938, *FRUS*, Diplomatic Papers, 1938, 1: 396.

89 R minute, 27 July 1942, "Attitude of the United States to Austria," PRO, FO 371, 30942.

90 Berle, *Navigating the Rapids*, 169. This sort of immobilizing compromise recurred later in April 1938 over the British recognition of the Ethiopian conquest. Roosevelt personally supported nonrecognition, but following urgings from Chamberlain and Halifax, he announced that he saw British recognition of Italy's rule in Ethiopia with sympathetic interest because "it is proof of the value of peaceful negotiations." *FRUS*, 1938, Diplomatic Papers, 1: 143–8; and diary entries of April 18–24, 1938, Moffat Papers, Diplomatic Journal.

91 Diary entries of 14 and 15 March 1938, Moffat Papers, Diplomatic Journal.

92 Dieckhof to Foreign Office, Berlin, 15 March 1938, *Akten der Deutschen Auswärtigen Politik 1918–1945*, ser. D, 1: 391; Welles' memorandum "Recent Events in Austria," 14 March 1938, in Schewe, *Roosevelt and Foreign Affairs*, 2: no. 920; and diary entry of 12 March 1938, Moffat Papers, Diplomatic Journal.

93 Messersmith to Wiley, 16 March 1938, Messersmith Papers, no. 969.

94 Wiley to Moffat, 25 March 1938, FDR, Wiley Papers, 2.

95 Ibid., Wiley to Moffat, 1 April 1938.

96 Hull, *Memoirs*, 1: 575 and 578; and *New York Times*, 12 March 1938.

97 Diary entries of 16 and 18 February 1938, FDR, Berle Diary, Box 8.

98 Diary entry of 19 March 1938, Berle, *Navigating the Rapids*, 168.

99 Diary entry of 14 March 1938, Moffat Papers, Diplomatic Journal.

100 Ibid., diary entry of 15 March 1938.
101 Hull's press statement of 15 March 1938, Department of State, *Press Releases*, 1: no. 133; transcript of press conference of 15 March 1938, in Schewe, *Roosevelt and Foreign Affairs*, 2: no. 919; also entry of 15 March 1938, Moffat Papers, Diplomatic Journal.
102 Diary entry of 17 March 1938, Moffat Papers, Diplomatic Journal.
103 Hull's speech, in the State Department's *Our Foreign Policy*, 2 and 10.
104 Diary entry of 17 March 1938, Moffat Papers, Diplomatic Journal.
105 Press clippings in FDR, OF, 1275.
106 Ibid., *Newsweek*, 28 March 1938.
107 Ibid., *Commonweal*, 5 April 1938.
108 Nevins, *America in World Affairs*, 115; and Smith, *America and the Axis War*, 142.
109 *New York Herald Tribune*, 12 March 1938, and *Survey 1938*, 1: 595.
110 Jacobs, "Influence of World Events on 'Neutrality Opinion'," 48ff; Toynbee and Ashton-Gwatkin, eds., *The World in 1939*, 3; and Brunner, *Mandate from the People*, 9ff.
111 Hillgruber, *Hitlers Strategie*, 91; and Jacobs, "Influence of World Events on 'Neutrality Opinion'," 51.
112 Dieckhoff to Auswärtiges Amt, Berlin, 7 December 1937 and 18 April 1938, *Akten der deutschen Auswärtigen Politik 1918–45*, ser. D, 1: nos. 401 and 423.
113 Francis Gill Wickware, "What We Think About Foreign Affairs," *Harper's*, September 1939, 397–406.
114 Diary entry of 23 March 1938, Moffat Papers, Diplomatic Journal.
115 Ibid., 23 March 1938.
116 Ibid., 16 March 1938.
117 Ibid., 17 March 1938.
118 Stimson, *The Far Eastern Crisis*.
119 Devine, *The Reluctant Belligerent*, 16.
120 Morison, *Turmoil and Tradition*, 464.
121 Ibid., 282.
122 Stimson's letter to the editor of the *New York Times*, 7 October 1937.
123 J.H. Holmes, C.H. Strong, G. Macdonald and R.M. Schwartz to Stimson, telegram of 21 March 1938; Stimson's reply stated, "I think for me to join in urging upon the government the non-recognition policy at this delicate time would be both immodest and embarrassing to the government. They must decide the question entirely on what they know of the situation without any pressure from me." Stimson Papers, Box 27, file 9; also Levinson's letters to Stimson, 13 and 25 April 1938, to which Stimson did not even respond, ibid., file 20; also Stimson and Bundy, *On Active Service in War and Peace*, 234ff.
124 Diary entries of 24 March and 4 April 1938, Stimson Papers, Diary, 28 (see

appendix 2).
125 Ibid., diary entry of 24 March 1938 (see appendix 2).
126 Diary entry of 29 March 1938, Moffat Papers, Diplomatic Journal.
127 Hackworth memorandum, 18 March 1938, quoted in his memorandum of 10 September 1943, NA, RG 59, 863.01/769.
128 Entries of 29 March and 5 April 1938, Moffat Papers, Diplomatic Journal.
129 Ibid., diary entry of 5 April 1938.
130 FRUS, 1938, 1:473 and 2:483–4 (see appendix 2).
131 Diary entry of 5 April 1938, Moffat Papers, Diplomatic Journal.
132 Quoted in Shapardson, ed., *The United States in World Affairs*, 44–5.
133 Welles, *The Time for Decision*, 6–7 and 330–1.
134 Offner, "Appeasement Revisited," 381.
135 Ambassador Wilson, 16 April 1938, State Department, *Press Releases*, 1: no. 486 (see appendix 2).
136 Ickes, *Secret Diary*, 2: 344.
137 Dulles and Armstrong, "Legislating Peace," 2.
138 Hackworth to A. Ornstein, 30 March 1940, and Hull to Haight, 30 March 1940, NA, RG 59, 863.01/636 and 637.
139 Ibid., 863.01/628, Berle to Burleigh and Beckworth, initialled by Hackworth, Moffat, and J. Dunn.
140 Ibid., 863.01/769, Hackworth to Secretary of Labour, quoted in Hackworth's memorandum on Austria of 10 September 1943.
141 Ibid., 763.72113/2838, Hull to Attorney General, 27 April 1939.
142 Ibid., 863.01/648, P.T. Culbertson to S.R. Wachtell, 20 June 1941.
143 Bemis, "The Memoirs of Cordell Hull," 317–18; and Brune, "Considerations of Force in Cordell Hull's Diplomacy," 389–405.
144 British Ambassador in Washington, R.J. Campbell, to W. Strang, Foreign Office, London, 8 August 1942, PRO, FO 371, C8007/1364/18.
145 Cannon to Atherton, 1942, "The record shows that we accepted the Anschluss as accomplished although with some misgivings [concerning the use of force] ... voiced by other western nations." NA, RG 59, 863.00/5–2252.
146 State Department internal planning paper "P-UND" 18, 2 April 1942, NA, RG 59, H. Notter Papers, 58.
147 Jellinek, *System des subjektiven öffentlichen Rechtes*, 321.
148 Morgenthau, "The Problem of Neutrality," 111.

CHAPTER THREE

1 Diary entries of 12 September and 2 November 1939, Moffat Papers.
2 Reynolds, *Creation of the Anglo-American Alliance*, 77–8.
3 Loewenheim, Langley, and Jonas, eds., *Roosevelt and Churchill: Their Secret Correspondence*.
4 Hall, *North American Supply*, 60–8.

5 Leigh, *Mobilizing Consent*, 48–9.

6 Sherwood, *Roosevelt and Hopkins*, 236 and 243; Harbutt, "Churchill, Hopkins, and the 'Other' Americans." These personal, direct channels of communication bypassed the ambassadors, the State Department, and, to a lesser extent, the Foreign Office. Ibid., 239.

7 Butler, *Grand Strategy*, 2: chapters 20 and 22; Collier, *The Defence of the United Kingdom*, 504–5.

8 Diary entries of 25 May and 5 June 1941, Long, *The War Diaries*, ed. Israel; Stimson Diary, vol. 32, 133, vol. 33, 3, Stimson Papers; Ickes, *Secret Diary*, 3: 422–3; diary entry of 9 June 1941, Berle Diary, Berle Papers, FDR; diary entry of 9 June 1941, Moffat Papers.

9 Mastny, *Russia's Road to the Cold War*, 307.

10 Butler, *Grand Strategy*, 2: 423–7; Leutze, *Bargaining for Supremacy*, chapters 13–15.

11 Berle to Roosevelt and reply, 21 and 26 June 1941, FDR, PSF, 90; diary entry of 19 June 1941, FDR, Berle Diary; Eden to Cripps, 17 November 1941, PRO, FO 371, 29471; Sherwood, *Roosevelt and Hopkins*, 311.

12 Stafford, *Britain and European Resistance*; Keyserlingk, "Otto Strasser in Churchills Strategie der nationalen Erhebungen"; Medlicott, *The Economic Blockade*, 2 vols; Milward, *War, Economy and Society, 1939–1945*, 23–30; Hinsley, *British Intelligence in the Second World War*, 63–73.

13 Maimann, *Politik im Wartesaal*; Goldner, *Das einsame Gewissen*. Maimann dealt mainly with Austrian exile groups in Great Britain, Goldner with those in the United States.

14 "Internationales Symposium zur Erforschung des öster reichischen Exils," 2 and 52, for a bitter attack on Helene Maimann's claim that Austrian communist exiles had not really favoured a reestablished and independent Austria; Bollmus, "Österreichs Unabhängigkeit im Widerstreit," 56–75; Maimann, *Politik im Wartesaal*, 190 and 236.

15 Mankin minute to Robert, September 1940, and PM minute of 23 November 1942, PRO, FO 371, C10392/96/18 and C12132/46/18. The monarchist Free Austria Movement in Canada should not be confused with the Communist-dominated Free Austria Movement in Great Britain.

16 Ibid., C5627/30/3, Statement by Sir James Crigg in the House of Commons, 29 April 1944.

17 Ibid., 24376, Categories of exemptions from the tough enemy alien restrictions.

18 Maimann, *Politik im Wartesaal*, 14–16.

19 Ibid., 191.

20 Harrison minutes, 8 and 15 December 1943, PRO, FO 371, 34421.

21 Ibid.

22 Ibid., C4523/2951/18, C11816/321/18, Anthony Eden, secret Foreign Office print, "Free Austrian and Free German Movements," 18 June 1941.

23 Ibid.

24 Ibid., C3729/31/18, Secret Foreign Office print, "Free Austrian and Free German Movements," June 1943; also "The Future of Austria," mid-1943; ibid., C6930/30/3, Foreign Office Research Department paper, 19 May 1944.

25 Ibid., C1083/36/3, PM minute M311/5, 8 April 1945, and Cullis minute, 23 February 1945. Oliver Harvey, Eden's private secretary and in 1943 head of the Central Department of the Foreign Office, documented Eden's discomfort – and his own – with Churchill's personal style of foreign policy and rivalry on this issue with Eden. See entries of 30 July, 3 and 11 August, and 27 October 1941, *Harvey Diaries*. "A.E. worried as usual about P.M.'s method of running the war. He is convinced it cannot go on," ibid., 2 April 1941; "The P.M. is untamable. He cannot leave well enough alone," ibid., 29 October 1943; "I am only afraid the P.M. may rush to their rescue ... He is very definitely on the side of fallen royalty, Habsburg, Hohenzollern or Glucksburg," ibid., 26 April 1945.

26 C. W. Cannon memorandum, 19 November 1942, and Division of Foreign Activity Correlation to Berle, same date, NA, RG 59, 863.01/11–1942.

27 Ibid., 863.01/84, C.W. Cannon memorandum, 30 April 1942.

28 Department of State, *Press Releases*, 5: 24 November 1942.

29 Berle's record of conversation with the British Minister [*sic*], August 1942, NA, RG 59, 811.2221/3071 and 853.01/758.

30 Ibid., 811.2221/307, War Department memorandum, 29 August 1942.

31 Ibid., 863.00/6–642, John Wiley to Ray Atherton, European Division, Department of State, 6 June 1942.

32 G. Stanley, "Great Britain and Austria," 70–4.

33 Stimson to Roosevelt, April 1943, with FDR's handwritten "ok" to the suggestion to close down the battalion, FDR, PSF, 32A; ibid., OF, 5309, Biddle to FDR, 23 April 1943; Otto von Habsburg to Roosevelt, 1 June 1943, NA, RG 59, 863.01/779.

34 Biddle to Roosevelt, 23 April 1943, FDR, OF, 5039; a great deal of the detail is in Goldner, *Das einsame Gewissen* and also in Ingram, "Die konservative Emigration aus Österreich"; on the failed British experiment, see Stanley, "Great Britain and Austria," 60, 66–71.

35 Berle memorandum, 3 September 1943, FDR, Berle Papers, 58.

36 Breckinridge Long memorandum to the Committee on Political Planning, Department of State, 5 May 1943, NA, RG 59, Notter Papers, 46.

37 Berle memorandum to Sir Ronald Campbell, British Embassy, 9 January 1942, FDR, Berle Papers, 213.

38 J.C. Dunn memorandum to Berle, 25 September 1942, NA, RG 59, 863.01

39 See 36 above.

40 Secretary of War Stimson to Eden, 12 November 1940, PRO, FO 371, C12858/1419/62; Stanley, "Great Britain and Austria," 55; Wagnleitner, "Wiedererrichtung Österreichs," 156.

41 Berle memorandum of 1 January 1942, copy in FDR, Berle Diary, 213.
42 Federal Bureau of Investigation, "Austrian Activities in the United States," May 1943, FDR, OF, 23, 116ff.
43 Ibid., 12ff.
44 OSS report, 16 June 1943, NA, RG 59, 863.01/782.
45 Ibid., 863.01/822, Berle memorandum, 6 January 1944.
46 Lord Halifax to Foreign Office, 1 March 1942, PRO, FO 371, C2281/1304/18.
47 Bennett minute, 16 October 1944, and a long file on this question before the High Court in 1944, ibid., C10210/30/3.
48 Ibid.
49 Herbert Morrison statement, 16 December 1943, *Parliamentary Debates (Commons)*, 5th ser., vol. 395.
50 Austrian National Committee to Hull, 28 July 1942, NA, RG 59, 863.01/679.
51 Hoover, "Alien Enemy Control," 398.
52 Francis Biddle interview in "Taking No Chances," *Colliers*, 21 March 1942; Hoover, "Enemy Alien Control," 400–3.
53 *Newsweek*, 22 December 1941 and 6 January 1942.
54 See 50 above.
55 James G. McDonald, Chairman, Presidential Advisory Committee on Political Refugees, to Roosevelt, 10 January 1942, FDR, OF 3186.
56 Ibid., OF 133, H.G. Harrison, special assistant to the attorney general, press release of 6 January 1942.
57 Biddle memorandum to Roosevelt, 6 February 1942, FDR, Biddle Papers, 1.
58 Ibid., Biddle memorandum to Roosevelt, 7 October 1942.
59 Office of Wartime Information, Bureau of Intelligence, "Survey of Intelligence Materials, # 30," 1 July 1942, FDR, PSF 173.
60 Matthew telegram from the US Embassy, London, to the Secretary of State, 28 July 1942, NA, RG 59, 863.01/697.
61 Ibid., 740.00115EW39/3248, Welles memorandum to Berle, 27 February 1942.
62 Ibid., Berle to Welles, 27 February 1942.
63 Ibid., 740.00115EW39/3248, Welles memorandum to Berle, 27 February 1942.
64 Ibid., 863.01/6–342, Hackworth memorandum to R. Atherton, 3 June 1942.
65 Ibid., 863.00/1816 1/2, F. Czernin of Austrian Action, with 2 1/2 pages of collected signatures, to Roosevelt, 10 May 1942.
66 Ibid., 863.00/5–2142, John C. Wiley to Hull, 21 May 1942.
67 Ibid., 740.00115EW39/4119, C.W. Cannon memorandum, 30 May 1942.
68 Ibid., 863.00/5–2242, C.W. Cannon report to Ray Atherton, 22 May 1942.
69 Ibid.
70 Ibid., Ray Atherton to Hackworth, 2 June 1942.
71 Ibid., 863.01/6–342 and 863.00/2242, Hackworth to Atherton, 3 June 1942, and Visa Division circular, 3 June 1942.

72 Ibid.

73 Ibid., 863.00/5–2242, Atherton to Berle, 29 June 1942.

74 Ibid., 863.00/7–2542, Atherton to Hull, 25 July 1942.

75 Hull's statement is in Department of State, *Bulletin*, 6, no. 386, 660; R. Atherton to Hull, 25 July 1942, NA, RG 59, 863.00/7–2542; Ibid., 740.00114EW39/7962, Flournoy memorandum, 1 November 1943.

76 Ibid., 863.01/697, M. Fuchs and F. Czernin to Hull, 28 July 1942, and W.M. Plöchl and F. Engel-Janosi to Roosevelt.

77 Ibid., 863.01/778, Hackworth to S.W. Merwick, 28 July 1942.

78 Ibid., 863.01/703, Hackworth to B.H. Conner, 19 September 1942.

79 Ibid., 740.00115EW39/7423, Solicitor General Fahy to Hull, 29 September 1943.

80 Ibid., 740.00115EW39/4158, Rabbi Yasipol, Nashville, to Hull, 9 October 1942.

81 Ibid., 863.00/7–2042, *Washington Times-Herald*, 16 July 1942; B.H. Conner to Hull, 5 August 1942.

82 Ibid., and 863.01/703, Conner to Hull, 5 August 1942.

83 Ibid., R.W. Flournoy, State Department Legal Department, to Hackworth, 8 September 1942.

84 Ibid., Hackworth to Conner, 19 September 1942.

85 Ibid., 863.01/712, Biddle to Hull, 23 August 1943.

86 Ibid., transcript of the judgment of the United States Court of Appeals of the Second Circuit, August 1943.

87 Ibid.

88 Ibid., 863.01/792, Biddle to Hull, 23 August 1943.

89 Ibid., 740.00115EW39/7960, Flournoy memorandum of 27 August 1943.

90 Transcript of the United States Circuit Court of Appeals for the Second Circuit, 18 August 1943, in Government of Canada, Department of External Affairs, 2915–40C.

91 Ibid.

92 Flournoy memorandum, 27 August 1943, NA, RG 59, 740.00115EW39/7960.

93 W.S. Bennett to Department of State, Legal Division, 10 August 1942, NA, RG 59, 740.00115EW39/4134.

94 Ibid., Hackworth to Bennett, 16 September 1943.

95 Ibid., Flournoy memorandum to Hackworth, 8 September 1942. Ibid., 740.00115EW39/7432, also his memorandum of 10 November 1943.

96 Ibid., 740.00115EW39/4134, Harrison, Department of Justice, to Hackworth, 9 December 1942.

97 Bennett to Hon. Marvin H. McIntyre, 9 June 1943 [which began "Dear Mac"], FDR, OF 166a.

98 Flournoy memorandum, 27 August 1943, NA, RG 59, 740.00115EW39/7960.

99 Transcript of the United States Circuit Court of Appeal, 18 August 1943.

100 Biddle to Hull, 23 August 1943. NA, RG 59, 863.01/792.

101 Ibid., 863.01/796, "Position of the Department Respecting the Incorporation of Austria into the German Reich," 10 September 1943.
102 Ibid., E.J. Ennis, Director, Alien Enemy Control Division, Department of Justice, to Hackworth, 21 August 1943.
103 Ibid., 863.01/792, Biddle to Hull, 23 August 1943.
104 Ibid.
105 Ibid., 740.00115EW39/7432, Fahy to Hull, 29 September 1943.
106 Ibid., 740.00115EW39/7960, Flournoy memorandum, 27 August 1943.
107 Ibid., 740.00115EW39/7962, Flournoy memorandum, 1 November 1943.
108 Ibid., Flournoy memorandum, 6 November 1943.
109 Ibid., 381.1143/Rosenthal, Maud/7–1144, Legal Adviser memorandum, "German Denationalization Decrees, July 11, 1941."
110 Ibid., 863.01/792, Hull to Biddle, 2 October 1943. This letter was approved and initialled by the main divisions within the Department of State responsible for this sort of problem, including the Legal Division.
111 Ibid., R.C. Alexander, Department of State, Visa Division, 27 September 1943.
112 Langer and Clute claimed that the Austrian declaration influenced the final decision; *Seizure of Territory*, 171–3; *International Legal Status of Austria*, 67–68.
113 Department of Justice to the War Department, 9 August 1944. Ibid., 740.00115EW39/8–944.
114 Ibid., 381.1143/Rosenthal, Maud/7–1144, Legal Adviser memorandum, "German Denationalization Decrees, 11 July 1941."
115 Diary entry of 3 April 1943, *Harvey Diaries*, 243.
116 Central Department to Chancery, 11 August 1942, PRO, FO 371, 30942.
117 Ibid., Harrison minute, 30 July 1942.
118 Ibid., C.H. Fone, "Attitude of the United States towards the Absorption of Austria."

CHAPTER FOUR

1 Stadler, *Austria*, 21.
2 Rostow, "The Planning of Foreign Policy," 3.
3 Rothstein, *Planning, Prediction and Policy Making in Foreign Affairs*. For a discussion of various models of foreign policy planning, see *The Domestic Context of American Foreign Policy*, 226–31.
4 Madar, "Foreign Policy Planning," 5. Madar, for some reason, assumes that long-range planning in the State Department began only in May 1947 under Secretary of State George Marshall, but perhaps refers only to the postwar period. Ibid., 2.
5 Rostow, "Planning of Foreign Policy," 4.

6 “”Seldom have two world leaders worked so closely together or attained such a degree of intimacy.” Lowenheim, Langley, and Jones, eds., *Roosevelt and Churchill*, 3.
7 Eisenhower, *Allies*, xxi.
8 Thorne, *Allies of a Kind*. Towards the end of the war Churchill came to see that his dream of a postwar Anglo-American condominium was not to be realized, whereupon his resentment increased. This cooling of relations was underlined by Churchill’s nonattendance at Roosevelt’s funeral, a decision he later regretted. Grigg, *1943*, 15–18.
9 Craig, “The Democratic Roots of American Diplomatic Style,” 117; Dallek, *The American Style of Foreign Policy*, xiiiff; Kissinger, “Domestic Structure and Foreign Policy,” 29ff.
10 Krakau, “American Foreign Relations.”
11 Matloff and Snell, *Strategic Planning*, and Matloff’s *Strategic Planning*.
12 Howard, *Studies in War and Peace*, 12ff.
13 Resis, “The Churchill-Stalin ’Percentages’,” 368ff; Lunderstadt claimed that he did accept the notion of “areas of gravitation.” *The American Non-Policy towards Eastern Europe*, 92–3.
14 Feis, *Churchill-Roosevelt-Stalin*, 125.
15 Entry of 6 October 1941, *Harvey Diaries*, 49.
16 As late as mid-1943 Eden’s secretary complained that “A.E. [Eden] himself has only superficial ideas of what our future plans are and is not anxious to commit himself.” 24 August 1943, ibid., 286. Hull was more personally involved in the actual planning process, even if he was keen to avoid peacetime commitments during wartime.
17 Kucklick, “The Genesis of the European Advisory Commission,” 189.
18 Stanley, “Great Britain and the Austrian Question,” 85ff; Wagnleitner, “Grossbritainnien und die Wiedererichtung der Republik Oesterreich,” ivff. Early wartime committees included the Armistice and Civil Committee, Ministerial Armistice and Terms Committee, and the Civil Administration Committee under Attlee, which in 1944 became the Armistice and Postwar Committee.
19 Stanley, “Great Britain and the Austrian Question,” 85ff.
20 Toynbee had contracted dysentery while travelling in Greece before the war. A.J. Toynbee, *Acquaintances*, 161ff. According to Christopher Seton-Watson, “In fact, Tyrrell was the director and Headlam deputy director; and there were at least five other members (Bailey, Bevan, Powell, Sauders, and Simpson). And Toynbee is wrong in stating that my father [Robert W.] was his colleague in PID: they were in fact colleagues from May 1917 to March 1918 in the Intelligence Bureau of the Department of Information.” Letter to author, 17 May 1987.
21 Toynbee, (Blue Book) *The Armenian Massacres in the Ottoman Empire*, also in French; *The German Terror in Belgium*, *The German Terror in*

France, 2 vols. "I worked in it [propaganda] myself, and can remember the relief of getting out of propaganda into work where one's business once more was to find out and state the truth." A.J. Toynbee to G. Gathorne-Hardy, 31 March 1938, A.J. Toynbee Papers, Bodleian Library, Oxford, Box 38. Wilson, "Lord Bryce's Investigation into Alleged German Atrocities in Belgium, 1914–1918"; Saunders and Taylor, *British Propaganda during World War One*, 137ff; Walter Lacqueur has blamed this type of World War I propaganda, later unmasked as being largely false, as one of the chief reasons why the World War II Jewish massacres received so little credence. *The Terrible Secret*, 9. Toynbee admitted as much: " ... we were also naïvely sure that our cause was one hundred percent righteous ... we behaved irresponsibly in shutting our eyes to the possible long-term consequences of our hand-to-mouth acts." *Experiences*, 304–5.

22 Toynbee, *Nationality and War*; *The New Europe*.

23 Stromberg, *Arnold J. Toynbee*, 8. As the CFR explained in its 1937 history, *The Council on Foreign Relations: A Record of Fifteen Years*, 5: "Under the pressure of a public opinion, which was impatient to be done with war-making and peace-making, decisions had to be taken in haste; and the minds of diplomats, generals, admirals, financiers, lawyers and technical experts were not sufficently well furnished to enable them to function satisfactorily on critical issues at top speed."

24 Toynbee, *Experiences*, 61ff; Dockrill, "The Foreign Office and the Proposed Institute of International Affairs, 1919," 667; CFR, *Record of Twenty-Five Years*, 5ff.

25 Temperley, ed., *A History of the Peace Conference of Paris*, 1: vi.

26 Toynbee, "Was Britain's Abdication Folly?" 227; Nicolson, *Peacemaking 1919*, 352.

27 Watt, "The Foundation of the Round Table," 425–33.

28 Shoup and Minter, *Imperial Brain Trust*, 14,

29 Curtis hoped that "the British and American branches would work together like Siamese twins and that other branches would grow like potatoes in various parts of the world." Lionel Curtis to W.H. Shepardson, 24 October 1919. RIIA Archives, 3/6/COU B. CFR *Handbook* (1919), 3–5.

30 Toynbee, *Eperiences*, 63; Dockrill, "The Foreign Office," 667, 669.

31 Toynbee, "Research at Chatham House," 2 February 1932. Toynbee Papers, Box 39; Knapp, "Fifty Years of Chatham House Books," part of a special fiftieth anniversary issue. Christopher Seton-Watson questions Toynbee's claim that Robert W. Seton-Watson's books came out under RIIA sponsorship. Letter to author, 17 May 1987.

32 Toynbee, *Acquaintances*, 167–8; RIIA published its *Survey* from 1927 on, and the CFR issued a similar report from 1928 on.

33 Toynbee, *The Western Question in Greece and Turkey*; Kitsikis, *Propagande et pressions en politique internationale*, 454–7; Clogg, *Politics and*

the Academy, 53ff.

34 Toynbee, *Toynbee on Toynbee*, 57; idem, *Acquaintances*, 110f. See his bitter RIIA talk against Munich, Toynbee Papers, Box 43. Many members opposed publishing the talk, including C.A. Macartney, E.L. Woodward and Michael Balfour. Sir Charles Petrie accused him of advocating war against Germany. Ibid., Box 75. The talk was finally published by Toynbee in the 1939 *International Affairs* as "After Munich."

35 Taylor, *The Projection of Britain*, 218ff and 271ff; Hinsley, *British Intelligence in the Second World War*, 1: 5, 10, and 17.

36 Taylor, " 'If War Should Come'," 43–7; Balfour, *Propaganda at War*, 90.

37 Toynbee to Geoffrey Gathorne-Hardy, 31 March 1938, and Gathorne-Hardy's reply of 1 April 1938, Toynbee Papers, Box 39. For summaries of FRPS's establishment and activity, see FRPS Committee, 1st meeting, 7 May 1941, annex 1, and Toynbee, "Why FRPS Has Been Set Up," RIIA Council, meeting of 13 May 1942, appendix A, RIIA, 2/1/6b and 2/1/7b.

38 Macartney, *Hungary and Her Successors, 1919–1937*, and *National States and National Minorities*; Morrow, *The Peace Settlement and the German-Polish Borderlands*; Wiskemann, *Czechs and Germans*; R.W. Seton-Watson, *A History of the Rumanians*, and *Treaty Revision and the Hungarian Frontiers*; Toynbee's *A Study of History*, 6 vols., also *The Problem of International Investment*, and *Central and Southeastern Europe*.

39 See 37 above for histories of FRPS. Also RIIA, "The Institute, FRPS and FORD, 1939–1948," 2/1/7a. The press surveys were published in *The Review of the Foreign Press*, 27 vols.

40 R.H.L.B. (Foreign Office) to Robert Seton-Watson, 12 October 1939, PRO, FO 898, Political Warfare, 29. Toynbee had earlier written: "Robert Seton-Watson's studies of the problem of nationalities in the Habsburg monarchy on the eve of the Great War ... were recognized at once as the standard works on the subject, and it is no exaggeration to say that the published results of Seton-Watson's researches affected the course of European history." "Research at Chatham House," 2 February 1932, Toynbee Papers, Box 39.

41 F. Ashton-Gwatkin report, 10 January 1941, PRO, FO 898, 29.

42 For 1939 attacks on the RIIA, especially the Earl of Tankerville's questions in the House of Lords in November and December 1939, see RIIA, 2/1/6a. FRPS accounts and organization are in ibid., 2/1/7a.

43 Quoted in Stafford, *Britain and European Resistance*, 34.

44 Ibid.; and Wheeler, "The SOE Phenomenon." By 1943, the socialist Hugh Dalton had lost the propaganda-sabotage group Special Operations Executive to the Political Warfare Executive controlled by the Foreign Office as well as his position as minister of economic warfare.

45 FRPS (German Section) memorandum, 9 November 1940, PRO, FO 898, 29.

46 Toynbee-Carr correspondence from December 1939, Toynbee Papers, Box

81; Toynbee's FRPS coordinating committee consisted of himself, Sir J. Hope Simpson, and Professors Paton and Price. Eleven subcommittees were established including "The German State and Nazi Regime," "Regional New Orders," and *"The Danubian Countries: States and Peoples"* [author's emphasis]. F. Ashton-Gwatkin, report on FRPS, 10 January 1941, PRO, FO 898, 29.

47 "Political Aspects of a German Defeat by Russia," 7 July 1941, PRO, FO 371, N3718.

48 Ibid., FO 898, 29, memorandum on FRPS, 9 November 1940.

49 Thorne, "Chatham House, Whitehall and Far Eastern Issues," 8.

50 Eden's secretary explained to him that "we have a staff of professors at Balliol working on our behalf in close touch with the departments, but they require a directive ... A.E. was interested and agreed." Entry of 6 October 1941, *Harvey Diaries*, 49.

51 FRPS memorandum, 9 November 1940, PRO, FO 898, 29.

52 W. Selby to O. Harvey, and Walford to Harvey, PRO, FO 371, 26538.

53 Ibid., 26537, R. Shackle to F.T. Ashton-Gwatkin, 18 June 1941, and 23 July 1941 note.

54 Stanley, "British Policy and the Austrian Question," 22ff.

55 Toynbee, *Survey of International Affairs*, 153; Toynbee speech to the Conference of Institutes for the Scientific Study of International Relations, Copenhagen, June 1931, in RIIA, 2/1/6a.

56 R.W. Seton-Watson, *Treaty Revision and the Hungarian Frontiers*, 69–71.

57 H. Seton-Watson, *Eastern Europe between the Wars*, 411.

58 RIIA, *South-Eastern Europe*.

59 Toynbee to R. Makins, enclosing Laffan's draft FRPS memorandum on Austria – one copy for Eden, 2 October 1941, PRO, FO 371, 26538.

60 The 1943 war cabinet decision read: "There was general agreement that we should aim at a Central European or Danubian Group centred in Vienna ... " PRO, CAB 65/34, WM 86(43), 92–93, 218 of 25 May 1943.

61 Memorandum on Austria, 2 October 1941, PRO, FO 371, 26538.

62 Ibid.

63 Ibid.

64 FRPS internal working paper "Austria – Economic Possibilities," 3 September 1941, PRO, FO 371, 30942.

65 Ibid., C.W. Harrison notes of 23 January 1942 and 31 January 1942.

66 Ibid., G. Counsell, FRPS, to R. Heppel, 2 February 1942, and T.H. Marshall to R. Makins, 17 February 1942.

67 Diary entry of 28 August 1943, *Harvey Diaries*, 286–7.

68 RIIA council meeting, 15 April 1942, chairman, Lord Astor, with Toynbee in attendance, and RIIA staff in January 1943, RIIA, 2/1/7b.

69 Ibid., draft letter, Lord Astor to Anthony Eden ("Dear Anthony"), 2 November 1942.

70 Ibid., draft heads of agreement between the RIIA and the Foreign Office, November and December 1942; Ronald (Foreign Office) to Macadam (Secretary, RIIA), 21 November 1942; Astor-Eden letters, December 1942.

71 Ibid., Jebb to Secretary, RIIA, 23 January 1943; Terms of Agreement, 1 April 1943; FORD staff circular on FRPS move from Oxford to London, 25 May 1943.

72 Foreign Office memorandum, 3 April 1943, PRO, FO 371,34466.

73 Stafford, *Britain and European Resistance*, 34; Foreign Office telegram to Moscow, 25 September 1943, and Dominions Office print to Dominions, 19 July 1943, PRO, FO 371, 34466.

74 M. Wright, "Eastern Europe," 206ff. Ashton-Gwatkin, the volume's editor, had been the Foreign Office official responsible in 1942 for recommending attachment of FRPS to the Foreign Office. F. Ashton-Gwatkin report on FRPS, 10 January 1941, PRO, FO 898, 29.

75 Toynbee and Ashton-Gwatkin, *Survey*, 236.

76 Macartney and Palmer, *Independent East Europe*. See also RIIA, *The Balkans together with Hungary*; A.J. and A.V. Toynbee, *The War and the Neutral*; Hugh Seton-Watson, *The "Sick Heart" of Europe*.

77 Between 1945 and 1967, 83 major books and 366 learned articles were published by the new breed of North American Habsburg scholars. See survey in "The Nationality Problem in the Habsburg Monarchy in the Nineteenth Century," *Austrian History Yearbook* (1967). Also in ibid., reports on Habsburg studies in Europe and the United States by Paul. W. Schroeder, Fritz Fellner, and Adam Wandruszka. Robert A. Kann explained that he picked the Habsburg Empire for his thesis, which became *The Multinational Empire*, 2 vols., because of its exemplary multinational format.

78 Murphy, *Diplomat among Warriors*; Mosley, *The Kremlin and World Politics*; Kennan, *Memoirs*, 123, 164, 171–3, 214–15 and 221; Bohlen, *Witness to History*, 210–11; and Acheson, "The Decline of the State Department," 593–606.

79 Loewenheim, Langley, Honas, eds., *Roosevelt and Churchill*, 3ff.

80 Entry of 12 June 1944, *Harvey Diaries*, 344.

81 Burns, *The Lion and the Fox*, 382–3; Dallek, "Franklin D. Roosevelt as War Leader," 1503ff; also idem, *Roosevelt and Foreign Policy*, 421; on Roosevelt's administrative techniques, see ibid., 29, 34, 84, and 421.

82 Stimson and Bundy, *On Active Service*, 361ff.

83 Sherwin, "The Atomic Bomb and the Origin of the Cold War"; Villa, "The United States Army, Unconditional Surrender and the Potsdam Proclamation."

84 In his *Memoirs*, Hull tried to show that his relationship with Roosevelt had been consistently close, 1: 195, 200; 2: 1474, 1609–10; Drummond, "Cordell Hull"; Blum, ed., *From the Morgenthau Diaries: The War Years*,

241–2.

85 Dallek, *Roosevelt and Foreign Policy*, 421.

86 Elsey memorandum "The Map Room Files of Franklin D. Roosevelt, 1941–1945," quoted in Loewenheim et al., *Roosevelt and Churchill*, 73n4; Welles, "Two Roosevelt Decisions," 182–90; Feis, "Some Notes on Historical Record-Keeping," 106.

87 Stimson and Bundy, *On Active Service*, 563.

88 Dallek, *Roosevelt and Foreign Policy*, 421. Dallek showed that public opinion polls, which Roosevelt studied, reflected general domestic lack of interest in postwar political programs. See also Steel, "The Pulse of the People," 195–216. Roosevelt's style is described in A.M. Schlesinger, *The Imperial Presidency*.

89 Lunderstadt, *American Non-Policy towards Eastern Europe*, 92–3.

90 Feis, *Churchill-Roosevelt-Stalin*, 125.

91 Gelfand, *The Inquiry*.

92 Eisenhower, *Allies*, 15–16.

93 Matloff and Snell, *Strategic Planning for Coalition Warfare, 1941–1942*, 100.

94 Churchill, *The Second World War*, 3: 684; Sherwood, *Roosevelt and Hopkins*, 447.

95 Diary entries of 30 April 1942 and 28 December 1944, Berle, *Navigating the Rapids*, 410 and 511.

96 Dallek, *Roosevelt and Foreign Policy*, 421.

97 Diary entry of 26 June 1941, Berle, *Navigating the Rapids*, 372.

98 Cabinet notes, 20 November 1942, FDR Biddle Papers, 1.

99 Notter, draft of "Postwar Foreign Policy Planning," chapter 1, 37–73, NA, RG 59, Notter Papers, 4.

100 Berle memorandum to the President and the Secretary of State, 23 November 1942, FDR, Berle Papers, 58; "The President was opposed to any formal Anglo-American discussion on postwar questions." British Embassy, Washington, to Foreign Office, 12 August 1942, PRO, FO 371, 31627/F5716/54/10.

101 Berle to Hull and Roosevelt, 23 and 26 November 1942, FDR, Berle Papers, 58.

102 Notter, "Postwar Foreign Policy Planning," 517 and 520, NA, RG 59, Notter Papers, 4.

103 Ibid., chapter 3.

104 General Hilldring to State Department, April 1945, *FRUS*, 1945, 6: 545; Stimson and Bundy, *On Active Service*, 560; Hayes, "Coordination of Military and Civil Affairs Planning," 267.

105 Mayo, "American Wartime Planning for Occupied Japan," 7.

106 Notter to Duggan, 3 September 1938, and Notter memorandum to Welles, 13 November 1939, NA, RG 59, Notter Papers, 108; diary entries of 20

December 1939 and 4 January 1940, Berle, *Navigating the Rapids*, 280–1.

107 Pasvolsky, *Economic Nationalism in the Danubian States.*

108 Notter, *Postwar Foreign Policy Planning*, 39–45 and 56–81.

109 Stuart, *The Department of State*, 376–407.

110 Notter, "Postwar Foreign Policy Planning," chapter 3, 10ff and 20ff, NA, RG 59, Notter Papers, 4.

111 The mood in the United States had changed, becoming anti-Versailles and anti-British. Shepardson to E.C. Carter, 4 February 1920; Shepardson to Curtis, 11 March 1920; and Curtis to Shepardson, 18 October 1920. RIIA, 3/6/COU B.

112 CFR, *Handbook* (1919), 3–5, and *By-Laws and List of Officers and Members* (1922); Fish Armstrong, *Peace and Counterpeace*, 181f.

113 For instance, Angell, *The Recovery of Germany*; Feis, *Europe the World's Banker*; Stimson, *The Far Eastern Crisis*; Dulles and Armstrong, *Can We Be Neutral?*; Shepardson, *The Interest of the United States as a World Power.*

114 CFR, *A Record of Fifteen Years*, 22–5. A solid overview, if aggressively Marxist in perspective, is Shoup and Minter, *Imperial Brain Trust*, see 22–8.

115 Dulles and Armstrong, *Can We Be Neutral?*

116 CFR, Records of Groups, vol.8 (1936–8), section C.

117 Bowman to Lionel Curtis, 2 November 1939, FDR, PPF, 5575.

118 Messersmith's memorandum of conversation, NA, RG 59, Notter Papers, 19; ibid., 811.43 CFR/2220, Hamilton Fish Armstrong's memorandum for Stettinius, 24 November 1943, Shoup and Minter, *Imperial Brain Trust*, 119.

119 CFR, *War and Peace Studies of the CFR, 1939–1945*, 19–24.

120 Hull to Norman Davis, 12 November 1940 and 1 October 1941, NA, RG 59, 811.43 CFR/119.

121 Pasvolsky to Hull, 12 September 1941, ibid., Notter Papers, 4; Notter, *Postwar Foreign Policy Planning*, 466–7.

122 CFR representatives were Hamilton Fish Armstrong, Isaiah Bowman, Herbert Feis, and Norman Davis. State CFR members were Welles, Pasvolsky, Berle, and Benjamin V. Cohen. Notter, *Postwar Foreign Policy Planning*, 64–5.

123 Minutes of the joint organizational meeting of the subcommittees on political, territorial, and security problems, 21 February 1942, NA, RG 59, Notter Papers, 77. Philip Mosley, research secretary for the CFR's territorial group from 1940 to 1945, became research secretary of the parallel State Department subcommittee, and moved directly into the department in November 1942 as one of Pasvolsky's Division of Special Research assistant chiefs. Shoup and Minter, 155ff. Members of the important Political Subcommittee were Welles as chairman, Adolf Berle, H. Fish Armstrong, Isaiah Bowman, Ben Cohen, C.H. Hackworth, Anne O.H. O'Cormack, Myron Tay-

lor, and Pasvolsky. Berle, *Navigating the Rapids*, 54.

124 Notter to Pasvolsky, 14 September 1942, NA, RG 59, Notter Papers, 4.

125 American Interest in War and Peace Project, EN C6, 11 October 1941, CFR, Summaries of the Peace Aims Group; ibid., Records of Groups, vol. 16, British-American meeting, "Economic and Political Reconstruction of the Liberated Areas in Europe," 5 April 1945.

126 Ibid., Records of Groups, vol. 12(a), United States Interests in European Reconstruction, 1941–2, meetings of 2 December 1941, 6 January and 30 March 1942.

127 Ibid., Summaries, T-B7, "The Interests of the United States in the Fate of Small Nations-States in Europe," 20 May 1940, and T-B55, "Russia and East European Federations," 26 October 1942.

128 Ibid., P-B71, "European Regionalism and Post-War World Organization," 27 September 1943.

129 Ibid., T-B55, "Russian and East European Federations," 26 October 1942.

130 Ibid., A-B82, "Soviet Interests in Europe Affecting Post-War Security," 12 February 1943.

131 Ibid., Record of Groups, vol. 16, Study Group on American-Russian Relations, 1945–6, and William Schubert to group chairman, 20 May 1946.

132 Ibid., Summaries, EN-B4, 14 July 1941; ibid., B5, 5 August 1941; ibid., EN-C4, 4 October 1941.

133 Ibid., B-14, 26 July 1943.

134 P-UND (Political Planning Committee document) 18, 2 April 1942, NA, RG 59, Notter Papers, 58.

135 Ibid.

136 Ibid., 56, P-UND 6 to 11, April and May 1942.

137 Ibid., 55, P chronological minutes 5, 4 April 1942.

138 Ibid., 55 and 56, P-UND 6 to 11, April and May 1942, and P chronological minutes 5.

139 Ibid., 55, P chronological minutes 5, 4 April 1942, and P chronological minutes 7, 18 April 1942.

140 Ibid., P chronological minutes 8, 25 April 1942.

141 Ibid., P chronological minutes 6, 11 April 1942.

142 Ibid., P chronological minutes 7 and 8, 18 and 25 April 1942.

143 Ibid., P chronological minutes 10 and 12, 9 and 23 May 1942.

144 Ibid., 56, P chronological minutes 17, 20 June 1942.

145 Ibid., 55, P chronological minutes 8, 25 April 1942.

146 Ibid., 56, P chronological minutes 11, 16 May 1942.

147 Ibid., 54, Notter memorandum to Wadleigh, 6 October 1942.

148 Ibid., Pasvolsky suggested the economic study. P chronological minutes 13, 16, 17, and 23, 30 May, 20 and 25 June, and 22 August 1942.

149 Ibid., 56, P chronological minutes, 7 April 1943.

150 Ibid., 54, 3rd meeting of the Security Technical Committee, Division of

Special Research, 6 January 1943.

151 Ibid., 6th meeting, Security Technical Committee, 27 January 1943.

152 Ibid., 7th meeting, Security Technical Committee, 3 February 1943.

153 Ibid., 79, 152, 155, H31, H17, H86 (preliminary), H4 documents.

154 Ibid., 54, P (final recommendation) 214C, 10 March 1943.

155 Ibid., P214 "European States," 12 March 1943.

156 Ibid., 55, 45th meeting, Policy Planning Subcommittee, minutes, 20 February 1943.

157 Diary entry of 2 February 1943, Berle, *Navigating the Rapids*, 431.

158 On eastern European unions or confederations, P204, 10 February 1943, P202, 5 February 1943, and P205, 19 February 1943. Notter Papers, 57.

159 Ibid., 56, Policy Planning document 14, "Soviet Interest in the Middle Zone," 23 September 1943; ibid., 7, Notter, "Postwar Foreign Policy Preparations," 119.

160 White memorandum to Morgenthau, 23 June 1943, FDR, Morgenthau Diaries, 542.

161 Notes of Roosevelt-Halifax conversation, 22 May 1943, FDR, MR, 7A.

162 Note of 10 March 1943, NA, RG 59, General Records, Office of European Affairs, 11.

163 British Foreign Office print, "The Future of Austria," 12 July 1943, sent to the Department of State 28 August 1943; Division of European Affairs evaluation of the print, 9 October 1943, NA, RG 59, 863.01/29.

164 Meeting of Hull, Pasvolsky, Dunn, Hackworth, Matthews, and Stettinius with Roosevelt, 5 October 1943, NA, RG 59, Notter Papers, 54; also P206A, "The Soviet Attitude towards East European Unions," 18 February 1943, NA, RG 59, Office of European Affairs, 16. Also Davis, *The Cold War Begins*, 22ff.

165 Boyle, "The British Foreign Office View of Soviet-American Relations," 307–10.

166 "Soviet Attitudes on Regional Organizations in Eastern Europe," 23 September 1943, Policy Group paper in preparation for the Moscow Conference, NA, RG 59, Notter Papers, 119.

167 Mark, "Charles E. Bohlen and the Acceptable Limits of Soviet Hegemony in Eastern Europe," 201–6.

168 Chronological minutes, Subcommittee on Problems of European Organization, R-12, 18 February 1944, Notter Papers, 84; Mark, "Charles E. Bohlen," 205.

169 Lundestad, *American Non-Policy*, 92ff.

170 Quoted in ibid., 76.

CHAPTER FIVE

1 J. Lambert, 25 July 1943, PRO, FO 372, 34465/C7012.

2 Entry of 13 October 1943, Stimson Diary, 44/192.

3 Paul Mellon, 4 November 1943, *New York Journal-American*. For this article and more, see "Excerpts from Leading Newspaper Editorials Concerning the Results of the Moscow Conference" (November 2–4), NA, RG, 59, Pasvolsky Papers, 1.

4 Ibid., David Sentner, 2 November 1943, *New York Journal-American*.

5 Scipio, *100,000,000 Million Allies*; Donovan and Mowrer, *Fifth Column Lessons for America*.

6 Morrison, *Fortress without a Roof*, 4ff; Webster and Frankland, *The Strategic Air Offensive against Germany*; and Hasting, *Bomber Command*.

7 Jong, *The German Fifth Column*, 91–4, 202–6, 241–2; Hinsley et al., *British Intelligence in the Second World War*, 1: 167; Smith, *The Shadow Warriors*, 3–20.

8 Stafford, *Britain and European Resistance*, llff; Hinsley, *British Intelligence*, 1: 64–5.

9 Medlicott, *The Economic Blockade*, 1 and 48.

10 Klein, *Germany Prepares for War*; Milward, *The German Economy at War*; and Carroll, *Design for Total War*.

11 Stephen Hall-King to S.G. Tallents, 5 September 1938, PRO, FO 898, 2; Goldman, "Stephen Hall-King and the Newsletter Controversy of 1940"; Cruikshank, *The Fourth Arm*, 2ff; Balfour, *Propaganda*, 53ff and 89.

12 "We do not suggest personal attacks on him [Hitler], but we consistently treat him as a pawn of events and personal influences, rather than the active master of his country's fate." EH review for the War Cabinet, 25 February 1940, PRO, FO, 898, 3. Ibid., "In regard to Hitler, insulting attacks on his personality are still calculated to arouse resentment [among Germans]." Sir Campbell Stuart, "Publicity to Enemy Countries," 6 January 1940.

13 A/Director to the Minister of Information, "Propaganda in Enemy Countries (draft)," 2 May 1940. In 1940 EH first moved to Duff Cooper's Ministry of Information, then to SOE. Balfour, *Propaganda*, 89–90.

14 Department EH review for Cabinet, 25 February 1940, PRO, FO 898/3.

15 PRO, War Cabinet, CAB 65/1, 28(39).

16 Bruce Lockhart, Political Warfare Executive, and PID, 11 November 1941 and W. Strang note, 16 November 1941, PRO, FO 371, 30128; C.W. Harrison draft answer for Eden, 2 March 1942, ibid., 30928; Keyserlingk, "Political Warfare Illusions," 71ff.

17 Secret British paper, "Political Warfare," 1942; Most Secret paper on political warfare by Air Commodore P.R. Groves of PWE, London, 30.4.1943; "The Progress of Economic Warfare," United States Memoranda and Economic Notes, No. 137, 1.10.1942; in Department of External Affairs Archives, Ottawa, 5404–40C.

18 Keyserlingk, "Which Fatherland in War?" 139.

19 W. Strang minute, 16.11.1941, PRO, FO 371, 34476, 10433; Eden print on Free German movements, 18.6.1941, Public Archives of Canada (PAC), William Lyon Mackenzie King Papers, MG 26, J4, 358. This file contains the Foreign Office prints on psychological warfare to 1943; Stafford, "The Detonator Concept"; and his *Britain and European Resistance*, 200ff; Deacon, *A History of the British Secret Service*, 288–343; Winterbottom, *Secret and Personal*, 162; and Balfour, *Propaganda in War*, 438–9, who rightly called this policy a failure.

20 Stafford, *Britain and European Resistance*, 19ff; Cruikshank, *The Fourth Arm*, chapters 1 and 4.

21 "Political Warfare Executive. The Place of Propaganda in Political Warfare against Germany," approved by the Standing Ministerial Committee, 7 October 1941, PRO, FO 898, 181; and Balfour, *Propaganda in War*, 91–2.

22 Diary entry of 20 November 1942, FDR, Biddle Papers, 1; Roosevelt meeting with the JCS, 10 August 1942, Records of the JCS, Part 1 (1942–5), ed. Paul Kesaris, microfilmed at Frederick, Maryland, 1983 (hereafter JCS Records), in the University of Ottawa Library, Meetings, reel 1; Davis, *The Cold War Begins*, 37–42 and 87.

23 For the official OSS history, see Kermit Roosevelt, a nephew of President Roosevelt and ex-member of OSS, ed., *War Report of the (Office of Strategic Services)*; Smith, *Shadow Warriors*, 21–4, 85, and 116; and Smith, *OSS*.

24 K. Roosevelt, *OSS War Report*, 55ff.

25 Executive Order of 23 February 1943, in JCS Records, Strategic Issues, reel 11; Secretary of War Stimson wrote rather petulantly about the OSS, "I have never been made fully acquainted with [the OSS]." Diary entry of 25 November 1943, Stimson Diary, 45/62.

26 Winkler, *The Politics of Propaganda*, 73ff; Smith, *OSS*, 140ff.

27 Smith, *OSS*, 78, 209, and 272.

28 K. Roosevelt, *OSS* War Report, 98–9. The Joint Psychological Warfare Committee reported through the Joint Staff Planners to the JCS.

29 K. Roosevelt, *OSS War Report*, 106–111; and Winkler, *Politics of Propaganda*, 125–6.

30 "Fundamental Plan of Propaganda to Germany," March 1941, Joint Planning Staff, and "PWE German Propaganda and Policy Plans 1941," September 1941, PRO, FO 898, 181.

31 Biddle memorandum to Berle, 17 January 1942, FDR, Berle Papers, 17; and "The German Military and Economic Position," 12 December 1941, FDR, PSF 4, 163, and 173.

32 The State Department's Adolf Berle, who sat on the Joint Planners' Intelligence Committee, shared this optimistic view. *Navigating the Rapids*, 408–11.

33 "Proposed Basic Estimates on Psychological Warfare," 22 August 1942, JCS Records, Strategic Issues, Reel 11.

34 "Operation Roundup," British military paper submitted to the Joint Planning Staff, 24 December 1941, JCS Records, European Theatre, Reel 1.

35 Ibid., Combined Staff Planners, "Offensive Operations Europe," 3 April 1942.

36 Ibid., Strategic Issues, Reel 11, "Psychological Warfare," 13 February 1942.

37 "The German Military and Economic Position," 12 December 1941, FDR, PSF, 4 and 163; and ibid., 173, "Elements of Disunity," Survey of Intelligence Materials No.28, 17 June 1942.

38 Joint United States Intelligence Committee, "Morale in Germany," 1 October 1942, JCS Records, European Theatre, Reel 9.

39 Quoted in Eisenhower, *Allies*, 235.

40 *The Papers of Dwight David Eisenhower*, 2: 1096.

41 Diary entry of 27 May 1943, Stimson Diary, 43/76.

42 Minutes of CCS for 1943, FDR, MR, 27.

43 "Overall Strategic Plan for the United States' Psychological Warfare," 1 March 1943, JCS Records, Strategic Issues, Reel 11.

44 Four were technical-security staff, while the other six represented parallel Anglo-American political warfare organizations – Foreign Office/State Department, OWI/PWE, OSS/SOE. JCS No. 231, "Policy for Coming Operations regarding Propaganda and Subversive Activities," 2 March 1943; ibid., Algiers to War Department, 1 March 1943; and "Deception Policy 1943 (Germany and Italy)," 3 April 1943.

45 CCS, "Defeat of the Axis Powers in Europe," 17 May 1943; Joint Staff Planners, "Comparison of Various Post-Husky Operations in Relation to Allied Air Capabilities," JCS No. 223, 3 July 1943; Joint Staff Planners, No. 438, "Estimate of the European Situation, 1943–1944. European-Mediterranean Area," 4 August 1943: JCS Records, European Theatre, Reel 1.

46 For instance, "Germans Are Deserting," *New York Times*, 20 September 1943; "U-Boat Mutinies Reported Growing," ibid., 4 October 1943.

47 J. Wheeler-Bennett's 54–page paper "On What To Do with Germany," 30 June 1943; and "The Dismemberment of Germany," 13 October 1943, PRO, FO 371, 34459, C6683 and C12101.

48 Joint Intelligence Committee, "Morale in Germany," 22 September 1943, 18–23, FDR, Hopkins Papers, 227.

49 Post-hostilities Planning Subcommittee, Military Subcommittee, Progress report of 31 July 1943, War Cabinet minutes of 29 September 1943, DEA, 7–AC(s).

50 CCS No. 310, "The CCS Propaganda Committee," 15 August 1943, FDR, MR 27.

51 Memorandum for the United States Chiefs of Staff, "Propaganda Committee," 15 August 1943, JCS Records, Strategic Issues, Reel 10.

52 Ibid., CCS No. 310/1, Memorandum from the British Chiefs of Staff, 2 September 1943.

53 CCS memorandum to the President and Prime Minister, 23 August 1943;

Operations Division, War Department, GS, 20 October 1943, FDR, MR 46.

54 "Washington Committee for the Emergency Coordination of Propaganda Policy," 6 November 1943, JCS Records, Strategic Issue, Reel 10.

55 Ibid., CCS memorandum for information No. 171, "Emergency Propaganda Committees," 23 December 1943.

56 Ibid., Telegram No. 378, Secretary of State to American Embassy, London, 14 January 1944.

57 Joint Staff Planners' report, January 1944, ibid.; on the functioning of the London group's Algiers component at Eisenhower's headquarters, see Macmillan, *Blast of War*, 310: " ... we have the great propaganda machine here."

58 The code name RANKIN was subtitled "A" to "C," ranging from the most distant to the most imminent German internal collapse. In 1943, as German disintegration was considered just around the corner, RANKIN "C" was the most popular version. JCS No. 290/1, "Conduct of the War in 1943–1944," 8 May 1943, JCS Records, Strategic Issues, Reel 13.

59 Ibid., Reel 10, JCS information No. 155, 16 November 1943, with R.A. Atherton letter to Admiral Leahy and American Embassy, London, telegram to Secretary of State, 5 November 1943.

60 Ibid., Winant, American Embassy, London, to Secretary of State, 5 November 1943. Winant was the State Department representative on the London political warfare group.

61 See ibid., on the "Hardcrust" line.

62 Ibid., Meetings, Reel 2, Minutes of Roosevelt's meeting with his chiefs of staff en route to Cairo and Teheran, 19 November 1943.

63 Ibid., European Theatre, Reel 7, JCS No. 577, "Europe-Wide Rankin," 8 November 1943. According to Stimson, the only reason Roosevelt even considered involving Americans in the temporary administration of occupied areas was to stop the British from "laying down a Mediterranean empire as a result of HUSKY (the Italian invasion)." Entry of 4 June 1943, Stimson Diary, 43/84, and Stimson and Bundy, *On Active Service*, 560.

64 Grigg, *1943*.

65 W.J. Donovan to Roosevelt, "Austria," 17 December 1941, FDR, PSF, 163.

66 OSS Bern report, 10 July 1943, FDR, MR 72.

67 Joint Intelligence Committee, "German Opposition to the Nazis," 11 April 1943, FDR, Hopkins Papers, 227.

68 OSS report, "Austria: Violent Anti-Nazi Sentiment Developing," 11 December 1943, FDR, MR 72.

69 *New York Times*, 19 October 1942, and ibid., "Guerrilla Actions Spread in Austria," 6 November 1943.

70 Ibid., "17 More Austrians Executed by Nazis," 15 March 1943; ibid., "Austrian Executions by Nazis Rise to 125," 27 April 1943.

71 Ibid., "Vienna Clashes Reported," 29 July 1943; ibid., "Austria Fears Ruhr Fate as Nazi Industry Pours In," 4 August 1943.

72 Ibid., "Liberators Hit Wiener Neustadt," 2 October 1943; ibid., "Plant in Austria Bombed to Ruins," 4 November 1943.

73 Ibid., "Tells of Unrest in Austria," 10 January 1943; ibid., "Austrians Report a Freedom Front," 23 May 1943.

74 OSS report, "Austria: Violent Anti-Nazi Sentiment Developing," 11 December 1943, FDR, MR 72.

75 Berle memorandum, 19 October 1943, NA, RG 59, 863.01/808; for a realistic judgment about the Austrian resistance, see Stanley, "Great Britain and the Austrian Question," 136ff.

76 Roosevelt memorandum to his secretary Marvin ("Mac") McIntyre, 22 October 1942, FDR, OF, 19.

77 Ibid., Roosevelt to Hon. Roy North, Assistant Postmaster General, 23 March 1943, "I approve the suggestion of the Under-Secretary of State that Austria and Albania be included in the list of overrun nations."

78 Ibid., Roy North memorandum to Roosevelt, 19 March 1943, and Roy North memorandum to the Postmaster General, 14 April 1943. Stephan Verosta mistakenly saw this as proof that the Americans saw Austria as occupied. "Aussenpolitik," in Weinzierl and Skalnik, *Das Neue Oesterreich*, 92.

79 Roy North to the Postmaster General, 14 April 1943, FDR, 19.

80 Ibid., Postmaster General F.C. Walker memorandum to Roosevelt with Roosevelt's scribbled "FW, OK, FDR," 14 April 1943.

81 PWE's proposed Austrian propaganda statement, and Foreign Office negative reactions, January 1943, PRO, FO 371, 34464, C321, especially 13 and 20 January 1943.

82 Foreign Office draft paper on Austria, 4 April 1943, ibid., C3729.

83 Realistic postwar economic planning for Austria started only in November 1943, following the Moscow Declaration on Austria, rather than before, and then largely on the basis of postwar relief. For instance, ibid., C12857.

84 Ibid., 34462, C13599, Harrison minute, 18 November 1943.

85 Ibid., Eden note, 21 November 1943.

86 E.g., Stourzh, *Geschichte des Staatsvertrages*, 2–3.

87 O.G. Sargent to Lord Cranborne, Dominions Office, 9 October 1943, PRO, FO 371, 34466/C11389; ibid., C14085, Harrison memorandum, 28 November 1943.

88 Ibid., C7012/321/18, "The Future of Austria," 12 June 1943.

89 Ibid.

90 Ibid.

91 Stanley, "Great Britain and the Austrian Question," 136ff.

92 Scarlett minute, 5 January 1943 and PWE minute, 13 January 1943, PRO, FO 371, C321/321/18 and C487/55/18.

93 Ibid., 34465/ C8235, H.C. Bowen, PID, to Harrison, 16 July 1943, and A. Allen minute, 20 July 1943.

94 Ibid., C8235/321/18, Bower, PID, to Harrison, 16 July 1943.

95 Quoted and commented upon in Stanley, "Great Britain and the Austrian Question," 108–9.

96 Joint Intelligence summary No. 46, 24 November 1943, 17–22. FDR, MR 227.

97 P.N. Loxley to Sir Charles Hambro, 9 June 1943, PRO, FO 371, 34465/ C6772. The same draft sent to the Dominions can be found in DEA 7–P(s).

98 Harrison minutes, 15 September 1943, PRO, FO 371, 34466/ C11201.

99 Ibid., 34465/ C9546, and 34466/ C11609, 14 August 1943 telegram from Moscow to Foreign Office.

100 Secret memorandum of October 1943 with draft declaration, and Cannon memorandum, "Evaluation of the British Foreign Office Secret Paper, 'The Future of Austria'," 23 September 1943, NA, RG 59, 863.014/29.

101 Diary entry of 2 February 1943, Berle, *Navigating the Rapids*, 433.

102 Mark, "Charles E. Bohlen," 204.

103 PG (Policy Group)-14, "Soviet Attitudes on Regional Organizations in Eastern Europe," NA, RG 59, Notter Papers, 119.

104 Davis, *The Cold War Begins*, 58–9.

105 In October 1943 Roosevelt told Stimson as they left a cabinet meeting, "Remember, no more Balkans." Diary entry of 29 October 1943, Stimson Diary, 44/234. See also Averell Harriman's story of his lunch with Roosevelt, in Harriman and Abel, *Special Envoy to Churchill and Stalin*, 226–8.

106 Leffler, "The American Conception of National Security," 349–81; Sherry, *Preparing for the Next War*, viii-ix; Stoler, "From Continentalism to Globalism," 305–6.

107 Diary entry of 8 September 1943, Stimson Diary, 44/108.

108 Secret memorandum with the draft declaration of October 1943, NA, RG 59, 863.014/29.

109 Donovan memorandum on Austria to Roosevelt, 19 October 1943, FDR, PSF, 167; ibid., MR, 72, OSS Bern report No. 71, 22 October 1943.

110 Diary entry of 1 October 1943, Stimson Diary, 44/164.

111 Dallek, *Roosevelt and Foreign Policy*, 411.

112 Ibid., 415–16; Matloff and Snell, *Strategic Planning for Coalition Warfare*, 2: 210–30; *FRUS, 1943*, Conferences at Washington and Quebec, 894–9, 914–15, 1211–15; Harriman, *Special Envoy*, 218; and Stoler, "From Continentalism to Globalism," 312.

113 "Foreign Ministers Conference and Russia's Western Frontiers," 5 September 1943, PRO, FO 371, 37028/N5267/3666/38; Sir Ronald Campbell to Foreign Office, ibid., 37028/N5364/3666/38; *FRUS, 1943*, 1: 540–2; Dallek, *Roosevelt and Foreign Policy*, 419.

114 United States, House of Representatives, House Resolution No. 458, reported on by Mr. Jarman, report No. 1228, 3 March 1943, House Misc Documents, No. 10845.

115 Plöchl had tried unsuccessfully to have himself recognized in the United States as the head of an Austrian government-in-exile. The very useful Plöchl

papers, especially his extensive collection of American newspapers, are located in the Dokumentationszentrum für österreichischen Widerstand in Vienna.

116 Wright, *The Attitude of the United States towards Austria.*

117 Ibid., 15–18.

118 For instance, his "The Legality of the Annexation," 621–35.

119 HLH memoranda, 15 and 22 March 1943, FDR, Hopkins Papers, 7, 329; Roosevelt press conference No. 888, 30 March 1943, ibid.

120 HLH letter to Adolf Berle, 23 March 1943, FDR, Hopkins Papers, 7, 329. itnah and Erickson wrongly state that Roosevelt told Eden that he did have the power to affirm support of Austria without the Senate's approval. *The Occupation of Austria*, 5.

121 Ibid.

122 Ibid., Berle's three-page answer to Hopkins, 25 March 1943.

123 Ibid.

124 OWI intelligence report No. 58, 15 January 1943, FDR, OF, 5015.

125 Stourzh, *Geschichte des Staatsvertrages*, 214.

126 Neville Butler, 30 July 1943, PRO, FO 371, C7012/321/18.

127 Ibid., C11609/321/18, Sir Mark Kerr, Moscow, 4 October 1943.

128 Ibid., 34466/C11389, text in Dominion Office telegram of 16 September 1943.

129 Ibid.

130 Ibid.

131 Secret Foreign Office circular No. D 434 to the Dominions, 19 August 1943, DEA 7–P(s).

132 State Department draft of the declaration and comments, 9 October 1943, initialled by eight divisions, NA, RG 59, 863.014/29.

133 Ibid.

134 Ibid.; Moscow Conference document 21, in *FRUS, 1943*, 1: General, 724. Rauchensteiner notes wrongly in his *Sonderfall*, 19, that the Americans wanted inclusion of the reference to the Atlantic Charter and opposed the war guilt notion in paragraph 3.

135 Fellner, "Die aussenpolitische und völkerrechtliche Situation Österreichs 1938," 70; Stourzh, *Geschichte des Staatsvertrages*, 4.

136 "The idea of an Austrian declaration, which was in reality a middle – and southeast European declaration ... " Rauchensteiner, *Der Sonderfall*, 19.

137 British Moscow Conference draft agenda, 3 September 1943, FDR, MR 32: Secretary of State to Sir Alexander Cadogan, 15 September 1943, NA, RG 59, Office of European Affairs, 16.

138 United States draft agenda for the Moscow Conference, 14 September 1943, FDR, MR, 32.

139 Ibid., draft Soviet agenda for the Moscow Conference, 2 October 1943, also, *FRUS, 1943*, The Moscow Conference, 1: 537–8.

140 Anglo-American draft agenda, 18 September 1943, NA, RG 59, Notter Papers, 18; ibid., Office of European Affairs, 16, copy of telegram from Eden to HM Ambassador, Moscow, 18 September 1943.

141 Vandenberg, ed., *The Private Papers of Senator Vandenberg*, 34–5, 37–43, 58, 90–106; Dallek, *Roosevelt and Foreign Policy*, 417–23.

142 "For the President: Tri-Partite Conference Moscow 1943," Minutes and Conversations, NA, RG 59, Notter Papers, 18.

143 Hull, *Memoirs*, 2: 1315.

144 Harriman, *Special Envoy*, 234. Looking at the Moscow Conference from outside, historian Gordon Craig exaggerated the Big Three's decisional results there by comparing them to the Allies' 1814 meeting while attempting to overthrow Napoleon. "The Technique of Peacemaking," 113–28.

145 Ibid., 177–8. Roosevelt explained that he had refused to take Hull to Casablanca because Hull was "forceful, stubborn, difficult to handle. He had some rigid ideas and would be a nuisance at the conference." Notter, *Foreign Policy Preparation*, 124–7.

146 Notter, "Foreign Policy Preparation (draft)," Notter Papers, NA, RG 59, 52.

147 Harriman, *Special Envoy*, 236.

148 Ibid., 244.

149 Minutes of 25 October 1943, Minutes and Conversations, Moscow 1943, NA, RG 59, European Advisory Commission; Harriman to Under-Secretary of State, 25(?) October 1943, FDR, MR, 35.

150 *FRUS, 1943*, 1: 638–9.

151 See 149 above, minutes of 25 October.

152 Harriman, *Special Envoy*, 236.

153 *FRUS, 1943*, 1: 633.

154 Ibid., 3: 553–6; Howard, *Grand Strategy*, 4: 523; and Lundestad, *American Non-Policy towards Eastern Europe*, 81ff.

155 Feis, *Churchill, Roosevelt and Stalin*, 208–9.

156 On his return from Moscow, Hull hopefully spoke of an end to spheres of influence and balance of power arrangements, probably because no territorial agreements were reached in Moscow. Department of State, *Bulletin*, 20 November 1943, 341–5.

157 Protocol of 1 November 1943 meeting, item No. 7, FDR, Hopkins Papers, 7.

158 Ibid., HB report to Hopkins, 29 October 1943.

159 Clark Kerr, Moscow, 28 October 1943, PRO, FO 371, C12794/321/18; Stanley, "Great Britain and the Austrian Question," 121.

160 25 October minutes, Tri-Partite Conference of Foreign Secretaries, Moscow, NA, RG 59, European Advisory Commission, 29.

161 Harriman to State Department, 25 October 1943, FDR, MR, 32.

162 Harriman to State Department, 31 October 1943, FDR, Special Files, 32; also

FRUS, *1943*, 65, 152–4.

163 British Embassy, Washington, to Foreign Office, 31 October 1943, PRO, FO, 371, 34466/C11820.

164 Ibid., C12794, Allen minute, 31 October 1943.

165 Mosley, "The Treaty with Austria," 227; Stanley, "Great Britain and the Austrian Question," 121.

166 British Embassy, Moscow, to Foreign Office, 31 October 1943, PRO, FO, 371, C12795.

167 *FRUS*, *1943*, 1: 761. For State Department translations into German, see Verosta, *Die internationale Stellung Österreichs*, 52–3, and Stourzh, *Geschichte des Staatsvertrages*, 214.

168 *Christian Science Monitor*, 1 November 1943; *Washington Star*, 2 November 1943; *Washington Times-Herald*, 3 November 1943. These and the following newspaper excerpts were collected in NA, RG 59, Pasvolsky Papers, 1.

169 Ibid., *New York Journal-American*, 4 November 1943.

170 Ibid., *New York Journal-American*, 2 November 1943; and *Washington Post*, 5 November 1943.

171 Ibid., *New York Herald Tribune*, 2 November 1943.

172 Ibid., *New York Post*, 2 November 1943.

173 Ibid., *Wall Street Journal*, 5 November 1943.

174 Diary entry of 13 October 1943, Stimson Diary, 44/192.

175 Ibid., 44/231, 28 October 1943.

176 Department of State, Memorandum of Press and Radio Conferences No. 105, 15 November 1943, NA, RG 43, World War Two Conferences, 1A. According to Whitnah and Erickson, Hull signed the declaration on Austria because he was so seriously convinced that Austria was a victim of Nazi aggression. *The Occupation of Austria*, 264.

177 Diary entries of 5 and 12 November 1943, Stimson Diaries, 45/20 and 45/43.

178 "Attitudes towards the Moscow Conference and International Cooperation," Bureau of Special Services, Survey Division, memorandum No. 96, 11 December 1943, FDR, OF 4647, 63.

179 William Bennett, Attorney for Austrian Action, to Adolf Berle, 20 December 1943, FDR, Berle Papers, 215.

180 Quoted in Stanley, "Great Britain and the Austrian Question," 143.

181 Amended PWE directive, March 1944, PRO, FO 371, C3652/2802/3.

182 Ibid., C8260/2802/3, Col. Thornley to Harrison, 16 June 1944; Stanley, "Great Britain and the Austrian Question," 150ff.

183 Harvey minute, 4 July 1944, PRO, FO 371, C8260/2808/3.

184 "Austria and the Moscow Conference," Joint Intelligence Weekly Survey No. 46, 24 November 1943, 17–22.

185 Algiers to War Department, 29 December 1943, FDR, MR, 46.

CHAPTER SIX

1 Admiral W.D. Leahy to Roosevelt, 18 November 1943, including the British Joint Planning Staff's paper, "Disintegration of Axis. Areas of Immediate Occupation." FDR, MR 35. CCS, 320/4, "Operation Rankin," 2 December 1943; JCS, 577/4, "Rankin," Joint Staff Planners, 28 December 1943, JCS Records, European Theater, 1, Reel 7; Butcher, *My Three Years with Eisenhower*, 447–8.

2 Rose, *Dubious Victory*, 1, 6–7.

3 Waibel, *Kapitulation in Norditalien.*

4 Rauchensteiner, *Der Sonderfall*, 15–45, and *Krieg in Österreich 1945*.

5 Grigg, *1943*, 186ff.

6 Col. C.B. Hazeltine, Allied Forces HQ, Psychological Warfare Branch, 9 November 1943, PRO, FO 898/216.

7 U.S. Algiers to the War Department, telegram 3 January 1944, FDR, MR 46.

8 PWE Central Directive, 18 November 1943, and attached "The Effects of the Moscow Conference," DEA, 5404–A–40C.

9 Ibid., PWE Central Directives, 23 September and 4 November 1943.

10 OSS report from Bern, 19 January 1944, FDR, MR 73.

11 Ibid., OSS report on Austria, 26 January 1944.

12 OSS Research and Analysis Branch report, "Materials for an Austrian Leaflet Campaign," 29 January 1944, NA, RG 59, OSS.

13 PWE Austrian reports of 9 January 1944, "Opinion and Morale in Austria," 23 April 1943, "Austrian Attitudes to Germany, the War and Future," and 12 June 1944, "Austria: Some Conclusions for Political Warfare," FO 898/216.

14 Ibid., PWE, "Austria: Some Conclusions for Political Warfare," 12 June 1944, FO 898/216.

15 Ibid., "Recent Trends in Russian Propaganda to Austria," December 1943.

16 Foreign Office, Political Intelligence Department, PWE Political Warfare Directives, 19 October 1944 and 12 April 1945, DEA, 5405–A–400.

17 CCS No. 454, "Monthly Review of Conditions in Europe," 1 January 1944, JCS Records, European Theatre, Reel 7; OSS report, 26 January 1944, FDR, MR 73.

18 OSS report, 19 January 1944, FDR, MR 73.

19 CCS No. 545, "Outline Plan for Political Warfare-Overlord," 13 April 1944, JCS Records, 1, Strategy Issues, Reel 10.

20 Ibid., Memorandum from Lt. Col. Stanley, Liaison Officer JCS, to OWI, 25 April 1944.

21 Ibid., JCS No. 836/1, "Outline Plan for Psychological Warfare-Overlord," 18 May 1944.

22 Elmer Davis, OWI Director, to Roosevelt, 24 May 1944: E. Stettinius to Roosevelt, 3 June 1944, on which the Roosevelt instruction "to file" can

be noted, FDR, MR 73.

23 "Austrian Rising Urged," *New York Times*, 24 July 1944; "Vienna's Well-Armed Underground Bides Its Time," *New York Post*, 16 October 1944; "Viennese Reported Battling Gestapo," *New York World-Telegram*, 2 December 1944.

24 'Reds Ask Austria to Rebel at Once," *New York World-Telegram*, 24 April 1944; "Moscow Calls Austrians to Revolt against Nazis," *New York Times*, 4 September 1944; "Viennese Revolt Urged by Moscow," *New York World-Telegram*, 14 December 1944.

25 "Hull Demands Austrians Turn on Reich Now," *New York Herald Tribune*, 12 September 1944.

26 "Riots Reported in Vienna after Eisenhower's Call," *New York World-Telegram*, 2 October 1944; "Austrians Told to Prepare for Arrival of Allies," *New York Times*, 2 October 1944.

27 Eisenhower meeting with PWE, BCOS, and Foreign Office, 2 February 1945, NA, RG 59, Office of European Affairs, 10.

28 "Austrians Urged to Seek Freedom," *New York Times*, 11 March 1945; ibid., "Hopes for Austria," 13 March 1945.

29 Rauchensteiner, "The Rebirth of Austria as a Military Problem," 7–8.

30 "The Provisional Austrian National Committee and the Austrian Underground," 19 April 1945, FDR, Hopkins Papers, 228; Stanley, "Britain and the Austrian Question," 108ff.

31 Memorandum of conversation, Mr A. Visson (*Time* magazine) and Mr Adams of CE [Central European Division], 7 March 1945, United States, Department of State Archives, Austria Desk, 1945–9.

32 PWE Central Directive, 12 April 1945, DEA, 5404–B–40C.

33 Ibid., PWE Central Directive, 26 April 1945.

34 JCS No. 980, "Prospects of a German Collapse or Surrender," 5 August 1944; CCS No. 660, same title, 28 August 1944, JCS Records, European Theater, Reel 1.

35 Ibid., CCS No. 660/3, "Estimate of the Enemy Situation -Europe," 26 January 1945.

36 Ibid., CCS No. 660/4, "German Capabilities for Continued Resistance in the South," 7 April 1945.

37 "The Provisional Austrian National Committee and the Austrian Underground," 19 April 1945, spoke of 20–50,000 members in POEN (Provisional Austrian National council), but admitted that its information was slim and Nazi rule still firm. FDR, Hopkins Papers, 228.

38 Draft memorandum to the Secretary of State, 2 February 1945, NA, RG 59, Office of European Affairs, 10.

39 "Austrian Revolution against Nazis Near," *New York World-Telegram*, 16 January 1945; ibid., "Anti-Nazis Get Ready in Austria," 15 February 1945.

40 Verbatim report of General Bedell Smith's sitrep of 21 April 1945, in

Butcher, *My Three Years with Eisenhower*, 806–5. Eisenhower's opinion in this regard was based on OSS and Ultra reports. *Eisenhower: At War*, 729. For the occupation question, see ibid., 630.

41 *Eisenhower: At War*, 768–9, 790. Rauchensteiner, *Krieg in Österreich*, chapters 11–14; *Les grandes unite'es francaises*, 779–98.

42 Rauchensteiner, "The Rebirth of Austria," 8.

43 Minot, *The Fortress That Never Was*.

45 First CCS draft on Austria, CCS No. 481, "Civil Affairs in Austria," 2 February 1944, with annex, "Political Guide," April 1944, Records of JCS, I, European Theater, Reel 13.

46 Macmillan and Murphy in conversation, *The Blast of War*, 521; Anderson, *The United States, Britain and the Cold War*, 1ff.

47 "Essentials of an American Policy," 21 March 1944, PRO, FO 371, AN 1538/16/45; Boyle, "The British Foreign Office View of Soviet-American Relations," 307.

48 Stoler, "From Continentalism to Globalism," 316–17.

49 Peterson, *The American Occupation of Germany*, 54ff.

50 Harrison minute, 22 February 1944, PRO, FO 371, C3398/2802/3; Stanley, "Great Britain and Austria," 184ff; Wagnleitner, "Grossbritannien und die Wiedererrichtung Österreichs," 5.

51 PWE paper, "Austria: Attitudes to Germany, the War and the Future," 23 April 1944, NA, EAC, 100 (see appendix 4).

52 Sir H.W. Malkin, Foreign Office legal expert, minute of 20 January 1945, quoted in Stanley, "Great Britain and Austria," 82.

53 Sargent to Lord Cranborne, Dominions Office, 9 October 1945, PRO, FO 371, 34466/C11389.

54 Ibid., C14085/321/18, Foreign Office circular dispatch of 31 December 1943,

55 Ibid., 38827/C1338, Viscount Halifax telegram to Foreign Office, 28 January 1944, passed to War Cabinet, also aide-mémoire to United States, 2 February 1944.

56 Stoler, *The Politics of the Second Front*, 157.

57 JCS meeting with Roosevelt, 10 August 1944, Records of JCS, 1, Meetings, Reel 1.

58 Ibid.

59 Dilks, ed., *Diaries of Sir Alexander Cadogan*, 597; *FRUS*, 1944, 4: 1035–7; Sir L. Woodward, *British Foreign Policy in the Second World War*, 5: 291.

60 Woodward, Sir L., *British Foreign Policy in the Second World War*, 5: 244–251.

61 "Report of the Interdepartmental Committee on Postwar Economic Policy towards Austria," 16 October 1944, DEA 7–PC(S).

62 Churchill to Roosevelt, No. 801, 22 October 1944, FDR, MR 32; also *FRUS, 1944*, 4: 1022–4.

63 Overseas Reconstruction Committee, 11 July 1945, PRO, FO 371, C3940/134/

3.

64 Stanley, "Die britischen Vorbehalte gegenüber der provisorischen Regierung Renner 1945," 38–46.

65 Hackworth memorandum for Hull, 23 November 1943, NA, RG 59, 863.01/814 (appendix 4).

66 Ibid., 863.01/854, Division of European Affairs memorandum, 10 December 1943.

67 State Department memorandum to Roosevelt, 20 April 1944, FDR, PSF, 32A.

68 Berle memorandum to Hull, 4 January 1944, FDR, Berle Papers, 59.

69 Ibid., Berle to Hull, 3 January 1944.

70 Stettinius to Miss Tully, White House, 20 October 1944, FDR, PSF, 32A.

71 Stettinius to United States Embassy, Paris, 16 March 1945, *FRUS, 1945*, 2: 562–3.

72 Mosley, "The Occupation of Germany," 580–604; Erikson, "The Zoning of Austria," 106–13; "Austria," in Balfour and Muir, eds., *Four-Power Control in Germany and Austria*, 283–6; Dorn, "The Debate over American Occupation Policy," 487; Snell, *The Wartime Origin of the East-West Dilemma over Germany*; Rauchensteiner, *Der Sonderfall*.

73 Belush, *He Walked Alone*, 191ff.

74 "Winant found himself shaken and embarrassed, handicapped as he was by inadequate, infrequent directives from Washington and publicly circumvented and ignored by his own government." Strang, *At Home and Abroad*, 208.

75 For details on the frustrations of SWNCC and WSC until late 1944, see Hammond, "Directives for the Occupation of Germany," 313–464; Hayes, "Coordination of Military and Civilian Affairs Planning," 267; Stimson and Bundy, *On Active Service*, 560.

76 Steefer, "American Attitudes and the Development of Policy towards Austria," 142ff.

77 JCS to Roosevelt, 18 November 1943, FDR, MR 35; "Europe-Wide RANKIN," JCS No. 577, 8 November 1943, and "Policies With Respect to the Military Considerations in Dealing with Neutral, Liberated and Occupied Countries," JCS No. 575, 8 November 1943, Records of JCS, 1, European Theater, Reel 7.

78 Roosevelt wrote to Churchill: "I can only add that political considerations in the United States make my decision conclusive." Roosevelt to Churchill, No. 457, 7 February 1944, FDR, OF 35.

79 "Operation RANKIN – Demarkation of Boundaries after Surrender of Germany," JCS No. 577/7, 22 February 1944, Records of JCS, I, European Theater, Reel 7.

80 Ibid., "Occupation of Certain Areas in the Mediterranean Theater under RANKIN 'C' Conditions," JCS No. 577/13, 20 May 1944, and Rigdon note, 25 May 1944.

81 Roosevelt to Hull, 30 April 1944, ibid.; Roosevelt to Churchill, No. 545, 30 April 1944, 27 May 1944, FDR, OF 35.

82 See 80 above.

83 "The Future Status of Austria," 30 September 1944, NA, RG 59, Notter Papers, 155.

84 Ibid., 4, Notter, draft "Foreign Policy Perparation," chapters 3 and 8.

85 Dallek, *Roosevelt and Foreign Policy*, 482–4.

86 JCS, "Occupation of Certain Areas in the Mediterranean Theater under RANKIN 'C' Conditions," 20 May 1944, Records of JCS, I, European Theater, Reel 7.

87 Ibid., Winant to Hull, 17 June 1944, 577/15, 21 June 1944.

88 Hull to Miss Tully, 27 June 1944, FDR, PSF, 32A; Belush, *He Walked Alone*, 202; Muir, "Austria," 283–6.

89 Hull to General Hilldring, 21 June 1944, in JCS 577/15, "American Participation in the Occupation and Control of Austria," 2 July 1944, Records of JCS 1, European Theater, Reel 7.

90 See 87 above.

91 Hull to Roosevelt, 24 June 1944, with Roosevelt's handwritten comment on this change, "CH, OK, FDR"; Hull to Miss Tilly, White House, 21 June 1944, with enclosed PWC (Postwar Committee) paper No. 217a, "Summary: The Treatment of Austria: Policy Recommendations," FDR, PSF, 32A. Compare this to CAC No. 210 (preliminary), "The Treatment of Austria," 31 May 1944, NA, RG 59, Notter Papers, 115.

92 PWC 217a, "Summary: The Treatment of Austria: Policy Recommendations," 21 June 1944, NA, RG 59, Notter Papers, 115.

93 Dallek, *Roosevelt and Foreign Policy*, 487–8.

94 Hull to Senator Vandenberg, 26 August 1944, NA, RG 59, 863.01/8–1844.

95 OSS Research and Analysis (R & A) preliminary draft document No. 2111.1, "The Revival of Austrian Political and Constitutional Life under Military Government," 6 January 1944, NA, RG 59, OSS (appendix 4).

96 PWC 218 (CAC 210) on Austria, 8 June 1944, FDR, PSF, 32A.

97 Ibid., PWC 217a, "Summary: The Treatment of Austria: Policy Recommendations," 21 June 1944.

98 OSS, R & A, 2111, "The Implementation under Military Occupation of the Moscow Declaration on Austria," 14 August 944, NA, RG 59, OSS.

99 H194, "The Future Status of Austria," NA, RG 59, Notter Papers, 155, and FDR, PSF, 32A.

100 Ibid.

101 Ibid.

102 Ibid., MR, 35, Roosevelt to Acting Secretary of State Stettinius, 3 August 1944, FDR, OF, 35; CCS – SHAEF, 19 August 1944.

103 CCS No. 481/5, "Planning for Military Government in Austria," September 1945, Records of JCS, I, European Theater, Reel 13.

104 American Forces HQ, Caserta, Italy, to War Department, 16 October 1944, FDR, MR 35; Roosevelt to Stettinius about Erhardt, 2 November 1944, FDR, PSF, 32A.

105 CAC No. 317, 1 November 1944, approved by the Postwar Program Committee, NA, RG 59, Notter Papers, 115.

106 Winant to Secretary of State, 4 and 8 December 1944; Roosevelt to Secretary of State, 8 December 1944, FDR, PSF, 32A.

107 JCS No. 1169/1, "Acceptance by the United States of a Zone of Occupation in Austria," 15 December 1944, Records of JCS, 1, European Theater, Reel 13.

108 JCS to Commanding General, AFHQ, Caserta, Italy, 28 December 1944, FDR, MR 35.

109 Ibid., CCS to Commanding General, AFHQ, Caserta, Italy, 16 March 1945; AFHQ, Italy, to War Department, 26 March 1945.

110 Ibid., SHAEF to War Department, 6 April 1945.

111 CCS No. 481, "Civil Affairs in Austria," 2 February 1944, in which Austria still appeared as enemy territory and a belligerent, Records of JCS, 1, European Theater, Reel 13; ibid., Reel 1, Joint Planning Staff No. 610/D, "OSS Mission for Germany," 12 February 1945, with Exhibit C, OSS, R & A civil affairs guides for Germany and Austria, including papers on "Political Differences between Germany and Austria Affecting Military Government," and "The Feasibility of an Administrative and Economic Separation of Austria from Germany under Military Government."

112 R.W. Flournoy, legal division, to Hackworth, 17 April 1945, NA, RG 59, 711.63/4–1745; ibid., 863.00/5–145, L.A. Merchant memorandum, 12 January 1945.

113 Ibid., 863.00/121–1946, Secret telegram from Dean Acheson to the American legation in Vienna, 19 November 1946.

114 Ibid., 863.00/10–1846, Coburn Kidd memorandum to Hickerson and Riddelberger, 10 August 1946.

115 Ibid., 711.63/7–2148, R.T. Yingling, legal division, to A. Gould, 9 August 1948.

116 F.T. Williamson memorandum to OE, ADO, DRE, "Policy and Information Statement – Austria," 18 June 1948, State Department Archives, Austrian desk, 1945–9.

117 Combined Civil Affairs Committee on Austia, "Civil Affairs in Austria: Political Guide," 30 May 1944, NA, RG 59, EAC, 100.

118 O'Neil minute, 16 August 1944, agreed to by Strang and two others, PRO, FO 371, 38838/C10298.

119 Ibid., W. Strang to Winant, 10 October 1944, with British draft proclamation.

120 Ibid., 39003/13387, Sir Cyril Hurst, Minutes of the War Crimes Commission, 2 October 1944, and J.C. Wadrop minute.

121 L.A. Merchant memorandum, 12 January 1945, NA, RG 59, 863.00/5–145.

122 P. Deen minute, October 1944, PRO, FO 371, 39003/13387.

123 For instance, the New Zealand opinion in June 1946: "In our view, Austria has not deserved, nor can she legally claim, a treaty more favorable than that applied to other active supporters of Germany and even Italy. She will, in any case, fare better than Germany herself because settlement will be earlier and more lenient." New Zealand Minister of External Affairs to the Canadian Acting Secretary of State for External Affairs, 12 June 1946, DEA, 7–D(s); see Keyserlingk, "Policy or Practice: Canada and Austria, 1938–1949," 25–30.

124 "The Revival of Austrian Political and Constitutional Life under Military Government," 6 January 1944, OSS, R & A, 2111.1; ibid., "Implementation Uunder Military Government of the Moscow Declaration on Austria," 14 August 1944 (appendix 4); ibid., "A Civil Affairs Guide for Austria and the Applicability of the German Guides." NA, RG 59, OSS, R & A Branch.

125 "Treatment of Austria," 11 January 1945, NA, RG 59, Office of European Affairs, 10 (appendix 4).

126 Overseas Reconstruction Committee report, 11 July 1945, PRO, FO 371, C3940/134/3.

CONCLUSION

1 Harbutt, *The Iron Curtain*, 24–8; see also Kitchen, *British Policy towards the Soviet Union during the Second World War.*

2 M. Gurfein and M. Janowitz, "Trends in Wehrmacht Morale," 78.

3 *Toynbee on Toynbee*, 48.

APPENDIX 1

1 *Documents on British Foreign Policy 1919–1939*. 3rd ser.(1938), 1: 18–19.

2 Ibid., 25–6.

3 Ibid., 29.

4 "The Anschluss," Chamberlain's official statement of 14th March 1938 in the House of Commons, quoted in Chamberlain, *In Search of Peace*, 69–76.

5 *Parliamentary Debates. House of Lords*, 5th ser., 108: 16 March 1938, 178–80.

6 Speech at a Unionist meeting, quoted in Chamberlain, *In Search of Peace*, 97–9.

APPENDIX 2

1 Collection of statements by the Department of State's Legal Adviser, 10 September 1943, NA, RG 59, 863.01/796.

2 *FRUS, 1938*, 1: 473.

3 Entry of 4 April 1938, Stimson Papers, Diary, vol.28.
4 *FRUS, 1938*, 1: 473.
5 Ibid., 483–4.

APPENDIX 3

1 *FRUS, 1943*, 1: 515–17.
2 Ibid., General, 549–50. This version was presented by the British to the Moscow Conference, becoming conference document no. 21. Ibid., 724.
3 Ibid., 761, Annex 6 to the Secret Protocol.

APPENDIX 4

1 NA, RG 59, 863.01/814.
2 Preliminary Draft, "The Revival of Austrian Political and Constitutional Life under Military Government," 6 January 1944, 1 and 56–7, NA, RG 59, OSS, R & A Branch, 2111.1.
3 "Austria: Attitudes to Germany, the War and the Future," Political Warfare Directive, 23 April 1944, PWE, German and Austrian Intelligence Section, PRO, FO 898/216.
4 "The Implementation under Military Occupation of the Moscow Declaration on Austria," 14 August 1944, NA, RG 59, OSS, R & A, 2111.
5 "Treatment of Austria," Secret, 11 January 1945, Department of State, NA, RG 59, Office of European Affairs, 11.
6 Circular D.47, Secret, 18 January 1946, Secretary of State for Dominion Affairs to Secretary of State for External Affairs, Canada, DEA, 7–DG(s).
7 Quoted from Karl Gruber, *Between Liberation and Liberty*, 82.
8 Circular D. 1013, Secret, 9 November 1946, Secretary of State for Dominion Affairs to the Secretary of State for External Afairs, Canada, DEA, 7–P(s).

Bibliography

PRIMARY SOURCES

Council on Foreign Relations Archives, New York

Annual Reports of the Executive Director, 1921–41

Records of Conferences

Records of Groups

Records of Meetings

War and Peace Studies, 1939–45

Department of External Affairs Archives, Ottawa

General Diplomatic Files

Dokumentationszentrum des österreichischen Widerstandes, Vienna

Robert Heine-Geldern Papers

Wilobad Plöchl Papers

W. Wunsch Papers

Photostat collection of British Foreign Office and American Department of State papers

Franklin D. Roosevelt Library, Hyde Park

Adolf A. Berle Jr Diary and Papers

Francis Biddle Papers

Charles Fahy Papers

Henry Hopkins Papers

Map Room Papers (MR)

Henry Morgenthau Manuscript Diary and Papers

President's Alphabetical File
President's Official File (OF)
President's Personal File (PPF)
President's Press Conferences
President's Secretary's File (PSF)
Rosenman Papers
John C. Wiley Papers
John G. Winant Papers

Harvard University, Houghton Library
J. Pierrepont Moffat Manuscript Diary and Papers
Joseph C. Grew Mauscript Diary and Papers

Library of Congress, Washington
Cordell Hull Manuscripts

National Archives, Washington
RG 43 World War II Conferences
RG 59 General Records of the Department of State
RG 208 Records of the Office of War Information
RG 218 Records of the United States Joint Chiefs of Staff
RG 226 Records of the Office of Strategic Services

Public Archives of Canada, Ottawa
RG 25 Department of External Affairs
MG 26 William Lyon Mackenzie King Papers
MG 26L Louis St Laurent Papers
E165 Norman Robertson Papers

Public Record Office, London
CAB 65: War Cabinet Conclusions and Minutes
CAB 66: War Cabinet Memoranda
CAB 79: Chiefs of Staff Minutes
FO 371: Foreign Office Political and Diplomatic Files
FO 898: Political Warfare Executive
PREM 3: Prime Minister's Operational Files
PREM 4: Prime Minister's Confidential Files

Royal Institute of International Affairs Archives, London
Arnold J. Toynbee file
Annual Reports of the Executive Director, 1922–46

Council on Foreign Relations file
Royal Institute general files

United States, Department of State Archives, Washington
Classified papers, EUR/WE [Europe, West], Austria Desk, 1945–9

University of Delaware Library, Manuscript Division
George S. Messersmith Papers

University of Oxford, Bodleian Library
Arnold J. Toynbee Papers

Yale University
Henry L. Stimson Manuscript Diary and Papers

SECONDARY SOURCES

Books

Adams, Henry H. *Harry Hopkins: A Biography*. New York 1977.
Aichinger, Wilfried. *Sowjetische Österreichpolitik, 1943–1945*. Wien 1981.
Allen, H.C. *Great Britain and the United States: A History of Anglo-American Relations, 1783–1952*. London 1954.
Allied Commission for Austria. *A Guide, Background, Principles and Procedures*. Vienna 1949.
Alsop, Stewart, and Thomas Braden. *Sub Rosa: The OSS and American Espionage*. New York 1946.
Ambrose, Stephen E. *Eisenhower and Berlin*. New York 1967.
– *The Supreme Commander: The War Years of General Dwight D. Eisenhower*. Garden City, NY 1970.
– *Eisenhower: A Life*. New York 1983.
Anderson, Terry H. *The United States, Great Britain and the Cold War, 1944–1947*. Columbia, Mo. 1981.
Andics, E.C. *Der Staat der keiner wollte: Österreich 1918–1938*. Wien 1962.
– *Der Fall Otto Habsburg: Ein Bericht*. Wien, München 1965.
– *Fünfzig Jahre unseres Lebens: Österreichs Schicksal*. Wien 1968.
Angell, H. *The Recovery of Germany*. New York 1929.
Armstrong, Anne. *Unconditional Surrender: The Impact of the Casablanca Policy upon World War II*. New Brunswick, NJ 1961.

Armstrong, Hamilton Fish. *The New Balkans*. New York 1926.
– *Where the East Begins*. New York 1929.
– *Versailles in Retrospect*. New York 1932.
– *Hitler's Reich*. New York 1933.
– *Europe between Wars?* New York 1934.
– *We or They: Two Worlds in Conflict*. New York 1936.
– *When There Is No Peace*. New York 1939.
– *Those Days*. New York 1963.
– *Peace and Counterpeace: From Wilson to Hitler*. New York 1971.
Austria. *Rot-Weiss-Rot Buch*. Wien 1947.
– *Austria Documentation: Austria – Permanently Neutral: Austrian Foreign Policy since 1945*. Vienna 1985.
Backer, John H. *The Decision to Divide Germany*. Chapel Hill, NC 1978.
Bader, William B. *Austria between East and West, 1945–1955*. Stanford 1966.
Baird, Jay W. *The Mythological World of Nazi War Propaganda, 1939–1945*. Minneapolis 1974.
Balfour, Michael. *Propaganda at War*. London 1917.
– and J. Muir, eds. *Four-Power Control in Germany and Austria, 1945–1946*. London 1956.
Ball, Mary. *Post War German Austrian Relations*. London 1937.
Barker, Elizabeth. *Austria, 1918–1972*. London 1973.
– *British Policy in South-East Europe in the Second World War*. London 1976.
Bauer, Ludwig. *Und Österreich. Ein Staat sucht ein Volk*. Paris 1933.
Bauer, Otto. *Acht Monate auswärtige Politik*. Wien 1919.
– *The Austrian Revolution*. Vienna 1923.
Beesly, Patrick. *Very Special Intelligence*. London 1977.
Beevor, J.G. *SOE: Recollections and Reflections*. London 1981.
Belush, Bernard. *He Walked Alone: A Biography of John Gilbert Winant*. The Hague, Paris 1968.
Berle, Beatrice, and Travis B. Jacobs, eds. *Navigating the Rapids, 1918–1971: From the Papers of Adolf A. Berle*. 2 vols. New York 1973.
Bethouart, Marie Emile. *Die Schlacht um Österreich*. Wien 1967.
Betts, R.R., ed. *Central and South East Europe*. London 1950.
Biddle, Francis. *In Brief Authority*. New York 1962.
Bluhm, William T. *Building an Austrian Nation: The Political Integration of a Western State*. New Haven 1973.
Blum, John Morton, ed. *From the Morgenthau Diaries: Years of Crisis, 1928–1938*. Boston 1959.
– *From the Morgenthau Diaries: Years of Urgency, 1938–1941*. Boston 1966.
– *From the Morgenthau Diaries: Years of War, 1941–1945*. Boston 1967.
– *The Price of Vision: The Diary of Henry A. Wallace, 1942–1946*. Boston 1973.
Blumenson, Martin. *Breakout and Pursuit: United States Army in World War II: The European Theater of Operations*. Washington 1961.

– ed. *The Patton Papers 1940–1945*. 2 vols. Boston 1972–4.

Bock, Fritz. *Der Anschluss an Europa: Gedanken, Versuche, Ergebnisse*. St Pölten 1978.

Bohlen, Charles. *The Transformation of American Foreign Policy*. New York 1969.

– *Witness to History, 1929–1969*. New York 1973.

Bornstein, Joseph, and Paul R. Milton. *Action against the Enemy's Mind*. Indianapolis 1942.

Botz, Gerhard. *Die Eingliederung Österreichs in das Deutsche Reich: Plannung und Verwirklichung des politisch-administrativen Anschlusses (1938–1940)*. Wien 1977.

– *Wien vom "Anschluss" zum Krieg: Nationalsozialistische Machtübernahme und politisch-soziale Umgestaltung am Beispiel der Stadt Wien, 1938/39*. Wien 1978.

Boyle, Andrew. *The Climate of Treason*. London 1979.

Bradley, Omar, N. *A Soldier's Story*. New York 1951.

– and Clay Blair. *A General's Life*. New York 1983.

Braunder, Wilhelm, and Friedrich Lachmayer. *Österreichische Verfassungsgeschichte*. Wien 1976.

Braunthal, Julius. *The Future of Austria: A Plea for the United States of Europe*. London 1943.

– *The Tragedy of Austria*. London 1948.

Briggs, Asa. *The War of Words*. London 1970.

Brown, Anthony Cave. *Bodyguard of Lies*. New York 1975.

Brunner, Jerome S. *Mandate for the People*. New York 1944.

Bryant, Arthur. *The Turn of the Tide: A History of the War Years Based on the Diaries of Field-Marshal Lord Alanbrooke, Chief of the Imperial General Staff*. Garden City, NY 1957.

– *Triumph in the West: Based on the Diaries and Autobiographical Notes of Field-Marshal Lord Alanbrooke*. London 1959.

Buchbender, Ortwin, and Horst Shuh. *Heil Beil: Flugblattpropaganda im Zweiten Weltkrieg. Dokumentation und Analyse*. Stuttgart 1974.

Bullitt, Orville H., ed. *For the President: Personal and Secret: Correspondence between Franklin D. Roosevelt and William C. Bullitt*. Boston 1972.

Bullock, John. *MI5. The Origin and History of the British Counter-Espionage Service*. London 1963.

Burnham, James. *The Web of Subversion*. New York 1954.

Burns, James MacGregor. *Roosevelt: The Lion and the Fox*. New York 1956.

– *Roosevelt: The Soldier of Freedom*. New York 1970.

Butcher, Henry C. *My Three Years with Eisenhower: The Personal Diary, 1942–1945*. New York 1946.

Butler, J.R.M. *Grand Strategy*. London 1957.

– *Lord Lothian, 1882–1940*. London 1960.

Buttinger, J. *In the Twilight of Socialism* New York 1953.

Byrnes, James F. *Speaking Frankly*. New York 1947.

Calvocoressi, Peter. *Top Secret Ultra*. New York 1980.

Campbell, John C. *American Policy toward Eastern Europe: The Choices Ahead*. Minneapolis 1965.

Campbell, Thomas M., and George C. Herring, eds. *The Diaries of Edward R. Stettinius Jr., 1943–1946*. New York 1975.

Cantril, Hadley, and Mildred Strunk, eds. *Public Opinion, 1935–1946*. Princeton, NJ 1951.

Carroll, B.A. *Design for Total War*. Mouton 1968.

Carsten, Francis L. *Fascist Movements in Austria from Schoenerer to Hitler*. London 1977.

Chandler, Alfred D., Jr, and Stephan E. Ambrose, eds. *The Papers of Dwight David Eisenhower: The War Years*. 5 vols. Baltimore, London 1970.

Chen, Ti-Chang. *The International Law of Recognition*. London 1951.

Churchill, Winston S. *The Second World War*. 6 vols. Boston 1953ff.

Clark, Mark W. *Calculated Risk*. New York 1950.

Clay, Lucius D. *Decision in Germany*. Garden City, NY 1950.

Clogg, Richard. *Politics and the Academy: Arnold Toynbee and the Koraes Chairs*. London 1986.

Clute, R.E. *The International Legal Status of Austria, 1938–1955*. The Hague 1962.

Cohen, Bernard. *The Public's Impact on Foreign Policy*. Boston 1973.

Cole, T. *The Recognition Policy of the United States since 1901*. Baton Rouge, La. 1928.

Cole, Wayne S. *America First: The Battle against Intervention, 1940–1941*. Madison, Wis. 1953.

– *Senator P. Nye and American Foreign Relations*. Minneapolis, Minn. 1962.

Coles, Harry L., and Albert K. Weinberg. *Civil Affairs: Soldiers Become Governors*. Washington 1964.

Collier, Brian. *The Defence of the United Kingdom*. London 1957.

Collingwood, R.G. *The Idea of History*. Oxford 1956.

Colvin, Ian. *Chief of Intelligence*. London 1951.

– *Vansittart in Office: An Historical Survey of the Origins of the Second World War Based on the Papers of Sir Robert Vansittart*. London 1965.

Complete Presidential Press Conferences of Franklin Delano Roosevelt. 25 vols. in 12. New York 1972.

Cookridge, E.H. *Inside SOE*. London 1966.

Cooper, Duff. *Old Men Forget*. New York 1954.

Correspondence between the Chairman of the Council of Ministers of the USSR and the Presidents of the United States and the Prime Ministers of Great Britain during the Great Patriotic War of 1941–1945. 2 vols. Moscow 1957.

Council on Foreign Relations. *Handbook*. New York 1919.

– *By-Laws and List of Officers and Members*. New York 1922.
– *By-Laws and List of Officers and Members*. New York 1924.
– *The Council on Foreign Relations: A Record of Fifteen Years*. New York 1937.
– *By-Laws and List of Officers and Members*. New York 1938.
– *Annual Report of the Executive Director*. New York 1940.
– *Annual Report of the Executive Director*. New York 1943.
– *The War and Peace Studies of the Council of Foreign Relations, 1939–1945*. New York 1946.
– *The Council on Foreign Relations: A Record of Twenty-five Years, 1921–1946*. New York 1947.
Craig, Gordon A., and Felix Gilbert, eds. *The Diplomats, 1919–1939*. 2 vols. New York 1965.
Cronin, Audrey K. *Great Power Politics and the Struggle over Austria*. Ithaca, NY 1986
Cruickshank, Charles. *The Fourth Arm: Psychological Warfare, 1938–1945*. London 1977.
Csa'ky, Eva-Marie. *Der Weg zur Freiheit und Neutralität. Dokumentation zur österreichischen Aussenpolitik 1945–1955*. Wien 1980.
Dachs, H. *Österreichischer Geschichtswissenschaft und Anschluss, 1918–1930*. Salzburg 1974.
Dallek, Robert. *Democrat and Diplomat: The Life of William E. Dodd*. New York 1968.
– *Franklin D. Roosevelt and American Foreign Policy, 1932–1945*. New York 1979.
– *The American Style of Foreign Policy: Cultural Politics and Foreign Affairs*. New York 1983.
Dalton, Hugh. *The Fateful Years: Memoirs, 1931–1945*. Vol. 2. London 1957.
– *High Tide and Afterwards: Memoirs, 1945–1960*. Vol.3. London 1962.
Daugherty, William W., and M. Janowitz. *A Psychological Warfare Casebook*. Baltimore 1958.
Davidson, Eugene. *The Death and Life of Germany: An Account of the American Occupation*. New York 1961.
– *The Trial of the Germans*. New York 1966.
Davies, Joseph E. *Mission to Moscow*. New York 1941.
Davis, Elmer, and Byron Price. *War Information and Censorship*. Washington 1943.
Davis, L.E. *The Cold War Begins: Soviet-American Conflict over Eastern Europe*. Princeton, NJ 1974.
Deacon, R. *History of the British Secret Service*. London 1969.
Deane, John R. *The Strange Alliance: The Story of Our Efforts at Wartime Co-operation with the Russians*. New York 1946.
De Jong, Louis. *The German Fifth Column in the Second World War*. Chicago 1956.

Delmar, Sefton. *Black Boomerang: An Autobiography.* 2 vols. London 1962.

De Santis, Hugh. *The Diplomacy of Silence: The American Foreign Service, the Soviet Union and the Cold War, 1933–1947.* Chicago 1981.

Deutsch, Julius. *Was wollen die Sozialisten?* Wien 1949.

– *Ein weiter Weg: Lebenserinnerungen.* Zürich 1960.

Diamant, Alfred, *Austrian Catholics and the First Republic: Democracy, Capitalism and the Social Order, 1918–1934.* Princeton, NJ 1960.

Dilks, David, ed. *The Diplomatic Diaries of Sir Alexander Cadogan, 1938–1945.* London 1971.

Divine, Robert A. *The Illusion of Neutrality.* Chicago 1962.

– *The Reluctant Belligerent: America's Entry into World War Two.* New York 1965.

– *Second Chance: The Triumph of Internationalism in America during World War II.* New York 1967.

– *Roosevelt and World War II.* Baltimore, Md. 1969.

Dodd, Martha. *Through Embassy Eyes.* New York 1939.

Dodd, William E., and Martha Dodd, eds. *Ambassador Dodd's Diary.* London 1941.

Dokumentationszentrum des österreichischen Widerstandes, *Österreicher im Exil 1934 bis 1945. Protokoll des internationalen Symposiums zur Erforschung des österreichischen Exils von 1934 bis 1945.* Wien 1977.

Donnison, F.S.V. *History of the Second World War: Civil Affairs and Military Government in North-West Europe, 1944–1946.* London 1961.

– *History of the Second World War: Civil Affairs and Military Government: Organisation and Planning.* London 1966.

Donovan, William J., and Edgar Mowrer. *Fifth Column Lessons for America.* Washington 1941.

Doob, Leonard. *Propaganda: Its Psychology and Technique.* New York 1935.

– *Public Opinion and Propaganda.* New York 1948.

Douglas, Roy. *From War to Cold War.* New York 1981.

Drummond, Ian S. *British Policy and Empire, 1919–1939.* London 1972.

– *Imperial Economic Policy, 1917–1939.* London 1974.

Dulles, Allan W. *The Craft of Intelligence.* New York 1965.

– *The Secret Surrender.* New York 1966.

– and Hamilton Fish Armstrong. *Can We Be Neutral?* New York 1936

Dunlop, Richard. *Donovan, America's Master Spy.* Chicago 1982.

Eden, Anthony, *The Memoirs of Anthony Eden, Earl of Avon: Facing the Dictators.* Boston 1962.

– *The Memoirs of Anthony Eden, Earl of Avon: The Reckoning.* Boston 1965.

Edinger, Lewis. *German Exile Politics.* Berkeley 1956.

Ehrman, John. *History of the Second World War: Grand Strategy.* Vols 5 and 6. London 1956.

Eichstädt, Ulrich. *Von Dollfuss zu Hitler: Geschichte des Anschlusses Öster-*

reichs, 1933–1938. Wiesbaden 1955.
Eisenhower, David. *Eisenhower: At War 1943–5*. New York 1986.
Eisenhower, Dwight. *Crusade in Europe*. London 1948.
– *Letters to Mamie*, edited by John Eisenhower. New York 1978.
– *The Eisenhower Diaries*, edited by Robert Ferrell. New York 1981.
Eisenhower, John D. *Allies: Pearl Harbor to D-Day*. New York 1982.
Eppel, Peter, ed. *Österreicher im Exil: USA 1938–1945. Eine Dokumentation*. Wien 1987.
Erickson, John. *The Road to Berlin*. New York 1983.
Ermacora, Felix. *Österreichs Staatvertrag und Neutralität*. Frankfurt/Main 1957.
– *Oesterreichische Verfassungslehre*. Wien, Stuttgart 1970.
European Resistance Movements, 1939–1945. First International Conference on the History of Resistance Movements. New York 1960.
Ewing, Blair G. *Peace through Negotiation: The Austrian Experience*. Washington 1966.
Farago, Ladislas. *German Psychological Warfare: A Critical, Annotated and Comprehensive Survey and Bibliography*. New York 1941.
– *The Game of Foxes*. New York 1971.
Feilchenfeld, E.H. *The International Law of Belligerent Occupation*. Washington 1942.
Feiling, Keith. *The Life of Neville Chamberlain*. London 1946.
Feis, Herbert. *Europe the World's Banker*. New York 1930.
– *Churchill-Roosevelt-Stalin*. Princeton, NJ 1967.
– *From Trust to Terror: The Onset of the Cold War, 1945–1950*: New York 1970.
Fellner, Fritz, and Heidrun Maschl, eds. *St. Germain im Sommer 1919*. Salzburg 1977.
Ferrell, R.H. *Frank B. Kellogg – Henry L. Stimson*. New York 1963.
Field, John C.W. *Aerial Propaganda Leaflets*. Sutton/Coldfield 1954.
Figl, Leopold. *Österreich kämpft um den Staatsvertrag*. Wien 1947.
Fischer, Alexander. *Sowjetische Deutschlandpolitik im Zweiten Weltkrieg, 1941–1945*. Stuttgart 1975.
Fischer, Ernst. *Das Ende einer Illusion: Erinnerungen 1945–1955*. Wien 1973.
Fischer, Heinz. *Das politische System Österreichs*. Wien 1974.
Foot, M.R.D. *SOE in France*. London 1966.
– *Resistance*. London 1978.
Ford, Corey. *Donovan of OSS*. Boston 1976.
Franckenstein, Sir George. *Diplomat of Destiny*. New York 1940.
François-Poncet, André. *The Fateful Years: Memoirs of a French Ambassador in Berlin, 1933–1938*. New York 1949.
Fraser, Lindley M. *Propaganda*. London: 1957.
Freedman, Max, ed. *Roosevelt and Frankfurter: Their Correspondence, 1928–1945*. Boston 1967.
Friedrich, Karl J. *American Experience in Military Government in World War*

II. New York 1948.

Fuller, Jean Overton. *The German Penetration of SOE: France 1941–1944*. London 1975.

Gaddis, John Lewis. *The United States and the Origins of the Cold War, 1941–1947*. New York 1972.

Galambos, Louis, ed. *The Papers of Dwight Eisenhower*. Vols. 7–9. Baltimore 1978.

Galloway, L.T. *Recognition of Foreign Governments: The Practice of the United States*. Washington 1978.

Gallup, George H. *The Gallup Poll: Public Opinion, 1935–1971*. Vol. 1 (1935–48). New York 1972.

Gardner, L.C. *Economic Aspects of New Deal Diplomacy*. Madison, Wis. 1964.

Garland, Albert N., and Howard Smythe. *Sicily and the Surrender of Italy*. Washington 1965.

Garlinski, Josef. *Poland, SOE and the Allies*. London 1969.

Gedye, G.E.R. *Betrayal in Central Europe: Austria and Czechoslovakia, The Fallen Bastions*. New York, London 1939.

Gehl, Juergen. *Germany and the Anschluss, 1931–1938*. London 1963.

Gelfand, E. *The Inquiry: American Preparations for Peace, 1917–19*. New York 1963.

George, Alexander L. *Propaganda Analysis: A Study of Inferences Made from Nazi Propaganda in World War II*. White Plains, NY 1959.

Germany. Foreign Office. *Documents on German Foreign Policy, 1918–45*, Series D, edited by R.J. Sonntag. Washington 1949–54.

Germany. Auswärtiges Amt. *Dokumente der deutschen auswärtigen Politik, 1918–45*, Series D, edited by Klaus Hohlfeld. Bonn 1950–.

Gilbert, Martin. *Britain and Germany between the Wars*. London 1966.

– and Richard Gott. *The Appeasers*. Boston 1963.

Gimbel, John. *The American Occupation of Germany: Politics and the Military, 1945–1949*. Stanford 1968.

Gladwyn, Hubert. *Memoirs*. London 1972.

Goebel, J. *The Recognition Policy of the United States*. New York 1915.

Goldinger, Walter. *Geschichte der Republik Österreich*. Wien 1962.

Goldner, Franz. *Das einsame Gewissen: Die österreichische Emigration, 1938 bis 1945*. Wien, München 1972.

– *Dollfuss im Spiegel der U.S.Akten*. St Pölten 1979.

Gorlich, Ernst J. *Die österreichische Nation und der Widerstand*. Wien, Frankfurt, Zürich 1967.

Graebner, Norman A., ed. *An Uncertain Tradition: American Secretaries of State in the Twentieth Century*. New York 1961.

Graham, Dominick, and Shelford Bidwell. *Tug of War: The Battle for Italy, 1943–1945*. London 1986.

Grayson, Cary Travers. *Austria's International Position, 1938–1953: The Re-*

establishment of an Independent Austria. Geneva 1953.
Great Britain. House of Commons. *Parliamentary Debates*, 1937–45. Vols, 330–423.
Great Britain. House of Lords. *Parliamentary Debates*, 5th Series, 1937–8. Vol. 108.
Great Britain. Foreign Office. *Documents on British Foreign Policy, 1919–1939*, 3rd series, edited by E.L. Woodward and Rohan Butler. 9 vols. London 1949–57.
Greenfield, Kent Robert, ed. *The History of the European Theater of Operations*. Vol. 4. Washington 1954.
– *Command Decisions*. New York 1959.
Grew, Joseph C. *Turbulent Era: A Diplomatic Record of 40 Years, 1904–1945*. Boston 1952.
Grigg, John. *1943: The Victory That Never Was*. New York 1980.
Gruber, Karl. *Politik der Mitte*. Zurich 1946.
– *Über Auswärtige Angelegenheiten*. Wien 1946.
– *Österreich in Moskau*. Wien 1947.
– *Zwischen Befreiung und Freiheit: Der Sonderfall Österreichs*. Wien 1952.
– *Ein politisches Leben*. Wien n.d.
– *Between Liberation and Liberty: Austria in the Postwar World*. New York 1962.
Guingand, Sir Francis de. *Operation Victory*. London 1947.
– *Generals at War*. London 1964.
Gulik, Charles Adams, *Österreich von den Habsburgs bis Hitler*. 5 vols. Wien 1948–9.
Gwyer, J.M.A., and J.R.M. Butler. *History of the Second World War: Grand Strategy*. Vol. 3 (June 1941–August 1942). London 1964.
Habsburg, Otto von. *Briefe aus der Verbannung*. Leipzig 1935.
Hagen, Louis. *The Secret War for Europe*. New York 1969.
Halifax, The Earl of. *Fulness of Days*. London 1957.
Hall, H. Duncan. *North American Supply*. London 1955.
Hamilton, Nigel. *Monty: The Making of a General, 1887–1942*. London 1980.
– *Master of the Battlefield: Monty's War Years, 1942–1944*. London 1983.
Hannak, Jacques. *Karl Renner und seine Zeit: Versuch einer Biographie*. Wien 1965.
Hantsch, H. *Österreich: Eine Deutung seiner Geschichte*. Innsbruck 1934.
Harbutt, Fraser J. *The Iron Curtain: Churchill, America, and the Origins of the Cold War*. New York 1986.
Harriman, W. Averell. *America and Russia in a Changing World: A Half Century of Personal Observation*. New York 1971.
– and Elie Abel. *Special Envoy to Churchill and Stalin, 1941–1946*. New York 1975.
Harvey, John, ed. *The Diplomatic Diaries of Oliver Harvey*. London 1970.

Hastings, Max. *Bomber Command.* New York 1979.

Hathaway, Robert H. *Ambiguous Partnership: Britain and America, 1944–1947.* New York 1981.

Heer, Friedrich. *Der Kampf um die österreichische Identität.* Wien, Köln, Graz 1981.

Hellbling, E.C. *Österreichische Verfassungs- und Verwaltungsgeschichte.* Wien, New York 1974.

Hertz, Friedrich. *Zahlungsbilanz und Lebensfähigkeit.* München 1925.

– *The Economic Problem of the Danubian States.* London 1947.

Higgins, Trumbull. *Soft Underbelly.* London 1968.

Hillgruber, Andreas, *Hitlers Strategie: Politik und Kriegsführung 1940–1.* Frankfurt/Main 1965.

Hindinger, Gabriele. *Das Kriegsende und der Wiederaufbau demokratischer Verhältnisse in Oberösterreich im Jahre 1945.* Wien 1945.

Hinsley, F.H., E.E. Thomas, et al. *British Intelligence in the Second World War: Its Influence on Strategy and Operations.* 3 vols. New York 1979–81.

Hiscocks, Richard. *The Rebirth of Austria.* Oxford 1956.

Hoare, Sir Samuel. *Ambassador on Special Mission.* London 1956.

Hoettl, W. *The Secret Front.* London 1954.

Hölzle, Erwin. *St. Germain, Das Verbot des Anschlusses: Gesamtdeutsche Vergangenheit.* München 1938.

Hoffmann, Peter. *Widerstand, Staatsstreich, Attentat: Der Kampf der Opposition gegen Hitler.* München 1969.

Holborn, Hajo. *American Military Government.* Washington 1948.

Holborn, Louise W., ed. *War and Peace Aims of the United Nations.* 2 vols. Boston 1943 and 1947.

Hollander, Richard. *The Psychological Warfare Division, Supreme Headquarters, Allied Expeditionary Force: An Account of Its Operation in the Western European Campaigns, 1944–1945.* Bad Homburg 1945.

Holt, Robert T., and Robert W. van der Velds. *Psychological Operations and American Foreign Policy.* Chicago 1960.

Hooker, Nancy H., ed. *The Moffat Papers: Selections from the Diplomatic Journals of Jay Pierrepont Moffat, 1919–1943.* Cambridge, Mass. 1956.

Hoor, Ernst. *Österreich 1918–1938.* Wien 1966.

Howard, Michael. *The Mediterranean Strategy in the Second World War.* London 1968.

– *Studies in War and Peace.* New York 1970.

– *History of the Second World War: Grand Strategy.* Vol. 4 (August 1942–September 1943). London 1972.

Howarth, Patrick. *Undercover: The Men and Women of Special Operations Executive.* London 1980.

Hübmer, Hans. *Österreich 1933–1938: Der Abwehrkampf eines Volkes.* Wien 1949.

Hughes, Barry H. *The Domestic Content of American Foreign Policy*. San Francisco 1978.

Hull, Cordell. *Our Foreign Policy*. Washington 1948.

– *The Memoirs of Cordell Hull*. 2 vols. New York 1948.

Hyde, C.C. *International Law: Chiefly as Interpreted by the United States*. 3 vols. New York 1951.

Hyde, H. Montgomery. *Secret Intelligence Agent*. London 1982.

Hymoff, Edward. *The OSS in World War II*. New York 1972.

Ickes, Harold L. *The Secret Diary of Harold L. Ickes: The Inside Struggle, 1936–1939*. New York 1954.

– *The Secret Diary of Harold L. Ickes: The Lowering Clouds, 1939–1941*, New York 1954.

Ind, Allison. *Allied Intelligence Bureau*. New York 1958.

Institut für Österreichkunde. *Die Entwicklung der Verfassung Österreichs vom Mittelalter bis zur Gegenwart*. Wien 1970.

International Military Tribunal. *The Trial of the Major War Criminals by the International Military Tribunal at Nuremberg, 14 November 1945 – 10 October 1946*. 42 vols. London 1946–7.

Irving, David. *The War between the Generals*. New York 1981.

Ismay, Hastings. *The Memoirs of General Lord Ismay*. New York 1960.

Jedlicka, Ludwig. *Der 20. Juli 1944 in Oesterreich*. Wien, München 1966.

– *Vom alten zum neuen Österreich: Fallstudien zur österreichischen Zeitgeschichte, 1900–1975*. St Pölten 1975.

Jeger, S.W., and Maurice Orbach. *Austria 1946*. London 1946.

Jellinek, G. *System des subjektiven öffentlichen Rechtes*. Tübingen 1905.

Jessup, P.C. *A Modern Law of Nations*. New York 1948.

Johnson, A.C. *Sir Anthony Eden*. London 1955.

Jonas, Manfred. *Isolationism in America, 1935–1941*. Ithaca, NY 1966.

Jones, R.V. *Most Secret War*. London 1978.

Kahn, David. *Hitler's Spies*. New York 1978.

Kann, Robert. *The Multinational Empire: Nationalism and National Reform in the Habsburg Monarchy, 1848–1918*. 2 vols. New York 1950.

– *A History of the Habsburg Empire, 1526–1918*. New York 1975.

– *Die Restauration als Phänomen in der Geschichte*. Graz 1974.

– and Friedrich E. Prinz, eds. *Deutschland und Österreich*. München 1980.

Katzenstein, Peter J. *Disjointed Partners: Austria and Germany since 1915*. Berkeley 1976.

Kelsen, Hans. *Die Staatsrechtliche Durchführung des Anschlusses Österreichs an das Deutsche Reich*. Wien 1928.

– *Austria: Her Legal Status and Re-establishment as an Independent State*. Berkeley 1944.

– *Principles of International Law*. Berkeley 1952.

Kennan, George F. *Memoirs, 1925–1950*. Boston 1967.

Kerekes, Lajos. *Anschluss 1938*. Budapest 1963.

Kertesz, Stephen D. *The Fate of East Central Europe*. Notre Dame 1956.

Keyserlingk, Robert W. *Unfinished History*. London 1948.

Kimball, Warren F. *Swords or Ploughshares? The Morgenthau Plan for Defeated Nazi Germany, 1943–1946*. Philadelphia 1976.

– *Churchill and Roosevelt: The Complete Correspondence*. 3 vols. Princeton 1984.

Kirchner, Klaus. *Flugblätter: Psychologische Kriegsführung im Zweiten Weltkrieg in Europa*. München: 1974.

– *Flugblattpropaganda im Zweiten Weltkrieg: Flugblätter aus England 1939–42*. Erlangen 1974.

– *Flugblattpropaganda im Zweiten Weltkrieg: Flugblätter aus den USA 1943/1944*. Erlangen 1974.

Kitchen, Martin. *British Policy towards the Soviet Union during the Second World War*. New York 1986.

Kitsikis, Dimitri. *Propagande et pressions en politique internationale: La Grèce et ses revendications à la Conference de Paix*. Paris 1963.

Klein, Burton H. *Germany's Preparations for War*. Cambridge Mass. 1959.

Kleinwächter, F.F.G. *Der deutsch-österreichische Mensch und der Anschluss*. Wien 1926.

– *Selbstbestimmung für Österreich*. Stuttgart 1928.

– *Von Schönbrunn bis St. Germain: Die Entstehung der Republik Österreich*. Graz 1964.

– and Hans Paller, *Die Anschlussfrage in ihrer kulturellen, politischen und wirtschaftlichen Bedeutung*. Wien 1930.

Klemperer, Klemens von. *Ignaz Seipel: Christian Statesman in a Time of Crisis*. Princeton NJ 1972.

Klusacek, C., Herbert Steiner, and K. Stimmer, eds. *Dokumentation zur österreichischen Zeitgeschichte, 1938–1945*. Wien 1971.

Kolko, Gabriel. *The Politics of War: The World and United States Foreign Policy, 1943–1945*. New York 1968.

Konrad, Helmut, ed. *Sozialdemokratie und Anschluss: Historische Wurzeln. Anschluss 1918 und 1938: Nachwirkungen*. Vienna 1978.

Kovrig, Bennett. *The Myth of Liberation: East Central Europe in U.S. Diplomacy and Politics since 1941*. Baltimore 1973.

Kreisky, Bruno [Observator], *Der lange Weg zu Österreichs Freiheit*. Wien 1956.

– *Die Zeit in der wir leben: Betrachtungen zur internationalen Politik*. Wien, München, Zürich, Innsbruck 1978.

Kreissler, Felix. *Von der Revolution zur Annektion: Oesterreich 1918 bis 1938*. Vienna 1970.

– *La Prise de conscience de la nation autrichienne, 1938–78*. 2 vols. Paris 1980.

Krock, Arthur. *Memoirs: Sixty Years on the Firing Line*. New York 1968.

Kucklick, B. *American Policy and the Division of Germany: The Clash with*

Russia over Reparations. Ithaca, NY 1972.

LaFaber, Walter. *America, Russia and the Cold War, 1945–66*. New York 1967.

Lamb, Richard. *Montgomery in Europe, 1943–1945*. Franklin Watts 1984.

Langer, Robert. *Seizure of Territory: The Stimson Doctrine and Related Principles*. Princeton, NJ 1947, 1967.

– *The Austro-Yugoslav Problem*. New York 1951.

Langer, William L., and S. Everett Gleason. *The Challenge to Isolation, 1937–1940*. New York 1952.

– *The Mind of Adolf Hitler: The Secret Wartime Report*. New York 1982.

– *In and Out of the Ivory Tower*. New York 1977.

Laqueur, Walter. *The Terrible Secret*. London 1980.

Lash, Joseph P. *Eleanor and Franklin*. New York 1971.

– *Roosevelt and Churchill, 1939–1941*. New York 1976.

Lasswell, Harold D. *Propaganda Technique in the World War*. New York 1927, 1938.

– and R.D. Casey and B.C. Smith. *Propaganda, Communications and Public Opinion: A Comprehensive Reference Guide*. Princton, NJ 1946.

Latour, Conrad F., and Thilo Vogelsang. *Okkupation und Wiederaufbau: Die Tätigkeit der Militärregierung in der amerikanischen Besatzungszone Deutschlands, 1944–1947*. Stuttgart 1973.

Lauterpracht, H. *Recognition in International Law*. Cambridge 1947.

Lavine, Harold. *War Propaganda and the United States*. New York 1972.

Layton, W.T., and Charles Rist. *The Economic Situation of Austria*. Geneva n.d.

Leahy, William D. *I Was There: The Personal Story of the Chief of Staff to Presidents Roosevelt and Truman Based on His Notes and Diaries Made at the Time*. New York 1950.

Leichter, Otto. *Zwischen zwei Diktaturen: Österreichs revolutionären Sozialisten, 1934–1938*. Wien, Frankfurt, Zürich 1968.

– *Otto Bauer*. Wien 1970.

Leigh, Michael. *Mobilizing Consent: Public Opinion and American Foreign Policy, 1937–1947*. Westport, Conn. 1976.

Leiss, Amelia C., and Raymond Denett. *European Peace Treaties after World War II*. Boston 1954.

Lerner, Daniel. *Skywar: Psychological Warfare against Germany: D-Day to VE-Day*. New York 1951.

Les grandes unitées francaises: Campagne de France et l'Allemagne (1944–5). 3e Parties. Paris 1976.

Leutze, James R. *Bargaining for Supremacy: Anglo-American Naval Relations, 1937–1941*. Chapel Hill, NC 1977.

Levering, Ralph B. *American Public Opinion and the Russian Alliance, 1939–1945*. Chapel Hill, NC 1976.

Lewin, Ronald. *Churchill as Warlord*. London 1973.

– *Ultra Goes to War*. New York 1978.

Liddell Hart, B.H. *History of the Second World War* New York 1970.

Lockhart, Robert Bruce. *Comes the Reckoning*. London 1947.

Loewenheim, Francis L., Harold D. Langley, Manfred Jonas, eds. *Roosevelt and Churchill: Their Secret Wartime Correspondence*. New York 1975.

Long, Breckenridge. *The War Diaries: Selections from the War Years, 1939–44*, edited by Fred C. Israel. Lincoln, Neb. 1966.

Lorenz, Reinhold. *Der Staat wider Willen: Österreich 1918–1940*. Berlin 1940.

Louis, William Roger. *Imperialism at Bay: The United States and the Decolonization of the British Empire*. Oxford 1977.

Low, Alfred D. *The Anschluss Movement 1918–1919 and the Paris Peace Conference*. Philadephia 1974.

– *The Anschluss Movement 1918–1938: Background and Aftermath. An Annotated Bibliography of German and Austrian Nationalism*. New York, London 1984.

– *The Anschluss Movement, 1931–1938, and the Great Powers*. Boulder, Col. 1985.

Lucas, John A. *The Great Powers and Eastern Europe*. New York 1953.

Ludwig, Edward. *Österreichs Sendung im Donauraum*. Wien 1954.

Lundestad, Gier. *American Non-Policy towards Eastern Europe*. Oslo 1978.

Lutz, Radomir. *Austro-German Relations in the Anschluss Era*. Princeton, NJ 1975.

Macartney, C.A. *Hungary and Her Successors, 1919–1937*. London 1937.

– *National States and National Minorities*. London 1937.

– *Problems of the Danube Basin*. London 1944.

– *October Fifteenth: A History of Hungary, 1929–1945*. 2 vols. Edinburgh 1956, 1957.

– *The Habsburg Empire, 1790–1918*. London 1969.

– and A.W. Palmer. *Independent East Europe*. London 1962.

MacDonald, Charles B. *The Siegfried Line Campaign: United States Army in World War II: The European Theater of Operations*. Washington 1963.

– *The Mighty Endeavor: American Armed Forces in the European Theatre in World War II*. New York 1969.

Macdonald, Mary. *The Republic of Austria: A Study in the Failure of Democratic Government*. London 1946.

McMahon, M.M. *Conquest and Modern International Law*. Washington 1940.

Macmillan, Harold. *The Blast of War, 1939–1945*. New York 1967.

McNeil, William H. *America, Britain and Russia: Their Co-operation and Conflict, 1941–1946*. London 1953.

Madder, D.R. *Foreign Policy Planning: Its Practice and Problems in the United States Department of State*. Toronto 1977.

Maimann, Helene. *Politik im Wartesaal: Österreichsexilpolitik in Grossbritannien 1938 bis 1945*. Wien 1975.

Maisky, Ivan. *Memoirs of a Soviet Ambassador: The War 1939–1943*. London

1967.

Maleta, Alfred. *Die Amnestie für Nationalsozialisten: Ein ERfolg der Österreichischen Volkspartei*. Wien 1948.

Malina, Peter, and Gustav Spann. *Bibliographie zue österreichische Zeitgeschichte 1918–1978: E A.* Wien 1978.

Mamety, Victor S. *The United States and East Central Europe, 1914–1918: A Study in Wilsonian Diplomacy and Propaganda*. Princeton, NJ 1957.

Marek, K. *Identity and Continuity of States in International Public Law*. Geneva 1969.

Masc, Walter B. *Country without a Name: Austria under the Nazi Rule, 1938–1945*. New York 1979.

Masterman, J.C. *The Double-Cross System in the War of 1939 to 1945*. New Haven 1972.

Mastny, Vojtech. *Russia's Road to the Cold War: Diplomacy, Warfare and the Politics of Communism*. New York 1979.

Matloff, Maurice, and Edwin M. Snell. *United States Army in World War II: Strategic Planning for Coalition Warfare, 1941–1942*. Washington 1953.

– *United States Army in World War II: Strategic Planning for Coalition Warfare, 1943–1944*. Washington 1959.

Medlicott, W.N. *The Economic Blockade*. London 1952, 1959.

Meissl, Sebastian, Klaus-Dieter Mulley, and Oliver Rathkolb, *Verdrängte Schuld, verfehlte Sühne: Entnazifizierung in Österreich 1945–1955*. Wien 1986.

Meyer, Henry Cord. *Mitteleuropa in German Thought and Action, 1815–1945*. The Hague 1955.

Messner, Johannes, *Dolfuss*. Wien 1935.

Middlemas, K. *Diplomacy of Illusion: The British Government and Germany, 1937–1939*. London 1972.

Mikoletzky, Hans L. *Österreichische Zeitgeschichte vom Ende des Ersten Weltkrieges bis zum Staatsvertrag*. Wien 1962.

Milward, Alan. *The German Economy at War*. London 1965.

– *War, Economy and Society, 1939–1945*. London 1977.

Minot, Rodney C. *The Fortress That Never Was*. New York 1964.

Molden, Otto. *Der Ruf des Gewissens: Der österreichische Freiheitskampf, 1938–1945*. Wien, München 1970.

Montgomery of Alamein, Viscount. *The Memoirs*. London 1958.

Moran, Lord. *Churchill: Taken from the Diaries of Lord Moran*. New York 1966.

Morrison, Elting E. *Turmoil and Tradition: A Study of the Life and Times of Henry L. Stimson*. Boston 1960.

Morrison, Wilbur H. *Fortress without a Roof*. New York 1982.

Morrow, I.D.F. *The Peace Settlement and the German Borderlands*. London 1936.

Mosley, Philip E. *The Kremlin and World Politics*. New York 1960.

Mowrer, Edgar A. *The Nightmare of American Foreign Policy*. New York 1948.

Muchitsch, Max. *Die Partisangruppe Loeben-Donawitz*. Wien, Frankfurt, Zurich 1966.

Muenzenberg, Willi. *Propaganda als Waffe*. Paris 1937.

Murphy, Robert. *Diplomat among the Warriors*. Garden City, NY 1964.

Neck, R. *Anschluss 1938*. Munich 1981.

– and A. Wandruszka, eds. *Beiträge zur Zeitgeschichte*. St Po'lten 1976.

Neugebauer, Wolfgang, ed. *Widerstand und Verfolgung in Wien*. 3 vols. Wien 1975.

Nevins, Alan. *America in World Affairs*. New York 1941.

Notter, Harley. *Postwar Foreign Policy Preparation, 1939–1945*. Washington 1949.

Oberleitner, Wolfgang. *Politisches Handbuch der Republik Österreich 1945–1960*. Wien 1960.

O'Connor, Raymond G. *Diplomacy for War: FDR and Unconditional Surrender*. New York 1971.

Offner, Arnold A. *American Appeasement: United States Foreign Policy and Germany, 1933–1938*. Cambridge, Mass. 1976.

Ovendale, Richard. *"Appeasement" and the English-Speaking World: Britain, United States and the Dominions and the Policy of Appeasement*. Cardiff 1975.

Padover, Saul. *Experiment in Germany: The Story of An American Intelligence Officer*. New York 1946.

Passant, E.J. *The Problem of Austria*. Oxford Pamphlets on World Affairs, No. 72. London 1945.

Pasvolsky, Leo. *Economic Nationalism of the Danubian States*. New York 1928.

Pauley, Bruce. *The Habsburg Legacy, 1867–1939*. New York 1972.

– *Hitler and the Forgotten Nazis: A History of Austrian National Socialism*. Chapel Hill, NC 1981.

Peterson, Edward N. *The American Occupation of Germany: Retreat to Victory*. Detroit 1977.

Pichler, Franz. *Die Donaukommission und die Donaustaaten: Kooperation und Integration*. Wien, Stuttgart 1973.

Pinson, Koppel S. *Modern Germany: Its History and Civilization*. New York, London 1966.

Pogue, Forrest C. *The Supreme Command*. Washington 1954.

– *George C. Marshall: Ordeal and Hope, 1939–1942*. London 1968.

– *George C. Marshall: Organizer of Victory, 1943–1945*. New York 1973.

Pollack, Oscar [Paul Oscar]. *Underground Europe Calling*. London 1942.

– *It Started in Vienna*. London 1944.

Pratt, Basil. *Cordell Hull*. 2 vols. New York 1964.

Preradovich, Nikolaus von. *Der nationale Gedanke in Österreich, 1866–1938*. Göttingen 1968.

– *Die Wilhelmstrasse und der Anschluss Österreichs 1918–1933*. Berne, Frankfurt/Main 1971.

Ransom, Harry Howe. *The Intelligence Establishment*. Cambridge, Mass. 1970.

Rauchensteiner, Manfred. *Krieg in Österreich, 1945*. Wien 1970.

– *1945: Entscheidung für Österreich*. Graz 1975.

– *Der Sonderfall: Die Besatzungszeit in Österreich 1945 bis 1955*. Graz, Wien, Köln 1979.

Rebhann, Fritz. *Das braune Glück zu Wien*. Wien, München 1973.

Reihmann, Viktor *Bruno Kreisky: Das Portrait eines Staatmannes*. Wien 1972.

Renner, Karl. *Österreich, St. Germain und die kommende Friede*. Wien 1946.

– *Denkschrift über die Geschichte der Unabhängigkeitserklärung Österreichs und die Einsetzung der provisorischen Regierung der Republik*. Wien 1947.

----- *Österreich von der ersten zur zweiten Republik*. Wien 1952.

Reynolds, David. *The Creation of the Anglo-American Alliance: A Study in Comparative Cooperation*. Chapel Hill, NC 1982.

Riedelsperger, Max. *The Lingering Shadow of Nazism: The Austrian Independent Movement since 1945*. New York 1978.

Rollins, Alfred B., Jr. *Roosevelt and Howe*. New York 1962.

Roosevelt, Eleanor. *This is My Story*. New York 1937.

– *This I Remember*. New York 1949.

Roosevelt, Elliott, ed. *F.D.R: His Personal Letters, 1928–1945*. Vol. 4. New York 1950.

– and James Brough. *An Untold Story: The Roosevelts of Hyde Park*. New York 1973.

Roosevelt, Kermit, ed. *The War Report of the OSS*. New York 1976.

– ed. *The War Report of the OSS: The Overseas Targets*. New York 1976.

Rose, Leslie A. *The American Occupation of Germany: Retreat to Victory*. Detroit 1977.

Rosenman, Samuel I. *Working with Roosevelt*. New York 1952.

– ed. *The Public Papers and Addresses of Franklin Delano Roosevelt*. 13 vols. New York 1938–50.

Rostow, Walt W. *Pre-Invasion Bombing Strategy*. Austin 1981.

Rothschild, K.W. *Austria's Economic Development between the Two Wars*. London 1947.

Rothstein, Robert. *Planning, Prediction and Policy Making in Foreign Affairs*. Boston 1972.

Royal Institute of International Affairs. *Survey of International Affairs*, edited by Arnold J. Toynbee. London 1925–.

– *The Problem of International Investment*. London 1937.

– *Central and South-Eastern Europe: Syllabus for a Study Group*. London 1938.

– *Southeastern-Europe: A Political and Economic Survey*. London 1939.

– *The Balkans together with Hungary*. London 1945.

– *Europe in 1939*, edited by A.J. Toynbee and F.T. Ashton-Gwatkin. London

1954.
– *The Review of the Foreign Press, 1939–1945*. 27 vols. Munich 1980.
Ryan, Cornelius. *The Last Battle*. New York 1966.
Saunders, M.C., and P.M. Taylor. *British Propaganda during World War One, 1914–1918*. London 1982.
Sawyers, Michael. *Sabotage! The Secret War against America*. New York, London 1942.
Schärf, Adolf. *Zwischen Demokratie und Volksdemokratie: Österreichs Einigung und Wiederaufrichtung im Jahre 1945*. Wien 1950.
– *Österreichs Wiederaufrichtung im Jahre 1945*. Wien 1960.
– *Österreichs Erneuerung 1945–1955: Das erste Jahrzehnt der zweiten Republik*. Wien 1955.
– *Erinnerungen aus meinem Leben*. Wien 1963.
Schausberger, N. *Der Griff nach Österreich: Der Anschluss*. Wien 1978.
Scheu, Friedrich. *Die Emigrationspresse der Sozialisten, 1938–1945*. Wien, Frankfurt, Zürich 1968.
Schewe, R., ed. *Roosevelt and Foreign Affairs, 1937–1939*. 11 vols. New York 1979–.
Schilcher, Alfons. *Österreich und die Grossmächte: Dokumente zur österreichischen Aussenpolitik 1945–1955*. Wien, Salzburg 1980.
Schlesinger, Arthur M., Jr, Lloyd C. Gardner, and Hans J. Morgenthau. *The Origins of the Cold War*. Waltham, Mass. 1970.
Schlesinger, Rudolf. *Federalism in Central and Eastern Europe*. London 1945.
Schluzinger, Robert D. *The Wise Men of Foreign Policy: The History of the Council on Foreign Relations*. New York 1984.
Schmitt, H.A., ed. *United States Occupation in Europe after World War II*. Lawrence, Kans. 1978.
Schnaebel, F. *The History of the Joint Chiefs of Staff: The Joint Chiefs of Staff and National Policy*. Vol. 1 (1945–1947). Wilmington, Del. 1979.
Schuschnigg, Kurt von. *My Austria*. New York 1938.
– *Farewell Austria*. London 1938.
– *Austrian Requiem*. New York 1946.
– *Im Kampf gegen Hitler: Die Überwindung der Anschlussidee*. Wien 1969.
Schwarzenberg, K. von. *The Holy Roman Empire*. New York 1968.
Scipio [pseud.]. *100,000,000 Allies – If We Want Them*. London 1940.
Selby, Sir Watford. *Diplomatic Twilight, 1939–1940*. London 1953.
Seton-Watson, Hugh. *Eastern Europe between the Wars, 1918–1941*. London and Hamden, Conn. 1943, 1962.
– *The "Sick Heart" of Modern Europe: The Problem of the Danubian Lands*. Seattle 1975.
– and Christopher. *The Making of a New Europe*. London 1981.
Seton-Watson, Robert W. *A History of the Rumanians*. London 1934.
– *Treaty Revision and the Hungarian Frontiers*. London 1934.

Sharp, Tony. *The Wartime Alliance and the Zonal Division of Germany*. Oxford 1975.

Shepard, Gordon. *The Austrian Odyssey*. London 1957.

– *Anschluss: The Rape of Austria*. London, Toronto 1963.

– *Engelbert Dollfuss*. Wien, Köln 1961.

Shephardson, Whitney H., ed. *The United States in World Affairs: An Account of American Foreign Relations*. New York, London 1939.

– *The Interests of the United States as a World Power*. Claremont, Calif. 1942.

– *The Early History of the Council on Foreign Relations*. Stanford 1960.

Sherry, Michael S. *Preparing for the Next War: American Plans for Postwar Defense, 1941–1945*. New Haven 1977.

Sherwood, Robert H. *Roosevelt and Hopkins: An Intimate History*. New York 1948.

Shoup, Lawrence, and William Minter. *Imperial Brain Trust: The Council on Foreign Relations and U.S. Foreign Policy*. New York, London 1977.

Siegler, Heinrich. *Österreichs Weg zur Souveraenität, Neutralität, Prosperität*. Bonn 1969.

Smith, Bradley F. *The Shadow Warriors: OSS and the Origins of the CIA*. New York 1983.

Smith, D. *America and the Axis War*. London 1942.

Smith, Gaddis. *American Diplomacy during the Second World War, 1941–1945*. New York 1965.

Smith, R. Harris. *OSS: The Secret History of America's First Central Intelligence Agency*. New York 1972.

Snell, John L. *The Wartime Origins of the East-West Dilemma Over Germany*. New Orleans 1959.

Sorensen, Thomas C. *The Word War: The Story of American Propaganda*. New York 1968.

Speier, Hans. *Psychological Aspects of Foreign Policy*. San Francisco, Calif. 1954.

Srbik, Heinrich Ritter von. *Metternich: Der Staatsmann und Mensch*. München 1924.

– *Österreich in der deutschen Geschichte*. München 1936.

Stadler, Karl. *Österreich 1938–1945 im Spiegel der NS-Akten*. Wien, München 1966.

– *The Birth of the Austrian Republic*. Leyden 1966.

– *Austria*. London 1971.

– and Maria Szecsi. *Die NS-Justiz in Österreich und ihre Opfer*. Wien 1962.

Stafford, David. *Britain and the European Resistance, 1940–1945*. London 1980.

Stalin's Correspondence with Churchill, Attlee, Roosevelt and Truman, 1941–1945. 2 vols. Moscow 1957.

Stamps, T. Dodson, and Vincent J. Esposito, eds. *A Military History of World War II*. Vol. 1: *Operations in the European Theater*. West Point 1953.

Stearman, William. *The Soviet Union and the Occupation of Austria*. Bonn

1961.

Steele, Richard W. *The First Offensive, 1942: Roosevelt, Marshall, and the Making of American Strategy*. Bloomington, Ind. 1973.

Steiner, Herbert. *Zum Tode verurteilt: Österreicher gegen Hitler*. Wien 1964.

– *Gestorben für Österreich: Widerstand gegen Hitler* Wien, Frankfurt, Zürich 1968.

Steiner, Kurt. *Politics in Austria*. Boston 1972.

Stettinius, Edward R. *Roosevelt and the Russians: The Yalta Conference*. Garden City, NY 1949.

Stimson, Henry L. *The Far Eastern Crisis*. New York 1936.

– and McGeorge Bundy. *On Active Service in Peace and War*. New York 1954.

Stoler, M.A. *The Politics of the Second Front: American Military Planning and Diplomacy in Coalition Warfare, 1941–3*. Westport, Conn. 1977.

Stolper, Gustav. *Deutsch-Österreich als Sozial- und Wirtschaftsproblem*. München 1921.

Stourzh, Gerald. *Geschichte des Staatsvertrages, 1945–1955: Österreichs Weg zur Neutralität*. Graz, Wien, Köln 1980.

Strang, Lord William. *At Home and Abroad*. London 1956.

Stromberg, R.N. *Arnold J. Toynbee: Historian for an Age of Crisis*. Carbondale, Ill. 1972.

Strong, Sir Kenneth. *Intelligence at the Top: The Recollections of a British Intelligence Officer*. Garden City, NY 1968.

Stuart, G.H. *The Department of State: A History of Its Organization, Procedure and Personnel*. New York 1949.

Suval, Stanley. *The Anschluss Question in the Weimar Era: A Study of Nationalism in Germany and Austria, 1918–1932*. Baltimore 1974.

Tansill, Charles C. *Back Door to War: The Roosevelt Foreign Policy, 1933–1941*. Chicago 1952.

Tautscher, Anton, and Ernst Kübler. *Die Lebensfähigkeit Österreichs: Untersuchungen und Ausblicke*. Wien, Graz 1946.

Taylor, Edmond Lapierre. *The Strategy of Terror*. Boston 1940.

Taylor, P.M. *The Projection of Britain, British Overseas Publicity and Propaganda, 1919–1939*. Cambridge 1981.

Temperley, H.V. *A History of the Peace Conference*. 6 vols. London 1920–3.

Thorne, Christopher. *Allies of a Kind: The United States, Britain and the War Against Japan, 1941–1945*. London 1978.

Toynbee, Arnold J. *Nationality and War*. London 1915.

– *The Armenian Massacres in the Ottoman Empire*. London 1916.

– with Lord Bryce. *The German Terror in France*. 2 vols. London, New York 1917.

– *The New Europe*. London 1917.

– *The Western Question in Greece and Turkey*. London 1922.

– *Experiences*. London 1966.

– *Acquaintances*. London 1967.
– *Toynbee on Toynbee: A Conversation between A.J. Toynbee and G.R. Urban*. New York 1974.
– and Frank T. Ashton-Gwatkin, eds. *The World in 1939*. Oxford 1952.
– and A.V. Toynbee. *The War and the Neutrals*. London 1956.
Tully, Grace. *FDR: My Boss*. Chicago 1949.
Ulam, Adam B. *Expansion and Coexistence: The History of Soviet Foreign Policy, 1917–1967*. New York 1968.
– *The Rivals: America and Russia since World War II*. New York 1971.
Ulrich, Johann. *Der Luftkrieg über Österreich, 1939–1949*. Wien 1967.
United States. Army, Propaganda Branch, Intelligence Division. *A Syllabus of Psychological Warfare*, edited by Paul M.M. Linebarger. Washington 1946.
United States. Congress, House of Representatives. Wright, Herbert. *The Attitude of the United States toward Austria: A Study of the Legality of the Annexation of Austria by Germany under International Law and the American Constitution and the Policy of the United States toward the Annexation*. House Document No. 477, 78th Congress, 2nd session. Washington 1944.
– *Special Committee on Postwar Economic Policy and Planning: Hearings*. Washington 1944 and 1945.
– *The OWI, June 13, 1942 to September 15, 1945*. Elmer Davis Report to the President. Foreign Operations and Government Information Subcommittee of the Committee on Government Operations. 88th Congress, 1st session. Washington 1963.
United States. Department of State. *Peace and War: United States Foreign Policy, 1931–41*. Washington 1943.
– *The United States in the Allied Administration of Austria*. Washington 1947.
– *The Austrian State Treaty: An Account of the Post-War Negotiations together with the Related Documents*. Washington 1957.
– *Bulletin*. Washington 1943–5.
– *Digest of International Law*, edited by Green H. Hackworth. 9 vols. Washington 1940–4.
– *Digest of International Law*, edited by Marjorie M. Whiteman. 6 vols. Washington 1960–.
– *Foreign Relations of the United States, 1940–5*. Washington 1957–71.
– *Press Releases*. Washington 1938–45.
– *Psychological Warfare in Support of Military Operations*. Washington 1951.
Vandenberg, Arthur H., Jr. *The Private Papers of Senator Vandenberg*. Boston 1952.
Vansittart, Sir Robert. *The Mist Procession*. London 1958.
Vasari, Emilio. *Dr. Otto Habsburg oder die Leidenschaft für Politik*. Wien, München 1972.
Verdross, A. *The Permanent Neutrality of Austria*. Vienna 1978.
Verosta, Stephan. *Die internationale Stellung Österreichs, 1938–1947: Eine*

Sammlung von Erklärungen und Verträgen aus den Jahren 1938–1947. Wien 1947.

Wagner, D., and G. Tomkowitz. *Anschluss: The Week Hitler Seized Vienna.* New York 1978.

Wagnleitner, Reinhold, ed. *Understanding Austria: The Political Reports and Analyses of Martin F. Herz, Political Officer at the US Legation in Vienna 1945–1948.* Salzburg 1984.

Wandruszka, A. *Geschichte der Republik Österreich.* Wien 1954.

Wathen, Mary A. *The Policy of England and France toward the Anschluss of 1938.* Washington 1954.

Webster, Charles, and Noble Frankland. *The Strategic Air Offensive against Germany, 1939–45.* London 1961.

Weigley, Russell F. *Eisenhower's Lieutenants.* Bloomington, Ind. 1981.

Weinzierl, Erika, and Kurt Skalnik, eds. *Das neue Österreich: Geschichte der Zweiten Republik.* 2 vols. Graz, Wien, Köln 1975.

Welles, Sumner. *The Time for Decision.* New York 1944.

– *Seven Decisions That Shaped World History.* New York 1950.

Wendt, B.J. *Economic Appeasement: Handel- und Finanzpolitik in der britischen Deutschland-Politik.* Düsseldorf 1971.

Wheeler-Bennett, John. *The Pipe Dream of Peace.* New York 1935.

– and Anthony Nicholls. *The Semblance of Peace: The Political Settlement after the Second World War.* New York 1974.

Whitnah, David R., and Edgar L. Erickson. *The American Occupation of Austria: Planning and Early Years.* Westport, Conn., London 1985.

Wilmot, Chester. *The Struggle for Europe.* London 1952.

Wilson, Henry Maitland. *Eight Years Overseas, 1939–1947.* London 1949.

Wilson, Hugh. *Diplomat between Wars.* New York 1941.

Wilson, R., Jr. *A Career Diplomat.* New York 1960.

Winkler, Alan M. *The Politics of Propaganda: The Office of War Information, 1942–1945.* New Haven 1978.

Winks, Robin W., ed. *The Historian as Detective: Essays on Evidence.* New York 1969.

Winter, Ernst Karl. *Monarchie und Arbeiterschaft.* Wien 1936.

Winterbottom, F.M. *Secret and Personal.* London 1969.

– *The Ultra Secret.* London 1974.

Wiskemann, Elizabeth. *Czechs and Germans.* London 1938.

– *The Europe I Saw.* London 1968.

Wolfe, Robert, ed. *Americans as Proconsuls: United States Military Government in Germany and Japan, 1944–52.* Carbondale and Edwardsville, Ill. 1984.

Woodward, C. Vann. *American Attitudes to History.* Oxford 1955.

Woodward, Sir Llewellyn. *British Foreign Policy in the Second World War.* 4 vols. London 1970–5.

Yergin, Daniel. *Shattered Peace: The Origins of the Cold War and the National Security State*. Boston 1977.

Young, Kenneth, ed. *The Diaries of Sir Robert Bruce Lockhart 1939–1965*. 2 vols. London 1980.

Ziemke, Earl. *Stalingrad to Berlin: The German Defeat in the East*. Washington 1968.

– *The United States Army of Occupation of Germany, 1944–1946*. Washington 1975.

Zink, Harold. *American Military Government in Germany*. New York 1947.

– *The United States in Germany, 1944–1951*. New York 1957.

Zöllner, Erich. *Histoire de l'Autriche des origines à nos jours*. Lyon 1965.

Articles, Theses

Acheson, Dean. "The Eclipse of the State Department." *Foreign Affairs* 49 (1971): 593–606.

Akino, A. "Soviet Policy in Eastern Europe, 1943–1948. A Geo-Political Analysis." *East European Quarterly* 17 (1983): 257–66.

Bader, W.B. "Österreich in Potsdam." *Österreichische Zeitschrift für Aussenpolitik* 2 (1962).

Baylis, John. "British Wartime Thinking about a Post-war European Security Group." *Review of International Studies* 9 (1983): 265–82.

Beer, Siegfried. "Allierte Planung, Propaganda und Penetration, 1943–1945: Die künftigen Bezatzungsmächte und das wiederzuerrichtende Österreich, von der Moskauer Deklaration bis zur Befreiung," in *Das Burgenland im Jahre 1945*. Eisenstadt 1985.

Bemis, S.F. "The Memoirs of Cordell Hull." *Journal of Modern History* 21 (1949): 317–18.

Benson, George C.S. "American Military Government in Austria, May 1945–February 1946," in Carl S. Friedrich, ed., *American Experiences in Military Government in World War II*. New York 1948.

Bernbaum, John A. "Nazi Control in Austria: The Creation of the Ostmark, 1938–1940." Doctoral dissertation, University of Maryland, 1972.

– " 'The New Elite': Nazi Leadership in Austria, 1938–1945." *Austrian History Yearbook* 14 (1978): 145–58.

Bernstein, Barton J. "The Quest for Security: American Foreign Policy and International Control of Atomic Energy, 1942–1946." *Journal of American History* 60 (1973–4): 1003–44.

Boehm, Eric H. "Free Germans in Soviet Psychological Warfare." *Public Opinion Quarterly* (1950): 285–95.

Boll, M. "Reality and Illusion: The Allied Control Commission for Bulgaria." *East European Quarterly* 17 (1983): 417–28.

Bollmus, Reinhard. "Österreichs Unabhängigkeit im Widerstreit: Neuere Arbeiten über das politische Exil in Grossbritannien und der Sowjetunion." *Zeitgeschichte* 4 (1976): 56–75.

– "Staatliche Einheit trotz Zonentrennung: Zur Politik des Staatskanzlers Karl Renner gegenüber den Besatzungsmächten in Österreich im Jahre 1945," in *Soziale Bewegung und politische Verfassung*. Stuttgart 1976.

Botz, Gerhard. "The Changing Patterns of Social Support for Austrian National Socialism," in Stein Larsen et al., *Who Were the Fascists? Social Roots of European Fascism*. Bergen 1980.

– "Die österreichischen NSDAP Mitglieder. Probleme einer quantitativen Analyse der NSDAP Zentralkartei im Berlin Documentation Center," in Reinhard Mann, ed. *Die Nationalsozialisten: Analysen faschistischer Bewegungen*. Stuttgart 1980.

Bouchard, Edwin. "Recognition and Non-recognition." *American Journal of International Law* 36 (1942): 108–10.

Boyle, P. "The British Foreign Office's View of Soviet-American Relations, 1945–1946." *Diplomatic History* 3 (1979): 307–20.

Braddick, H.B. "A New look at American Foreign Policy during the Italo-Ethiopian Crisis." *Journal of Modern History* 34 (1962): 64–73.

Brown, Philip M. "The Effects of Recognition." *American Journal of International Law* 36 (1942): 106–7.

– "The Legal Effects of Recognition." *American Journal of International Law* 44 (1950): 617–40.

Brune, L. "Considerations of Force in Cordell Hull's Diplomacy." *Diplomatic History* 11 (1978): 384–405.

Bruntz, George G. "Allied Propaganda and the Collapse of German Morale in 1918." *Public Opinion Quarterly* 2 (1938): 61–76.

Bryant, Arthur. "Factors Underlying British Foreign Policy." *International Affairs* 3 (1946): 338–51.

Bucky, Evan B. "The Nazi Party in Linz, Austria, 1919–1939: A Sociological Perspective." *German Studies Review* 1 (1978): 302–25.

– "Hitler's Hometown under Nazi Rule: Linz, Austria, 1938–1945." *Central European History* 16 (1983): 171–86.

Campbell, John C. "Diplomacy on the Danube." *Foreign Affairs* 27 (1949): 315–28.

– "The European Territorial Settlement." *Foreign Affairs* 25 (1947): 196–219.

Chandler, H. "The Transition to Cold Warrior: The Evolution of W. Averell Harriman's Assessment of the USSR's Polish Policy, October 1943 – Warsaw Uprising." *East European Quarterly* 10 (1976): 229–45.

Clauss, E.M. "The Roosevelt Administration and Manchukuo, 1933–1941." *The Historian* 59 (1954): 513–42.

Craig, Gordon A. "The Technique of Peacemaking." *Yale Review* 34 (1944): 133–8.

– "The Democratic Roots of American Diplomatic Style," in H. Berding et al., *Vom Staat des Ancien Regimes zum modernen Parteienstaat*. München, Wien 1978.

Crossman, Richard. "Psychological Warfare." *Journal of the Royal Service Institution* 26 (1952): 319–23.

Current, R.N. "The Stimson Doctrine and the Hoover Doctrine." *American Historical Review* 59 (1954): 513–42.

Dallek, Robert. "Beyond Tradition: The Careers of William E. Dodd and George S. Messersmith." *South Atlantic Quarterly* 66 (1967): 233–54.

Davis, Elmer, et al., "The Office of War Information." *Public Opinion Quarterly* 7 (1943): 3–138.

Diamant, A. "The Group Basis of Austrian Politics." *Journal of Central European Affairs* 18 (1958): 134–56.

Dilks, David. "Baldwin and Chamberlain," in Lord Butler, ed., *The Conservatives: A History from Their Origins to 1965*. London 1977.

Dockrill, M.L. "The Foreign Office and the Proposed Institute of International Affairs." *International Journal* 50 (1980): 665–72.

Doob, Leonard. "The Utilization of Social Scientists in the Overseas Branch of the OWI." *American Political Science Review* 41 (1947): 649–62.

– "Goebbels' Principles of Propaganda." *Public Opinion Quarterly* 13 (1949–50): 419–42.

Dorn, Walter L. "The Debate over American Occupation Policy in Germany in 1944–1945." *Political Science Quarterly* 72 (1957): 484–501.

Douglas, Roy. "Churchill and Eden, 1937–1938." *Journal of Contemporary History* 13 (1978): 97–116.

Drummond, Donald F. "Cordell Hull," in Norman A. Graebner, ed., *An Uncertain Tradition: American Secretaries of State in the Twentieth Century*. New York 1961.

Dulles, A.W., and H.F. Armstrong. "Legislating Peace." *Foreign Affairs* 17 (1938): 1–12.

Dusek, Peter. "Nachkriegskonzeptionen für Österreich: Der Exilwiderstand und die nationale Frage," in *Österreicher im Exil, 1934–1945*. Wien 1977.

Emerson, William. "Franklin Roosevelt as Commander-in-Chief in World War II." *Military Affairs* 22 (1958–9): 181–207.

Erickson, Edgar L. "The Zoning of Austria." *The Annals of the American Academy of Political and Social Sciences* 267 (1950): 106–13.

– "Austria," in M. Balfour and J. Muir, eds., *Four-Power Control in Germany and Austria, 1945–6*. London 1956.

Feis, H. "Some Notes on Historical Record-Keeping, the Role of the Historian and the Influence of Historical Memoirs during the Era of the Second World War," in F.L. Loewenheim, ed., *The Historian and the Diplomat: The Role of History and Historians in American Foreign Policy*. New York 1967.

Fellner, Fritz. "Österreich in der Nachkriegsplannung der Alliierten, 1943–

1945," in *Österreich und Europa*. Wien 1964.
– "Habsburg Studies in Europe." *Austrian History Yearbook* 3, pt.3 (1967): 296–307.
– "The Dissolution of the Habsburg Monarchy and Its Significance for the New Order." *Austrian History Yearbook* 4/5 (1968–9): 3–27.
– "Die aussenpolitische und völkerrechtliche Situation Österreichs 1938: Österreichs Wiederherstellung als Kriegsziel der Allierten," in Erika Weinzierl and Kurt Skalnik, eds., *Österreich: Die Zweite Republik*. Vol. 1. Wien 1972.
– "Österreich im Spannungsfeld des Ost-West-Konflikts: Materialen zur Geschichte Österreichs in der amerikanischen Aktenpublikation *FRUS*." *Österreichischer Zeitschrift für Aussenpolitik* 13 (1973): 203–21.
– "Teilung oder Neutralisierung? Zur österreichischen Geschichte des Jahres 1947 nach *FRUS*." *Österreichische Zeitschrift für Aussenpolitik* 14 (1974): 199–216.
Ferencz, B.B. "The United Nations Consensus Definition of Aggression: Sieve or Substance." *Journal of International Law and Economics* 10 (1975): 701–17.
Fletcher, R. "Karl Leuthner's Greater Germany: The Pre-1914 Pan-Germanism of an Austrian Socialist." *Canadian Review of Studies in Nationalism* 9 (1982): 57–80.
Foster, H. Schuyler. "The Official Propaganda of Great Britain." *Public Opinion Quarterly* 3 (1939): 263–71.
Funk, Arthur L. "Churchill, Eisenhower and the French Resistance." *Military Affairs* 45 (1981): 29–33.
Gaddis, John Lewis. "The Emerging Post-Revisionist Synthesis on the Origins of the Cold War." *Diplomatic History* 7 (1983): 171–90.
Ganglmair, Siegwald. "Amerikanische Kriegspropaganda gegen das Deutsche Reich in den Jahren 1944/1945." Doctoral dissertation, University of Vienna, 1978.
Garner, J.W. "Non-Recognition of Illegal Territorial Annexations and Claims to Sovereignty." *American Journal of International Law* 30 (1936): 679–98.
– "Questions of State Succession Raised by the German Occupation of Austria." *American Journal of International Law* 32 (1938): 421–38.
– "Germany's Responsibility for Austria's Debts." *American Journal of International Law* 32 (1938): 766–75.
Garson, Robert. "The Atlantic Alliance, Eastern Europe and the Origins of the Cold War," in H.C. Allen and Roger Thompson, eds., *Contrast and Connections: Essays in Anglo-American History*. Athens, Ohio 1976.
Gazell, James A. "Arthur H. Vandenberg, Internationalism and the United Nations." *Political Science Quarterly* 88 (1973): 375–94.
– "The Position of Austria." *Contemporary Review* (November 1946): 257–62.
Gilbert, Felix. "Two British Ambassadors: Perth and Henderson," in Gordon A. Craig and Felix Gilbert, eds., *The Diplomats, 1919–1939*. Vol. 2. New York

1965.

Goldman, A. "Stephan Hall-King and the Newsletter Controversy of 1940." *Canadian Journal of History* 10 (1975): 209–30.

Gould, S. "Austrian Attitudes toward Anschluss, October 1918–September 1919." *Journal of Modern History* 22 (1950): 220–31.

Groehler, Olaf. "Die anglo-amerikanische Nachkriegspläne gegenüber Deutschland während des Zweiten Weltkrieges." *Zeitschrift für Geschichtswissenschaft* 13 (1965): 430–45.

Gruber, Karl. "Austria Holds On." *Foreign Affairs* 24 (1945): 478–85.

– "Austria Infelix." *Foreign Affairs* 26 (1947): 229–38.

– "Österreich 1945." *Zeitgeschichte* 2 (April 1975): 171–3.

Gurfein, Murray I., and Morris Janowitz. "Trends in Wehrmacht Morale." *Public Opinion Quarterly* 10 (1946): 78–84.

Haag, John. "Othmar Spann and the Quest for a True State." *Austrian History Yearbook* 3 (1967–8): 227–50.

Haas, H. "Neueste Forschungen über die Begründung der Republik Österreich." *Zeitgeschichte* 2 (1974): 189–95.

Habsburg, Otto von. "Danubian Reconstruction." *Foreign Affairs* 20 (1942): 243–52.

Hammond, Paul Y. "Directives for the Occupation of Germany: The Washington Controversy," in Harold Stein, ed., *American Civil-Military Decisions: A Book of Case Studies*. Birmingham 1963.

Hanisch, E. "Vierzig Jahre nach dem Anschluss: Neue wissenschaftliche Literatur." *Zeitgeschichte* 6 (1978–9): 117–27.

Harbutt, Fraser. "Churchill, Hopkins, and the 'Other' Americans: An Alternate Perspective on Anglo-American Relations, 1941–1945." *International History Review* 8 (1985): 236–62.

Harrison, Richard A. "Testing the Water: A Secret Probe towards Anglo-American Military Cooperation in 1936." *International History Review* 7 (1986): 214–34.

Hathaway, Robert M., Jr. "The Paradoxes of Partnership: Britain and America, 1944–1947." Doctoral dissertation, University of North Carolina, 1976.

Hausmann, Astrid. "Die amerikanische Aussenpolitik und die Entstehung der Republik Österreich, 1917–19." Doctoral dissertation, University of Vienna, 1973.

Hayek, F.A. von. "The Future of Austria." *The Spectator*, 6 April 1945, 306–7.

Hayes, E.J. "Coordination of Military and Civil Affairs Planning." in *Annals of the American Academy of Political and Socials Sciences* 267 (1950).

Heinrichs, Waldo. "President Roosevelt's Intervention in the Battle of the Atlantic, 1941." *Diplomatic History* 10 (1986): 311–22.

Heller, Victor. "The Economic and Political Background of Austrian Reconstruction." *Journal of Central European Affairs* 6 (1947): 283–300.

Herz, Martin F. (Chief Leaflet Writer for the Psychological Warfare Division,

SHAEF). "Some Psychological Lessons from Leaflet Propaganda in World War II." *Public Opinion Quarterly* 13 (1949–50): 471–86.

Hiscocks, Richard. "Austrian Prospects." *International Journal* 8 (1953): 240.

Hoff-Wilson, Joan. "The Future of American Diplomatic History." *Society of Historians of American Foreign Relations Newsletter* 16 (June 1985): 10–21.

Hoffmann, L.A. "Austria: Zones of Occupation," 21 April 1946, in U.S. Department of State *Bulletin* 14: 645–9.

Hoffmannsthal, E. de. " 'Austro-Hungarians'." *American Journal of International Law* 36 (1942): 292–4.

Holborn, Hajo. "The Final Dissolution of the Habsburg Monarchy." *Austrian History Yearbook* 3 (1967): 189–205.

Holdich, P.G.H. "A Policy of Percentages? British Policy and the Balkans at the Moscow Conference of October 1944." *International History Review* 9 (1987): 28–47.

Holmes, B.R. "Europe and the Hapsburg Restoration, 1930–1938." *East European Quarterly* 9 (1975): 173–84.

Hoor, Ernst. "Die österreichische Nation – Eine Realität." *Österreich in Geschichte und Literatur* 1 (1957): 193–200.

Houston, Douglas. "Karl Renner and Austria in 1945." *Austrian History Yearbook* 1 (1965): 122–48.

Hyde, C.C. "The Termination of Treaties of a State in Consequence of Its Absorption by Another – The Position of the United States." *American Journal of International Law* 24 (1932): 133–6.

"Independent Austria." *The International and Comparative Law Quarterly* 7 (1958): 94–8.

Ingram, E. "Die konservative Emigration aus Oesterreich in den Vereinigten Staaten von Amerika, 1938–1945." Hausarbeit bei Professor L. Jedlicka, University of Vienna, 1976.

Jablon, J. "The State Department and Collective Security." *The Historian* 33 (1971): 248–63.

Jacobs, Philip E. "The Influence of World Events on 'Neutrality' Opinion." *Public Opinion Quarterly* 4 (1940): 48–65.

Jakusch, K. "Die Entwicklung der theoretischen Beurteilung des Schicksals Österreichs zwischen 1938 und 1945." Doctoral dissertation, University of Vienna, 1966.

Jedlicka, Ludwig. "Verfassungs- und Verwaltungsprobleme, 1938–1945," in Institut für Österreichkunde, *Die Entwicklung der Verfassung Österreichs vom Mittelalter bis zur Gegenwart*. Wien 1970.

– "Ein unbekannter Bericht Kaltenbrunners über die Lage in Österreich im September 1944." *Österreich in Geschichte und Literatur* 21 (1973).

Jelevich, Charles, and R. John Rath. "The Conference." *Austrian History Yearbook* 3, pt. 1 (1967): 1–10.

Jessup, P.C. "The Reality of International Law." *Foreign Affairs* 18 (1940): 244–

53.

– "Force under the Modern Law of Nations." *Foreign Affairs* 25 (1946): 90–105.

Jones, J.M. "State Succession in the Matter of Treaties." *British Yearbook of International Law* 24 (1947): 360–75.

Kane, R. Keith. "The OFF" *Public Opinion Quarterly* 6 (1942): 204–20.

Kann, Robert. "Karl Renner (December 14, 1870 – December 31, 1950)." *Journal of Modern History* 23 (1951): 243–9.

– "The Defeat of Austro-Hungary in 1918 and the European Balance of Power." *Central European History* 2 (1969): 237–47.

– "The Case of Austria." *Journal of Contemporary History* 15 (1980): 37–52.

Kehm, H.D. "The Methods and Functions of Military Psychological Warfare." *Military Review* 26 (1947): 3–15.

– "Organization for Military Psychological Warfare in ETO." *Military Review* 26 (1947): 35–45.

Kelsen, Hans. "Recognition in International Law." *American Journal of International Law* 35 (1941): 605–17.

– "The International Legal Status of Austria to Be Established Immediately upon the Termination of the War." *American Journal of International Law* 38 (1944): 689–94.

Kempner, Robert M. "The Enemy Alien Problem in the Present War." *American Journal of International Law* 34 (1940): 443–58.

Kerekes, Lajos. "Österreich zwischen Anschlusspolitik und Donaukonföderation, 1918–19." *Vierteljahrshefte für Zeitgeschichte* 22 (1974): 18–45.

– "Die wirtschaftliche und soziale Lage Österreichs nach dem Zerfall der Doppelmonarchie," in R. Neck and A. Wandruska, eds. *Beiträge zur Zeitgeschichte.* St Pölten 1976.

Kettenacker, Lothar. "The Anglo-Soviet Alliance and the Problem of Germany, 1941–1945." *Journal of Contemporary History* 17 (1982): 435–58.

Keyserlingk, Robert H. "Political Warfare Illusions: Otto Strasser and Britain's World War Two Strategy of National Revolts against Hitler." *Dalhousie Review* 61 (1981): 71–92.

– "Anschluss oder Besetzung: Der 'Anschluss' Österreichs aus der Sicht der USA" *Zeitgeschichte* 9 (1982): 126–40.

– "Austrian Restoration and Nationalism: A British Dilemma during World War II." *Canadian Review of Studies in Nationalism* 9 (1982): 279–96.

– "Grundsatz oder Praxis? Kanada und Österreich, 1938–1945." *Zeitgeschichte* 10 (1983): 227–39.

– "Policy or Practice: Canada and Austria, 1938–1945," in Martin Kovacs, ed., *Roots and Realities among Eastern and Central Europeans*. Edmonton 1983.

– "Otto Strasser in Churchills Strategie der nationalen Erhebungen, 1940–1942." *Vierteljahrshefte für Zeitgeschichte* 31 (1984): 614–45.

– "Which Fatherland in War? The Canadian Government's View of German Canadians' Loyalties in World War Two," in T. Yedlin, ed., *Central and East*

European Ethnicity in Canada. Edmonton 1985.

– "Arnold J. Toynbee's Foreign Research and Press Service, 1939–43, and Its Post-War Plans for South-east Europe." *Journal of Contemporary History* 21 (1986): 539–58.

– "The Rehabilitation of the Austro-Hungarian Empire: British Postwar Planning in the Second World War." *Hungarian Studies Review* 23 (1986): 63–74.

– "Austria Abandoned: Anglo-American Propaganda and Planning for Austria, 1938–1945," in F. Parkinson, ed., *Austrian Nazism after the Anschluss*. Detroit, Mich. 1987.

Kimball, Warren F. "Naked Reverse Right: Roosevelt, Churchill, and Eastern Europe from TOLSTOY to Yalta – and a Little Beyond." *Diplomatic History* 9 (1985): 1–24.

Kissinger, Henry L. "Domestic Structure and Foreign Policy," in H. Berding et al. *Vom Staat des Ancien Regimes zum modernen Parteienstaat*. Munchen, Wien: 1978.

Klemperer, Klaus von. "On Austro-Fascism." *Central European History* 11 (1978): 313–15.

Klinghofer, H. "Die Moskauer Erklärung über Österreich," *Österreichische Zeitschrift für öffentliches Recht* (1953–5): 461–89.

Knapp, W. "Fifty Years of Chatham House Books." *International Affairs* 46 (1970), fiftieth anniversary issue.

Knight, Robert. "Britische Entnazifizierungspolitik 1945–1949." *Zeitgeschichte* 9/10 (1984): 326–44.

Kohn, Hans. "AEIOU: Some Reflections on the Meaning and Mission of Austria." *Journal of Modern History* 11 (1939): 513–27.

– "Reflections on Austrian History." *Austrian History Yearbook* 1 (1965): 4–22.

Kowalski, H.G. "Die 'EAC' als Instrument alliierter Deutschlandspolitik." *Vierteljahrshefte für Zeitgeschichte* 19 (1971): 261–93.

Kozenski, J. "The Discrediting of the Idea of Anschluss in the Years 1938–1945." *Polish Western Affairs* 9 (1968): 225–57.

Krakau, K. "American Foreign Relations: A National Style." *Diplomatic History* 8 (1984): 253–72.

Kramer, Paul. "Nelson Rockefeller and British Security Coordination." *Journal of Contemporary History* 16 (1981): 73– 88.

Kreisky, Bruno. "Austria Draws the Balance." *Foreign Affairs* 37 (1959): 269–81.

Kris, Ernst, and Nathan Leites. "Trends in Twentieth-Century Propaganda," in Daniel Lerner. *Propaganda in War and Crisis*. Cornwall, NY 1951.

Kucklik, P. "The Genesis of the EAC." *Journal of Contemporary History* 4 (1969): 189–201.

Large, David C. "Richard von Kralik's Search for Fatherland." *Austrian History Yearbook* 17/18 (1981/2): 144–55.

Lauterpracht, H. *Annual Digest and Reports of Public International Law* 9

(1938–40): 87–92.

– "De Facto Recognition, Withdrawal of Recognition and Conditional Recognition." *British Yearbook of International Law* 22 (1945): 164–90.

– "The Contemporary Practice of the United Kingdom in the Field of International Law – Survey and Comment." *International and Comparative Law Quarterly* 7 (1958): 94–5.

Lees, Lorraine M. "National Security and Ethnicity: Contrasting Views during World War II." *Diplomatic History* 11 (1987):113–26.

– and Sandra Treadway. "A Future for Our Diplomatic Past? A Critical Appraisal of the Foreign Relations Series." *Journal of American History* 70 (1983–4): 621–9.

Leffler, Melvyn P. "The American Conception of National Security and the Beginnings of the Cold War, 1945–1948." *American Historical Review* 89 (1984): 346–81.

Leser, Norbert. "Austria between the Wars: An Essay." *Austrian History Yearbook* 7/8 (1981–2): 123–42.

Lettner, Lyda. "Die französische Österreichpolitik von 1943 bis 1945." Doctoral dissertation, University of Salzburg, 1980.

Lewis, J. "Red Vienna: Socialism in One City, 1918–1927." *European Studies Review* 13 (1983): 335–56.

Lónne, Karl Egon. "Politische Romantik und die Krise der Zwischenkriegszeit." *Zeitgeschichte* 14 (1987): 135–46.

Low, A.D. "The Anschluss Movement (1918–19) in Recent Historical Writing: German Nationalism and Austrian Patriotism." *Canadian Review of Studies in Nationalism.* 3 (1976): 212–25.

– "Otto Bauer, Austro-Marxism and the Anschluss Movement, 1918–1938." *Canadian Review of Studies in Nationalism* 6 (1979): 33–57.

– "The Soviet Union, the Austrian Communist Party and the Anschluss Question, 1918–1938." *Slavic Review* 39 (March 1980): 1–26.

McGranahan, Donald V. "US Psychological Warfare Policy." *Public Opinion Quarterly* 4 (1946): 446–50.

MacNeil, William H. "Arnold J. Toynbee." *Proceedings of the British Academy* 63 (1977): 441–69.

Maddux, T. "Watching Stalin Manoeuver between Hitler and the West: America's Diplomats and Soviet Diplomacy, 1934–1939." *Diplomatic History* 1 (1977): 140–54.

Mader, D.R. "Foreign Policy Planning: Its Practice and Problems in the United States Department of State." Doctoral dissertation, University of Toronto, 1974.

Mamety, Victor S. "Legalizing the Collapse of Austria-Hungary at the Paris Peace Conference." *Austrian History Yearbook* 3 (1967): 206–37.

Maquis, Alice G. "Words as Weapons: Propaganda in Britain during the First World War." *Journal of Contemporary History* 13 (1978): 467–98.

Marcic, Rene. "Verfassung und Grundrechte," in Weinzierl and Skalnik, eds. *Österreich: Die Zweite Republik*. Vol. 2. Graz 1972.

Marks, Edward. "Charles E. Bohlen and the Acceptable Limits of Soviet Hegemony in Eastern Europe: A Memorandum of 18 October 1945." *Diplomatic History* 3 (1979): 201–14.

– "Today Has Been A Historical One: Harry S. Truman's Diary of the Potsdam Conference." *Diplomatic History* 4 (1980): 317–26.

– "American Policy toward Eastern Europe and the Origins of the Cold War, 1941–1946: An Alternate Interpretation." *Journal of American History* 68 (1981–2): 316–36.

Mastny, Vojtech. "Stalin and the Prospects of a Separate Peace in World War II." *American Historical Review* 77 (1972): 1365–88.

– "Soviet War Aims at the Moscow and Teheran Conferences of 1943." *Journal of Modern History* 47 (1975): 481–504.

Mayers, David. "Nazi Germany and the Future of Europe: George Kennan's Views, 1939–1945." *International History Review* 8 (1986): 550–72.

– "Soviet War Aims and the Grand Alliance: George Kennan's Views, 1944–1946." *Journal of Contemporary History* 21 (1986): 57–80.

Mayo, Marlene J. "American Planning for Occupied Japan: The role of the Experts," in Robert Wolfe, ed. *Americans as Proconsuls: United States Military Government in Germany and Japan,* 1944–52. Carbondale, Ill. 1984.

Merkl, A. "Der Anschluss Österreichs an das Deutsche Reich -eine Geschichtslegende." *Juristische Blätter* [Wien] 77, no.17 (1955).

Messer, R. "Paths Not Taken: The United States State Department and Alternatives to Containment, 1945–1946." *Diplomatic History* 1 (1977): 297–320.

Miscamble, W. "Anthony Eden and the Truman-Molotov Conversation of April 1945." *Diplomatic History* 2 (1978): 167–80.

Modisett, L.E. "The Four-Cornered Triangle: British and American Policy toward Yugoslavia, 1939–1945." Doctoral dissertation, Georgetown University, 1981.

Moltmann, G. "Die frühe Deutschland Plannung im 2. Weltkrieg." *Vierteljahrshefte für Zeitgeschichte* 5 (1957): 241–64.

Morgenthau, Henry J. "The Problem of Neutrality." *Kansas City Review* 7 (1938–9): 111–17.

Mosley, Philip "The Treaty with Austria." *International Organizations* 4 (1950): 224–37.

– "The Occupation of Germany: New Light on How the Zones Were Drawn." *Foreign Affairs* 28 (1950): 580–604.

– "Hopes and Failures: American Policy towards Eastern Europe, 1941–1947" *Review of Politics* 17 (1955): 461–85.

Moss, K. "George S. Messersmith: An American Diplomat in Nazi Germany." *Delaware History*, 17 (1976–7): 236–49.

Muir, L. "Austria," in Michael Balfour and L. Muir, eds. *Four-Power Control in Germany and Austria, 1945–1946*. London 1956.

Offner, A.A. "Appeasement Revisited: The United States, Great Britain and Germany, 1933–1940." *Journal of American History* 64 (1977): 373–93.

Oppenheimer, F.E. "Governments and Austhorities in Exile." *American Journal of International Law*. 36 (1942): 568–95.

Orde, Anne. "Grossbritannien und die Selbstständigkeit Österreichs, 1918–1938." *Vierteljahrshefte für Zeitgeschichte* 28 (1980): 224–48.

Ostrower, G. "Secretary of State Stimson and the League." *The Historian* 51 (1979): 467–82.

Padover, Saul K. "Psychological Warfare Policy." *The American Scholar* (Spring 1951): 151–61.

Pasvolsky, L. "Obstacles to the Union of Austria and Germany." *Current History* 31 (December 1929): 520–8.

Pauley, Bruce F. "A Case Study in Fascism: The Styrian Heimatschutz and Austrian National Socialism." *Austrian History Yearbook* 12/13 (1976–7): 251–73.

– "From Splinter Party to Mass Movement: The Austrian Nazi Breakthrough." *German Studies Review* 3 (1979): 7–29.

– "Fascism and Führerprinzip: The Austrian Example." *Central European History* 12 (1979): 272–96.

Peden, G.L. "A Matter of Timing: The Economic Background of British Foreign Policy, 1937–1939." *History* 69 (1984): 15–28.

Perkins, Dexter, "The State Department Speaks." *Journal of Modern History* 16 (1944): 124–36.

Pollard, John A. "Words Are Cheaper than Blood." *Public Opinion Quarterly* 9 (1945): 238–47.

Pollard, Robert. "Economic Security and the Origins of the Cold War: Bretton Woods, the Marshall Plan and American Rearmement, 1944–1950." *Diplomatic History* 9 (1985): 271–89.

Pollock, Oscar. "The Rebirth of Austria." *Contemporary Review* (March 1945): 146–51.

Possony, Stefan T. "Needed – A New Propaganda Approach to Germany." *Public Opinion Quarterly* 5 (1942): 335–50.

Propas, Frederic L. "Creating a Hard Line towards Russia: The Training of State Department Foreign Experts, 1927–1937." *Diplomatic History* 8 (1984): 209–26.

Rathkolb, Oliver. "US Entnazifizierung in Österreich zwischen kontrollierter Revolution und Elitenrestauration." *Zeitgeschichte* 11 (1984): 302–25.

– "NS-Problem und politische Restauration: Vorgeschichte und Etablierung des VdU," in S. Meissl et al., *Verdrängte Schuld, verfehlte Sühne*. Wien 1986.

Renner, Karl. "Austria: Key for War and Peace." *Foreign Affairs* 24 (1948): 589–603.

Resis, A. "The Churchill-Stalin Agreement on the Balkans, Moscow, October 1944." *American Historical Review* 83 (1978): 368–89.

Reut-Nicolussi, E. "The International Legal Status of Austria since 1918." *Transactions of the Grotius Society* 39 (1954): 119–31.

Riley, John W., Jr, and Leonard S. Cottrell, Jr. "Research for Psychological Warfare." *Public Opinion Quarterly* 21 (1957): 119–31.

Ritter, H. "Recent Writing on Interwar Austria." *Central European History* 12 (1979): 297–311.

Ross, R.J. "Heinrich Ritter von Srbik and 'gesamtdeutsch' History." *Review of Politics* 31 (1969): 88–107.

Rostow, E.W. "The Planning of Foreign Policy." *Department of State Newsletter* 38 (June 1964): 3–11.

Roth, R. "History and Citizenship Training: An Austrian Example." *Journal of Modern History* 21 (1949): 227–38.

Roucek, Joseph S. "The 'Free Movements' of Horthy's Eckhardt and Austria's Otto." *Public Opinion Quarterly* 7 (1943): 466–77.

Roy, Douglas. "Chamberlain and Eden, 1937–1938." *Journal of Contemporary History* 13 (1978): 97–116.

Salmon, Patrick. "British Plans for Economic Warfare against Germany 1937–1939: The Problem of Swedish Iron Ore." *Journal of Contemporary History* 16 (1981): 53–72.

Schauch, Wolfgang. "American Policy toward Germany 1945." *Journal of Contemporary History* 4 (1970): 113–29.

Schausberger,Norbert. "Der wirtschaftliche Anschluss Österreichs 1938." *Österreich in Geschichte und Literatur* 15 (1971): 249–73.

Schilling, Frederick Karl, Jr. "Germany and Her Future: British Opinion and Policy, 1939–1947." Doctoral dissertation, Indiana University, 1954.

Schmulowitz, Nat, and Lloyd D. Luckmann. "Foreign Policy by Propaganda Leaflets." *Public Opinion Quarterly* 9 (1945): 428–9 and 485–93.

Schroeder, Paul W. "The Status of Habsburg Studies in the United States." *Austrian History Yearbook*, 3, pt.3 (1967): 267–95.

Schulzinger, Robert D. "Whatever Happened to the Council on Foreign Relations?" *Diplomatic History* 5 (1981): 277–90.

Schuschnigg, Kurt von. "The National Minority Question in Austria before and after 1918." *Journal of Central European Affairs* 18 (1959): 367–79.

Selby, Sir Watford. "Austria before the Anschluss and a View of Her Future Prospects." *International Affairs* 4 (1945): 477–84.

Seton-Watson, Hugh. "The Danubian Satellites: A Survey of the Main Social and Political Factors in the Present Situation." *International Affairs* 2 (1946): 240–53.

Shafir, S. "George S. Messersmith: An Anti-Nazi Diplomat's View of the Jewish Crisis." *Jewish Social Studies* 35 (1973): 32–41.

Shils, Edward, and Morris Janowitz. "Cohesion and Disintegration in the Wehrmacht in World War II." *Public Opinion Quarterly* 12 (1948): 280–315.

Siegwald, Gangelmair. "Amerikanische Kriegspropaganda gegen das Deutsche

Reich in den Jahren 1944/1945." Doctoral dissertation, University of Vienna, 1978.

Siracusa, J. "The Night Stalin and Churchill Divided Europe." *Review of Politics* 43 (1981): 381–409.

Speier, Hans. "The Future of Psychological Warfare." *Public Opinion Quarterly* 12 (1948): 5–18.

Stadler, Karl. "The Disintegration of the Austrian Empire." *Journal of Contemporary History* 3 (1968): 177–90.

– "Österreich 1945: Neue Dokumente zur Politik der Alliierten." *Österreichische Zeitschrift für Aussenpolitik* 9 (1969): 88–110.

Stafford, David A. "Britain Looks at Europe, 1940: Some Origins of SOE." *Canadian Journal of History* 10 (1975): 231–48.

– "The Detonator Concept: British Strategy, SOE and European Resistance after the Fall of France." *Journal of Contemporary History* 10 (1975): 185–217.

Stanley, Guy. "British Policy and the Austrian Question." Doctoral dissertation, University of London, 1973.

– "Die britische Vorbehalte genenüber der provisorichen Regierung Renner 1945." *Zeitgeschichte* 3 (1975–6): 38–46.

Steefer, Herbert F. "American Attitudes and the Development of Policy towards Austria, 1938–1945." Doctoral dissertation, Tufts University, Fletcher School of Law and Diplomacy, 1967.

Steele, Richard W. "The Pulse of the People: Franklin D. Roosevelt and the Gauging of Public Opinion." *Journal of Contemporary History* (1974): 195–216.

Steiner, Senta G. "Österreich und die europäische Integration zwischen Moskauer Deklaration und Europakongress in den Haag." Doctoral dissertation, University of Salzburg, 1971.

Stoler, Mark., "From Continentalism to Globalism: General Stanley Embrick, the Joint Strategic Survey Committee and Military View of National Policy during the Second World War." *Diplomatic History* 6 (1982): 303–21.

Stourzh, Gerald. "Zur Entstehungsgeschichte des Staatsvertrages und der Neutralität Österreichs, 1945–1955." *Österreichische Zeitschrift für Aussenpolitik* 5 (1965): 301–36.

– "Die Regierung Renner, die Anfänge der Regierung Figl und die Alliierte Kommission für Österreich." *Archiv für österreichische Geschichte* 125 (1966): 339–47.

Strang, William. "Prelude to Potsdam: Reflections on War and Foreign Policy." *International Affairs* 46 (1970): 441–55.

Suval, Stanley. "The Search for Fatherland." *Austrian History Yearbook* 4/5 (1968–9): 275–99.

Sweet, P. "Seipel's View on the Anschluss: An Exchange of Letters." *Journal of Modern History* 19 (1942), 320–3.

– "The New Austria: Notes on the First Year." *Journal of Politics* 8 (1946): 350–

61.
– "Democracy and Counterrevolution in Austria." *Journal of Modern History* 22 (1950): 52–8.
Taborsky, Edward. "Benes and Stalin – Moscow 1943 and 1945." *Journal of Central European Affairs* 13 (1953): 154–181.
Taylor, P.M. "The Foreign Office and British Propaganda during the First World War." *Historical Journal* 23 (1980): 875–98.
– " 'If War Should Come': Preparing the Fifth Arm for Total War." *Journal of Contemporary History* 16 (1981): 27–53.
Thorne, C. "Chatham House, Whitehall and Far Eastern Issues, 1941–1945." *International Affairs* 54 (1978): 7–26.
Toynbee, A.J. "Is There a Crisis?" *International Affairs* 17 (1938): 1–28.
– "After Munich." *International Affairs* 18 (1938): 307–37.
– "Was Britain's Abdication Folly?" *The Round Table* 60 (1970): 352–70.
Villa, Brian. "The United States Army, Unconditional Surrender and the Potsdam Proclamation." *Journal of American History* 53 (1979): 66–92.
Vogelmann, Karl. "Die Propaganda der österreichischen Emigration in der Sowjetunion für einen selbstständigen österreichischen Nationalstaat (1938–1945)." Doctoral dissertation, Vienna University, 1973.
Wadlow, J.K. "United States Recognition Policy towards Coups d'etat: The Development of the Current Position." *Australian Journal of Politics and History* 24 (1978): 20–35.
Wagnleitner, Reinhold. "Diplomatische Dokumente zur Geschichte Österreichs, 1918–1945, im Londoner Public Records Office." *Scrinium* 12 (1975): 45–58.
– "Grossbritannien und die Wiederherstellung der Republik Österreich." Doctoral dissertation, University of Salzburg, 1975.
– "Die britische Österreichpolitik 1936 oder 'The Doctrine of Putting Off the Evil Day'," in L. Jedlicka and R. Neck, eds., *Das Juli Abkommen von 1936*. München 1977.
– "Die Kontinuität der britischen Aussenpolitik nach dem Wahlsieg der Labour Party im Jahr 1945." *Zeitgeschichte* 1 (1978): 35–40.
– "Die kulturelle Reorientierung Österreichs nach dem Zweiten Weltkrieg." *Zeitgeschichte* 11 (1984): 326–44.
Wandruska, A. "Grossdeutsche und kleindeutsche Ideologie," in Robert A. Kann and F.E.Prinz, eds. *Deutschland und Österreich*. München 1980.
Warner, G. "From Teheran to Yalta: Reflections on Franklin D. Roosevelt's Foreign Policy." *International Affairs*, 43 (1967): 530–36.
Watt, David. "The Foundation of the Round Table." *The Round Table* 60 (November 1970): 425–33.
Watt, Donald C. "Appeasement: The Rise of a Revisionist School?" *The Political Quarterly* 35 (1965): 191–213.
– "Roosevelt and Neville Chamberlain: Two Appeasers." *International Journal* 28 (1973): 185–204.

Weinberg, Sydney S. "Wartime Propaganda in a Democracy: America's Twentieth-Century Information Agencies." Doctoral dissertation, Columbia University, 1969.

Welles, Sumner. "Two Roosevelt Decisions: One Debit, One Credit." *Foreign Affairs* 29 (1951): 182–204.

Wheeler, B. "The SOE Phenomenon." *Journal of Contemporary History* 16 (1981): 513–20.

Wickware, Francis G. "What We Think About Foreign Affairs." *Harper's Magazine*, September 1939, 397–406.

Williams, Maurice. "The Aftermath of the Anschluss: Disillusioned Germans or Budding Austrian Nationals?" *Austrian History Yearbook* 14 (1978): 129–44.

– "German Imperialism and Austria, 1938." *Journal of Contemporary History* 14 (1979): 139–54.

– "Delusions of Grandeur: The Austrian National Socialists." *Canadian Journal of History* 14 (1979): 417–36.

– "Some Reflections on Austro-Nazis and their Brand of Nationalism before the Anschluss." *Canadian Review of Studies in Nationalism* 12 (1985): 285–306.

Wilson, Francis G. "Lord Bryce on Public Opinion: Fifty Years Later." *Public Opinion Quarterly* 3 (1939): 420–35.

Wilson, T.W. "Lord Bryce's Investigation into Alleged German Atrocities in Belgium, 1914–1918." *Journal of Contemporary History* 14 (1979): 420–35.

Winkler, Alan M. "Politics and Propaganda: The Office of War Information, 1942–1945." Doctoral dissertation, Yale University, 1974.

Wintergest, W. "Die staatsrechtliche Stellung Österreichs nach dem Anschluss." Doctoral dissertation, Freiburg i. Breisgau University, 1939.

Winters, Stanley. "The Forging of a Historian: Robert A. Kann in America, 1939–76." *Austrian History Yearbook* 17/18 (1981–2): 3–24.

Wright, Herbert "The Legality of the Annexation of Austria by Germany." *American Journal of International Law* 38 (1944): 621–35.

Wright, Michael R. "Eastern Europe," in A.J. Toynbee and F.T. Ashton-Gwatkin, eds., *The World in 1939*. London 1952. (1945): 73–8.

Wright, Quincy. "The Denunciation of Treaty Violators." *American Journal of International Law* 32 (1938): 526–34.

Zink, H. "American Military Government Organization in Germany." *Journal of Politics* 8 (1946): 329–49.

Index